Makeshift Chicago Stages

Makeshift Chicago Stages

A Century of Theater and Performance

EDITED BY

Megan E. Geigner, Stuart J. Hecht, and Jasmine Jamillah Mahmoud

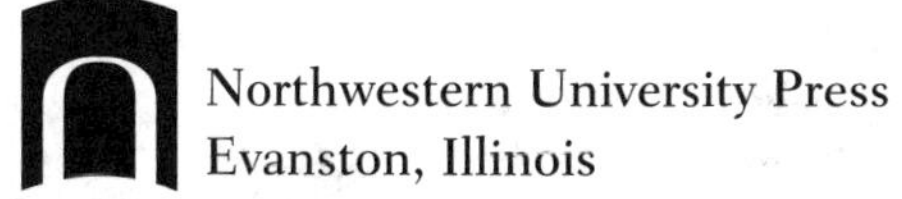

Northwestern University Press
Evanston, Illinois

Northwestern University Press
www.nupress.northwestern.edu

Printed in the United States of America

10 9 8 7 6 5 4 3 2 1

Library of Congress Cataloging-in-Publication Data

Names: Geigner, Megan E, editor. | Hecht, Stuart Joel, 1955– editor. | Mahmoud, Jasmine Jamillah, editor.
Title: Makeshift Chicago stages : a century of theater and performance / edited by Megan E Geigner, Stuart J Hecht, and Jasmine Jamillah Mahmoud.
Description: Evanston, Illinois : Northwestern University Press, 2021.
Identifiers: LCCN 2021011424 | ISBN 9780810143814 (paperback) | ISBN 9780810143821 (cloth) | ISBN 9780810143838 (ebook)
Subjects: LCSH: Theater—Illinois—Chicago—History. | Experimental theater—Illinois—Chicago—History. | Theater and society—Illinois—Chicago—History.
Classification: LCC PN2277.C4 M35 2021 | DDC 792.0977311—dc23
LC record available at https://lccn.loc.gov/2021011424

CONTENTS

ACKNOWLEDGMENTS

The editors of this volume would like to acknowledge the many people who made the book possible. We thank Sarah Zimmerman of the Chicago Public Library, who is a tireless champion of Chicago theater history. The collection at Harold Washington is a treasure, and we are grateful for Sarah's commitment to it. We also thank Lesley Martin, Russell Lewis, Archie Motley, Rosemary Adams, and the staff of the Chicago History Museum Research Center. We also thank the staff of the Newberry Library.

Much of this work developed from presentations and panels throughout the years at various professional organizations. We would like to thank Albert Williams, John Green, and Arvid (Gus) Sponberg for their years of work on Chicago theater history and for putting together the Columbia College Chicago Theatre Symposium, "Chicago: Theatre Capital of America—Past. Present. Future" in May of 2011. We would also like to thank the Mid-American Theatre Conference, the Association for Theatre in Higher Education, and the American Theatre and Drama Society for hosting panels of our work. Additionally, we thank the American Society for Theatre Research for awarding us the 2020 Collaborative Research Award.

Finally, we would like to thank our family, friends, and mentors for offering support through the process: Joel Hobson, Shirah W. Hecht, Zack Elway, Gianna Mosser, Harvey Young, Linda Walsh Jenkins, and Ramón Rivera-Servera, and Mary Trotter, who suggested this project.

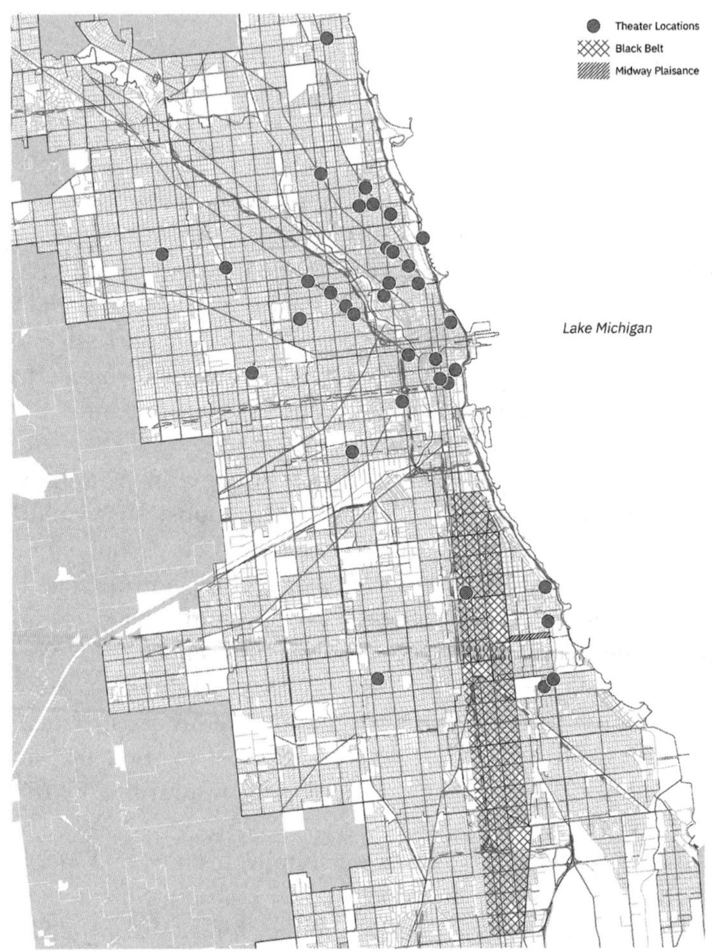

Chicago makeshift theater locations. Map created by Kelsey Rydland, Northwestern University Libraries, Geospatial and Data Services.

INTRODUCTION

Chicago Theater as Makeshift Performance

Megan E. Geigner, Stuart J. Hecht, and Jasmine Jamillah Mahmoud

In Chicago's beginning, there was makeshift theater and performance. Since the mid-1980s, Chicago theater productions and performers have gained national and even international recognition for the artistic excellence of their work. At present, Chicago sports some three hundred professional theaters demonstrating extraordinary community support, engagement, and appreciation for a style of work that stresses issues and ideas, emotion and theatricality. It is a grassroots theater, one peculiar to the city and its dynamics, rooted in what we call the "makeshift."

In one of the first buildings created by white settlers in the 1830s—the Sauganash Hotel at the bend of the Chicago River—the city's first theater company started in the dining room in 1837. As Richard Christiansen recounts in *A Theater of Our Own*, the producers "turned a place that was never intended for use as a playhouse into a small theater and put on a show."[1] Elsewhere during the city's first decade,[2] tavern theaters at private homes, barrooms, and lodges crammed attendees into repurposed spaces to watch ventriloquism, live music, monologues, and melodrama. At one bar during the 1830s, audience members included adults who paid fifty cents (half that for children) to watch productions.[3] Makeshift theater fashioned from spaces with non-theatrical purposes characterized Chicago's earliest years.

In the almost two centuries since the city's founding in 1833, makeshift has continued to define Chicago's theatrical landscape. By the mid-twentieth century, storefront theaters—spaces made from commercial buildings converted into performance venues that often battled restrictive zoning laws—became the quintessential Chicago theater space, blooming in neighborhoods across the city, from Lakeview to Hyde Park to Jefferson Park. Called the "soul of Chicago theatre,"[4] storefront theaters demonstrate the centrality of makeshift as a concept defining relationships among repurposed space, experimental ensemble-led work, municipal policy, and intimate viewing practices, with often fewer than one hundred audience members snugly seated in small spaces not originally meant to be theater venues.

This book examines the rise and proliferation of such improvised stages in Chicago. It considers the variety of organizations, dynamics, and forms of expression that emerged as a result, culminating today in a thriving Chicago theater community, which features its own ways of doing theater. This book includes chapters documenting noted twentieth-century storefront venues such as the 57th Street Artist Colony, Body Politic Theatre, and Kingston Mines Theatre, as well as other makeshift practices from the late nineteenth to the early twenty-first centuries, within and beyond the storefront: private homes, public parks, and even theater institutions.

Collectively, these chapters propose *Chicago theater as makeshift theater*. The word "makeshift" connotes the action of making shift, the state of being a temporary or "sufficient" substitute, expediency, and often the state "of an inferior kind" according to the *Oxford English Dictionary*. While many theaters in Chicago have permanent spaces and do more conventional work, our book shows how makeshift has animated many theaters' beginnings and that the ethos of the makeshift is still central to much of Chicago theater today.

In what follows, we first theorize "*makeshift*," the titular concept so important to this volume, in dialogue with space, race, tactics, repertoire, and aesthetics. There are connections, we assert, among Chicago theater space as makeshift, Chicago as a racially hyper-segregated city, and Chicago theater as aesthetically often hyperrealist, gritty, and ensemble-led. We then situate Chicago as an object of study in theater and performance history. As the chapters in this volume progress chronologically, we introduce how each case study collectively animates the *makeshift*.

Theorizing Makeshift: Space, Race, Tactics, Repertoire, and Aesthetics

Taverns, lodges, temporary exhibition buildings, and storefronts—Chicago performance has habitually taken place in spaces neither durable, nor zoned, nor fashioned for theater. Makeshift, then, spatially frames Chicago theater-making. Centering this concept as a spatial one follows a genealogy of scholarship that considers the role of staged performance on and beyond the stage.[5] This scholarship underpins a key contribution of this book: from architecture to routes of movement to traditional dramatic literature, the chapters here examine theater as a spatial practice that animates relationships among architecture, aesthetics, and embodiment.

Spaces carry a history of the people and the aesthetics that built them and still animate them. As scholars attuned to the sociological aspects of space have argued, space is a social product that changes as the bodies change that inhabit the space.[6] In other words, spatial meanings are ephemeral because space is always defined by the bodies using it. As the case studies here bear out, the various spaces of makeshift performance did not have meaning until people began circulating and using them. Stuart J. Hecht's analysis of the 57th Street Artist Colony, for example, describes how after the World's Columbian Exposition of 1893 ended, theater artists inhabited storefronts built on the fairground's spatial margins, imbuing these structures with new artistic life.

Our collective use of "makeshift" also entangles with the concept of "marginal." According to the *Oxford English Dictionary*, "marginal" means "relating to an edge, border, boundary, or limit; of, on, or relating to the edge or fringe of the field of consciousness; that which is on or close to a limit below or beyond which something ceases to be possible or desirable; or of an individual or social group: isolated from or not conforming to the dominant society or culture; (perceived as being) on the edge of a society or social unit; belonging to a minority group." Chicago is famously the "second city," marginal to New York City, and with the second most theaters per capita behind New York City; as of this writing Chicago is the third most populous city (with about 2.7 million residents) after New York City and Los Angeles.

The case studies also show intricate ideas of marginality as makeshift and relational, and as foundational to sustained and identifiable cultural practice in Chicago. In Chicago, "Off-Loop" is a term used to describe venues that exist spatially outside of Chicago's Loop. Theaters in Chicago's Loop—the downtown business district where elevated public transit trains loop overhead—often stage big-budget, touring "Broadway in Chicago" shows, and include the Goodman Theatre, now considered Chicago's top regional theater powerhouse. By contrast, "Off-Loop" describes spatially decentered, marginal neighborhoods where intimate, low-cost storefront theater thrives. Cat Gleason's chapter describes the origins of Off-Loop storefront theaters along North Lincoln Avenue, and interactions among aesthetics, race, and spaces fashioned from a former trolley barn (Kingston Mines Theatre) and bowling alley (Body Politic Theatre).

Another key aspect to makeshift is how it frames a continuum between itinerancy and permanence. While these poles usually refer to space, the chapters demonstrate an affective element as well. Many of the artists in these chapters did not or do not have permanent performance space. Some chapters, including Gleason's on the origins of Off-Loop storefronts, chronicle artists on a quest to develop a permanent space. Shannon Epplett details the performance history of early twentieth-century artists who sought permanence in the Fine Arts Building, namely "Uplifters" Anna Morgan and Donald Robertson and Chicago Little Theatre cofounders director Maurice Browne and actress Ellen Van Volkenburg, Browne's wife. In his chapter, Travis Stern details ImprovOlympic's long search for a permanent space in late twentieth-century Chicago. In hers, LaRonika Marie Thomas details the early twenty-first-century place-making of Theaster Gates. Other artists in these chapters choose not to have permanent space or have a complicated relationship with the idea of permanent space: the 57th Street Artist Colony, Teatro Vista, and the Chicago Home Theater Festival. To understand how space affects these artists, we consider the sociological connection of space and performance.

One prominent example of how humans define space is how race, especially in the United States, is spatialized. This is the argument made by sociologist George Lipsitz, who in his 2011 book *How Racism Takes Place* writes of connections between policy and the racialization of space; he illustrates how municipal zoning practices, highway construction, restrictive housing covenants, and other aspects of urban renewal negatively affected people of color, displacing them, confining them, and making them proximate to environmental hazards.[7] He cites major hallmarks of spatial racialization—the clearing of indigenous people, restrictive covenants, redlining, urban renewal (as the removal of Black people)—that starkly map onto Chicago, a city named from an indigenous word for "wild leeks" that grew in the area and, in the late twentieth and early twenty-first centuries, declared racially the "most hypersegregated"[8] city in the United States. As of this writing, Chicago's population is 29.7 percent white, 29.3 percent Black, and 29.7 percent Hispanic/Latinidad, which crosses racial categories.[9]

Beyond policy, the devices of theater and performance also animate and produce the social construction of race. As scholars such as Harry Elam, David Krasner, and Harvey Young demonstrate, marking out the difference between bodies onstage and those not onstage heightens awareness of otherness and invites both performers and audiences to consider the way identity is made through performance.[10] And the work of Joshua Chambers-Letson makes it clear that policy, law, and the aesthetics of theater and performance overlap and impact one another, creating shared racial knowledge.[11] The accounts that follow offer case studies of these arguments that performance creates embodied meanings of race and that ideas of race create certain kinds of performance.

Our volume builds on these ideas of the relationship between theater, space, and racialization. Aaron Krall's chapter reveals how both the Black characters in Theodore Ward's 1930s-era play *Big White Fog* and the Black audiences of this play performed within and against the racist structures of the time. Laura A. Lodewyck's chapter on Teatro Vista centers voices of the Latinx[12] theater company's members to reveal the importance of onstage representations to produce underrepresented offstage ideas and practices of Latinidad communities. Jasmine Jamillah Mahmoud's chapter on the Chicago Home Theater Festival shows how festival organizers used the intimate space of the home to combat and imagine beyond the civic reality of Chicago as a racially hyper-segregated city. Chicago theater and performance history also demonstrates the construction of whiteness through performance. Most notably, white immigrant group members who performed in ethnic theaters at the beginning of the twentieth century became racially unmarked stars no longer associated with the ethnic theater tradition as the franchise of whiteness grew from an Anglo-Saxon ideal to a more ecumenical non-Black ideal.[13] Furthermore, Latinidad theaters and artists struggle still to define themselves against Black/white racial paradigms. The very makeshift Chicago theater featured in this volume attests to how flexible-in-formation works are often best suited to both reflect racial norms and render racial underrepresentations, possibilities, and imaginations.

Those which are makeshift and that which is on the margins use tactics as part of their spatial and aesthetic practices. By tactics, we reference Michel de Certeau's idea that systems of operation dictate embodied usage, or that maps of roads and sidewalks tell people to walk in certain ways in cities. But as de Certeau also points out, "Users make innumerable and infinitesimal transformations of and within the dominant cultural economy in order to adapt it to their own interest and their own rules."[14] Users or artists employ tactics, or "a calculus which cannot count on a 'proper' (a spatial or institutional localization), nor thus on a borderline distinguishing the other as a visible totality."[15] In addition to tactics often being sideways, underneath, improper, and blurry, they are—as many of our chapters reveal—tied to engaging time, ephemerality, survival, and history. The Black characters in Theodore Ward's *Big White Fog* used responsive, attentive, and imaginative tactics to establish themselves in early twentieth-century Chicago where systems of racism prevented their full belonging, for instance. As Teatro Vista's history shows, expansive tactics were what made theater in a community center and a museum, and what kept the group staging productions in various Chicago spaces despite having a home at Victory Gardens Theater. Conceptual artist Theaster Gates's approach involved renovating houses on Chicago's South Side with wood from the ash trees that municipal workers pulled out of the ground due to the ash borer. The chapters in this volume attest to the power of tactics in theater and performance.

Two main tactics that Chicago theater and performance makers have developed in the last century include the use of ensemble and repertoire. Many of Chicago's theaters, both large and small, central and marginal, have an ensemble of artists who produce work and govern the theaters' choices. In their book *Ensemble-Made Chicago: A Guide to Devised Theater*, Chloe Johnston and Coya Paz Brownrigg explain that

> ensemble-based or devised process is a way of creating theater that welcomes the ideas and contributions of everyone in the room, that relies on a collective vision rather than the singular vision of a playwright or director. Ensemble process rejects a predetermined hierarchy in favor of figuring out what works best *this* time, with *these* particular people. It happens in the spaces between people, it responds to the space.[16]

As our case studies show, ensembles have been central within makeshift spaces: from the 57th Street Artist Colony and the Little Theatre movement of the early twentieth century, to those within the twentieth-century Body Politic Theatre and ImprovOlympic (later iO), to the collaborative work of the organizers of the early twenty-first-century Chicago Home Theater Festival.

Chicago theater and performance are also often described as "gritty," not always in content but often as a way of working wherein things are done on the fly, with hard labor, and by getting as many proverbial fingers in the pot at once. Johnston and Paz Brownrigg suggest the city itself undergirds this way of theater-making since it is a city of neighborhoods, each with its own theater or its own performance practice defined by the people who live there, which makes Chicago theater "flexible and resourceful."[17] Many of the performance venues and theater artists featured in this collection are "flexible and resourceful," bearing this out.

By repertoire, we mean two things. First, we cite Diana Taylor's conception of embodiment as a means of creating and sharing knowledge.[18] Chapter 1 shows how the habitus of the performers and spectators on the Columbian Exposition's Midway in 1893 may not be archived, but the behavior—the embodied nature of walking around in a carnival-like atmosphere, circulating with subjects from all over the globe, with a feeling of the tacit consumption of the exotic—remains and repeats in subsequent generations. The Chicago Home Theatre Festival, featured in chapter 10, may no longer run, but the embodiment of getting off the subway, moving through the Humboldt Park neighborhood following a guide, eating with strangers in an apartment, and attending to the performance endures. In many ways, the practice of Chicago theater is a repertoire, as it is embodied and practiced knowledge rarely written down in the official record. The act of making a bowling alley into the Body Politic Theatre (chapter 6) or an old bank into a gallery (chapter 9) is part of a Chicago performance repertoire in which the space records and transmits as much information as the performers occupying it do.

The second aspect of repertoire has to do with relationality of makeshift Chicago theater and performance. Part of the history of Chicago theater and performance is what we would now call "devised," as artists drew from pedestrian everyday movements and tasks to make the quotidian performative. In 1939, innovative leaders at Hull-House experimented in what we now call devised theater, and Chicago's theater and performance history runs thick with it, from the twentieth century to the twenty-first, including such Chicago icons as the Neo-Futurists, Frank Galati, Mary Zimmerman, and the Albany Park Theater Project, among many more. Even theater in Chicago that follows or followed a more traditional practice of putting movement and atmosphere with a prewritten text finds ways to devise the performance. For example, as chapter 8 explains, stage director Kyle Donnelly's concept of John Barton's adaptation of *The Rover* set in Trinidad (Aphra Behn's original is set in Italy) at the Goodman Theatre in 1989 formed the basis of the founding of Teatro Vista because Henry Godinez and Edward Torres's experience as actors embodying the production gave them the idea to start a Latinx theater of their own.

In the case of Chicago theater, space and race, along with tactics and repertoire, create an aesthetic. The Chicago makeshift manifests in certain hallmarks: experimentation, audience-actor intimacy, hyperrealist productions, and ensemble-based works. Collectively, these chapters propose *Chicago theater as makeshift theater*. While many theaters in Chicago have permanent spaces and do more conventional work, our book shows that the makeshift animated many theaters' beginnings and that the ethos of the makeshift is still centered in much of Chicago theater today. We argue that Chicago's unique makeshiftness exposes the politics and policies around how communities in Chicago engage in place-making and city ownership and the transgressive possibilities of theater and performance. By putting space at the center of an exploration of Chicago theater, these case studies revise traditional ideas of who holds power in Chicago, the distribution of city (and in some cases federal) resources, the desirability of permanency (versus itineracy), and various meanings made by "permanent" and "temporary." Furthermore, the collection includes case studies on the way racial and spatial dynamics central to understanding Chicago—as a hyper-segregated, dense, urban center—dialogue with performance practice. The essays consider how policies (i.e., zoning, fire codes) surround makeshift venues and affect the aesthetics of the stages and what happens on those stages in Chicago. By revisiting spaces on the margins, this book argues for distinct tactics and geographies of the makeshift, and for a theory of makeshift that engages tactics to subvert systemic, institutionalized power structures.

Chicago as Object of Study

This book demonstrates that Chicago's nearly two hundred years of theater history animates significant discussion in the fields of theater history, performance studies, and urban studies,[19] and yet few books are dedicated to the subject. Despite its influence and importance, long and varied history, myriad performance spaces, and thousands of performance texts and creators, Chicago's theater and performance history has not generated volumes of published texts. The *Chicago Tribune*'s two long-standing critics each authored a monograph about Chicago theater: one gives a narrative history of some of Chicago's theaters from the founding of the city, and the other offers an encyclopedia of *Chicago Tribune* articles about theater.[20] A handful of writers have examined a theater or two,[21] and other authors have explored certain styles of Chicago theater.[22] This book grows the recent scholarship and archival work on Chicago theater—work that chronicles actors, producers, writers, choreographers, directors, and other theater artists and their practices that have contributed to Chicago's theater and performance scene[23]—by positioning how theater and performance in Chicago from the late nineteenth century to the contemporary moment has continually made space in repurposed, marginal, temporary, and liminal, rather than just institutional, venues. Here we offer a brief history of Chicago theater, both so it exists in the field and so we can locate our chapters within it.

Since the mid-nineteenth century, Chicago has had both grassroots, makeshift theater and established, commercial theater. At times, these arts organizations were at odds with each other, but more often than not, Chicago proved a site where what started as amateur could become professional, where what was at the margins could become institutionalized, and where that which was community based became mainstream to the theater and performance scene in the city.

For example, while both the dining room at the Sauganash Hotel and the Rialto, a former auction house, ran as makeshift performance spaces in the 1830s and 1840s, Chicago entrepreneurs created legitimate and permanent theater spaces that hosted not only traveling troupes with commercial hits from the East Coast and Europe, but also local talent and new plays written in and about Chicago—spaces such as Rice's Theatre, McVicker's Theatre, and Crosby's Opera House. The end of the century saw more theater development; the Grand Opera House, Hooley's Theatre, the Auditorium Theatre, the Schiller, and Columbia Theatre hosted such greats as Joseph Jefferson, Sarah Bernhardt, Ellen Terry, Henry Irving, Ethel Barrymore, and Helena Modjeska.[24] But downtown theaters also hosted budding Chicago talent, such as Mary McVicker, child actress and daughter of the theater owner by the same surname, and local playwrights who wrote successful plays about life in Chicago.[25]

Chicago artists and creators also performed in more marginal settings. Perhaps the best example of this was the Midway Plaisance just to the west of the World's Columbian Exposition, which ran between May and October of 1893. The fairgrounds proper for the world's fair hosted educational exhibits on art, agriculture, fishery, machinery, transportation, and state and world governments. But the Midway, as chapter 1 explains, became a site where fairgoers could experience transgressive mixing of world populations, go on thrill rides, and attend cabaret performances. Furthermore, as chapter 2 explains, temporary concession buildings and souvenir stands built for the fair became home to Chicago's burgeoning bohemian artist collective. This desire to seek out performance in the margins remains a major part of what animates Chicago theater and performance in the twenty-first century.

Chicago stages in the twentieth century followed the pattern created in the nineteenth—major theater institutions running the business of theater popped up in the business district, while performances dedicated to developing new forms and types of artistic expression developed at the margins. By 1901, theater was big business in the Loop, with dozens of theaters drawing huge crowds and running shows year-round.[26] Like many urban theaters in the United States, many of these large playhouses were in business with the Syndicate, the vertically integrated theater business wherein the owners created a monopoly of plays, tours, actors, and theaters and wiped out the independent theater manager business.[27] Some theaters played minstrel shows and vaudeville instead of full-length plays, and many of the vaudeville theaters were part of circuits, too. In later years, the Shubert Brothers—Sam, Lee, and Jacob—also bought theaters and built one of their own in Chicago. These booking monopolies made sense commercially, but they did not help develop local talent.

Another contributing factor to Chicago's sense of makeshift theater—even in professional houses downtown—was the city's ongoing struggle with fire. McVicker's burned down three times and Hooley's (later Powers') burned at least twice. And yet artists and entrepreneurs rebuilt. The most famous Chicago theater fire was at the Iroquois in December 1903, when 602 people (mostly women and children) burned to death or were suffocated when a set piece lit a curtain on fire at a matinee showing of *Mr. Blue Beard*; this remains the deadliest theater fire in history.[28] The Iroquois Theater fire caused a major revision of theater architecture and fire safety codes. Even theaters in retrofitted buildings must be up to demanding codes, and the Chicago fire marshal visits all theaters without fixed seating prior to opening night to make sure that the codes are being followed.[29] These strict laws impeded the growth of theater in Chicago for years; few companies could meet the stringent demands placed on theaters in those buildings built solely to be theaters.

Theater makers at the margins also struggled with fire codes written for large auditoriums since many of their performance spaces were converted spaces rarely able to meet the requirements. But despite these issues, the twentieth century saw community-oriented, immigrant, club, and parish theaters grow up in the neighborhoods. In these settings, Chicagoans could attend foreign-language theater or art theater or dance and see new forms of dramatic expression and local talent onstage. As chapter 3 shows, pioneers of the Little Theatre movement set up in a renovated carriage showroom on South Michigan Avenue. Many of these artists had met and developed their work at the 57th Street Artist Colony outlined in chapter 2. One of the most important sites for art theater was Hull-House, a neighborhood theater that produced some of the most important theater in America at the turn of the century. Hull-House had multiple theater groups, but the Hull-House Players under the direction of Laura Dainty Pelham holds a significant place in U.S. theater history due to its production of art theater from such noteworthy playwrights as William Butler Yeats, Henrik Ibsen, and Nikolai Gogol. The group pioneered art theater and the Little Theatre movement.

Immigrant enclaves were another important site for noncommercial theater in the first few decades of the twentieth century. Chicago's immigrant groups—Germans, Central and Eastern European Jews, Italians, Irish, Poles, Lithuanians, Swedes, Greeks, Norwegians, and later Mexicans—produced theater, whether in club houses, church halls, or state-of-the-art auditoriums. For example, Chicago's Poles had one of the largest and most state-of-the-art theaters in the city at St. Stanislaus Kostka parish in what is now Wicker Park, and they even hosted Helena Modjeska on their stage for a Polish play written by a local, amateur Chicago playwright in 1892. Chicago's Jewish community has an enduring theater tradition with Glickman's Palace Theatre and the People's Music Hall on Twelfth Street (now Roosevelt Road) and the Douglas Park Auditorium on Ogden and Kedzie.[30] And Chicago's Czechs built Thalia Hall on Eighteenth Street and Allport Street in the Pilsen neighborhood—the building still functions as a performance venue today. As chapter 4 makes clear, some of these groups even helped bolster the fledgling Goodman Theatre in its early years. Furthermore, the growing African American community in Chicago had the first professional "colored" theater in America—from 1904 to 1924—where the Pekin Stock Company, made up of local Chicagoans, put on twenty-eight different musical comedies, not including revivals, between 1906 and 1908.[31]

Theater in the 1930s in Chicago faced the challenge of the Great Depression, which both economically stifled and creatively spurred theater development in the city. The larger playhouses struggled to keep large audiences, but the city was also home to several units of the Works Progress Administration's Federal Theatre Project (FTP). One of the most popular productions of the FTP came from Chicago—the *Swing Mikado*, which transferred to Broadway. Chapter 5 outlines another FTP production, that of *Big White Fog*, a show written by a Black Chicagoan about the Great Migration and the brutalities of city life for the African American community. A decade later, another Chicago playwright would make these themes famous: Lorraine Hansberry in her play *A Raisin in the Sun*. Other theater groups in Chicago made their way despite the economics of the Depression. One such case is the Chicago Workers Theater, a collective begun in 1931 who did social drama with amateur actors on a platform in a room above a bookshop at 505 North State Street.[32] In 1935, they changed their name to the Chicago Repertory Group (CRG), and Louis "Studs" Terkel was among their members. Terkel called the CRG a "club team of the Group Theatre" in New York; the group lasted until 1943 and helped launch Terkel's career.[33]

The mid-twentieth century saw a downturn in theater-making and theatergoing in Chicago. Most of the commercial theaters in the Loop hosted second-rate tours of commercial fare, and some converted into movie palaces. A few institutions kept theater alive in the city. The Goodman Theatre, for example, although it no longer produced professional shows, survived into the 1970s as a theater training school. Hull-House, long a trailblazer of avant-garde theater,[34] merged its many groups into an adult education division and produced art theater throughout the 1940s, 1950s, and 1960s.[35] In 1963, when much of the settlement house complex was demolished to build the campus of the University of Illinois at Chicago Circle (UICC, now the University of Illinois at Chicago), the theater moved to 3212 North Broadway into a former American Legion post in the Lakeview neighborhood under the innovative and energetic artistic direction of Robert Sickinger, whose work revitalized Chicago theater through the 1960s.

In 1953, the American Indian Center was founded in Chicago largely as a response to "the growing needs of a rapidly-expanding local American Indian population"[36] and the "selective termination of tribal status, in concert with the Indian Relocation program"[37] during the mid-twentieth century. Considered the "oldest urban-based Native membership community center," [38] the American Indian Center hosted and continues to host a wealth of traditional and nontraditional Native American arts, theater, and performance events, including powwows, dances, drum centers, and music. The center's midcentury founding attests to the city's growing indigenous population as well as the growth of indigenous performance practices in Chicago.

Mid-twentieth-century Chicago also saw the beginnings of improvisational theater, a form Chicago would later become famous for. Viola Spolin, Paul Sills, and Bernie Sahlins all started their work at this time, and The Second City opened in Chicago in December 1959. Chapter 7 outlines some of the history of improv in Chicago. Spolin had been a student at Hull-House as a child, and Sills, her son who also did theater as a child, helped create Playwrights Theatre Club, a theater that brought together such Chicago theater greats as Sills, Sahlins, Joyce and Byrne Piven, and Sheldon Patinkin. In addition to changing the trajectory of American comedy, The Second City also demonstrated the possibility of a hybrid between commercial and art theater. They were a small, ensemble-driven performance group like the Chicago Little Theatre and the Chicago Repertory Group, but they were not a not-for-profit group.[39] While The Second City got a new space, other theater spaces—such as Hull-House's Jane Addams Theatre, usurped by the construction of the University of Illinois at Chicago Circle—were lost in the 1960s.

Small, ensemble-driven theater companies began springing up throughout the 1960s, 1970s, and 1980s, making new performance spaces. Christiansen notes that despite Chicago Mayor Richard J. Daley's attempts to create a centrally located performing arts center, "the city's culture, and particularly the culture of theater, was to grow organically, from the bottom up, in homes converted from former warehouses, bowling alleys, laundries, and bakeries."[40] Chapter 6 tells the story of two such companies—Kingston Mines Theatre and the Body Politic Theatre. Each group had been working in churches and other marginal spaces prior to transforming industrial buildings on North Lincoln Avenue in the Lincoln Park neighborhood into theater spaces. The storefront as we know it came into being.

By the 1990s, many of these storefront theaters faced precarity due to increased property values and zoning laws. In 1994, Wisdom Bridge Theatre—first established in 1974 in Chicago's Rogers Park neighborhood on the Far North Side—left its home and relocated to the Ivanhoe Theater, then in Lakeview.[41] Two years earlier, in 1992, the theater—"once one of the crown jewels of the Chicago theater scene"—had its board suspend paychecks to all staff to recoup more than six figures of debt.[42] Yet despite precarious financial times and the financial difficulty of running a theater, theaters in Chicago continued to incubate and grow; by the early twenty-first century, Chicago had over three hundred theater companies.

The boom in theaters—both spaces and companies—in the latter part of the twentieth century was significant, and we cannot name all of them in this introduction, much as we have failed to name all the theaters in Chicago up to this point. But a few game changers stand out. Since 1985, five theaters in Chicago have been recognized for their excellence by garnering the Regional Theatre Tony Award. The first to win was Steppenwolf Theatre Company. Steppenwolf began in 1974 when a group of high school and college students put on plays in a church basement in suburban Deerfield, and it was the make-shift nature of the shows that excited the group and pushed them to continue.[43] After being itinerant for nearly two decades, in 1991, Steppenwolf built a new, state-of-the-art theater at 1650 North Halsted Street. Thirty years later, the new complex includes multiple theaters.

The second theater to win a Regional Theatre Tony was the Goodman Theatre in 1992 under the artistic direction of Robert Falls, who has led the theater since 1985; Falls had previously worked with Wisdom Bridge. As chapter 4 outlines, the Goodman mounted productions in the auditorium built for them at the Art Institute of Chicago for seventy-five years before moving into a renovated set of buildings—on sites that once hosted live theaters but had been converted to movie theaters mid-century—at 170 North Dearborn Street in 2000. The next Chicago theater to win a Regional Theatre Tony was Victory Gardens Theater in 2001 under the artistic direction of Dennis Začek. Victory Gardens started in 1974 and had an itinerant existence for nearly two decades. The company, which is dedicated to producing new work, renovated the Biograph Theater—formerly a movie theater—at 2433

North Lincoln Avenue, near the spaces discussed in chapter 6. In addition to the large theater on the first floor, Victory Gardens has a smaller theater upstairs that is home to Teatro Vista—chapter 8 outlines the contours of that relationship—and other itinerant theater companies.

In 2008, Chicago's largest theater in terms of size and budget, Chicago Shakespeare Theater, won the Regional Theatre Tony Award. Chicago Shakespeare Theater began in 1986 when Barbara Gaines staged a production of *Henry V* on the rooftop of the Red Lion Pub at 2446 North Lincoln Avenue. Today, Chicago Shakespeare Theatre has three theaters and a huge facility on Chicago's Navy Pier. (Barbara Gaines remains at the helm.) The last Chicago theater to win a Regional Theatre Tony as of the writing of this book is Lookingglass Theatre Company in 2011. Lookingglass began in 1988 when a group of Northwestern University theater students devised a new adaptation of Lewis Carroll's *Through the Looking-Glass, and What Alice Found There*, which they titled *Through the Lookingglass*, to stage at the Edinburgh Festival Fringe. The company's later adaptation of Carroll's book remains one of the theater's signature shows (now called *Lookingglass Alice*) and has been remounted several times.

We mention these major theaters because each began on the margins in makeshift conditions, and today each is a major Chicago theater institution. This has also been the case with Jackie Taylor's Black Ensemble Theater, and, as of an announcement in spring 2019, TimeLine Theatre: they are theaters whose success and popularity have allowed them to build or launch their own permanent spaces. While countless other Chicago theater and performance groups formed in the middle and latter parts of the twentieth century are equally important—Court Theatre, Skyloft Players, Tempo Players of Washington Park, Congo Square Theatre, Pegasus Players, the Neo-Futurists, Mary-Arrchie Theatre, Strawdog Theatre Company, Apple Tree Theatre, Lifeline Theatre, the Hypocrites, Chicago Dramatists, Stage Left Theatre, Famous Door Theatre Company, A Red Orchid Theatre, About Face Theatre, Redmoon Theater, Aguijón Theater, and UrbanTheater Company, to name just a few—the move from margins to center, itinerant to permanent, demonstrates the argument of our book: Chicago theater is unique in its adaption of makeshift and marginal spaces that create a method and style of theater and performance celebrated nationwide. And as much as this book is about makeshift or unorthodox or marginal performance efforts, it is important not to lose sight of the growth of Chicago as a thriving conventional theater community, especially starting in the 1970s and continuing to this day. What is remarkable is that the same dynamics and impulses that led to makeshift, to the unorthodox, also led to the orthodox—a place where Bernie Sahlins, cofounder of The Second City, and Del Close, a theater artist who performed and directed at The Second City, then went on to coach *Saturday Night Live* comedians and act in major motion film productions.

Not yet mentioned are the many performance spaces in Chicago not associated with a single theater company, spaces that have allowed itinerant performance groups to exist: Little Black Pearl, the Greenhouse Theater Center, the Chopin Theatre, the Den Theatre, Stage 773 (previously known as Theatre Building Chicago), the Athenaeum Theatre, and the many spaces affiliated with churches, universities, museums, and cultural associations. Equally important are the many theaters that do not aim to move from marginal to center. Many Chicago theaters through the years invested in their makeshift theater tactics as a way of engaging in community and art- and space-making with no designs on new buildings or expanded seasons. Chicago continues to cultivate and celebrate that as a legitimate form of theater and performance, too.

Chapter Summaries

The ten chapters in this book are arranged chronologically to enable readers to draw conclusions about change over time. That said, the book could have been arranged by theme instead: many of the chapters connect to one another in relation to themes of dramatic literature, regional theater, spatial racism, itinerancy, dramatic versus postdramatic theater, and geography. We have also divided the chapters into three sections.

The first section explores how theater in Chicago at the turn of the nineteenth to the twentieth century rose from the ashes of the Great Chicago Fire in 1871 to produce world-renowned artistic movements and forms. Chapter 1 by Rosemarie K. Bank gives a new account of the theory of the Midway Plaisance at the World's Columbian Exposition of 1893. Most scholars of turn-of-the-century world's fairs attribute their spatial organization to social Darwinism, or the belief that white Northern and Western Europeans and white Americans were the height of civilization, with all other races and ethnic groups being less developed. Bank intervenes to show that the actual map of the Midway does not support this interpretation, and that the manager of most of the acts booked for the Midway, Sol Bloom, was more invested in business entrepreneurship than racial ideology. Furthermore, Bank shows how rather than siloing racial groups by perceived levels of savage versus civilized, the Midway allowed both performers and spectators transgressive space to circulate among one another.

Stuart J. Hecht's chapter investigates the 57th Street Artist Colony that took up residence in leftover souvenir stands from the World's Columbian Exposition at the turn of the nineteenth to the twentieth century. This group of notable Chicago architects, writers, theater makers, and visual artists—including Mary Aldis, Margaret Anderson, Sherwood Anderson, Maxwell Bodenheim, Floyd Dell, Theodore Dreiser, Arthur Davison Ficke, Alice Gerstenberg, Kenneth Sawyer Goodman, Ben Hecht, Vachel Lindsay, Edgar Lee Masters, Harriet Monroe, B. J. O. (Bror) Nordfeldt, and Carl Sandburg—revived the forgotten space. Hecht analyzes the artists and art made in conjunction with this makeshift space to point out that while the Victorian-inspired neoclassicism of the Columbian Exposition's White City faded within a year or so of the fair, the makeshift and modern style of the 57th Street Artist Colony's buildings endured and created new forms of American art.

Shannon Epplett's chapter tells the story of the Fine Arts Building on South Michigan Avenue as it transformed from a carriage company showroom and workshop to a home for musicians, architects, writers, publishers, illustrators, bookbinders, bookstores, art supply retailers, musical instrument repair and sales shops, sheet music publishers, piano showrooms, and, ultimately, theater artists in the first two decades of the twentieth century. Chicago theater reformers, as Epplett calls them, brought art theater—or theater meant to inspire and uplift—to the building's smaller spaces, which were not built to be theaters. Epplett catalogs the work of such Chicago theater pioneers as Anna Morgan, Donald Robertson, Arthur and Mary Aldis, Arthur Bissell, Hobart Chatfield-Taylor, Alice Gerstenberg, Kenneth Sawyer Goodman, Maurice Browne, and Ellen Van Volkenburg as they create the Chicago Little Theatre and deal with the challenges of the building and one another.

The second section reveals how theater movements in Chicago in the middle of the twentieth century grappled with definitions of ethnicity and race in the city; it also deals with transitions between spaces meant for and spaces converted into use for theater and performance. The four chapters in this section illustrate how theater and performance made in and between communities and the codifying neighborhoods and spaces from the 1920s to the 1970s revealed hyper-segregation but also—at times—produced new possibilities for collaboration and reaching new audiences. Megan E. Geigner's chapter explores the many non-Goodman productions on the brand-new Goodman Theatre stage at the Art Institute of Chicago during the first years of its existence, from 1925 to 1933. She argues that the Goodman's hosting of Hull-House play transfers, immigrant theater and performance groups, amateur theater tournaments, and benefit performances upheld the artistic practice of its namesake—Kenneth Sawyer Goodman—by inviting marginalized groups into a central and monied theater, and that doing so helped Chicago theater audiences associate these types of theater with professional and worthwhile theater endeavors in the city. She also outlines how this type of theatrical cultural exchange set a precedent for the way theaters in Chicago work today.

Aaron Krall's chapter catalogs the production by the Chicago Negro Unit of the Federal Theatre Project of Theodore Ward's *Big White Fog* in 1939. The play tells the story of the Mason family—Great Migration transplants to Chicago—and the difficulties they face in a city inhospitable to African Americans. Krall interprets the plot and characters of the play through the fraught production history of the show. It started in the Loop at the Great Northern Theatre, but for reasons that are unclear, Chicago's Federal Theatre Project management transferred it to the DuSable High School auditorium on the city's South Side, where the production failed to draw an audience. Krall argues that makeshift theatrical spaces on the city's margins were precarious locations for ambitious but marginalized communities to tell their stories in the early twentieth century.

Cat Gleason's chapter gives the account of the Kingston Mines Theatre and the Body Politic Theatre transforming a trolley barn, bowling alley, and slicing machine workshop into performance venues in the late 1960s and early 1970s. Deconstructing the mythology of the first few storefronts, Gleason shows how these spaces were at the intersection of racist urban renewal projects, community activist groups, city fire codes and building policy, and theater in Chicago. By giving a detailed history of the two theaters and their pioneers—June Pyskacek, Paul Sills, and James Shiflett—Gleason argues that the theaters' abilities to position themselves between the forces of urban renewal and community resistance set a new standard for Chicago theater and ushered in the era of the storefront theater.

Travis Stern's chapter relays the intricate history of ImprovOlympic (later called iO after the United States Olympic Committee threatened to sue them over their name), improv's development in Chicago from the 1960s through the 1990s, and the group's quest to find a permanent space. By tracing not just the ways that improv styles and performers changed over the years, but also the different types of spaces, performance times, and audiences for the form, Stern shows the relationship between improvised theater forms and improvised performance spaces.

The third section of the book examines the potency of itinerancy. Troubling the assumption that theater and performance artists desire a theater to call their own, these chapters explore artistry that calls into focus Chicago's legacy of racism. Furthermore, they offer a critique of linear trajectories of "arrival," wherein artists with permanent, recognized, and unchanging work get reviewed and codified by institutional power. Laura A. Lodewyck's chapter offers the first account of the founding and trajectory of one of Chicago's longest-running Latinx theaters in the city, Teatro Vista. Through interviews with some of the theater's prominent artists throughout the years, including Sandra Marquez, Henry Godinez, Edward Torres, Carlos Tortolero, Nilda Hernandez, Ricardo Gutiérrez, and Sandra Delgado, Lodewyck counters the idea that ending itinerancy and finding a permanent theater space is the goal. Instead, the chapter, through its reading of Teatro Vista's earliest performances in 1991 along with two other productions in the last few decades, argues that itineracy allows for more sustained community contact.

LaRonika Marie Thomas's chapter illustrates the racial, spatial, and aesthetic significance of the work of Theaster Gates, the Chicago-based urban planner and artist. Through interviews and aesthetic observation, Thomas focuses on how Gates's work produced the Stony Island Arts Bank and the Dorchester Projects, repurposed makeshift spaces on the city's South Side. Through her concept of "civic dramaturgy," Thomas argues that Gates's spatial practice—which had made arts spaces of former homes, banks, and other non-arts venues—amalgamates meanings across the private and the public to reveal how political, racial, and aesthetic systems filter and produce relationality in the city.

Jasmine Jamillah Mahmoud's chapter offers a participant observer's account of attending the Chicago Home Theater Festival in 2015 and interviews with four of the festival's founders and lead producers—Irina Zadov, Laley Lippard, Aymar Jean Christian, and Meida McNeal—that record their experiences with the festival between 2012 and 2017. In so doing, her chapter archives how the private space of the home acted as fertile public ground for producing theater, for contesting long histories and practices of spatial racism in Chicago, and for practicing, however temporarily, a more intimate, engaged way of making home.

Finally, the epilogue addresses the way Chicago theater and performance makers dealt with both the COVID-19 pandemic beginning in the spring of 2020 and the social uprising about racial inequality in the early summer of 2020.

Makeshift: A Work in Progress

While much of what follows offers a historical lens, makeshift Chicago theater and performance promises to continue. Perhaps Chicago playwright Ike Holter puts it best: "I think the city knows it's a work in progress, and I think that's exciting. Some cities think that they are all the way there, whereas Chicago is always, I think, cautiously moving toward progress. We've fallen sometimes, but the idea that we're not at the end point is important. . . . Chicago has a feel of, OK, cool, so we're *all* working on this, we're *all* doing this, right. Instead of, like, it's done, everything is great."[44] While the following chapters provide insight into this "city on the make," to quote Nelson Algren, we look forward to the yield of the makeshift in the coming centuries.

Notes

1. Richard Christiansen, *A Theater of Our Own: A History and a Memoir of 1,001 Nights in Chicago* (Evanston, IL: Northwestern University Press, 2004), 7.

2. Chicago was officially incorporated in 1833. That said, many nations of Native Americans—the Algonquin, Iroquois, Illiniwek, Potawatomi, and Sauk—called what we now call "Chicago" home for centuries prior to white settlement.

3. Arthur W. Bloom, "Tavern Theatre in Early Chicago," *Journal of the Illinois State Historical Society (1908–1984)* 74, no. 3 (Autumn 1981): 217–21, 223–29.

4. Bob Bullen, "On Making Chicago America's 'Theater Capital,'" *Chicago Theatre Addict (blog)*, June 23, 2010.

5. Marvin Carlson, *Places of Performance: The Semiotics of Theatre Architecture* (Ithaca, NY: Cornell University Press, 1993); Una Chaudhuri,

Staging Place: The Geography of Modern Drama (Ann Arbor: University of Michigan Press, 1995); D. J. Hopkins, Shelley Orr, and Kim Solga, eds., *Performance and the City* (New York: Palgrave MacMillan, 2009).

6. See Henri Lefebvre, *The Production of Space* (Hoboken, NJ: Wiley-Blackwell, 1974); Shannon Jackson, *Lines of Activity: Performance, Historiography, Hull-House Domesticity* (Ann Arbor: University of Michigan Press, 2000).

7. George Lipstiz, *How Racism Takes Place* (Philadelphia: Temple University Press, 2011.)

8. Spencer Rich, "Black in Baltimore, 9 Other Cities 'Hypersegregated.'" *The Washington Post*, August 5, 1989.

9. Tanveer Ali, "Hispanics Pass Blacks as Chicago's 2nd Largest Racial, Ethnic Group: Census." DNAinfo.com, September 14, 2017.

10. Harry J. Elam Jr., "The Device of Race: An Introduction," in *African American Performance and Theatre History: A Critical Reader, ed.* Harry J. Elam Jr. and David Krasner (New York: Oxford University Press, 2001); Harvey Young, *Theatre & Race* (New York: Palgrave McMillan, 2013).

11. Joshua Chambers-Letson, *A Race So Different: Performance and Law in Asian America* (New York: New York University Press, 2013), 4.

12. We recognize this term is from US Anglophone English and that it is a contested term for those who identify as part of Latinidad and by those who study the work of Latin American theater and performance. For more discussion on "Latinx" as a term, see Lordes Torres, "Latinx?," *Latino Studies* 16 (2018): 283–85; and Salvador Vidal-Ortiz and Juliana Martínez, "Latinx Thoughts: Latinidad with an X," *Latino Studies* 16 (2018): 384–95.

13. For more on the expansion of whiteness in the twentieth-century United States, see Nell Irvin Painter, *The History of White People* (New York: W. W. Norton, 2011).

14. Michel de Certeau, *The Practice of Everyday Life* (Berkeley: University of California Press, 1984), xiii-xiv.

15. de Certeau, *The Practice of Everyday Life*, xix.

16. Chloe Johnston and Coya Paz Brownrigg, *Ensemble-Made Chicago: A Guide to Devised Theater* (Evanston, IL: Northwestern University Press), x.

17. de Certeau, *The Practice of Everyday Life*, ix.

18. Diana Taylor, *The Archive and the Repertoire: Performing Cultural Memory in the Americas* (Durham, NC: Duke University Press, 2003), 21.

19. This book also contributes to sociology and urban sociology. It should be noted that many cite the beginnings of urban sociology as rooted in the city of Chicago, due to the direction of sociologist Robert Park, who taught at the University of Chicago's Department of Sociology and Anthropology

from 1914 to 1933. Given the city's entanglements with race, it must be noted that Park previously worked with noted African American educator Booker T. Washington, and that W. E. B. Du Bois's urban sociology work predated Park's by twenty years but was largely ignored at the time because Du Bois was Black. For more, see Mitchell Duneier, Philip Kasinitz, and Alexandra K. Murphy, eds., *The Urban Ethnography Reader* (Oxford and New York: Oxford University Press, 2014), 9–21.

20. Christiansen, *A Theater of Our Own;* Chris Jones, *Bigger, Brighter, Louder: 150 Years of Chicago Theater as Seen by Chicago Tribune Critics* (Chicago: University of Chicago Press, 2013).

21. Thomas Bauman, *The Pekin: This Rise and Fall of Chicago's First Black-Owned Theater* (Urbana-Champaign: University of Illinois Press, 2014); Janet Coleman, *The Compass: The Story of the Improvisational Theatre That Revolutionized the Art of Comedy in America* (New York: Knopf, 1990); John Mayer, *Steppenwolf Theatre Company of Chicago: In Their Own Words* (London: Bloomsbury, 2016).

22. Jeffrey Sweet, *Something Wonderful Right Away* (Newark, NJ: Limelight Editions, 2004); Mark Larson, *Ensemble: An Oral History of Chicago Theatre* (Evanston, IL: Agate Midway, 2019).

23. Harvey Young and Queen Meccasia Zabriskie, *Black Theater Is Black Life: An Oral History of Chicago Theater and Dance, 1970–2010* (Evanston, IL: Northwestern University Press, 2013); Johnston and Paz Brownrigg, *Ensemble-Made Chicago*.

24. Christiansen, *Theater of Our Own*, 24–27.

25. Christiansen, *Theater of Our Own*, 13. Sadly, the *Chicago Daily Tribune*, which Christiansen cites, fails to enter the playwrights' names in its articles.

26. A survey of the *Chicago Daily Tribune* from 1901 lists the following theaters: the Academy, Auditorium, Cleveland's, Columbus, Dearborn, Garrick (previously the Schiller), Great Northern, Haymarket, Hopkin's, Illinois, McVicker's, Olympic-Clayton, People's, Powers' (previously Hooley's), Studebaker, and Tracadero Theatres, and the Chicago Opera House, the Grand Opera House, the Orpheum Music Hall, and Middleton's Clark Street Museum.

27. Jack Poggi. *Theater in America: The Impact of Economic Forces 1870–1967* (Ithaca, NY: Cornell University Press, 1968).

28. Jones, *Bigger, Brighter, Louder*, 39–40.

29. One example of a retrofitted theater built to meet Chicago fire codes is the Francis X. Kinahan Theater on the third floor of the Reynolds Club student union building on the University of Chicago's campus. Named for

an English professor who supported student theater, the converted student lounge has a double layer of drywall on each outer wall in compliance with Chicago fire codes for theaters. Current theaters, such as Lookingglass's Water Tower Theatre, get visits from the Chicago fire marshal before each opening.

30. Christiansen, *Theater of Our Own*, 54.

31. Bauman, *Pekin*, xvii.

32. Christiansen, *Theater of Our Own*, 80–83.

33. Christiansen, *Theater of Our Own*, 83.

34. Stuart J. Hecht, "Hull-House Theatre: An Analytical and Evaluative History," (PhD diss., Northwestern University, 1983).

35. Hecht, "Hull-House Theatre," 90–92.

36. "History," American Indian Center, https://www.aicchicago.org/history.

37. "History," American Indian Center.

38. AICChicago website, https://aicchicago.org/.

39. Although The Second City was an evolution of the Compass Players, when it formed in 1959, Sahlins used his money from selling his business to invest in The Second City as a producer rather than setting up the funding through a not-for-profit board of directors and donations. See Coleman, *Compass*, 255–56.

40. Christiansen, *Theater of Our Own*, 123.

41. Sid Smith, "Wisdom Bridge Theatre Moving to New Town," *Chicago Tribune*, April 15, 1994.

42. Lewis Lazare, "Further Crumbling at Wisdom Bridge/Phone Tix: Theater League Tries Convenience/Cultural Center Update," *Chicago Reader*, January 23, 1992.

43. Mayer, *Steppenwolf Theatre Company*, 18–19.

44. Quoted in Larson, *Ensemble*, 479.

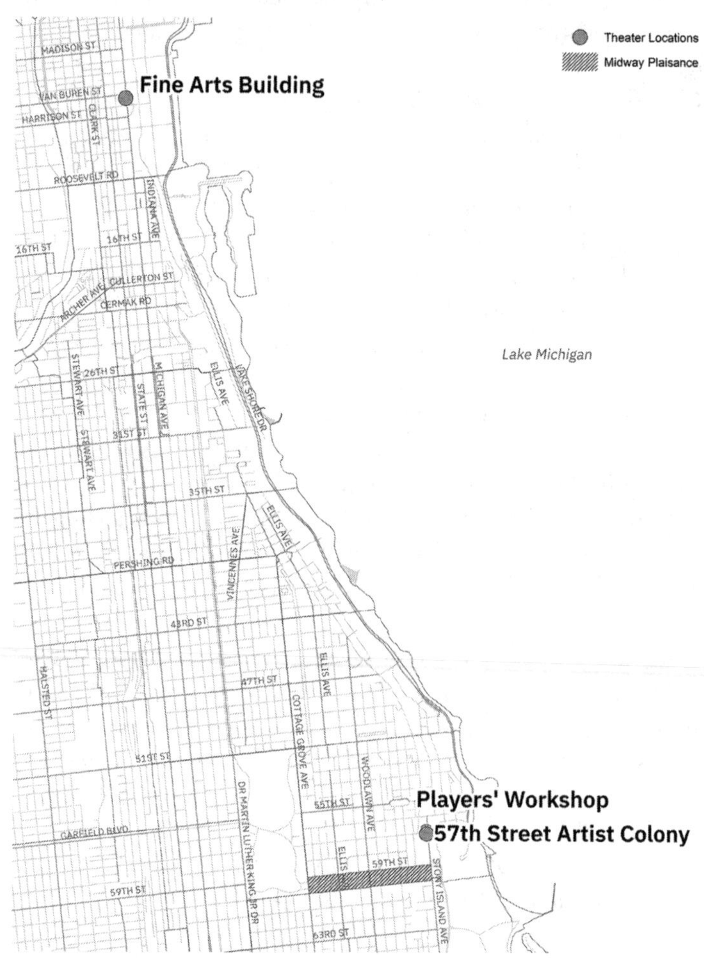

Part 1 theater locations. Map created by Kelsey Rydland, Northwestern University Libraries, Geospatial and Data Services.

Part 1

Theater: Artistry Born of Ashes

Stuart J. Hecht

Chicagoans are a hearty people. They live in a city whose history is one of destruction, some self-inflicted and some acts of God. Its people are resilient: they have always found opportunity in change. From the start buildings were built only to be razed, then replaced with newer buildings, which in turn were torn down or reconfigured for alternate use. When Chicago first prospered, it built blocks of grand mansions and miles upon miles of apartment dwellings—and storefront businesses. The mansions are long gone, but the apartments and storefronts remain, attesting to shifts in fortune and fate, and the ongoing demand for cheap rental space.

Chicago began in 1833 as a small village but quickly grew thanks to its location, ambition, and imaginative resourcefulness. As Liesl Olson, director of Chicago studies at the Newberry Library, has noted, the city's business was closely tied to farmland (and transportation); like farmers, Chicagoans learned to make nothing into something. City engineers miraculously redirected the Chicago River to remove urban stench but could not avoid fire. The Civil War enabled Chicago businesses to prosper and the downtown population to soar. But the great fire of 1871 left most of the city charred and its peoples displaced.

This catastrophe burned out much of the old, yet made way for the new—or at least that is how civic leaders approached it. It was only a quarter century since Chicago's founding; boosterism became the city's hallmark. Rather than crumble in defeat, Chicago reinvented itself. Though still stockyard rough-and-tumble, Chicagoans built new buildings upon the muck, marvels of engineering and art: thus began the city's tradition of cutting-edge architecture. Wanting to celebrate its rebirth—and to silence East Coast snobs who sniffed at this Midwest upstart's vulgarity—Chicagoans again decided to build, this time constructing an entirely faux "White City" over swamplands on the South Side. Hence arose the World's Columbian Exposition of 1893, which drew some twenty-seven million attendees. The exposition lasted but a summer; the winter after it closed its structures succumbed to fire—the second blaze of our story.

From this second fire emerged a bohemian arts community dedicated to new ideas and forms. This signals another, corresponding theme. Though Chicago did sport a number of often-impressive theater buildings beginning in the nineteenth century, those structures had little impact on local Chicago artistry. Most of the productions seen at Chicago's established theaters were transfers, heading to or coming from commercial Broadway, and were rarely woven into the fabric of the city itself. What ultimately proved meaningful or lasting in Chicago more often came from indigenous, grassroots beginnings. The bohemia that emerged at the Fifty-Seventh Street community offered something different and new: homegrown theatrical art that was modest, enduring, imaginative, and fresh.

A third major fire hampered the construction of Chicago theaters for most of the twentieth century. In December 1903 star comedian Eddie Foy was performing in *Mr. Blue Beard*, a touring musical, at the brand-new Iroquois Theater. Fire broke out. Poor design resulted in over 600 deaths, many of them children. Calls for reform led to the implementation of stringent guidelines for theaters nationwide. In Chicago the codes were so strict that they squelched efforts to use alternative spaces as theaters. Ironically, this forced Chicago theater makers to find new ways to perform, often in unorthodox settings, finding "Loop" holes to survive; it would also eventually contribute to the city's peculiar—and special—aesthetic: unadorned, realistic, and imaginatively raw.

Old buildings continued to give way to the new. For over a hundred years tenements and abandoned neighborhoods have provided sites for Chicago's artistic initiatives. In 1889 Jane Addams and Ellen Gates Starr moved into a run-down mansion situated in the heart of a multiethnic immigrant slum neighborhood to undertake a reclamation project designed to aid the poor—again, the concept of making nothing into something. They built their Hull-House settlement into a social service institution garnering national and international renown. As part of this, the settlement began several theaters led by in-house "residents," but whose actors were locals: the working poor. Hence social work resulted in often-significant art: the Hull-House Players were probably America's first "little theater," and they inspired a host of others, including Maurice Browne, founder of the Chicago Little Theatre a dozen years later. Hull-House's children's theater attracted literally hundreds of participants, some going on to productive, cultured lives and others making their mark in professional theater. It was here that Neva Boyd and her star pupil Viola Spolin first studied children at play, and it was here that Spolin first experimented with improvisational games; her methods later evolved via her son Paul Sills, first into the Playwrights Theatre and its offshoot, the venerable Second City improv company, and still later into Sills's influential Story Theater. When in 1962 Mayor Richard J. Daley decided to bulldoze that neighborhood—along with Hull-House itself—in the name of urban renewal, Hull-House reorganized, morphing into several small centers scattered throughout the city. Robert Sickinger was hired to run its newly reestablished theater and built an impressive, dynamic program, featuring four separate theaters and a touring company, earning national recognition for his inventive directorial artistry, and training both actors (e.g., Mike Nussbaum) and playwrights (e.g., David Mamet and Jim Jacobs). Sickinger also cultivated audiences for then cutting-edge dramas by the likes of Pinter, Beckett, and Albee. The result would be Chicago's "Off-Loop" theater movement that began in the 1970s and still thrives today.

The Great Depression paradoxically played to Chicago's strengths, despite its obvious hardships. The city responded with another world's fair, this one in 1933. As was the case with the 1893 exposition, this newer edition featured technological advances, traditional art (like a recreated Globe Theatre), and, comparable to the older fair's scandalous dancer Little Egypt, there was the notorious fan dancer Sally Rand. In another important development, the Chicago branch of the Federal Theatre Project emerged, headed for a time by playwright Susan Glaspell. Though short-lived, it did birth the controversial play *Spirochete*, as well as a significant African American play explored here in chapter 5. Resilient Chicagoan artists built from the detritus of economic disaster.

Robert Sickinger's Hull-House success inspired other entrepreneurs, many of them baby boomers, to attempt small-scale theater in Chicago. Some utilized Sickinger's abandoned theaters; others turned to alternative sites, refashioning them into performance spaces. The Second City skirted the old, still-restrictive fire codes by setting up tables and serving drinks; thus a new configuration for performance—and a style of performance itself, sophisticated and hip—was born. It was an aesthetic peculiar to Chicago. This spirit of invention would later find expression artistically through various theatrical forms, but perhaps most notably in the Viola Spolin-based methods of The Second City, its improvisational flavor characterized by the title of Jeffrey Sweet's book *Something Wonderful Right Away: An Oral History of The Second City and The Compass Players*.

The predominant Chicago theater characteristic is its emphasis on community. Perhaps this goes back to Hull-House or perhaps to that Fifty-Seventh Street bohemian community. But Chicago theater is often about issues or ideas, not scenery. Rather than the East Coast and West Coast systems of individual actors seeking fortune and fame, nomads moving from show to show, in Chicago theater artists favor the ensemble. Usually, groups of friends have started theaters together, as a company—or compact community—congregating around a shared ideal. From Sickinger came a taste for strong directorial imagery and wild theatrical invention; such over-the-top showmanship appealed to a city famous for its entrepreneurs, journalists, politicos, gangsters, and Barnumesque carnies. But Chicago audiences have also always felt part of the event; as scholar Julie Jackson has noted, unlike the East Coast where the theater event ends at the curtain line, in Chicago the onstage production reaches out to include its spectators.

Chicago theatergoers are hungry to listen and debate, to dissect and explore the latest dramatic expression of Chicago's grit. Without their adventurous support Chicago theater would not have blossomed forth and continue to do so today. In Chicago, theater is community.

All of Sickinger's theaters are now gone; one became a parking garage, another was remodeled into expensive condos. One once housed Steppenwolf Theatre's breakthrough 1982 production of Sam Shepard's *True West* with John Malkovich swinging away at Jeff Perry (replaced by Gary Sinise in the acclaimed New York production). Ashes to ashes, dust to dust. Elsewhere once-ramshackle storefronts still enable acting ensembles to morph, moving into impressive, formal theaters; others have been demolished, only to be replaced by a new generation of ensembles operating in new makeshift sites: newer populations, new ways of performing Chicago lives. The creative embers still glow.

It is then with some measure of irony that one of contemporary Chicago's preeminent theater companies, the Tony Award–winning Lookingglass Theatre, found its eventual home in a fire's relic. Begun in 1988 and initially performing in makeshift spaces, Lookingglass

View southwest from the roof of the Manufacturers and Liberal Arts Building, 1893. Photograph by C. D. Arnold, Ellsworth-Arnold Photograph Album Collection, vol. 3, image 138, Special Collections, Chicago Public Library. Courtesy of the Chicago Public Library.

eventually proved sufficiently successful that, in 2003, it moved into a new state-of-the-art theater constructed for it within the nineteenth-century Chicago Water Tower and Pumping Station building on fashionable Michigan Avenue. This meant refurbishing a historic Chicago landmark, one of the few structures to survive Chicago's great fire of 1871. The building is a long-cherished civic reminder of that past devastation: Chicago survived its fires and rebuilt from the ground up—and the city's homegrown theater emerged alongside it, with vitality.

Phoenixes from ashes rise.

From Marginal to Mainstream

This same spirit of improvisation and ingenuity, of reworking the old to fit new purposes, permeates the city's artistry. Part of this is born from a certain desperation: the flip side of Chicago is its lack of nostalgia; the old is readily torn down to make way for the new. But if a structure can be reconfigured, then it—and its resident artists—might survive another day; perhaps thus the makeshift might become the permanent. There is no guarantee though that even makeshift theaters can survive indefinitely; most either close down entirely or feature companies that achieve sufficient success to move on to nicer accommodations.

In a sense we can see this evolutionary pattern over the course of the first three chapters of our book as traced by a trio of theater historians who have excavated Chicago archives and unearthed once-lost gems. In the first chapter scholar Rosemarie K. Bank describes how unorthodox performance forms appeared at the World's Columbian Exposition of 1893. The great bulk of that fair was intended to impress, a testimony to nineteenth-century American technology, business, and culture. Yet what was generally remembered by those who attended the exposition were its entertainments and oddities, rather than its ersatz temples to the dominant culture. Yes, the so-called White City was memorialized in countless postcards and souvenirs, spectacularly accentuated by newfangled electric bulbs that made it stand out at night. Bank points out the various forms that appeared on that fair's midway, off to the side, that have endured far longer in America's popular imagination. The carny, not the concertmaster, eventually held sway. Still, it was the massive neoclassical buildings that elicited the most oohs and aahs—if only for that one summer.

According to our paradigm this impressive world's fair must give way—and give way it did. My own chapter follows next. I examine how small, jerry-rigged structures built on the margins of the great fair ironically ended up as more enduring sites than the fair they were intended to serve. Here we see Chicago's initial effort to reconstitute abandoned, preexisting buildings so as to provide inexpensive work and living space where unorthodox artists could congregate. The informality of their daily interactions and their lack of concern with material gain generated art in sharp contrast to the fair's materialism, and established both bohemia and modernism in Chicago. The impromptu studios on Fifty-Seventh Street formed an artist enclave, instigating forward-looking creativity within a mutually inspirational, supportive community. In other words, these unimpressive storefront spaces helped Chicagoans discover their own indigenous art. The 57th Street Artist Colony became a hotbed of the Chicago Renaissance in art and letters, as well as a site for theatrical and dramatic and eventually performative invention, the echoes of which resonate throughout the rest of this book.

Since the 57th Street Artist Colony arose in buildings built at the margins of the World's Columbian Exposition, the geography of the two overlap. The full fairgrounds were vast, whereas the colony was limited to only a few blocks. Frederick Law Olmsted designed the original fair on what had been largely swampland on Chicago's South Side; the bohemian artists' enclave thus benefited from this reclamation, being literally built upon its foundations.

Our third chapter, written by Shannon Epplett, picks up our story from Fifty-Seventh Street's community of artists. One of the colony's makeshift studios was rented by sculptor Lou Wall Moore. Moore allowed a recent émigré—English director Maurice Browne, along with his wife, actress and Chicago native Ellen Van Volkenburg—to use her studio for play rehearsals. Browne found actors among the colony members for his intended production of Euripides's tragedy *The Trojan Women*. Browne's martinet approach alienated some participants, but his reputation caught the attention of a Chicago impresario, who consequently invited Browne to move the company—and their production—into his Fine Arts Building, prominently located in downtown Chicago. There he had already transformed an automobile dealership into a fairly substantial theater space. But Browne wanted to recreate the makeshift sensibility, evident in every aspect of the 57th Street Artist Colony. Rather than use the Fine Arts Building's large, preexisting stage, Browne insisted that an intimate space be constructed elsewhere in the building, a space that would recreate the dynamics found in Lou Wall Moore's tiny studio. So the intimate Chicago Little Theatre was consequently constructed there to serve these performance dynamic needs.

This then forms a third step in our account of makeshift Chicago theater's evolution: from the Columbian Exposition's off-to-the-side entertainments to bohemia with its explorations, and then from bohemia to actively spurning a preexisting conventional theater space and instead shaping a non-theatrical space so as to recreate those more informal, improvised theatrical dynamics. Along the way, augmented by Hull-House's dramatics, Chicago theater began to make a stir beyond its borders, finding national attention and acclaim, inspiring others to follow its example through the construction of little theaters and makeshift experimentation as a fresh means of creative expression. Chicago's makeshift sensibilities would go on to inspire East Coast experiments and, consequently, those of the nation as a whole.

I

Entertaining People

The 1893 Columbian Exposition Midway Plaisance

Rosemarie K. Bank

The use of people *in propria persona* as figures of entertainment has a long history. When the corporate directors of the World's Columbian Exposition at Chicago decided they would follow the lead of the 1889 Paris Universal Exposition and incorporate concessions into their plans, they expected those concessions to make money for the corporation's stockholders. Because the "Colonial City" of simulated Asian and African villages had been Paris's most financially successful concession, the Columbian Exposition directors had human exhibits in view from their initial planning. They also had, as a cautionary lesson, the example of the 1876 Centennial Exhibition at Philadelphia, where an unregulated shantytown "Centennial City" warred with the elevated aims of that fair's organizers. The Columbian Exposition's Committee on Ways and Means determined that its entertaining people could achieve "ethnological and historical significance" under the authority of the Department of Ethnology and Archaeology (known as Department M), headed by Frederic Ward Putnam, director of Harvard's Peabody Museum of American Archaeology and Ethnology.[1]

The results of this decision have been far-reaching. The Columbian Exposition, intended by its creators to celebrate what had been wrought since 1493 on the territory that was to become the United States—and in Chicago since the great fire of 1871—has been seen through the lens of ethnology, particularly that displayed on its Midway Plaisance, a mile-long, 600-foot-wide strip of land on Chicago's

South Side between Stony Island and Cottage Grove Avenues, sutured to the western flank of the exposition between Fifty-Ninth and Sixtieth Streets, where concessions were consolidated. The joining of anthropology, entertainment, and commerce has given the World's Columbian Exposition and its Midway Plaisance a very bad reputation in our own times as sources for and popularizers of theories of racial hierarchy. Those views were considered "progressive" in the 1890s, a reconciliation, as social scientists saw it, of cultural with biological evolution, and a substantial body of evidence supports the existence of hierarchical racist views in 1890s anthropology and allied fields and the damage they have done.

There is, however, another story to place beside this dominant narrative, one that dismantles the master's (progressive) house without using the master's (progressive) tools, a spatial rather than a temporal historiography. In the case of the Midway Plaisance, it is a story of the margins and the popular, a tale of class and of a space of escape from the hyper-ordered White City of the fair itself and its temporal determinism. Rather than seeing the landscape of the Midway as a design to illustrate racial hierarchy, spatial historiography sees the Midway as a place of transgression and border crossing, an alternative to the power narratives of the architects of the White City. In the process, the Midway emerges not as a marginal case, the domain to which race and gender have been exiled, but as the central place from which these discourses speak their histories.[2]

In 1889, an American teenager from San Francisco named Sol Bloom had earned enough through hard work and an eye for business to treat himself to a world tour. He made it as far as Paris, where the Universal Exposition brought all the world to him. He explored the fair systematically and judged the exposition "a very good show." Bloom's interest was captured not by the exhibits, however, but by the entertaining people (no surprise, since Bloom's chief enterprises in San Francisco had been in show business), specifically by the fifty entertainers of the Algerian Village. Though he doubted "anything resembling it was ever seen in Algeria," Bloom signed an exclusive contract to exhibit the troupe in the Americas, and, shortly after the fair closed, he left for New York. Bloom failed to drum up any interest in the Algerian Village there, instead learning of the Columbian Exposition planned for Chicago. Bloom rushed to "Paris on the prairie" too early (in 1890) for anything but schmoozing. He made a return trip to Chicago from San Francisco in 1891 to find construction of the fair under way, but no structure established for concessions. In a few weeks, however, Bloom's persistence paid off, and he was appointed "manager for all the amusement concessions" at the World's Columbian Exposition, at a salary exceeding that of the president of the United States. At the time, Sol Bloom was twenty-one years old.[3]

History has not forgotten Sol Bloom, but accounts of his importance to the exposition are generally as brief as Bloom's own, and follow Robert Rydell's lead in seeing Bloom's work as separate from and lesser than Putnam's but characteristic of "an alliance between entertainment and anthropology replicated in subsequent fairs." When Bloom is quoted, it is this reflection that is cited:

> There never was any question about Professor Putnam's qualifications as head of the ethnological section, but to have made this unhappy gentleman responsible for the establishment of a successful venture in the field of entertainment was about as intelligent a decision as it would be today to make Albert Einstein manager of the Ringling Brothers and Barnum and Bailey Circus.

Rather than acting as Putnam's ally in establishing a "progressive" cultural hierarchy, Bloom pursued a business opportunity that had been his quarry since 1889, one focused solely on entertainment. While his brother wound down his businesses in San Francisco, Bloom moved to Chicago and expanded opportunities there, using the Midway Plaisance as his calling card. Taking advantage of Putnam's absence in Cambridge, Bloom appealed to the exposition's president, Harlow N. Higinbotham, to speed construction of the Midway. Higinbotham passed the ball to Daniel Burnham, the fair's architect and urban planner, who, Bloom reports, told him, "You are in complete charge of the Midway. Go ahead with the work. You are responsible only to me. I will write orders to that effect." Bloom was now an independent agent.[4]

Managing the Midway involved both concessions and architecture. The footings for the Ferris wheel, the first of its kind, had to be built (and they are still underground on Chicago's South Side). Structures to house the Algerian Village and Streets of Cairo exhibits, restaurants, a circus, two panoramas, glass works, and a range of other special fee entertainments needed to be erected, while Bloom went about the business of securing concessions. He got to know most of the people in show business and allied industries in Chicago (restaurants, saloons, hotels, vice and the underworld, and, of course, politics). Bloom reported, "None of the physical work got underway until the spring of 1892, and though perhaps half of the structures were completed by the end of the summer, the heaviest pressure didn't come until 1893." (The fair was dedicated in October 1892 and opened on May 1, 1893, as specified in the act of Congress creating the exposition.) The Algerian Village began hosting performances in midsummer 1892 for the "many visitors who came daily to the grounds at Jackson Park for a preview of the fair, and the concessionaires who got set up early did a thriving business." (Bloom was out of the red by September 1892, a month before the exposition was dedicated.) Theatrical advertising had been one of Bloom's businesses in San Francisco, and, he wrote, he "was always called in when there was a publicity matter under discussion or when a statement was requested by the press."[5]

Toward the end of a long career in entertainment, music publishing, commodities trading, real estate, and politics, Sol Bloom looked back on his Columbian experience with pride. He had established himself, "through my successful management of the Midway, as an enterprising young man with a knack for making money." He had "attracted favorable attention among experienced businessmen," and proven that, "whatever else a man may lack, he will always be sought after by other men if he knows how to make money." The Midway was Bloom's springboard to a post-fair career in Chicago and, by the early twentieth century, in New York and Washington. Unfortunately, however, he says little more about the Midway in his autobiography than this:

> Throughout the six months that the exposition lasted, the affairs of my own concession occupied only a small part of my time. My biggest job was to see that the whole Midway ran smoothly, and that meant doing all sorts of things not specified in my contract. I was the trouble shooter, and when something went wrong, or threatened to go wrong, I was expected to know how to straighten out the difficulty.

No one has yet doubted that Bloom did so successfully, especially in contributing to the exposition's overall financial success.[6]

Sol Bloom clearly did not view the Midway Plaisance as an anthropologist might, though he shares their casual racism, referring to Amerindians as "redskins," for example, craving "firewater" and prone to "scalping." Bloom approached the Midway as a popular space of entertainment, an escape from the pedagogical orientation of the fair itself, just as he had found "spiritual intensity" and a higher plane of culture at the Paris exposition in the performance of an Arabian sword swallower or a Bedouin acrobat rather than in a medieval tapestry or an ancient example of "ethnological and historical significance." Being under Department M's jurisdiction had little impact upon how the Midway was built, staffed, or operated; indeed, Department M had its own entertaining people to manage, and its director was not alone among fairground scholars who became showmen. I have elsewhere discussed the exposition's living displays—for example, the Bureau of Indian Affairs' schoolhouse full of Amerindian children, or Department M's commercial "Esquimaux Village" near the North Pond and its own fee-free "Anthropological Village" near the out-of-the-way Anthropology Building, staffed with Amerindian docents from cultures ranging from Alaska to Mexico. Similarly, the Smithsonian's Navajo weaver worked in the Women's Building, and a still unknown number of entertaining people demonstrated crafts in state and foreign displays.[7]

Location was key to the Midway's success. It was an enclosed area with three entry points: from the fairground on the east at Stony Island Avenue, at Woodlawn Avenue near the Ferris wheel at the strip's midpoint, and from the cable car stop on Cottage Grove Avenue to the west. It was a circus- or carnival-style entertainment mall—crowded, dirty, noisy, smelly, and expensive, but also exciting, eclectic, fun, entertaining, even instructive. You could walk its mile-long Plaisance, or rent a sedan chair, a camel, a donkey, or a rickshaw (or you could buy a seat on the sliding railway running along the Sixtieth Street boundary). The sounds of band music, street hawkers, and show barkers would accompany you as you jostled through crowds of people headed toward numerous attractions: a fashion museum of pretty girls in ethnic costumes, a panorama of the Bernese Alps or of Kilauea, a balloon ascension, the Ferris wheel, Hagenbeck's circus, the ice skating rink, immersion in the Natatorium, a nursery and farm exhibit, models of the Eiffel Tower, St. Peter's, Blarney Castle, or a Moorish palace, the Libbey, Bohemian, and Venice-Murano glass studios, an electric theater, a working man's home, or a log cabin. And you could shop 'til you dropped—footsore, dusty, and thirsty—into one of the Midway's many restaurants (one of the German ones—there were two—accommodated eight thousand people) or settled for an ice or a glass of French cider. This was the familiar atmosphere of P. T. Barnum's circus, and, like that circus, it was spiced with performers from all around the world.[8]

Despite the clear differences between the Midway and the fairground itself, there was a sustained effort to colonize the concessions as part of the exposition's mission to illustrate the progress of civilization by hierarchizing the world's cultures. This effort came in two forms. Among anthropologists and those anxious to legitimize that field and other new scholarly disciplines, the exhibits at the Columbian Exposition and its Midway illustrated the work of the many national and international scholarly "congresses" meeting at Chicago's new Art Institute building, including congresses of folklore, archaeology, anthropology, religion, languages, history, and ethnology. The second type of hierarchizing served more general social and political ends. The *Chicago Tribune*, reflecting on the Midway late in 1893, expressed this social scheme: "What an opportunity was here afforded the scientific mind to descend the spiral of evolution, tracing humanity in its highest phases down almost to its animalistic origins." Among such ideologues, Rydell locates a literary critic who lays out this descent geographically, placing European exhibits on the Midway nearest the White City to the east, exhibits of Asians at its midpoint, and "the savage races, the Africans of Dahomey and the North American Indians," at the western edge of the Plaisance.[9]

As is often the case, hierarchy privileges temporal ideology over spatial reality. A more reliable geography can be derived from maps of the Midway. These vary over time, so it is useful to compare an early example, such as the management-authorized guide *The Best Things to Be Seen at the World's Fair*, published in 1893 at the fair (and likely before it opened), and Hubert H. Bancroft's oversized, two-volume *The Book of the Fair*, published as a memorial album in 1894, after the fair had closed. Their maps show Midway exhibits divided into lots, portions of lots, and double and triple lots, the largest single area a German Village/Concert Garden/Museum/Restaurant space of perhaps five lots. The lots were separated north from south by a broad east-west walkway, the "Plaisance" itself, with only the Ferris wheel and a Vienna café initially located on it. *The Best Things* is the more detailed map, as would be expected of a guidebook, and it indicates water closets, exhibit fees, and theaters omitted from the later publication. Both maps contain voids and both indicate exhibits bearing both city and national names. Only one cultural exhibit disappears from the earlier map (the Brazil Concert Hall), while four are added to the later map: an East Indian Village (occupying a void at the western end of the Midway); an American Indian exhibit (where the Brazilians had been, and next to the

East Indians); a very large Dutch Settlement exhibit (east of the German Village, incorporating the spaces earlier assigned to the Javanese Village and, across the Plaisance from it, the spaces where the Java lunch room, the Johor exhibit, and the South Sea Islanders concession had been); and a Moroccan Village (in a void just west of the Ferris wheel).[10]

As Sol Bloom supposed, and as the fair managers hoped, ethnic concessions were both profitable and geographically stable parts of the Columbian Exposition's Midway Plaisance. Maps clearly demonstrate, however, that the Midway was not a spatial "illustration of evolution." The Irish Industries exhibit, for example, was indeed close to the fairground on the east, but the "German Ethnographic Village" (its official name) was near the center of the Midway. The Austrian Village was well to the west, next to the Dahomey Village, with Dahomey flanked by the Lapland Village to its west, and the Hungarian National Orpheum west of the Laps and next to the military camp (subsequently an agricultural nursery), which marked the western end of the Midway. There was no "civilized to savage," "high to low" cultural plan for the Midway privileging culturally European white people. There was, rather, a commercial plan and a "first come, first served" ethic at work, signaled by Sol Bloom locating his own Algerian Village early and at the middle of the Midway, near the Woodlawn Avenue entrance and the fair's most popular concession, the Ferris wheel. Bloom's neighbors were the Streets of Cairo exhibit, the Moorish Palace, the Turkish and German Villages, the Persian tent, and non-ethnic concessions and eateries. If the Middle East was here at the midpoint, the Far East and Asia were farther *east* on the Midway, where the hierarchy advocates wanted Europe and high culture to be, while substantial European exhibits remained well to the *west* of the Ferris wheel.[11]

Attempts to replicate on the Midway the Colonial City of the 1889 Paris Exposition, and its "living connection between men and things" as an illustration of ethnological theory, were bound to fail, and did. In part, that failure was due to the radically different organization of the two fairs. The exhibits on the Midway did not represent the U.S. government's colonial holdings, as France's Colonial City had done; indeed, most of the Midway concessions did not connect to governments at all—China, for example, declined to participate in the fair, in reaction to the Chinese Exclusion Acts beginning in 1876, thus the Midway's Chinese concessions were wholly commercial ventures, as was the Dahomey Village (Dahomey, now called Benin, was then a

French possession). As far as I have been able to ascertain, there was no direct U.S. government involvement in the Midway and no Department M exhibits on it.

In 1993, the Chicago Historical Society commemorated the Chicago World's Fair of 1893 with an exhibition and publication, which, among other things, confirmed Rydell's view of this (and other) U.S. fairs as "visions of empire" promulgating racial hierarchy. Certainly, protests—by Frederick Douglass and Ida B. Wells, for example, and Rain-in-the-Face and Simon Pokagon—underline the presence of such "visions" at the Columbian Exposition, visions encapsulated in 1895 by John Burgess, a political scientist at Columbia University, who wrote, "We must conclude that American Indians, Asiatics, and Africans cannot properly form any active, directive part of the political population which shall be able to produce modern political institutions and ideals."[12]

While protests against such views come increasingly to light, these ethnic performers of the past remain hidden, assumed to be mere dupes of unscrupulous managers, even when they fought and won against such managers in court, when they straightened out reputable managers (as happened to Sol Bloom), or when they managed themselves. That all ethnic performers were exploited, even in an age in which performers of all races and ethnicities had few protections as to hours of work, number of shows a day, time or days off, working conditions, or pay, may well cause scholars outside theater to think no person would willingly take on such work. Yet, entertaining people not only did so, they did so with an eye toward what made a good attraction, even when that fed stereotypes. Condemnations of their work often mask thinly veiled, anti-theatrical prejudices and cultural hierarchies of the sort still circulating today around ethnic performances and plays. Moreover, these condemnations continue to marginalize performances central to a grittier, nuanced, and contradictory history, a history from the marginalized center of historical discourse. An assumption of righteous hierarchy privileging our own temporal ideology over another era's spatial reality fails to recognize that entertaining people at the margins tell a truer history of cultural diversity than progressive class-biased hierarchies and hierarchizing progressive historiographies allow us to do.[13]

Notes

1. Robert W. Rydell, *All the World's a Fair: Visions of Empire at American International Expositions, 1876–1916* (Chicago: University of Chicago Press, 1984), 34 for Philadelphia, 62 for the quote, 55 for Putnam's appointment.

2. Spatial historiography looks for the occasions in history when multiple events break the surface at the same time. These events provoke a broad-scale investigation of the historical context, exposing the relationships at work. Where historiography concerns the arrangement of the record (historiographia), spatial historiography seeks historical relationships not in global theories about history, but in specific historical spaces (which may indeed contain, reflect, or generate such theories). In this view, time is a function of how we measure historical space, not the space we measure. For more about spatial historiography, see the introduction to and essays in Rosemarie K. Bank and Michal Kobialka, eds., *Theatre/Performance Historiography: Time, Space, Matter* (New York: Palgrave Macmillan, 2015). In the present essay, the historical relationships in the space of the Columbian Exposition's Midway are the ones under the lens. These relationships include those seeking to marginalize people (for a *variety* of reasons, including race), but these "entertaining people" are the center of the history—they tell it—rather than being marginal to their own story.

3. Sol Bloom, *The Autobiography of Sol Bloom* (New York: G. P. Putnam's Sons, 1948), 105–18. According to Bloom, the president, Grover Cleveland, was paid an annual salary of $50,000. Bloom asked for, and got, $1,000 a week.

4. Rydell, *All the World's*, 63; Bloom, *Autobiography*, 119–20.

5. Bloom, *Autobiography*, 120–23. Before his concession opened to the public, Bloom quartered the Algerian Village entertainers on the Midway, and he employed a number of the men as laborers and "two or three of the women in the office" (123). In those pre-union days, no entertainer was paid while not playing, so other work was necessary. Bloom "most emphatically denies," in his autobiography, "that I had anything whatever to do with a female entertainer known professionally as Little Egypt. At no time during the Chicago fair did this character appear on the Midway" (136). Belly dancers were, however, part of the Algerian Village and of other Middle Eastern companies. "The crowds poured in," Bloom gleefully remarks of his own success. "I had a gold mine" (135).

6. Bloom, *Autobiography*, 141 for the shorter quotes, 136 for the "trouble shooter" quote. (Bloom cites: resolving complaints from Buffalo Bill's

Wild West—camped near the fair and Midway—that performers in the Algerian Village were selling Cody's Indian performers alcohol; handling a shortage of ostrich eggs for omelets; getting the Ferris wheel running, delayed until late June 1893, but "the biggest attraction of the fair" [138]; and converting an unused swimming pool into a venue for boxing acts.)

7. For Bloom on Amerindians, see 136–37. Contemporary sources tell us Department M's exhibits, forced by overcrowding out of the centrally located Manufacturers and Liberal Arts Building and into a lately completed and unattractive building of its own at the southeastern margin of the fairground, were patronized by "only a comparative sprinkling [of visitors]" and those who made "a hasty survey of this region from the Intramural railway," *The Columbian Gallery: A Portfolio of Photographs from the World's Fair* (Chicago: Werner, 1894), unpaginated, but see the "Down by the Windmill" section. For Amerindian performers on the fairground, see Rosemarie K. Bank, "Telling a Spatial History of the Columbian Exposition of 1893," *Modern Drama* 47, no. 3 (Fall 2004): 349–66; Rosemarie K. Bank, "The Savage Other: 'Indianizing' and Performance in Nineteenth-Century American Culture," in *Interrogating America through Theatre and Performance*, ed. William W. Demastes and Iris Smith Fischer (New York: Palgrave Macmillan, 2007), 11–27; Rosemarie K. Bank, "Representing History: Performing the Columbian Exposition," in *Critical Theory and Performance*, rev. ed., ed. Janelle G. Reinelt and Joseph R. Roach (Ann Arbor: University of Michigan Press, 2007), 223–44 [reprint of an article in *Theatre Journal* 54, no. 4 (Winter 2002): 589–606]; and Rosemarie K. Bank, "Show Indians/Showing Indians: Buffalo Bill's Wild West, The Bureau of Indian Affairs, and American Anthropology," *Journal of Dramatic Theory and Criticism* 26, no. l (Fall 2011): 149–58.

8. The Barnum analogy is apt, since the Barnum and Bailey Circus exhibited an ethnological collection by 1884. Though Barnum died in 1891, the 1880s and 1890s were the big top's most successful decades. The cultures represented on the Midway were (I use the names that appear on maps) Algeria (and Tunis), American Indian, Austria, Brazil, Cairo, China, Dahomey, Dutch (see note 10 for its colonial possessions), East Indian, Germany, Hungary, Ireland, Japan, Lapland, Morocco, Persia, and Turkey. Some non-ethnic concessions that were solely commercial exhibits are omitted from this list.

9. Rydell, *All the World's*, 43–45, on progress as the unifying theme for the fair, a contribution of G. Brown Goode of the Smithsonian. The best integrator of the scholarly congresses and the fair was William F. Cody. When Amerindians from Buffalo Bill's Wild West illustrated a presentation

about sign language at the Art Institute, Cody used the occasion to distribute free tickets to his show. Presenters at the congresses who were involved in the fair (e.g., Otis Mason and Frederic Putnam) also urged conveners to visit their anthropological exhibits and ethnographic villages.

10. John J. Flynn, comp., *The Best Things to Be Seen at the World's Fair* (Chicago: Columbian Guide Company, 1893), the Midway map is front matter, the description of the Midway, 167–82 (not everything mapped is described); Hubert H. Bancroft, *The Book of the Fair*, 2 vols. (New York: Bancroft Books, 1894), 1:55 for its Midway map. The South Seas exhibit on the *Best Things Midway* map included Java, Sumatra, Borneo, Fiji, Samoa, New Zealand (presumably Maori), Tonga, and Hawaii. I do not know how many of these cultures were incorporated into the "Dutch Settlement."

11. See the Midway maps. Because there was so little movement, new concessions either went into voids on earlier maps (the East Indian and Morocco exhibits), took over vacated spaces (the American Indian exhibit, where the Brazil Concert hall had been), or incorporated existing exhibits (the Dutch Settlement). *The Book of the Fair* Midway map shows that "Orange Judd" (an agricultural publisher) and farm/nursery exhibits have disappeared at the easternmost end of the Midway, along with a log cabin exhibit and the electric theater. Only a circular railway tower has been added (the elevated Illinois Central Railroad tracks crossed here), creating several voids.

12. Neil Harris, Wim de Wit, James Gilbert, and Robert W. Rydell, *Grand Illusions: Chicago's World's Fair of 1893* (Chicago: Chicago Historical Society, 1993); John Burgess, "The Ideal of American Commonwealth," *Political Science Quarterly* 10, no. 3 (September 1895): 406.

13. I have elsewhere discussed the "Esquimaux" troupe on the fairground that successfully sued its manager and thereafter ran its own concession (the incident is discussed in Harris et al., *Grand Illusions*, 158–60, and see my sources cited in note 7). See Bloom, *The Autobiography*, 122–23, for his chastening by one of his Algerian performers.

2

From Marmalade to Gingerbread

The Columbian Exposition, Chicago's 57th Street Artist Colony, and the Theaters They Spawned

Stuart J. Hecht

Chicago hosted a monumental world's fair during the summer of 1893. By year's end it was gone. Designed in anticipation of a new century, the fair and its buildings better served as a tribute to the past. But out of the fair's rubble emerged an arts colony, lacking the fair's pretense and housed in humble dwellings, yet better suited to the needs of the coming age. In retrospect, the World's Columbian Exposition, built to impress along Victorian lines, faded in significance; the small arts colony that replaced it, outwardly modest, planted the seeds for twentieth-century theatrical art in Chicago and beyond.

The Great Fair: Progress and Publicity

Popular memory recalls the World's Columbian Exposition of 1893 as the "White City," a utopian vision of pristine neoclassical structures overlooking placid lagoons. Others remember the more sensationalistic Midway, with its Ferris wheel and the scandalous belly dancer "Little Egypt." Between 1850 and 1925 world's fairs appeared almost annually throughout Europe and America.[1] America hosted one prior to Chicago's, in Philadelphia to celebrate the nation's centennial. But we tend to remember Chicago's best. Built on 633 acres of land, it was roughly four times the size of the 1890 fair held in Paris, and it drew some 27.5 million visitors, who came away with stories and mementos.[2]

Fair organizers employed the nation's finest architects and artists; Frederick Law Olmsted designed the grounds, and the firm of Burnham and Root supervised a national team of architects, including several leading Chicago designers. Sculptor Augustus Saint-Gaudens reportedly said to Burnham during a planning session, "Do you realize that this is the greatest meeting of artists since the fifteenth century?"[3]

But for all its prominence, the World's Columbian Exposition was not built to last. The huge white palaces, constructed upon frameworks of steel, iron, and wood, were covered with what appeared to be stonework but was in fact "staff," a plaster-like impermanent substance shaped to resemble neoclassical cornices, cupolas, fluted columns, and the like. The central buildings looked solid, but were only intended to survive the summer. Of the almost $12 million it cost to build the fair, half a million was raised by selling in advance as scrap the steel used to support many exposition buildings.[4]

Still, the fair was built to impress. Chicago's leaders promoted the fair to demonstrate not only the city's reemergence following its disastrous 1871 fire, but also the idea that Chicago was more than "hog-butcher to the world," that the city valued culture and civilization and thus could compete successfully with its East Coast rivals. Similarly, America viewed the fair as a chance to prove to Europe that America valued culture and was as civilized as its European counterparts.[5]

To Victorian minds, steeped in machinery and Darwin, civilization meant progress.[6] This attitude was exacerbated by the American elite's acceptance of the so-called genteel tradition. From such a perspective, the fair embodied high culture and was an effort to "uplift and civilize" its visitors in the Matthew Arnold tradition of providing "the knowledge of the best that has been thought and said in the world."[7] Thus the fair ultimately asserted prestige more than artistry or innovation.

Looking Backward

On the verge of a new century, rather than looking ahead, fair planners paid homage to their own recent past. Rather than imagining the *future*, the fair instead asserted a *present* defined largely as the culmination of nineteenth-century sensibilities. It celebrated the past to legitimize the present. Hence its classically inspired architectural facades covered otherwise dull, over-large buildings, whose insides were unimaginatively designed empty spaces, crammed with as many displays as possible. The Florentine exteriors thus misled; the outside promised the rebirth of an expansive, idealized humanism. But the innards asserted a cluttered, mechanized, depersonalized, materialistic present.[8]

Not everyone regarded the fair fondly. Noted Chicago architect Louis Sullivan, who designed the Transportation Building (one of the few major palaces that featured any color in its design), later raged at the exposition's subsequent impact:

> Meanwhile the virus of the World's Fair . . . began to show unmistakable signs of the nature of the contagion. There came a violent outbreak of the Classic and the Renaissance in the East, which slowly spread westward, contaminating all that it touched. . . . The selling campaign of the bogus antique was remarkably well managed through skillful publicity and propaganda, by those who were first to see its commercial possibilities. . . . The damage wrought by the World's Fair will last for half a century from its date, if not longer. It has penetrated deep into the constitution of the American mind, effecting there lesions significant of dementia.[9]

Others voiced similar concerns. They argued that the fair's influence discouraged attempts to create afresh, along more indigenous lines. Reliance on the past served to counter new forms of artistic expression that favored fresh individuality. Instead the fair conservatively clung to mimicry of the long-familiar.

Burning Down the House

The World's Columbian Exposition closed quietly in October 1893 with flags at half-mast. The day before, Chicago's popular mayor, Carter Harrison, was assassinated by a disgruntled office worker. The realities of economic depression soon hit the fairgrounds. That winter the homeless moved in. The following summer, when striking railway workers clashed with police, fires broke out that destroyed most of the fair structures.[10] The few that survived remained empty. Years later the Palace of Fine Arts was transformed into Chicago's Museum of Science and Industry, but for the most part the cavernous relics proved useless, with almost all either destroyed by fire or razed.[11]

From Peacock to Phoenix

Out of the ashes of the great fair emerged the beginnings of twentieth-century Chicago art, a bohemian community whose work pointed ahead toward modernism. It is ironic and somehow fitting that the seeds of the new grew directly out of the decay of the old, for the modernist values proved to be an inversion of Victorian sensibilities. This inversion was evident in the layout of the fair itself.

The Columbian Exposition's geographical layout was a reflection of Victorian cultural priorities. Designers Burnham and Root designed the fairgrounds so that the most important and impressive structures were grouped together around a basin at the southeast corner. Almost a microcosm of period values, those buildings closest to this centerpiece represented what was considered the age's highest achievements, and those buildings farthest away represented its lowest and least important.[12]

Of least significance were those structures just beyond the fairgrounds themselves. Just outside the northwest entrance to the fair, literally at its margins and thus farthest from its geographical and cultural hub, stood two rows of plate glass window storefronts used to sell souvenirs and refreshments. Built two years earlier in anticipation of the business generated by the exposition, these eighteen modest, one-story shops lined the northwest and southwest corners of Stony Island Boulevard Avenue where it met Fifty-Seventh Street, strategically placed between the Illinois Central train stop and the northwest gateway to the fair to greet visitors coming or going, eager for refreshments or knickknacks. This prime location brought unduly high rent, but business boomed and the shops flourished. But when the fair closed, business evaporated, and the shops closed and were abandoned.[13]

Ironically, where onetime "important" exposition palaces proved to be dinosaurs, these "unimportant" concession buildings found new life. In part this was because they were well situated. To one side was scenic Jackson Park and on another the still-new University of Chicago, all along the vast, blue expanse of Lake Michigan. Rent was cheap and the long, narrow, high-ceilinged storefronts held great possibilities.

In 1903 B. J. O. (Bror) Nordfeldt, a Swedish immigrant artist teaching at the Chicago Academy of Fine Arts, moved into one. He convinced his friend, iconoclastic University of Chicago professor Thorstein Veblen, later known for his theories on conspicuous consumption, to move into another.[14] Gradually the storefronts filled, inhabited mostly by artists, writers, and students. Occupants hung curtains over the windows for privacy, enabling the transformation from storefront into combination living quarters and studio space. Never intended as housing, the storefronts lacked cellars, and each relied feebly (given the nearby lake's bitterly cold winter winds) on a single coal-burning stove for heat. Plumbing was crude. Still, only fifteen dollars a month rent brought the inhabitants adequate room, good light, and a shady backyard. By 1911 these rickety, gingerbread-fronted structures housed a thriving bohemian arts community, Chicago's first ever.[15]

La Boheme, or Community and Art

Appearances mattered little to members of this community, now called "the Corner," unlike the fair that spawned it. And unlike the massive exposition, the 57th Street Artist Colony seemed indifferent to the outside world and its conventions. Discounting the past, colony artists concentrated on creating anew, experimenting with ideas and form, defying formal disciplines. And rather than overwhelm with scope and numbers, the emphasis among the colony's artists was thoughtful appreciation of individual creativity, one object or idea at a time.[16]

This of course marks a radical shift from the fair's attitudes toward the function of art. Where the fair sought to overwhelm, the arts colony nurtured. Colony members socialized together, truly forming a creative community. In the evenings people met mostly to drink and talk, exchanging stories and observations. This in turn contributed to the nature of individuals' artistic output as the artists influenced each other, sometimes even serving as subjects for each other. For example, Nordfeldt painted portraits of the poet Arthur Davison Ficke and the essayist Floyd Dell, both of whom in turn described Nordfeldt in their writing.[17] And whereas the fair offered the categorization of knowledge as some sort of accomplishment in and of itself, thus reinforcing the illusion of a fixed order, Corner members tended to focus on the question at hand and approach it without concern for the imposed rules of formal disciplines. The informality of their living situation and interpersonal interactions resulted in a comparable open exploration of questions and discoveries, of invention and creativity. In other words, their living arrangements and interactions became reflected in the art they produced.

The Fifty-Seventh Street environment nurtured artistry. And while the majority of its inhabitants were painters, sculptors, etchers, and musicians, the colony's writers earned the greatest national recognition. Though only a few actually lived there, many spent considerable time at the Corner to socialize and to present and discuss their work. Schoolteacher Margery Currey and her then husband, the aforementioned Floyd Dell, moved into Veblen's former apartment and set up their place as a salon. Among the regular visitors to the Currey-Dell flat were novelist Sherwood Anderson; poet Vachel Lindsay; essayist, poet, and playwright (and attorney) Edgar Lee Masters; poet and troubadour Carl Sandburg; poet and playwright Arthur Davison Ficke; novelist Theodore Dreiser; journalist, playwright, and provocateur Ben Hecht and his bohemian cohort; poet Maxwell Bodenheim; and Chicago high-society playwrights Kenneth Sawyer Goodman, Alice Gerstenberg, and Mary Aldis. Other regulars included Harriet Monroe, founder and editor of *Poetry* magazine (which was first to publish Sandburg, Robert Frost, T. S. Eliot, and Ezra Pound), and Margaret Anderson, founder and editor of *The Little Review* (which first introduced James Joyce to America). It was said that free verse was first suggested and discussed here. Others in attendance included the prominent defense attorney (and law partner of Masters) Clarence Darrow, anarchist Emma Goldman, playwright Lawrence Langner, and Dell's good friends from Iowa, arts guru George Cram Cook and his significant other, playwright Susan Glaspell.[18]

In the 1930s historian Albert Parry composed a study of bohemian communities in which he contextualized this era of Chicago's as follows: "The university [of Chicago] bells to the West punctured the outside silence late into the night and early into the dawn. The white hope of American arts was being born. Chicago was supplanting Boston and perhaps New York as the mainspring of American letters! There was at that time a keen awakening in the Mid-Western lands. The young of America did not want to wait till middle age to claim their values. They wanted values right away. And their values were not those of their elders. . . . The young were ready to be not only Americans but citizens of the world. And what was the geographic heart of the country, and of every new feeling in the land, if not the Middle West? So it was that on Chicago fell the honorable duty of having a more thoughtful Bohemia than other provincial localities of America. In Chicago, the new cenacles of youth were formed not only in the name of vague goodfellowship and pleasant drink and love, but also in the name of serious discussion of What Is Art and how is it produced."[19]

Yet Parry also makes an important cultural distinction that marked the Chicagoans in contrast to their Greenwich Village cohorts: "The Chicago rebels remained to rebel mainly in the arts, to issue manifestoes to poets and not to workers, to argue Imagism rather than Marxism, and Free Verse rather than Free Speech."[20]

The Corner's Two Theaters

It was an extraordinary group. In a few years most would move on to New York, where they helped shape the Greenwich Village bohemian scene. George Cram Cook, Glaspell, Dell, and Nordfeldt would go on to help found the Provincetown Players and revolutionize American noncommercial theater. Langner, building on their work, helped found the Washington Square Players and later the Theatre Guild.

But understand that the Fifty-Seventh Street community in which they participated sponsored its own small theaters first; the Fifty-Seventh Street theaters offered experimental prototypes for these more famous, later theatrical efforts. Furthermore, the institutional organization and the artistic approaches practiced by the emerging Fifty-Seventh Street theater groups proved both an extension and an expression of that community's cultural sensibilities.

Chicago Theatrical Begettings

In September 1912, Lou Wall Moore, a well-to-do sculptor and would-be dancer, invited director Maurice Browne, a recent English émigré, and his actress bride Ellen Van Volkenburg to use her studio to rehearse.[21] The Brownes hoped to start a theater and needed a space to work. All Moore asked in exchange was that she be in the play. The play was Euripides's *The Trojan Women*, and so Browne cast the overage Moore as Cassandra. Also representing the Corner community, Chicago playwright Alice Gerstenberg had a small part playing one of Euripides's suffering women. A neighbor described overhearing them rehearse:

> The vibrant, emotion-packed chanting of a female Greek chorus filled a Jackson Park store-front studio and wafted through

> the open doors and back windows. . . . Passersby paid little heed. Not that Greek choruses were ordinary in Chicago, nor that the chanted words of Euripides were familiar to Chicago ears. In a colony of poor artists unconventional behavior was simply taken for granted. When the director interrupted with clipped, frenzied outcries—well, no artist should be denied his temperament.[22]

The Englishman Maurice Browne may have been a martinet director, but he was well connected; his Chicago Little Theatre soon moved away, having been offered space in the ritzier, downtown Fine Arts Building (see chapter 3). The Corner had provided a spawning ground enabling their initial work, but Browne quickly leaped on the opportunity to have a "real" theater, even if small. The Fine Arts space offered better resources for Browne to develop his artistic vision. His company's work—and his personal connections—helped gain international recognition for the Chicago Little Theatre's poetic productions, hallmarked by simple yet striking visuals.

Browne took some members of the arts colony with him to the new Fine Arts locale. This initially included Bror Nordfeldt as his theater's first stage designer. Nordfeldt not only designed several sets but also did portraits of Browne and of Browne's Andromache, Elaine Hyman. When Nordfeldt's work soon drew him away from stage design, he recommended to Browne as his replacement one of his students, also a Fifty-Seventh Street inhabitant, C. Raymond Johnson. Johnson's stage design contributed heavily to the Chicago Little Theatre's artistic reputation. In later years Johnson, too, abandoned the stage, dropped the "h" from his name (to become "Raymond Jonson"), and gained fame as a leading American modernist painter.[23]

Though Browne and company moved, they maintained the Corner's pattern of offering topical lectures and discussions alongside their productions, thereby underscoring an affinity between art and issues. So just as Browne revived *The Trojan Women* at Jane Addams's request to protest World War I, so too did the Chicago Little Theatre host polemic lectures by Emma Goldman and others. In fact, Goldman later published a collection of her talks on the social justice plays of writers like Henrik Ibsen and John Galsworthy, implying ties between their works and her anarchistic political beliefs.[24]

When this circle subsequently relocated to Greenwich Village, they took with them their practice of blending art and ideas: Cook and

Glaspell and Nordfeldt helped found the Provincetown Players, still staging new plays in new ways; Dell worked alongside Max Eastman as editor of the prominent socialist magazine *The Masses*. They now hobnobbed with the likes of radical journalist Jack Reed, his feminist girlfriend and fellow activist Louise Bryant, and poet Edna St. Vincent Millay, along with other Chicago transplants such as authors Theodore Dreiser and Sherwood Anderson, much as they had done back on Fifty-Seventh Street at the Corner.

The Players' Workshop

In 1916 a second theater emerged in the 57th Street Artist Colony: the Players' Workshop. Though not as well known as the Chicago Little Theatre, in its own day it proved very influential. It began when several former Chicago Little Theatre actresses, disgruntled with Browne, decided to quit his troupe to form their own theater.[25] One of them, Elizabeth Bingham, volunteered her storefront art studio, located at 1544 East Fifty-Seventh Street, to house the theater. Bingham installed a seventeen-by-fifteen-foot platform, hung a makeshift curtain (which unfortunately buckled as it went up sideways), and set up enough folding chairs to seat eighty, though as many as a hundred could squeeze in to see the amateur casts perform. In the spirit of the Corner colony, neighboring studio inhabitants provided talent and space to help construct costumes and paint sets. And while its membership came primarily from locals, a goodly number of high-society members also participated as artists and audience.[26]

Despite its name, the Players' Workshop specialized in producing exclusively the work of Chicago playwrights. In the third week of every month, they would present two, three, or four one-acts by writers such as Alice Gerstenberg, Ben Hecht, Kenneth Sawyer Goodman, Maxwell Bodenheim, Oren Taft Jr., and Elisha Cook Sr. The Players' Workshop lasted only fourteen months, but managed in that time to produce thirty-one plays.[27]

Unlike the lyrical Chicago Little Theatre, the Players' Workshop was entirely experimental. Playwrights felt free to fiddle with structure, characters, and language, with varying degrees of success. This openness to new ideas and forms directly reflected the Fifty-Seventh Street community. For instance, Alice Gerstenberg's work here featured the use of expressionistic, even surrealistic devices, whereas her earlier and later plays proved far more conventional. She later credited Bingham for creating the "most wonderful general atmosphere of 'belonging' without any visible effort." Gerstenberg added that Bingham established the "right beginning for consolidating a creative atmosphere for Chicago, and for one blessed year we could breathe! It has not been equaled since."[28]

Much like the rest of the arts colony, this transformed storefront's theater was primitive at best. Regardless, Ben Hecht, later a highly successful playwright and screenwriter, called his experience at this makeshift, amateur Players' Workshop his "happiest memories of the theatre," even though his play *Dregs* was yanked after three performances because of profanity. The plays done at the Players' Workshop ranged in subject matter from the lyric to the grittily realistic, from fantasies set in far-off places to grim dramas trapped in Chicago sweatshops. While Chicago critics rarely reviewed their work, *Theatre Arts Magazine* (bible of the nation's art theater movement) regularly reported on Players' Workshop activities.[29]

Also note that though they lived bohemian lives, some Corner residents and participants came from very affluent Chicago families. This was certainly the case with Alice Gerstenberg; it was also true of playwright Kenneth Sawyer Goodman and of playwright Mary Aldis, to name a few. As a result, when such authors' work was performed, it was common to see a long row of limousines lined up waiting outside the Players' Workshop Theatre, having transported wealthy family and friends to attend their makeshift productions. The Corner allowed rich and poor to rub elbows in their shared bohemia.

Meanwhile, Players' Workshop productions gained national recognition for their artistry, in part thanks to the work of a gifted designer. Demonstrating a remarkable versatility, J. Blanding Sloan designed sets and lights for all but four of the Players' Workshop productions. Sloan was another Nordfeldt student and roomed with Raymond Johnson nearby.[30] Except for one set design for the Chicago Little Theatre, there is no evidence of Sloan ever having a serious interest in theater prior to his work with the Players' Workshop, which suggests he followed Johnson's example in entering the theater. Still, like Johnson, Sloan gained national recognition for his theatrical artistry. His designs for Players' Workshop productions were included in several major exhibitions of the new stagecraft, alongside such twentieth-century luminaries of American stage design as Robert Edmund Jones, Lee Simonson, Norman Bel Geddes, Raymond Jonson, and Joseph Urban. *Theatre Arts*

Magazine featured Sloan's design work in several issues, clearly ranking him among the art theater's chief artistic innovators. This acclaim was particularly remarkable given the extremely limited space and resources available to him at the Players' Workshop.[31]

The Players' Workshop folded shortly after America entered World War I. Gerstenberg claimed it closed because some key members left to enlist. It is also true that the national mood discouraged "frivolousness" in the face of the war, causing many small theaters across the country to close. But though short-lived, the Players' Workshop made its mark. And the Players' Workshop's open-minded, communal approach to theater made it a better representation than its rival Chicago Little Theatre of the Corner colony itself—of its organization, values, and overall corresponding aesthetics.

Generational Change

Immediately following World War I, the original Fifty-Seventh Street community dissolved. A schism occurred among the Fifty-Seventh Street residents, between the radicals and the more conservative in the community. Most of the radicals moved out, migrating to Chicago's Near North Side. Many of the leading artists and writers had already moved east, where they tried to expand upon their bohemian lifestyles and art in Greenwich Village and Provincetown. But by the late 1920s a new generation replaced the old, and Chicago's bohemia resumed. Builders increased the number of storefronts to twenty-six, and an annual art fair was begun in the late 1930s. After several threats over the years to raze the old colony to make way for modern businesses, the site gave way to urban renewal in 1962. Still, every June, Chicago hosts its 57th Street Art Fair in Hyde Park.[32]

The World's Columbian Exposition of 1893 lasted six months; the buildings that became the 57th Street Artist Colony lasted seventy-one years. The juxtaposition of the two contrasting arts models is unusual and revealing. Together they present contrasting visions of what art is, what it is for, and how it comes about, and ultimately the two embody the battle over the shape and nature art would take in the twentieth century—and beyond.[33]

Looking back we can now see that the 57th Street Artist Colony's method of transforming small abandoned buildings into functioning arts studios and improvised theaters anticipated the trend that would become the hallmark of the Chicago theater boom that began in the 1960s and continues today: namely the so-called storefront theater. These were the first of a long line of makeshift theaters that later characterized the city's theatrical activities. Not only did they introduce the notion that theater could be done in small spaces, but they showed that they could effectively draw Chicago audiences to see their work performed there. No need for ersatz palaces to culture or the arts for theater to thrive; in Chicago the onstage work itself was sufficient to attract interest and support from locals. Furthermore, as we have seen in this example, audience interest ultimately was not based upon spectacle or design elements of the sort only possible in fully rigged "conventional" theaters. Since the Fifty-Seventh Street buildings were intended as storefronts to sell fairgoers knickknacks, no such formal theatrical equipment was evident or available. Audiences did not seem to mind; they focused instead on the plays and the players. While these conditions limited technical and design possibilities, they correspondingly freed playwrights, directors, and actors to experiment and invent, using little to express much. This rudimentary aesthetic remains a hallmark of Chicago's storefront theater to this day.

The Corner also anticipated a still more recent theatrical trend: the Chicago Home Theater movement (covered in chapter 10 of this book). Keep in mind that the initial appeal of the Fifty-Seventh Street studios was that they offered housing. Artists who moved into these units also then used them as artist studios, welcoming in neighbors and friends to view their work. That work might be a play or a painting, a poetry reading or a salon discussion of arts and society. But each unit held this dual purpose of home and presentation space. Their very informality fostered new aesthetic and interpersonal possibilities. Presentations or performances thus took place in the creative site itself: no separation of process from product here, any more than there was a separation between the private and the public.

Another key element that Chicago storefront theater (and most other makeshift theaters in the city) inherited from the Fifty-Seventh Street paradigm is the emphasis on community. The Corner developed a collective aesthetic, based in part on the interpersonal exchange among the mishmash of artists who peopled it, as well as the primitive buildings in which they congregated and worked. This sense of community anticipates Chicago's present-day emphasis on theater ensembles rather than the every-artist-for-themself systems that are standard practice in most other American cities. The Chicago norm is often a group of friends who start a theater together, either around an aesthetic or an ideal, subsequently selecting or developing plays that reflect their group sensibilities. This too has roots in the Corner's theatrical efforts.

The old storefronts are long gone, gone the way of the Columbian Exposition, as are a long list of Chicago storefront successors. But it never was about the buildings—was it?

Notes

1. Wim de Wit, "Building an Illusion: The Design of the World's Columbian Exposition," in Neil Harris, Wim de Wit, James Gilbert, and Robert W. Rydell, *Grand Illusions: Chicago's World's Fair of 1893* (Chicago: Chicago Historical Society, 1993), 41–98.

2. Norman Bolotin and Christine Laing, *The World's Columbian Exposition* (Washington, DC: Preservation Press, 2002), 4.

3. Neil Harris, "Memory and the White City," in Harris et al., *Grand Illusions*, 10–11; see also Helen Horowitz, *Culture and the City: Cultural Philanthropy in Chicago from the 1880s to 1917* (Chicago: University of Chicago Press, 1976), 86–87, 115–16. On page 115, Horowitz writes: "For all the fair's variety and amusement, what struck visitors most profoundly was the White City itself. The dramatic landscape was an overwhelming experience to those used to the multiplicity, even chaos, of the American city street. The Court of Honor had been consciously designed to be beautiful, the product 'of a desire for structures more noble and landscape effects more beautiful than any the world had hitherto seen.'"

4. Bolotin and Laing, *World's Columbian Exposition*, 4; see also transcript of the Federal Act Creating the World's Columbian Exposition of 1893 as found in R. Reid Badger, *The Great American Fair* (Chicago: Nelson-Hall, 1979), 133–36.

5. Bolotin and Laing, *World's Columbian Exposition*, 4; see also de Wit, "Building an Illusion," 61. Many other exposition buildings did not adhere to the Beaux-Arts style, but this mishmash of styles did not show the fair at its harmonious best. For promotional purposes official photographs concentrated on the neoclassical, especially on the central Court of Honor area, as best representing the fair. For more on this see James Gilbert, "Fixing the Image: Photography at the World's Columbian Exposition" found in Harris et al., *Grand Illusions*, 99–140.

6. Robert W. Rydell, *All the World's a Fair* (Chicago: University of Chicago Press, 1984).

7. Robert Muccigrosso, *Celebrating the New World: Chicago's Columbian Exposition of 1893* (Chicago: Ivan R. Dee, 1993), 96. Muccigrosso offers a useful analysis of the fair's architectural history and impact.

8. de Wit, "Building an Illusion," 68; see also Alan Trachtenberg, *The Incorporation of America: Culture and Society in the Gilded Age* (New York: Hill and Wang, 1982). Trachtenberg similarly notes the contrast between the external ornate facades and the buildings' technologically centered intent. But he views these exteriors as a devious "disguise" that masks the true techno-centric nature of the age. My argument differs in that I view this not so much as an attempt to deceive but rather as a desire to link technology to the tradition of classical culture and its positive cultural associations.

9. Louis H. Sullivan, *The Autobiography of an Idea* (New York: Dover, 1956), 324–25.

10. Badger, *Great American Fair*, 130.

11. Bolotin and Laing, *World's Columbian Exposition*, 154–55. It is not clear whether or not the scrap metal beams, sold in advance to raise monies to construct the fair, were recovered or destroyed in the fires that struck after the fair's closing, though the latter is most likely.

12. Trachtenberg, *Incorporation of America*, 212–13.

13. For regulations regarding use of concessions, see Moses P. Handy, *The Official Directory of the World's Columbian Exposition, May 1st to October 30th, 1893* (Chicago, W. B. Conkey, 1893), 212.

14. Significant here is the fact that Veblen had in 1899 published his classic study *The Theory of the Leisure Class* (London: Oxford University Press, 2009 reissue), in which he introduced the term "conspicuous consumption" to criticize those bent only on accruing material goods. So it is especially fitting that he lived for a time among the ruins of the Columbian Exposition.

15. See Paul Kruty, "Mirrors of a 'Post-Impressionist' Era: B. J. O. Nordfeldt's Chicago Portraits," *Arts Magazine*, 61 (January 1987): 27–33; see also Delia Austrian, "Society Folk and Artists Unite in Making Players' Workshop a Successful Experiment," *Fashion Art* 3 (April 1917): 17, 43; J. Z. Jacobson, *Thirty-Five Saints and Emil Armin* (Chicago: L. M. Stein, 1929), 100–112; Al Chase, "Stony Island's Old Art Center Property Sold," *Chicago Tribune*, October 18, 1946; Daniel M. MacMaster, ". . . And Here Was Bohemia," *Chicago Tribune*, March 14, 1954. Both *Chicago Tribune* clippings found in a Chicago Historical Society file entitled "Buildings.

Fifty-Seventh and Stony Island, NW & SW Corner." Bror Nordfeldt left Chicago in 1907 to study in Paris, returning to live in the Corner in 1911 as a member of the postimpressionist school. One wonders if he was exposed to the then latest theatrical trends in Paris as well, given his subsequent interest in little theaters. He later participated in other bohemian arts communities in America. He was an original member of the Provincetown Players and later lived and worked amid the artist colonies of New Mexico. Both Nordfeldt and his wife, a practicing psychologist, set up backyard tables on hot days for shared meals accompanied by beer and wine, "to aid the conversation." They paid fifteen dollars per month for the amenity of an inside toilet whereas most paid three dollars less for units relying on outhouses. See Dale Kramer, *Chicago Renaissance: The Literary Life in the Midwest, 1900–1930* (New York: Appleton-Century, 1966), 160–62.

16. See Kruty, "Mirrors of a 'Post-Impressionist'"; see also Austrian, "Society Folk and Artists Unite"; Kramer, *Chicago Renaissance*.

17. Kruty, "Mirrors of a 'Post-Impressionist'," 31; Trachtenberg, *Incorporation of America*, 37, 55. Trachtenberg argues that the late nineteenth century's "incorporation" of society tended to force people into functional molds. Perhaps the impulse toward bohemianism was a reaction against those growing pressures to conform, a rebellious reassertion of American individualism.

18. Allen Churchill, *The Improper Bohemians* (New York, E. P. Dutton, 1959), 178; for a far more detailed account of the personal networks among the literary inhabitants of the Corner, see Steven Watson, *Strange Bedfellows* (New York: Abbeville Press, 1991). For a closer look at the life and work of writer Floyd Dell, especially his Iowa roots alongside Jig Cook and Susan Glaspell, see Douglas Clayton, *Floyd Dell: The Life and Times of an American Rebel* (Chicago: Ivan R. Dee, 1994).

19. Albert Parry, *Garrets and Pretenders: A History of Bohemianism in America*. (New York: Dover, 1960), 188.

20. Parry, *Garrets and Pretenders*, 190. There were some exceptions to this, most notably Emma Goldman.

21. Parry, *Garrets and Pretenders*, 194–95. Parry writes also of "The Shop," a bohemian club begun by poet Maxwell Bodenheim and Lou Wall Moore, located in her studio, calling this the site of the "Players' Work Shop" theater. But it seems Parry is confusing the Maurice Browne company that rehearsed in Moore's studio with the later group, which was housed in Elizabeth Bingham's studio shortly thereafter. Still, see Parry's account of the hair-lipped Moore, "whom Bodenheim called Princess Lou. She was a sculptor and a dancer, one of the first interpretative dancers not

to emulate Isadora Duncan, but to apply a knowledge of sculpture to a series of posings which Princess Lou exhibited as dance. . . . In the season of 1907–1908 New York's Four Hundred imported her from Chicago and offered her dances [at] their parties. . . . [A]n unknown admirer [wrote of her]: 'Lou Wall Moore—ah, she has the soul of Chicago! She is Bohemia! She is generous, and kind, and truly fine; hospitable always to new things, and learned in the old, leaning to the bizarre and the colorful.'"

22. Kramer, *Chicago Renaissance*, 160.

23. Ed Garman, *The Art of Raymond Jonson, Painter* (Albuquerque: University of New Mexico Press, 1976).

24. Emma Goldman, *The Social Significance of the Modern Drama* (New York: CreateSpace, 2017).

25. The leader of this mutiny against Browne was no other than Alice Gerstenberg. For an account of Gerstenberg's actions here, see Shannon Epplett, "The Steppenwolf Scenario" (unpublished dissertation, University of Illinois at Urbana-Champaign, 2018).

26. See the Dale Kramer Papers, vol. 1, Chicago notebooks, Newberry Library, Chicago; see also the Ben Hecht Papers, Newberry Library, Chicago. Hecht's remarks appear as outtakes from an unpublished original draft of his autobiography, *A Child of the Century*. Also, see Austrian, "Society Folk and Artists Unite," 17, who reports that by spring 1917, active membership numbered seventy eight, with "a number of associate ones who make up the organization which finances itself. The active members write, act and produce the plays."

27. For more detail about the work of the Players' Workshop, see Alice Gerstenberg, "Come Back With Me" (unpublished autobiography), 337–38, found in the Alice Gerstenberg Papers, Chicago Historical Society; and Alice Gerstenberg, "The Players' Workshop of Chicago," *Theatre Magazine*, September 1917, 142–43.

28. Gerstenberg, "Come Back With Me," 337–38.

29. Ben Hecht, unpublished original draft of *A Child of the Century*; Bernard Duffey aligned the Players' Workshop with those Chicago literati who voiced what he called "The Liberation," which is to say a more radical point of view. Still, this radical group was relatively tame. Hecht's play *Dregs* opened with "Jesus Christ, I'm a cross-eyed son-of-a-bitch if I ain't!" from a drunk who then, confusing his own reflection in a barroom window with Christ, invites Christ to accompany him to a brothel for some warmth and comfort. Shocked audiences walked out each night, and critic Percy Hammond's review apparently condemned the "unbelievable squalor of the words." Hecht expressed alienation following the group's decision

to replace the play. Still, he later remembered his experiences fondly. See William MacAdams, *Ben Hecht: The Man behind the Legend* (New York: Charles Scribner's Sons, 1990), 36–37.

30. It may be becoming apparent here that Bror Nordfeldt (1878–1955) was a seminal figure in both bohemianism and artistry, well beyond what he has been credited with doing. In this chapter we see him as the first to inhabit the abandoned buildings and to encourage Veblen to join him. It was Nordfeldt and his wife who hosted nightly conversations in their backyard, long before Floyd Dell and his wife started their salon nearby. We see Nordfeldt encouraging his students to move to the Corner and offering them opportunities to do their work, including when Nordfeldt helped establish for Browne's Chicago Little Theatre its high standard of scenic design via his own work. We again see Nordfeldt as a cofounder of the Provincetown Players a few years later. In the Nordfeldt Papers (housed at the Smithsonian Institution Research Information System, aka SIRIS, Title: Bror Julius Olsson [B. J. O.] Nordfeldt papers, 1909–1989. Phy. Description: 3.5 linear ft. [partially microfilmed on 2 reels], reel D166–D167), there is mention of his widow and Ellen Van Volkenburg (Browne's widow) both expressing dismay following a group meeting with theater historian Travis Bogart, where Bogart wanted to credit only Eugene O'Neill with the Provincetown Players' founding (Bogart was an expert on O'Neill), thereby deliberately ignoring the contributions of others like Nordfeldt. Nordfeldt was also among the first to move from Greenwich Village to Santa Fe, New Mexico, again helping establish a bohemian arts community there. Apparently Nordfeldt was cantankerous, which did not sit well with many others, yet his contributions to this modernist movement are unmistakable and deserve recognition—and credit!

31. Unlike his friend Jonson, Sloan did not attain lasting artistic acclaim. By the 1930s he found work as a Disney cartoon illustrator, a job that did not require innovation or vision beyond pure technical skill.

32. Samuel Putnam, unknown magazine, April 20, 1926, Emil Armin Papers, Archives of American Art, Smithsonian Institution, Washington, DC. See also Robert Grimm, "Grieving of Evicted Ghosts Heard at Farewell Festival," *Chicago Tribune*, May 20, 1962, n.p. Special thanks to Susan Weininger for her help in locating this material.

33. It would be inaccurate to assume that the fair represented upper-class interests while the 57th Street Artist Colony represented lower-class interests, since members of the city's affluent set supported both the Chicago Little Theatre and the Players' Workshop. Some (Alice Gerstenberg, Mary Aldis) actively participated in each as artists, while others gave

financial assistance. In fact, many of these families also supported the Columbian Exposition. What can be said is that the well-to-do active in the arts colony and like endeavors tended to be the children of those who made the large family fortunes. In general, where these parents gave support to the fair, their children supported Chicago's bohemia. But this group represented a small portion of Chicago's affluent elite. For more on this, see Horowitz, *Culture and the City*. Also see Stuart J. Hecht, "Kenneth Sawyer Goodman: Bridging Chicago's Affluent and Artistic Networks," *Theatre History Studies* 13 (1993): 135–47.

3

All Passes—Art Alone Endures

Staging the New Drama at the Fine Arts Building

Shannon Epplett

Over the portal [. . .] magical words were inscribed, words which would strike home to my heart: "Art alone endures." As I entered the building I noticed that they were preceded by two other words [. . .] words ominous to would-be theatrical producers: "All passes."

—Maurice Browne

Inscribed above the entrances to Chicago's Fine Arts Building, the phrase "All Passes—Art Alone Endures" simultaneously evokes the ephemeral and the eternal; its placement not-so-subtly suggests that the entrant prepare to set foot upon hallowed ground. The Fine Arts Building, a ten-story Richardsonian Romanesque arts colony in downtown Chicago, opened in 1898. If not the first, it is certainly the most significant early example of commercial space being repurposed for the arts in Chicago's history. In this way, the building is itself a makeshift space. In the quest to stage the new drama emerging at the beginning of the twentieth century within the Fine Arts Building's walls, new practices of creating and utilizing makeshift stages developed, which have come to be emblematic of theater practice in Chicago.

The Development of the Fine Arts Building

The Fine Arts Building stands at 410 South Michigan Avenue, on the west side of the city's major north-south boulevard, which itself constitutes the eastern edge of "the Loop," the nickname for the downtown business district. Grant Park and Lake Michigan lie on the east side of the street, giving the buildings on Michigan Avenue's west side a spectacular view of the park and lakefront. The Fine Arts Building is situated two-and-a-half blocks south of the Art Institute of Chicago, the city's preeminent art museum and school, and next door to the Auditorium Building, the Adler and Sullivan–designed complex that included a concert hall that seated 4,200, a hotel, and an office building.[1] The Auditorium Theatre was the original home of the Chicago Symphony Orchestra, as well as touring opera productions, and the office building housed numerous music teachers, trade schools, and arts-related businesses. The Art Institute's building opened in 1887, the Auditorium Building in 1889; thus, when the Fine Arts Building opened in 1898, it was at the heart of the city's fine arts district—the home of music, opera, and the visual arts. Chicago's commercial theaters were safely sequestered within the Loop, a few blocks away.

The building was originally constructed in 1887 by the Studebaker Brothers Manufacturing Company as a showroom and workshop for their horse-drawn carriage business.[2] By 1896, the company had outgrown the building and moved, leaving the Studebakers with eight solidly built floors of vacant space. Charles C. Curtiss, music business impresario and "society acquaintance" of the Studebakers, proposed turning the building into a space for the arts (Swan, n.p.). Chicago urban historian Perry R. Duis notes Curtiss had observed that "artistic endeavors needed ample and inexpensive, yet conveniently located, space to accommodate patrons. Moreover, Curtiss had realized that the arts attracted one another."[3] Curtiss had already been successful with Weber Music Hall, a six-story building located in the Loop that housed a concert hall, retail space, and offices and studios for musicians. He convinced the Studebakers to remodel their building into a high-rise arts colony and appoint him manager, a position he would hold for the next thirty years.[4]

Substantial renovations began in November 1897 and were completed in just under a year: two floors were added and a six-story open air "Venetian Court" was created in the center of the building. The upper floors of the building were given over to artists' studios, galleries, retail spaces, and various club and assembly rooms. On the main floor, two opulent theater spaces were created.[5] The Studebaker Theatre was a traditional proscenium stage with a fly space, wings, an orchestra pit, and seating for 1,500 on three levels. The smaller Music Hall seated approximately 500.[6] Photos from 1911 show the Music Hall with a shallow stage framed by an arch-shaped and curtainless proscenium. The stage appears to have a permanent back wall punctuated by two doors, and a grand piano takes up about one-third of the stage. The auditorium had seating on the main floor and in a small, U-shaped gallery.[7] The Fine Arts Building was a showplace; Duis notes, "Its marble lobby walls were lined with paintings and exhibit cases. Ornate benches, palms, ferns, and statuary graced the halls."[8]

Chicago's Cultural Aspirations

When the building opened in the summer of 1898, it quickly became what Curtiss envisioned—a home to musicians, architects, writers, publishers, illustrators, bookbinders, bookstores, art supply retailers, musical instrument repair and sales shops, sheet music publishers, and piano showrooms. Music dominated the building, and given Curtiss's background, it is not surprising: in 1901, it was estimated that over ten thousand students studied music within the building, either with private teachers or at one of the two musical schools headquartered there.[9] The Fine Arts Building also housed many of the city's prominent social clubs and service organizations, with members drawn from Chicago's upper classes. The Chicago Woman's Club, the Chicago Literary Club, the Fortnightly, the Cordon Club, the Caxton Club, the Catholic Women's League, the Daughters of the American Revolution, Alliance Française, the College Club, the Wednesday Club, the Thursday Club, and the Illinois Equal Suffrage Association all called the building home (Swan, n.p.). As such, the building was a contact point between the working artists and writers of Chicago and the city's philanthropic, social elite—bringing them together in one space.[10] David Swan notes in the 2008 preface to *The Book of the Fine Arts Building*:

> As the Fine Arts Building matured over the course of Curtiss' tenure (1898–1929) it developed into a kind of civic forum for new ideas and social movements, while serving also as a superb and incredibly popular performance place. . . . It also served

> many important social organizations comprising clubs for both men and women with aspirations for civic improvement. As was noted just a year after the Fine Arts Building had opened, Curtiss had been instrumental in assembling under the roof of the Fine Arts Building "all that is best of the best side of Chicago life."[11]

The Fine Arts Building served as a conspicuous oasis of high culture and progressive thought, in a city then known primarily for its industry and enterprise.

Chicago at the turn of the century was seen as a raucous, uncouth, and uncultured boomtown; the creation of the Fine Arts Building was a manifestation of the efforts by the city's social and cultural elite to overcome this reputation. Chicago's population went from 350 to 300,000 between its incorporation in 1833 and the Great Chicago Fire of 1871.[12] The city rebuilt quickly after the fire, and became a hub for transportation, distribution, and manufacturing. The need for labor in the steel mills and slaughterhouses created an immigration-driven population explosion: in 1890, 79 percent of Chicagoans were either foreign-born or the children of immigrants.[13] In the face of this growth, educational and cultural amenities had not kept pace. At the end of the nineteenth century, Chicago was big and wealthy but rough and uncivilized compared to the cities of the Eastern Seaboard. This reputation extended to its citizenry and did not sit well with the upper echelons of Chicago society. To rectify this, in the 1880s and 1890s, Chicago's fortune makers engaged in an aggressive campaign to develop educational and cultural institutions. The Chicago Public Library, the University of Chicago, the Art Institute, and the Chicago Symphony Orchestra were established in the period between the great fire of 1871 and the turn of the century.[14] Establishing, supporting, and patronizing cultural institutions was also a way for the city's wealthiest citizens, such as the Fields, the Palmers, the Armours, and the McCormicks, to display their status under the guise of serving the public good. When the Fine Arts Building opened, the city's representative institutions of the "fine" or "high" arts of the day were firmly established, and the Fine Arts was yet more empirical evidence that Chicago was a city devoted to culture.

In keeping with the "fine arts" in its name, the Fine Arts Building's theaters were not intended for the kinds of work that filled the commercial theaters of the Loop. *The Book of the Fine Arts Building*, a promotional publication from 1911, recounts the performance history of the building: the Studebaker had been home to opera companies, touring Shakespeare productions, and appearances by Sarah Bernhardt and Alla Nazimova; the Music Hall had hosted lectures, "private musicales," and events for the many social clubs headquartered in the building. What *The Book of the Fine Arts Building* lists are the kinds of performances that the management of the building—Curtiss—wanted to promulgate. The programming reflects a nineteenth-century conception of the "great" or "high" performing arts, and would meet with the approval of Chicago's Gilded-Age patron class. As avant-garde movements in theater brought new types of plays and production methods to the fore, the Fine Arts Building seemed like the proper place for such work, yet the building's stages proved to be unsuitable, and this in turn fostered innovation in terms of staging, acting, lighting, and scenic design.

The opening of the Fine Arts Building coincided with the effort to shift public perceptions of theater from that of lowbrow popular entertainment toward a high art. Vaudeville, spectacles, and melodramas dominated Chicago's theaters, as they did everywhere else in the country at the time.[15] The commercial theater industry was almost entirely under the control of the New York–based Theatrical Syndicate, a monopoly of theatrical agents and producers that, by 1903, controlled booking and touring for most of the country. The syndicate was held responsible for the low quality of commercial theater, as the emphasis on the bottom line led to safe play choices, mindless spectacle, star vehicles, and low artistic standards (Czechowski, 13). Theater was popular entertainment for the masses—not "culture"—and no alternative existed to the commercial theater production model.

The Uplift Movement

Locally, the push to reform the stage intersected with the efforts of the city's social elite to make Chicago a modern cultural mecca to rival or outdo New York and Boston. Taking cues from Europe's independent theater movement, Chicago's theatrical reformers were known collectively and colloquially as the "Uplifters."[16] The uplift movement in Chicago had its beginnings in Jane Addams and Laura Dainty Pelham's Hull-House Dramatic Association, which began in 1897 with amateur production of melodramas, and by 1904 had developed into what would be called the first art theater.[17] The Uplifters were an informal group that included professional theater artists like Anna Morgan and Donald Robertson; wealthy and progressive arts patrons such as Arthur Aldis, Arthur Bissell, and Hobart Chatfield-Taylor; and some who bridged both categories, like "society" playwrights Alice Gerstenberg, Mary Aldis, and Kenneth Sawyer Goodman. An "art world," to use Howard Becker's term to describe the community that develops surrounding the production of art, coalesced around interest in the "new drama" and the related "new stagecraft" movements—a loose category that encompassed the plays of Ibsen, Yeats, Synge, and Maeterlinck and the design theories of Edward Gordon Craig and Adolphe Appia. The Fine Arts Building came to be a cornerstone of this art world.

This perception of the Fine Arts Building as a home for the arts is encoded within the architecture of the building itself. The phrase "All Passes—Art Alone Endures" above the entrances is derived from an 1852 poem, "L'Art," by Théophile Gautier, adapted into English by Henry Austin Dobson as "Ars Victrix," in 1876. The inscription is actually a misquote of one of the concluding stanzas. Dobson's version has it as:

> All passes. ART alone
> Enduring stays to us;
> The Bust outlasts the throne,—
> The Coin, Tiberius;[18]

The poem is a Romantic exhortation to artists to persist in their efforts, acknowledging that making art is hard, but the results eternal. By its placement above the front door, the phase seems to declare the building as a home for the arts, but the words' source—Gautier's poem—also reflects the nineteenth-century mindset that created the building. The Fine Arts Building's theaters were designed and built and programmed with existing performance genres in mind—opera, concert music, Shakespeare, classical tragedy. While the new drama was not exactly excluded from the building, its large and opulent stages proved not to serve it very well.

The financial realities of the Fine Arts Building determined the practices of the new drama in Chicago. The Studebaker and Music Hall proved to be too capacious and expensive for the small budgets and limited audiences drawn to the new drama. However, the Uplifters would find alternatives within the walls of the Fine Arts Building to stage the new drama, and these alternatives would become a part

The entrance to the Fine Arts Building. Photograph by Shannon Epplett, 2019. Courtesy of the author.

of the "habitus"—to use Pierre Bourdieu's term for cultural practices and traditions—of Chicago's alternative theater scene.[19] The Fine Arts Building served as a testing ground for two of the earliest advocates of the new drama in the city: Anna Morgan and Donald Robertson. Their initial efforts informed the later work of Maurice Browne and Ellen Van Volkenburg's Chicago Little Theatre in its approach to staging plays in a makeshift space.

Anna Morgan

Morgan (1851–1936) was one of Chicago's first advocates for the new drama. She began her career as a dramatic "reader" on the Redpath

Lyceum circuit in the late 1870s, and began teaching "elocution, physical culture, and general deportment on the stage" at the Chicago Conservatory of Music in 1884.[20] She was an authority on the Delsarte method, a then popular form of speech and movement training originally developed for actors and singers.[21] Her students were primarily young women from Chicago's well-off families hoping to acquire social graces. Morgan frequently staged recitals and public performances with her conservatory students—these events ranged from evenings of scenes and monologues to fully staged plays, depending on her students' abilities and interests. Some of these early productions point toward her interest in the new drama: in 1892, the conservatory staged Ibsen's *The Pillars of Society*, although it is not clear if Morgan directed this production.[22] In March 1895, she directed Ibsen's *The Master Builder* at Powers' Theatre with a cast of conservatory students and invited the press.[23] Her goal was to bring Ibsen's then controversial work to Chicago; unfortunately, the newspaper critic she was expecting—who was favorably disposed toward Ibsen—was unavailable, and his replacement savaged both play and playwright.[24] Morgan made another attempt at uplifting the public taste in February 1896, with Maurice Maeterlinck's symbolist drama *The Intruder*.[25] Again, the press was not receptive, with Morgan recalling: "The newspaper men for the most part sat on the back seats and grinned, regarding both it and me as being 'queer.'"[26] Morgan did not take this well: in her autobiography, written nearly twenty-five years later, she states, "I have dwelt at length on this, because I wish to record the lack of appreciation and encouragement I encountered from our critics on this and subsequent occasions" (Morgan, 45).

In 1898, Morgan left the Chicago Conservatory and started her own school, the Anna Morgan Studio, in the Fine Arts Building. She was one of the building's first tenants.[27] Her school occupied a suite of rooms on the eighth floor, the largest of which was a twenty-one-by-forty-five-foot space with a small proscenium stage at one end. It is clear from photos that the stage was a permanent fixture of the room, rather than a temporary platform or an improvised architectural afterthought. The stage was raised about one-and-a-half feet, with two steps leading down into the rest of the room. It was fifteen-and-a-half feet deep, with a proscenium sixteen feet wide and eighteen-and-a-half feet high.[28] The back wall was an exterior wall of the building, and had windows and a working fireplace—most likely covered by a drop curtain during performances. A traverse curtain ran across the proscenium arch. Lighting was accomplished with "room lamps and standing goose-necked student lamps which could be turned in any direction."[29] For performances, the main room was estimated to hold 125 on folding chairs (Sozen, 33). This space was used regularly for instruction and was usually referred to as a lecture hall or studio, but it could be converted into a theater for performances and recitals, which Morgan staged regularly.

Morgan's studio was often referred to as a school of elocution, but beyond poise, deportment, and etiquette, it offered a comprehensive training program in aesthetics and arts appreciation aimed at Chicago's social elite. In her study on Morgan, Joyce Sozen notes that Morgan's aim was "to give students social poise and wide knowledge and appreciation of literature and the arts, so they could gain more pleasure from life. Her instruction was not primarily dramatic instruction, but 'cultural' instruction" (Sozen, 37).

> According to a catalogue for 1915, a student would be required to gain an extensive knowledge of poetry and prose, of authors, and of classical and modern plays and playwrights. There were special courses for professional teachers, dramatic artists, and operatic career singers. Students showing talent were now encouraged to write dialogues, sketches, and plays, which, when worthy, would be presented at recitals. (Sozen, 50)

In this way, Morgan made theater—and particularly the new drama—acceptable and understandable to Chicago's upper classes; she modeled the idea of theater as an art form rather than popular entertainment, and helped build an audience for it among her students and their families.[30] Through the studio's regular recitals and performances, Morgan made it acceptable for "society girls" like playwright Alice Gerstenberg and Little Theatre cofounder Ellen Van Volkenburg to take to the stage.[31]

Prior to starting her studio, Morgan had staged her own productions of the new drama; she usually worked with amateur actors but booked commercial theater spaces, distributed tickets, and invited critics.[32] She later expressed regrets about not pursuing it further:

> At that time my presentation of the plays of Ibsen, Maeterlinck, Yeats and other dramatists had made a distinct impression and I imagined that some of my admirers would come forward and

> offer the money with which to provide an artistic playhouse. Time went on and the money did not come—and I did not ask for it. When I went into the Fine Arts Building I determined to abandon the giving of plays altogether and confine my efforts to educational and cultural work, the development of the speaking voice, interpretive readings, and the study of literature. My reasons were that I was not properly equipped to give plays on an adequate scale, and the worry and bother of trying to give them without adequate means was discouraging.[33]

It is worth noting that Morgan's main reason for stopping was financial: the negative reviews did not build public support for the new drama, and this translated into a lack of funding. Morgan recognized that there was not much of an audience for the new drama, and she set about developing one through her studio. She never abandoned her interest in the new drama, however, and continued to stage productions on her studio stage with her students. Although Morgan feared that too much emphasis on plays at her studio "gave the public the impression that [she] was conducting a preparatory school for the professional stage," she nevertheless encouraged her students who showed an interest in performing and writing for the stage, among them Van Volkenburg and Gerstenberg.[34]

Morgan viewed her studio productions as recitals, "the avenues through which the culture obtained in the general classes was displayed, the 'show work,' so to speak, of the school."[35] These were end-of-term showcases of her students' progress and were not necessarily intended for a wider public, yet they sometimes rose to this level by virtue of the material she selected. She interspersed plays by Shaw, Synge, Yeats, and Maeterlinck into her recital programs of scenes and monologues from classical plays, Shakespeare, poetry, and dramatic readings. All were presented on her small stage using minimal props, dark draperies for sets, and often all-female casts.[36] Shaw and Yeats in particular drew outside interest: in April 1899, her production of Shaw's *Candida* ran for nearly a month due to public attention. Sozen notes that "Miss Morgan said that the play was admirably suited to her small theater because the three acts of the play are in one setting. Devotees of Shaw came to see the production three, and in some instances, four times" (Sozen, 77–78).

Her staging of Yeats's *The Hour Glass* in 1905 earned praise for its scenic simplicity from James O'Donnell Bennett, theater critic for the *Chicago Record-Herald*:

> As it was, the draperies and the shadows, the desk of the scholar, which was so simple as to be quite unnoticed, and the hourglass in a dim recess, served all the purposes of a perfect investiture. Nothing seemed lacking, and yet nothing obtruded. What was equally profitable and pleasant there was opportunity for the free play of the spectator's fancy. He could create pictures for himself, projecting them against that gracious background, or, penetrating it, imagine glimpses of the busy village beyond the walls of the scholar's study. (Sozen, 83)

Morgan made a virtue of necessity; she surrounded her performers with dark fabric and lit them using desk lamps, effecting a stark scenic minimalism that was well suited to the new work. She was likely influenced by the new stagecraft of Craig and Appia. Morgan's small-stage, minimalist productions of the new drama provided a template for how to produce theater on a shoestring budget and in makeshift circumstances; in doing so, she set in place elements of alternative theater production in Chicago. Morgan recognized her own influence, even if no one else did: "Consequently, and in this place, I am going to take credit to myself for having originated and carried forward to this hour with unimpaired success the 'Little Theatre' idea."[37]

Donald Robertson

Following Morgan, Donald Robertson (1860–1926) is another person responsible for testing the suitability of the Fine Arts Building for the new drama. Robertson was born in Scotland in 1860, emigrated with his family to the United States at age thirteen, and made his acting debut in New York in 1879. After working for several years in London, he returned to the United States in the 1890s and established himself as a dramatic leading man in touring theater—best known for playing the lead role in his own adaptation of *The Man in the Iron Mask*.[38] Robertson became enamored with the new drama coming out of Europe and wanted to bring it to the American stage. During a two-week engagement in Chicago in 1904, he saw a performance at Hull-House, and decided that the city would be the perfect place to establish his "ideal" theater.[39] For Robertson, this meant an endowed or subscription-based professional repertory ensemble, performing the "poetic" drama.

His first attempt at establishing a company was ill-fated; in 1905, he was named artistic director of a proposed endowed theater sponsored by the Chicago Woman's Club. It was to be housed at the Fine Arts Building, in a renovated Music Hall.[40] The project came into competition with a similar venture, the New Theatre—an effort that originated among a group of prominent Chicago businessmen and arts patrons that included real estate developer Arthur Aldis, Arthur Bissell of the Bissell-Weisart Piano Company, and writer Hobart Chatfield-Taylor.[41] Both proposed theaters were to be professional ensembles performing the new drama for a subscription audience. Despite attempts to combine their efforts, the Woman's Club and the men behind the New Theatre could not reach an agreement. The Woman's Club eventually abandoned their plans, leaving Robertson with no prospects. The New Theatre was an artistic and financial failure, barely lasting a single season at Steinway Hall in 1906–1907.[42]

The next season, and without financial backing, Robertson announced that the Donald Robertson Company would present a season of twelve plays in repertory at Ravinia, a suburban amusement park, in September and October 1907.[43] The work was well received and garnered the support of several of the men involved in the New Theatre: Aldis, Bissell, and Chatfield-Taylor. With their support, Robertson's company obtained an engagement at the Garrick, a large commercial theater in the Loop, where the company performed their repertory as a matinee series four days per week.[44] Critics lauded the company, but the group failed to fill the 1,300-seat theater. In December, with the patronage of Aldis, Bissell, and Chatfield-Taylor, the company announced a move to the intimate Music Hall of the Fine Arts Building, performing Wednesday afternoons and Saturday evenings.

The Robertson company continued to receive favorable reviews but were not attracting an audience. *Chicago Tribune* critic Burns Mantle dramatized this fact in his review of *As the Leaves*:

> "I'm afraid," remarked Hobart Chatfield Chatfield-Taylor[45] yesterday afternoon as he reflectively surveyed the rows of empty seats in Fine Arts Music hall, where the Donald Robertson company was presenting "As the Leaves," one of the last plays written by the late Giuseppe Giacosa of Italy and the universe, "I'm afraid that if you were to place a sign at the entrance to this hall reading, 'The Higher Drama—Admittance Free,' no one would enter."

Chatfield-Taylor observes that "any reference to an 'art theater' seems to frighten rather than to attract playgoers."[46] Robertson proved that the audience for theatrical uplift was small: while it was not a surprise that the group could not fill the Garrick's 1,300 seats, they also had difficulty filling the 500-seat Music Hall. The smallest theater at the Fine Arts was too large and therefore financially untenable for the new drama. The next season, the Robertson company was offered rent-free use of a lecture hall at the Art Institute, where they remained in residence for two seasons.[47]

Reviews of Robertson's productions in the Music Hall do not mention lighting and scenic design, which implies that these elements were not noteworthy. Robertson seems to have been drawn to the new drama based on its literary merits and does not appear to have had much interest in the new stagecraft. Given his background as an actor on the nineteenth-century commercial stage, it seems likely that he produced the new drama within the older staging traditions to which he was accustomed. By contrast, Morgan incorporated the ideas of the new stagecraft and adapted her staging practices and production designs to suit her small space—which proved to work well with the new drama. By their efforts, both Morgan and Robertson showed the opportunities and limitations that existed within the Fine Arts Building's walls, lessons that Van Volkenburg and Browne took to heart.

The Chicago Little Theatre

Husband and wife Maurice Browne and Ellen Van Volkenburg established the Chicago Little Theatre in 1912. Browne (1881–1955) was an Englishman with a literary background; Van Volkenburg (1882–1975), the daughter of a salesman for Chicago's meatpacking industry, wanted to act. They had met in Europe, married after a whirlwind romance, and settled in Van Volkenburg's hometown of Chicago, where Browne tried to earn a living as a writer and teacher. He described the founding of the Little Theatre as driven by Van Volkenburg's ambition to be "a 'really-truly' actress," his own desire to write "masterpieces of poetic drama," and their shared disdain for the commercial theater. The Abbey Players' visit to Chicago in 1912 inspired the couple, and they received the following advice from Lady Gregory:

> By all means start your own theatre; but make it in your own image. Don't engage professional players; they have been spoiled

> for your purpose. Engage and train, as we of the Abbey have done, amateurs; shopgirls, school-teachers, counter-jumpers; cut-throat-thieves rather than professionals. And prepare to have your hearts broken.[48]

The couple had no real experience or money when they started.[49] They began by first finding a free place to rehearse: the studio of sculptor Lou Wall Moore, "an old ramshackle one-storied frame-building, far out on the city's south side."[50] Next, they found actors—initially all women, drawn from Van Volkenburg's circle of college friends—and based on that, decided on a play: Euripides's *The Trojan Women*.[51] Moore wished to play Cassandra, and since it was her studio, she did. Van Volkenburg played Hecuba and Browne directed (Browne, 118). They rehearsed nine hours a day for eleven months: "Presumably it was this long period of extraordinarily detached theatre—rehearsal as its own end and justification—that led Browne and his players to arrive at their ideas and ideals of drama."[52] At this point, the Little Theatre had no home other than Moore's studio and was rehearsing with no prospect of a performance in sight. As the piece came together, Browne recalled that "performance became a paramount necessity, a theatre an imperative need: we talked it all the time: finally we talked it into being." After coverage of the group's activities appeared in the press, they received an invitation from Curtiss, manager of the Fine Arts Building, to discuss renting space. Browne jumped at the opportunity: "Perfectly appointed and immaculately kept, it was the antithesis of Lou Wall's studio. I raced toward it."[53]

Curtiss offered the Little Theatre exclusive use of the Music Hall for $25,000 a year.[54] When Browne balked at the price, "Mr. Curtiss waved my scruples aside. I was young, brilliantly gifted; I would earn vast sums; Chicago was talking about me. 'To be perfectly frank,' the mellifluous voice continued, 'my building cannot afford to let you be housed elsewhere.'" Browne and Curtiss negotiated an alternative: a storage space at the back of the fourth floor for $3,000 a year—"and the space convertible, he assured me, for an infinitesimal outlay into an ideal small theatre." Browne used a $500 check—a wedding present—to procure their theater. The "infinitesimal" price of converting the space put the company $10,000 in debt.[55]

In their space on the fourth floor, Browne and Van Volkenburg created a small proscenium theater, with a stage fifteen feet wide by eighteen feet deep, and a proscenium opening of just under twelve feet.[56] The design and dimensions of their stage appear to have been borrowed from Anna Morgan's studio, but the audience experience at the Little Theatre was far more comfortable than Morgan's folding chairs. The Little Theatre's auditorium was long, narrow, carpeted, and tastefully decorated in understated shades of stone, beige, and olive. It seated ninety-one on fixed, upholstered seats, and also featured a tearoom that was open at intermission and post-show.[57] Although the space was noted for its elegance, some critics compared it to seeing a play performed in a hotel corridor.[58]

Browne primarily directed and Van Volkenburg acted, but both were involved in all aspects of running the theater—from administration to designing shows. Browne and Van Volkenburg continued to develop and refine the methods of scenic design and lighting that Morgan may have pioneered in Chicago. The Little Theatre usually staged five productions per season; many were evenings of one-acts. In all they produced forty-eight plays over the course of five years, including the Gilbert Murray translations of *The Trojan Women* and *Medea*; Ibsen's *Rosmersholm* and *Hedda Gabler*; Shaw's *Mrs. Warren's Profession*, *The Philanderer*, and *Candida*; Strindberg's *Creditors*, *Pariah*, and *The Stronger*; Synge's *Deirdre of the Sorrows*; and Yeats's *On Baile's Strand* and *The Shadowy Waters*.[59] Browne was influenced by Craig's ideas about directing, in that he believed a theater production needed to be the vision of one person controlling all elements (Dukore, 60). However, scenic design and lighting were generally approached as a collaboration among Browne, Van Volkenburg, and resident designer Raymond Jonson.

Browne and Van Volkenburg shared an avid interest in stage lighting, and were influenced by the ideas of Craig and Appia. Resident designer Raymond Jonson came to the Little Theatre from a position of complete naïveté. He was studying to be a painter at the time. Browne writes, "Raymond Jonson had been sent to us soon after the theater opened by Brör Nordfeldt, the painter, when we were desperately seeking a young Hercules who would masterfully unite in himself stage-designer, stage-manager, stage-carpenter, scene-painter, scene-shifter, electrician and, on occasion, actor."[60] Jonson's knowledge of scenic and lighting design was developed entirely at the Little Theatre, in response to specific challenges presented by the space.[61]

The design collaboration between Browne, Van Volkenburg, and Jonson led to a refined, minimalist stage aesthetic, in response to the space itself. Theater historian Bernard Dukore quotes Van Volkenburg on this front:

> The Chicago Little Theatre was opposed to the conventional type of scenery. It whole-heartedly adopted the aims and methods of the new stagecraft. This was done partly through intention (Maurice Browne had been influenced by and wanted to follow the path pointed out by Gordon Craig), partly through lack of funds (the company did not have the money to spend on lavish scenery), and partly through the limitations of the Little Theatre (the stage was very small). (Dukore, 69)

Browne notes, "We had learned to eliminate from the stage every object which had not both dramatic and visual meaning."[62]

Dukore characterizes the Little Theatre scenery as "simplicity and suggestion," driven by necessity but rooted in the ideas of Craig and Appia.[63] Like Anna Morgan's 1905 production of *The Hour Glass*, they often used draperies to create settings, and with their second production, Arthur Schnitzler's *Anatol*, they achieved noteworthy results:

> Four of the dialogues pass in rooms. These rooms, with no suggestion of actual walls, were hung with soft greenish or brownish hangings through which the players made their entrances and exits. Once these hangings seemed to enclose a window, or there was a hint in andirons and the like of a fireplace against them. . . . In each setting, sparse furniture gave the room the hangings were presumed to enclose a touch of the character of the occupant or suited the necessity of the action. In the one episode out of doors, there was no attempt whatever at scenic suggestion. Anatol and Gabrielle stood before no simulated shop; but against a big brown screen while brown hangings closed in the stage. Inevitably there was no illusion of place, except as the spoken words, Anatol's outspread umbrella and the calling of a taxi suggested it. . . . In the scenes within doors the illusion was satisfying to those that like simplicity in the theatre because it leaves leeway for the imagination.[64]

Browne noted that some critics assumed they had used five sets of velvet curtains in the show, when it was actually "one set of curtains throughout, made of flannelette, with differently coloured lights thrown on it for each scene."[65]

Their set for *The Trojan Women* was emblematic of their scenic simplicity.[66] It consisted of an upstage stone wall rent with a crack large enough to serve as an entrance. "Jonson's extremely simple and powerful design," said the *Indianapolis News*, "has as much of the towering dignity we have admired in the sketches of Gordon Craig, dwarfing the mortal figures until they seem but puppets in the hands of destiny."[67] The allusions to Craig were apt: although the Little Theatre was not the first to use simplified settings in America, they did so effectively, and they brought the practice to a wider audience through their 1915 tour of *The Trojan Women*.[68] Browne and Van Volkenburg later met Craig during a trip to Europe, where he accused them of stealing his ideas for using screens as scenery, a charge they denied: "Our screens bore no relation to his but had been copied from screens in Lou Wall's studio and modified in accord with a print by Shunyei."[69]

The "less is more" aesthetic worked well on their small stage but did not transfer well to larger ones. In 1916, Browne rented the Music Hall in the Fine Arts Building to stage *Mrs. Warren's Profession*. Due to budget constraints the set consisted of gray screens and minimal furniture, rearranged to indicate four different settings. The abstract setting for a realistic comedy was deemed too jarring by critics, a sentiment with which Van Volkenburg and Browne concurred: "[We] knew it was wrong. When it was designed, we had an eye to the clean line and the simplicity; but then we saw that we should have been more realistic, less abstract."[70]

The Little Theatre relied heavily on lighting to set the scene. The theater had a remarkable lighting setup, considering their small budget and the technology available at the time: eight dimmers with each running three-circuit strips (Dukore, 82). However, they often improvised lighting instruments out of "dishpans from the ten-cent store" for floods and "tin funnels" for spotlights.[71] They also eliminated footlights from their stage. Browne, Van Volkenburg, and Jonson lit their minimalist scenery to evoke setting, mood, and atmosphere. "We sought to make something out of—as nearly as possible—nothing: a wisp of cheesecloth, a flower in a vase, a shaft of light" (Browne, 158). In doing so, they created magic on their tiny stage:

> Sitting in his (Maurice Browne's) little corridor-like audience-room, which has slowly gone almost dark just before the play begins, you see the curtains parted on absolute darkness. You are in deep shadows—so you might be anywhere in that you do not feel the constraint of four walls—and the parting of the curtain has revealed an opening into blackness at the other end of the room—so that stage might be any size. In the darkness

> you hear the voice of a woman lamenting. . . . Slowly the darkness around her is shot with faint shafts of light. Sometimes the light seems to be suffusing the scene; at other times it is only a ray that falls across her or is reflected on her white arm.[72]

Under constant financial pressure, the group began to unravel in 1916; they had opened their doors already in debt due to renovations on the space, and with only ninety-one seats, there was little chance of ever earning enough income to meet expenses. World War I contributed to the end of the Little Theatre; audiences dwindled as the war progressed. It also did not help ticket sales that the Little Theatre was identified with the antiwar movement due to their 1915 tour of *The Trojan Women*, sponsored by the Women's Peace Party. Browne and Van Volkenburg gave up their space in the Fine Arts Building and tried to produce in another space—Central Music Hall—but folded in December 1917 (Dukore, 28–29).

A Legacy of Practice

The Little Theatre lent its name to a national movement. Despite its size, the group had a high profile: the *Trojan Women* tour brought their work to thirty-three cites, and Browne wrote several articles about the group, its work, and their ideas that appeared in *The Drama* magazine.[73] The group's longevity—they produced consistently over the course of five seasons—was also a significant factor in their notoriety. Chicago's art theater community faded away following the war—many of its members moved to New York, where George Cram Cook and Floyd Dell modeled the Provincetown Players on the Little Theatre.[74] Beyond their national significance, the Chicago Little Theatre created the template for Off-Loop theater production through their use of converted space and their innovation in terms of production design within the confines of their small space and budget.

Had they been able to afford it, Browne and Van Volkenburg likely would have taken Curtiss up on his offer of the Music Hall. Financial realities intervened, and Browne negotiated a makeshift space elsewhere in the building—and in the course of making it work, made history on its stage. Their alternative space required creativity, improvisation, and ingenuity. The Little Theatre's work at the beginning of the twentieth century has come to define some of the elements of alternative theater production in Chicago to the present day: makeshift and alternative spaces, small budgets, scenic simplicity, innovation, and collaboration. It is now part of the habitus of Chicago theater that when a "real" theater is unavailable or unaffordable, you can create your own. Within their makeshift space, on their makeshift budget, Browne, Van Volkenburg, and Jonson expanded upon what Morgan had started with her studio productions and evolved their own staging aesthetic, and at times they achieved scenic and lighting effects that transcended the limitations under which they were created. The Little Theatre's attention and innovation in this area has also become incorporated into Chicago's alternative theater ethos: the belief that something great can be created out of nothing. Perhaps most significantly, Browne and Van Volkenburg seemed never to have dwelt on the shortcomings of their space; rather, they focused on its possibilities—what it could be, rather than what it was not. This kind of aesthetic optimism in the face of adversity is also definitive of Chicago's theater culture.

A new approach to theater production emerged amid the marble tile and art nouveau embellishments of the Fine Arts Building, an approach that influenced a nationwide Little Theatre movement but also became the prototype for alternative theater production in Chicago. Not only was the Fine Arts building itself a makeshift space, but due to the legacy of creating makeshift performance space within its walls, it was instrumental in anchoring this particular element of Chicago's theater habitus. In this way—as the inscription above the doors suggest—the Fine Arts Building *is* hallowed ground: it is where some of Chicago theater's defining qualities first manifested.

Notes

Epigraph: Maurice Browne, *Too Late to Lament: An Autobiography* (Bloomington: Indiana University Press, 1956), 120.

1. The Auditorium Theatre is still in use; the Auditorium Building is now part of Roosevelt University.

2. David Swan, Elia Wilkinson Peattie, and Ralph Fletcher Seymour, eds., *The Book of the Fine Arts Building* (Chicago: Hyoogen Press, 2008), n.p.

3. Perry R. Duis, "'Where Is Athens Now?': The Fine Arts Building 1898 to 1918," *Chicago History* 6, no. 2 (1977): 66–78.

4. Perry R. Duis, "'All Else Passes—Art Alone Endures': The Fine Arts Building 1918 to 1930," *Chicago History* 7, no. 1 (1978): 40–51.

5. Swan, *Book of the Fine Arts Building*, n.p.

6. Both theaters have undergone several renovations that altered seating capacities. The Music Hall was also known as University Hall and the Playhouse at various times: at one point, it could seat up to 700, but probably seated approximately 500 when it opened. The Studebaker Theatre was renovated and reopened in 2016. It currently seats 740. "About the Studebaker Theater," Studebaker Theatre, https://www.studebakertheater.com; see also Joyce Lorraine Chalcraft Sozen, "Anna Morgan: Reader, Teacher, and Director" (PhD diss., University of Illinois, 1961), 36.

7. Swan, *Book of the Fine Arts Building*, n.p.

8. Duis, "Where Is Athens Now?," 69.

9. Swan, *Book of the Fine Arts Building*, n.p.

10. Duis, "Where is Athens Now?," 69; Swan, *Book of the Fine Arts Building*, n.p.

11. Swan, *Book of the Fine Arts Building*, n.p.

12. Karen Sawislak, "Fire of 1871," Electronic Encyclopedia of Chicago, Chicago Historical Society, 2005, http://www.encyclopedia.chicagohistory.org/pages/1740.html.

13. Walter Nugent, "Demography: Chicago as a Modern World City," Electronic Encyclopedia of Chicago, Chicago Historical Society, 2005, http://www.encyclopedia.chicagohistory.org/pages/962.html.

14. Wilma June Dryden, "Chicago Theatre as Reflected in the Newspapers 1900–1904" (PhD diss., University of Illinois, 1961), 17.

15. Jan Charles Czechowski, "Art and Commerce: Chicago Theatre 1900–1920" (PhD diss., University of Michigan, 1982), 34–35.

16. The independent theater movement included the Théâtre Libre in Paris, the Freie Bühne in Germany, J. T. Grein's Independent Theatre in London, the Moscow Art Theatre, and the Abbey Theatre in Dublin.

17. Jane Addams and Todd London, "How America's First Art Theatre Came to Be," *American Theatre*, January 2006, 82; Stuart J. Hecht, "Hull-House Theatre: An Analytical and Evaluative History" (PhD diss., Northwestern University, 1983), 301.

18. Edmund Clarence Stedman, ed., *A Victorian Anthology, 1837–1895: Selections Illustrating the Editor's Critical Review of British Poetry in the Reign of Victoria* (Boston: Houghton Mifflin, 1895), 489.

19. Pierre Bourdieu, *Outline of a Theory of Practice* (Cambridge: Cambridge University Press, 1977), 72.

20. Anna Morgan, *My Chicago* (Chicago: R. F. Seymour, 1918), 14; Sozen, "Anna Morgan," 4.

21. "Chicago Elocutionists: Teachers Who Give the Young Idea the Proper Trend," *Chicago Daily Tribune*, August 14, 1887, 17.

22. Sozen, "Anna Morgan," 69.

23. "Amusements," entertainment listing, *Chicago Daily Tribune*, March 22, 1895, 8.

24. Morgan, *My Chicago*, 45.

25. "Given the Name 'High Bohemia': Great Interest in Miss Anna Morgan's Studio Teas," *Chicago Daily Tribune*, February 16, 1896, 12.

26. Morgan, *My Chicago*, 48.

27. Sozen, "Anna Morgan," 5.

28. Sozen, "Anna Morgan," 36; Swan, *Book of the Fine Arts Building*, n.p.

29. Sozen, "Anna Morgan," 36.

30. Stuart J. Hecht, "Anna Morgan," in *Women Building Chicago 1790–1990*, ed. Rima Lunin Schultz and Adele Hast (Bloomington: Indiana University Press, 2001), 608.

31. Morgan, *My Chicago*, 61; Sozen, "Anna Morgan," 193. Sozen does not include Van Volkenburg among Morgan's students in her study. Her list of Morgan's students appears to be based on recital programs. Van Volkenburg is mentioned in a society column from November 1908 as appearing in a performance at Morgan's studio. Sozen shows no records from 1908. Based on this, it is assumed that Van Volkenburg was a student of Morgan and appeared in a recital in 1908. Hugh Stuart Campbell, "News of the Society World," *Chicago Daily Tribune (1872–1922)*, November 8, 1908, F6.

32. Sozen, "Anna Morgan," 70.

33. Morgan, *My Chicago*, 67–68.

34. Morgan, *My Chicago*, 67–68; Campbell, "News of the Society World," F6; "Give College Girl's Plays: Bryn Mawr Graduates Present Miss . . . ," *Chicago Daily Tribune (1872–1922)*, March 13, 1908, 3.

35. Morgan, *My Chicago*, 81.

36. Sozen, "Anna Morgan," 66.

37. Morgan, *My Chicago*, 69.

38. "Robertson, Noted Stage Veteran, Dies," *Chicago Daily Tribune*, May 21, 1926, 1.

39. Donald Robertson to Anna Titus Robertson, May 11, 1904, Donald Robertson Papers (1825–1947), Chicago History Museum Research Center; Donald Robertson, *The Player's Calling in Relation to Municipal Theatres* (Chicago: Manufacturers' and Dealers' Association of America, 1915), 6.

40. Part of the Chicago Woman's Club plan involved renovating Music Hall, which suggests it was not considered suitable for play production at this time.

41. L. France Pierce, "Chicago to Have Two Subsidized Playhouses," *The Theatre*, July 1906, 194–95; Chicago Woman's Club, *Annals of the Chicago Woman's Club for the First Forty Years of Its Organization, 1876–1916* (Chicago: Chicago Woman's Club, 1916), 239; "News of the Woman's Clubs," *Chicago Daily Tribune*, October 29, 1905, 1; James L. Highlander, "An Historical Study of the New Theatre and the Robertson Players of Chicago (1906–08)" (MA thesis, University of Illinois, 1951), 1; Kathy L. Privatt, "The New Theater of Chicago: Democracy 1; Aristocracy 0," *Theatre History Studies* 24 (2004): 98.

42. "A Theatrical Autopsy," *The Dial*, March 1, 1907, 129–131; J. Dennis Rich and Kevin L. Seligman, "The New Theatre of Chicago, 1906–1907," *Educational Theatre Journal* 26, no.1 (1974): 54.

43. Ravinia is now known as an outdoor summer music festival and the summer home of the Chicago Symphony Orchestra. In 1907, it was an amusement park that had been created to entice riders onto the commuter railroad that connected it to the city. "History of Ravinia," Ravinia, accessed March 15, 2019, https://www.ravinia.org/Page/History.

44. Highlander, "Historical Study of the New Theatre," 45.

45. This is his real name. He was usually referred to as "H. C. Chatfield-Taylor" in the press.

46. Burns Mantle, "News of the Theaters," *Chicago Daily Tribune*, February 6, 1908, 8.

47. Czechowski, "Art and Commerce," 90.

48. Browne, *Too Late to Lament*, 116.

49. Bernard Dukore, "Maurice Browne and the Chicago Little Theatre" (PhD diss., University of Illinois, 1957), 8–9.

50. Browne, *Too Late to Lament*, 118.

51. Two men were later added to the cast.

52. Charles Lock, "Maurice Browne and the Chicago Little Theatre," *Modern Drama* 31, no. 1 (1988): 108.

53. Browne, *Too Late to Lament*, 119.

54. It is not known what condition or configuration the Music Hall was in at this time. Browne's meeting with Curtiss likely occurred in early 1912. The photos appearing in *The Book of the Fine Arts Building* are from 1911 or earlier, and the theater does not appear to be suitable for the production of plays. Donald Robertson's company had produced plays in the Music Hall in 1907–1908. Either the stage may have been more versatile

than it appears in photos in *The Book of the Fine Arts Building*, or it may have been renovated around this period.

55. Browne, *Too Late to Lament*, 120.

56. Dukore, "Maurice Browne," 49.

57. Browne, *Too Late to Lament*, 120.

58. Czechowski, "Art and Commerce," 59.

59. Dukore, "Maurice Browne," 141–42.

60. Browne, *Too Late to Lament*, 122.

61. Dukore, "Maurice Browne," 69.

62. Browne, *Too Late to Lament*, 154.

63. Dukore, "Maurice Browne," 71.

64. H. T. Parker, "A Tragedy of Pity," *Boston Evening Transcript*, March 14, 1913, 14. Quoted in Dukore, "Maurice Browne," 74.

65. Browne, *Too Late to Lament*, 124.

66. *The Trojan Women* was the first production that Browne and Van Volkenburg rehearsed, although it was the third production to be presented by the company, in January 1913. A remounted version of the play toured the United States in 1915 under the auspices of the Women's Peace Party, as part of the antiwar movement. Dukore, "Maurice Browne," 141; Browne, *Too Late to Lament*, 178.

67. Dukore, "Maurice Browne," 74.

68. Dukore notes that Max Reinhardt's *Sumurun* in New York in 1911 and the Abbey Players on their 1912 tour used simplified scenery. Dukore, "Maurice Browne," 124.

69. "Screens" are wooden frames covered in fabric, similar to standard stage flats. They were freestanding and could be easily shifted to suggest different settings. Browne, *Too Late to Lament*, 172.

70. Dukore, "Maurice Browne," 80.

71. Browne, *Too Late to Lament*, 123.

72. Dukore, "Maurice Browne," 88.

73. Maurice Browne, "Temple of a Living Art, a Plea for an American Art Theatre," *Drama* 12 (1911): 160–178. Browne always credited Jane Addams, Laura Dainty Pelham, and the Hull-House Dramatic Association for being the first art theater. Donald F. Tingley, "Ellen Van Volkenburg, Maurice Browne and the Chicago Little Theatre," *Illinois Historical Journal* 80, no. 3 (1987): 131.

74. Stuart J. Hecht, "The Plays of Alice Gerstenberg: Cultural Hegemony in the American Little Theatre," *Journal of Popular Culture* 26, no.1 (1992): 5.

Part 2 theater locations. Map created by Kelsey Rydland, Northwestern University Libraries, Geospatial and Data Services.

Part 2

From Mainstream to Institutionalized

Megan E. Geigner

Theater and performance in Chicago hit its stride in the twentieth century. Several of the movements and theaters examined in chapters 4 through 7 illustrate how marginal whims from one or two people morphed into long-running theaters, productions, or movements. Megan E. Geigner (chapter 4) gives an account of how the 1918 death of a socialite-turned-playwright, Kenneth Sawyer Goodman, resulted in building the Goodman Theatre in 1925; it is now one of the United States' oldest and most revered regional theaters. Aaron Krall (chapter 5) details one of the remarkable productions of the Works Progress Administration's Federal Theatre Project (FTP), *Big White Fog*, made by the Chicago Negro Unit in the late 1930s. Someone unknown decided to move the production closer to the Black community, which thus foreshadowed the still-extant issue of racial segregation of the arts in the city. Cat Gleason (chapter 6) describes how in the late 1960s a handful of theater makers on Chicago's North Side worked to convert buildings along Lincoln Avenue to serve their theatrical purposes and thereby became pioneers in Chicago's Off-Loop theater movement. And Travis Stern (chapter 7) explains the decades-long evolution of iO (formerly ImprovOlympic) from a back room in a bar in the early 1980s to a permanent institution with a space, regular performances, and classes open to the public in 1995. (In June 2020, iO announced they would be closing.) Regional theater, African American theater, Chicago-style long-form improvisational ("improv") theater, and storefronts remain touchstones of Chicago (and American) theater today.

But as much as these chapters show theater coming into its own, makeshift production practices remain central in these stories. Even with a beautiful auditorium built to stage art theater, the Goodman Theatre struggled in its first decade: audiences were small, the endowment insufficient, and the critics unaccustomed to noncommercial theater. Although the FTP landed a major, commercial venue—the Great Northern Theatre—for the Chicago Negro Unit's production of *Big White Fog*, the show failed to draw large African American audiences. The industrial buildings converted into storefront theaters on Lincoln Avenue required battling with the city over fire codes on the one hand, and with the neighbors at odds with who was being represented onstage on the other. For years iO performed in dozens of spaces—from bars to restaurants to other ensembles' venues—before finally landing a theater of their own.

The content of these productions also illustrates how the makeshift animates Chicago theater. After the Goodman initially failed to attract audiences, it turned instead to one-off performances: charity benefits, ethnic festivals, and transfer productions from local amateur theaters. The play *Big White Fog* tells the story of a family who came north in the Great Migration only to discover a marginal life in Chicago that requires making do, never feeling settled. iO's signature performance form—"the Harold"—embodies the makeshift, as it changes nightly. And finally, the plays produced at the Lincoln Park theaters used Story Theater devices such as movement and gesture, rather than set pieces, to suggest scenery and effects. Ultimately, these four chapters demonstrate migrations: movement of forms from one theater to another, movement of people from one place to another, and movement as a way of making connections and exchanges between Chicago and other locales.

Chapters 4 through 7 expand upon the first three chapters as they show how theater and performance in Chicago between the 1920s and the 1990s grappled with definitions of ethnicity and race in the city. These decades saw rapid codification of neighborhoods and spaces, and Chicago's urban planning reinforced segregation. In the 1950s and 1960s, Chicago's Mayor Richard J. Daley oversaw the deliberate demolition of parts of the south, west, and northwest sides of the city with the construction of the interstates and the erection of University of Illinois at Chicago Circle's campus, both of which created permanent barriers between white and non-white neighborhoods and destroyed neighborhood business districts. And yet, as these chapters demonstrate, theater

Viola Spolin rehearses children on the Hull-House stage, circa 1940. The boy on the far right, holding the script, is her son, future theater innovator Paul Sills. Photograph courtesy of the estates of Viola Spolin and Paul Sills, www.violaspolin.org.

could be a site for reaching across boundaries. The Goodman Theatre's decision in the 1920s and 1930s to host the Hull-House Players and Marionette Players, Greek artists, and other artists from the margins of Chicago created collaboration between otherwise isolated groups of people. The FTP Chicago Negro Unit's initial downtown production of *Big White Fog* exposed mostly white audiences to the Black experience in Chicago but eventually fell victim to Chicago's segregational practices. As Krall explains, documents do not make clear why the show moved from Chicago's business district to a high school on the South Side, but as his reading argues, efforts at integration too often proved fleeting in this period.

Gleason's and Stern's chapters also expose some of the racial politics of twentieth-century Chicago, illustrating the relationship between space, race, and makeshift. The transformation on Lincoln Avenue of a trolley barn, bowling alley, and slicing machine workshop into performance venues was wrought because Lincoln Park was a locus for grassroots and integrational community activism as well as racist urban renewal municipal policies. Thus, the theaters were caught between community members' voices of protest and the harbingers of gentrification. Stern's chapter shows how improv's flexibility can create an expansive and inclusive environment for both performers and audiences; as a form, improv acknowledges the makeshift conditions of its performance by foregrounding each performance as uniquely created for its moment, location, and audience. Improv's roots trace back to wordless games played at Hull-House to overcome language barriers and to habituate new Chicagoans to socially accepted behavior. But at the same time, the improv archive relays mostly a story of white improv artists, which shows through omission the segregation and restraints of racial segregation in Chicago.

All four chapters engage in deep archival exploration, carefully crafting histories from short bits of newspaper articles, scrapbooks, play scripts, and other ephemera in special collections. Closely examining these few touchstones—the Goodman Theatre, the Federal Theatre Project and Chicago African American theater, storefront Lincoln Park theater, and improv—tells stories about the confluence of space, race, institutionalization, and art in twentieth-century Chicago. Although all these theaters and movements are now renowned beyond Chicago, these chapters show that the makeshift and institutionalization are not mutually exclusive but are always working in relational flows, much like performance itself.

4

Pillars of the Community

Reversing the Flow between the Goodman and Community and Immigrant Theater

Megan E. Geigner

The Kenneth Sawyer Goodman Memorial Theatre opened in 1925 at the Art Institute of Chicago. Following in the footsteps of its namesake, Kenneth Sawyer Goodman—who despite his upper-class status worked with makeshift theaters and theater artists throughout Chicago—the theater itself preserved his theatrical and community values. It was dedicated to teaching both students and audiences about the art of theater rather than focusing on creating blockbuster productions like the other theaters in downtown Chicago at the time. The Goodman created space for professional theater makers to teach drama students and play alongside them in productions in the Art Institute's new drama department. Using the copious resources of the Art Institute and the donor family, William and Erna Goodman, the drama department produced shows in a brand-new theater built to suit the needs of the school and its seasons of productions. The new theater had much going for it: it could borrow from the prestige of the Art Institute, the local press celebrated it, and it was located adjacent to Grant Park on the lakefront in downtown Chicago. Despite these advantages, the Goodman Theatre floundered in its first few years. In a surprising turn, the Goodman turned to settlement house, immigrant, and community theater to help bolster its early seasons and attract diverse audiences to the new venue. Between 1925 and 1933, the Goodman hosted various community and immigrant group performances, from an annual Chicago play competition and Polish literature readings to Hull-House play transfers and Greek dance festivals.

That the Goodman partnered with these groups in its early seasons is significant for three reasons. First, these partnerships show how marginalized communities have often been at the center of artistic development in American theater history, and telling this story moves them into the spotlight. Second, this history shows that resource sharing in cross-cultural and cross-class collaborations yields benefits for multiple communities and institutions. And third, rather than being a story of an established institution (the Goodman) including racial, ethnic,[1] and class-based minorities as evidence of its benevolence, this history demonstrates marginalized communities including the Goodman in their theater-making, and it shows a longer history of exchange in theater communities. Using resources from the Newberry Library's and Chicago Public Library's special collections and the *Chicago Tribune*, the newspaper of record for the city, this chapter documents the many community collaborations in the early years of the Goodman and, in doing so, illustrates the long history of equitable exchange between immigrant and community theater and the largest and oldest regional theater in Chicago. The chapter posits that the ethos of the Little Theatre movement in Chicago helped bring these diverse theaters together and provided a model for the way the Goodman and other Chicago theaters would work for years to come.

The Goodmans and Chicago's Little Theatre Movement

The Goodman Theatre was one of the first large, institutionalized sites for the growing Little Theatre movement. The Little Theatre movement took a different tactic than most American theater that preceded it: instead of focusing on making money or celebrity culture, theater within the movement was to be "spiritually and emotionally fulfilling, socially elevating, of civic importance, a site for assaying cultural change, and an enriching focus of cultural capital."[2] The theater's namesake, Kenneth Sawyer Goodman, had been a playwright, naval officer, and businessman invested in the mission of the Little Theatre movement. Goodman joined the Cliff Dwellers Club, an affluent social club dedicated to cultural philanthropy, and he became active in the Art Institute in 1909 and 1910.[3] While the Art Institute had no drama department until after Goodman's death, it did have a drama club that produced shows under the direction of Donald Robertson, and the school produced *A Pageant of the Italian Renaissance* performed by Art Institute students and directed by Thomas Wood Stevens.[4] Goodman attended these events—and he even acted in a drama club production—and became inspired by the idea of art theater. He sought out Stevens, and the two began collaborating.

Goodman created a community of art theater collaborators and friends, people such as directors Stevens and Robertson and playwrights Ben Hecht, Mary Aldis, and Alice Gerstenberg,[5] many of whom he worked with at the Players' Workshop, an amateur theater group on the city's South Side.[6] Goodman also wrote dozens of plays, some on his own and some cowritten with Stevens or Hecht.[7] Ultimately, Goodman had several pageants and workshops produced at the Art Institute, and he looked for ways to partner with other Chicago cultural organizations or create his own organizations to do theater. He wrote a masque for the Friends of our Native Landscape organization, he helped begin the Chicago Theatre Society within the Cliff Dwellers, he sought out Jane Addams of Hull-House to collaborate on a pageant there, and he proposed a collaboration with the Immigrants' Protective League (IPL), an organization designed to help new immigrants avoid exploitation in Chicago.[8] Goodman's interest in Hull-House and the IPL connects with a trend in the Little Theatre movement to appreciate the grassroots dedication found in immigrant theaters.[9] These collaborations illustrate that Goodman, despite his high-society standing, worked with a range of people from all different classes and so set the stage for the Goodman Theatre to do the same. He hoped to translate his many commitments to a sustained and permanent "workshop . . . under the roof and under the direct auspices of the Art Institute."[10] Furthermore, he emphasized in his plans that this project should be "an experimental theater" that had enough financial backing "PLEDGED TO COVER THE MINIMUM EXPENSES OF THE EXPERIMENT AS AN OUT AND OUT GIFT [all caps in the original]" in order to avoid another "bitter experience with short experiments and insufficient funds and over-confident estimate of box office returns."[11] In essence, Goodman was arguing for a transition from the makeshift Chicago Little Theatre of the 1910s to a permanent, centralized, institutional theater celebrating collaboration, incisiveness, and art theater.

When Goodman died suddenly at age thirty-five in 1918, his parents helped bring his dream to fruition. They donated $250,000 to the Art Institute to finance Kenneth's dream of a theater "arts university" and committed to an additional $10,000 to the department and theater yearly.[12] As Kenneth had hoped, the Art Institute tapped Stevens,

Donald Robertson, Thomas Wood Stevens, and Kenneth Sawyer Goodman, April 1912. Photograph by Kenneth Goodman, from *The Cliff Dwellers Photographic Album 1910–1940*, Newberry Library Modern Manuscripts. Courtesy of the Newberry Library.

who by then had created the first degree-granting drama department in the United States at the Carnegie Institute of Technology (later Carnegie Mellon University), to run the new wing of the Art Institute.[13] At the helm, Stevens developed a repertory company and the drama school. He made plans to produce dual seasons—a mainstage repertory season performed by faculty and students and a studio season performed exclusively by students—featuring classic plays rarely seen on commercial stages and new and experimental plays that would instruct the audience in the art of theater rather than simply entertain the masses.[14]

To house this new project, the Art Institute built a theater on the north side of its existing museum building with the express purpose of producing art theater. The theater was inspired by the ancient Greeks, with an arced seating plan and a sunken house that sat seven hundred. The Art Institute selected local architect Howard Van Doren Shaw to build the theater. Shaw was closely linked to the Little Theatre movement in Chicago as he was neighbors with Mary Aldis and her husband, Arthur, who served on the board of the Art Institute. (Shaw even built a theater on the Aldis property in Lake Forest.)[15] City of Chicago rules prohibited Shaw from building a traditional fly loft, so he designed a lateral scene-shifting system that could take place behind and in the wings of the playing space and installed a permanent eighty-foot cyclorama at the rear of the stage.[16] Instead of a lobby, the space just outside the theater was an art gallery. Hundreds of people enjoyed the new space when it officially opened with a production of three of Kenneth's one-acts—*Back of the Yards*, *The Green Scarf*, and *The Game of Chess*—in late October 1925.

From October to June of 1925–1926, the Goodman produced its first full season, with ten plays as part of their repertory season and five plays as part of their studio season. The repertory season was John Galsworthy's *The Forest*, Martinez Sierra's *The Romantic Young Lady*, Mary Aldis's *An Heir at Large*, Georg Kaiser's *Gas*, *Everyman*, John Masefield's *The Tragedy of Nan*, Shaw's *The Man of Destiny* and *The Dark Lady of Sonnets* in rep with Molière's *Don Juan, or the Stone Guest*, and Shakespeare's *A Midsummer's Night Dream*. The repertory company played on Thursday, Friday, and Saturday evenings and had a Friday matinee each week. Tickets were fifty cents for Art Institute members and a dollar for the public.[17] The price reflected the Art Institute's subsidizing of the project. The students also produced a large studio season, including Lady Gregory's *The Golden Apple*, Muriel Brown's *The Captive Princess*, and Charles S. Brooks's *Wappin' Wharf*—all plays for children—and St. John Hankin's *The Cassilis Engagement* and Euripides's *Iphigenia at Taurus*.[18]

But even with this robust schedule, the Goodman invited other groups onto its stage. Perhaps they did so to create a revenue stream to help finance their new theater,[19] or perhaps they did so to honor Kenneth Sawyer Goodman's collaborative artistic spirit, or perhaps they did so to consciously set a model for how regional theaters could create exchange with their neighbors.[20] Regardless, what the Goodman did was make an association between art theater, community theater, and immigrant theater at Chicago's first major professional not-for-profit theater. This is all the more significant given that the 1920s saw an uptick in vilification of immigrants and growing campaigns to make everyone "100% American."[21] Furthermore, the early years of inviting others onto its stage lifted up immigrant groups, amateur theaters, and local charities, suggesting that theater is a philanthropic arena in which cross-cultural bonds are made. In the following case studies—community theater events, ethnic theater events, and amateur theater competitions in the early years of the Goodman—the role of the community-based marginal theater groups and the large, monied, prominent institution are reversed; the established ethnic communities living in the margins of the city helped promote and support the fledgling Goodman.

Community Theater Events

The first community theater event the Goodman hosted after its October 1925 opening was the fall production of the Chicago Allied Arts Inc. Chicago Allied Arts Inc. "was an organization formed in 1924 for the purpose of presenting small-scale ballet and music performances in Chicago . . . modeled somewhat along the line of Serge Diaghilev's Ballets Russes . . . [and] funded through the guarantees of individual sponsors."[22] The Goodmans were one of the sponsors of the group.[23] In this case, the production aligned with the art-theater goal of the theater. The performance featured Chicago choreographer Adolph Bolm's dance company, Ballet Intime, dancing three ballets: *Mandragora*, *Bal des Marionettes*, and *The Rivals*.[24] *Mandragora* was a ballet originally created to accompany Molière's *Le Bourgeois Genthihomme*, and the *Chicago Tribune* described it as "a fantastic fantasy and humor combining Columbines and African kings."[25] The second ballet, *Bal des Marionette*, was described as a grotesque imitation of old dance forms such as the polka.[26] *The Rivals* was a reworking of a Chinese legend set to an original score by Henry Eichheim, and Chicago dancer Ruth Page danced a lead role in it.[27] Page also performed in a piece titled *Elopement* with music by Mozart. In addition to staging ballets accompanied by a live orchestra, Chicago Allied Arts Inc. also had a resident designer, Nicolas Remisoff, who designed original, "fun . . . [and] colorful scenery" for the ballets to be installed in the Goodman stage.[28] That the Chicago Allied Arts Inc. brought their own designer is particularly remarkable because this means that a designer not affiliated with the Goodman was actually the first to design in the theater. The commitment of Chicago Allied Arts Inc. to highbrow art, new ballets, and intricate design fits within the mission of the Goodman Theatre even if the shows did not include the drama school faculty or staff.

The Goodman also produced benefit performances on their stage in the first season that drew society audiences. The second performance outside their season was the Association of Housekeeping Centers' benefit production of *Moby Dick* on Wednesday, February 10, 1926. The Association of Housekeeping Centers' mission was to create schools in tenement districts where working girls, mothers, children, and others learned the essentials of American homemaking.[29] The chairwoman of the benefit was Mrs. Augustus Swift, wife of the Chicago stockyards magnate, and so like the work of the Chicago Allied Arts Inc., this production appealed to the arts donor class of Chicago. These types of society events in the new theater allowed those who helped sponsor the Art Institute and the new art theater time to bask in the glow of what they had created at the Goodman. That said, the choice to produce a full-length play performed by amateurs rather than the Goodman Drama School's talent was risky; undiscerning audience members could have confused the show as one of Goodman's own. (Today we call this "brand confusion.") The housekeeping association group's benefit differed from another charitable show the Goodman produced in the first season, that of the Blue Bird Club. The Blue Bird Club was a society of Chicago working women who collectively owned a cottage in Boulder, Colorado, where the membership could take a reduced-rate vacation.[30] The Goodman dedicated a portion of the ticket revenue from a few performances of their spring repertory productions of Molière's *Don Juan* and Shaw's *The Man of Destiny* in April 1926 to the group.[31]

In November 1932, the Goodman continued this pattern of hosting society benefits by producing *When Chicago Was Young*, a play written by Little Theatre dramatist Alice Gerstenburg and local newspaper columnist Herma Clark. The play was a historical fiction about the founding of Chicago and several important moments in its history. The prologue was set on the "banks of the Checagou River" in 1673, act 1 in the Tremont House in 1858, act 2 during the Great Chicago Fire of 1871, act 3 at Potter Palmer's house[32] in 1893 (the year of the World's Columbian Exposition), and an epilogue on Michigan Avenue in 1933.[33] This show brought in high society; the *Tribune* called it "a gala occasion," and Chicago's debutantes ushered.[34] Additionally, this production was a natural fit for the theater given Kenneth's interest in pageants and knowledge of Gerstenberg's work prior to his death. These gala performances did significant cultural work for the Goodman Theatre: they trained the cultural elite to think of the Goodman when they thought of theater; they participated in Chicago boosterism, which was popular among the elite class at the time; and they gave an opportunity for another Chicago little theater giant, Gerstenberg, to circulate among the Art Institute supporters. Although these productions did not showcase the drama department talent, they did elevate theater to an art and encourage a high-class crowd.

Immigrant Theater Events

Alongside these society events, the Goodman also began hosting productions associated with immigrants and Chicago's working class. In the spring of 1926, the Goodman produced two transfers from theater groups at Hull-House: the Hull-House Players and the Marionette Players. The Hull-House Players began in the late nineteenth century as a way to build community, teach English, and create art and entertainment in the Near West Side neighborhood that was home to mainly poor immigrant laborers and their families.[35] (Hull-House was located at the corner of Halsted Avenue [800 West] and Polk Street [800 South]. The neighborhood is now known as Little Italy or University Village since the University of Illinois at Chicago is there.) Originally, many of the Hull-House Players actors were members of the neighborhood's Irish community, but the group diversified over the years.[36] Still, the group had an affinity for the theater in the style of the Abbey Players, the famous Irish theater developed in the first few decades of the twentieth century. Jane Addams explained that a visit from the Irish dramatist and poet William Butler Yeats to Hull-House inspired the groups to "free . . . the stage from its slavery to expensive scene setting."[37] In fact, when the Abbey Players toured the United States (under the auspices of the Chicago Theatre Society), they visited Hull-House again, and the theaters remained in a partnership. By the time the Hull-House Players transferred Philpott's *The Farmer's Wife* (a play about an Englishman whose wife dies, and he finds himself in denial about being in love with his Irish housekeeper) to the Goodman, the well-regarded Little Theatre company had performed not only the works of William Shakespeare, Henrik Ibsen, John Galsworthy, and

GOODMAN MEMORIAL THEATRE

MONROE STREET AT THE LAKE

THE MARIONETTE PLAYERS

OF HULL-HOUSE

Under Direction of Edith de Nancrede

IN

"ANNA CHRISTIE"

By Eugene O'Neill

WEDNESDAY MAY 12th.

CURTAIN PROMPTLY AT 8:30 P.M.

Program from the Marionette Players of Hull-House production of Eugene O'Neill's *Anna Christie* at the Goodman Memorial Theatre, May 12, 1926. Playbill Collections: Goodman Theatre, Chicago History Museum Research Center. Courtesy of the Chicago History Museum.

Maxim Gorky, but also the plays of Yeats and Lady Gregory, most under the direction of Laura Dainty Pelham. Pelham died in 1924, so tickets for *The Farmer's Wife*, which cost one dollar, went to benefit the Laura Dainty Pelham memorial cottage, a countryside property in Waukegan that served as a day camp for the Hull-House neighborhood's inner-city children in the summers.[38]

A month later, the Goodman hosted Hull-House's Marionette Players on their main stage in a production of Eugene O'Neill's *Anna Christie*. The Marionette Players had formed as a group of children at Hull-House at the turn of the century, but when the group played at the Goodman in May 1926, most of the actors were in their twenties and thirties.[39] The group was more diverse than the Hull-House Players, with actors of Italian, German, Russian Jewish, and Irish backgrounds.[40] O'Neill himself "blessed" the production, saying, "I wish I could see your production. Your cast is extremely interesting. Please perform it with my blessing."[41] He also waived the royalties.[42] The *Chicago Daily News* suggested that the acting was particularly good because the lead actress, Agnes Davoren, who played the title role of a prostitute, was "born and brought up on famous Halstead street . . . with a born knowledge and keen observation of the type."[43] *Anna Christie* at the Goodman not only made a case for the expertise of lower-class actors, but showed a melting-pot ensemble of actors achieving success with one of America's rising playwright talents.

These Hull-House shows on Goodman's stage provide an example of early regional theater outreach within twentieth-century American theater history, and one that flips the narrative. Instead of illustrating exclusively the way a well-staffed and well-funded institution like the Art Institute's Goodman helped support neighborhood immigrant theater, these cases studies show how neighborhood immigrant theater helped build Goodman's reputation. Hull-House was a likely collaborator given Kenneth Sawyer Goodman's relationship with the settlement house and desire to produce art theater, which Hull-House was renowned for producing. Donald Robertson, the Art Institute's drama club director, had produced several shows at Hull-House prior to the founding of the Goodman Theatre, as well.[44] Thomas Wood Stevens's vision for the theater named for his friend and collaborator strove to emulate the successful theater work at Hull-House and the settlement house's existing reputation for producing difficult art-theater scripts. By transferring their shows to the Goodman, Goodman management hoped to share an audience with those from Hull-House and get people in the habit of attending the Art Institute to view and enjoy theater. In fact, the Goodman's debut production in the fall of 1925 was Galsworthy's *The Forest*, so collaborating with an already-established theater who had successfully produced Galsworthy's work in Chicago was a smart move. In other words, transfers from Hull-House had the potential to strengthen Goodman's reputation as a legitimate theater and attract new audiences.

Concurrent to the productions from Hull-House, Goodman also produced a Greek arts festival from April 11 through April 13, 1926, featuring demonstrations of Greek dances, music, and plays on the

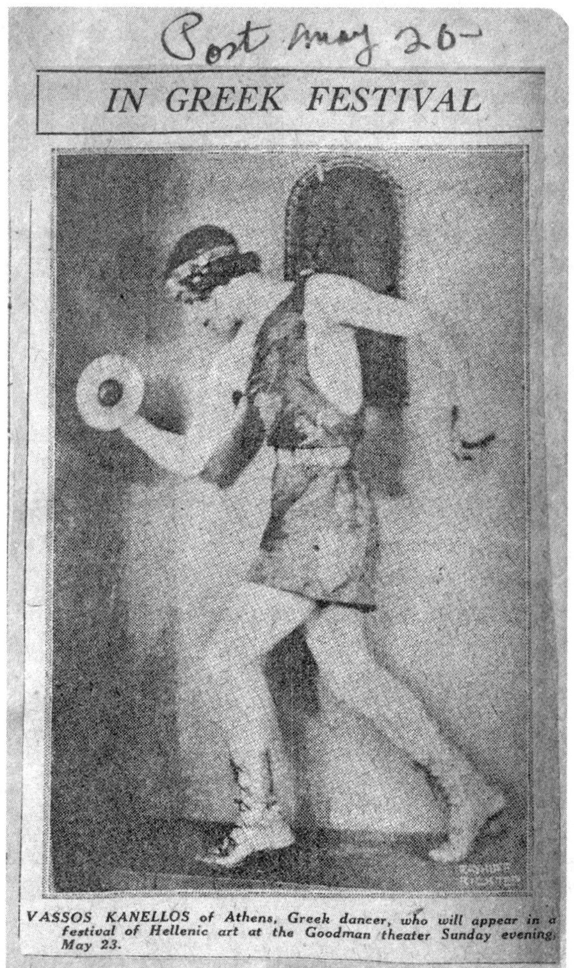

Post May 20–

IN GREEK FESTIVAL

***VASSOS KANELLOS** of Athens, Greek dancer, who will appear in a festival of Hellenic art at the Goodman theater Sunday evening, May 23.*

Greek dancer Vassos Kanellos in a May 1926 newspaper clipping for a Greek arts festival hosted by the Goodman Theatre. Photographer unknown. Goodman Theatre Archives, Publicity Scrapbook, 1926–1930, page 48, Chicago Theater Collection, Special Collections, Chicago Public Library. Courtesy of the Chicago Public Library.

Goodman stage and overseen by Vassos and Tanagra Kanellos. An article in the Greek-language Chicago newspaper, *Saloniki*, explained that the festival was a collaboration between a group of Chicago Greek-Americans of the Phil-Hellenic Committee and the management of the Art Institute.[45] Audiences could attend lectures about Greek painting (given by Tanagra), see Greek and Byzantine art on display in special galleries, watch Greek dancing, and attend a production of *Oedipus* with "a chorus moving to the words, as was done when the play was originally produced over 2,000 years ago in Athens."[46] This collaboration drew Chicago's Greek immigrant community—*Saloniki* reported that the "Greeks of Chicago do not fail to see the three performances"[47]—and the festival was so popular that it was reprised a month later, in May, but this time under Stevens's direction. The *Chicago Evening Post* reported that "the entire personnel of the [drama] school took part in the program, which was a very elaborate one, and they gave the [Kanelloses] splendid support; indeed, there was nothing to show that they had not always worked with their principals. Such work as this . . . shows not only versatility but extraordinary ability on the part of the student-actors and on the part of their directors."[48]

The Greek festival at the Goodman tied performance to visual art to show that the theater was a natural extension of the art museum and built a new audience. Furthermore, the reprise of the Greek play at the Goodman provided pedagogical value to the drama school. At a time when the idea of a theater school was still new, performing Greek plays alongside Greek experts validated the enterprise of a theater department, an idea Stevens himself originated in the United States. Furthermore, perhaps Stevens knew of the success *Athanasius Diakos*, a Greek play produced at Hull-House in 1905 that packed the house with the Greek community.[49] Finally, and with regard to the rep company, the play fulfilled the mission of theater, which, as etched on the theater itself, was "to restore the old visions and win the new." By performing Greek theater in its presumed original form, the students not only got firsthand experience with "the old visions," but performed next to their professional counterparts in the rep company. In this case, immigrant theater served a teaching purpose that tied theater school to classical education models.

These productions also gave the Goodman a cosmopolitan reputation; in the theater's first few years it hosted Greek, German, Swedish, Polish, Mexican, and Spanish productions. In May 1926, the Goodman hosted the Teutonic Players of America's German-language production of Karl Schönherr's *Der Weibsteufel* (*A Devil of a Woman*). In November 1926, the theater was the site of a benefit performance to celebrate the fifty-year career of Swedish actor and Chicago immigrant Ida Anderson-Werner.[50] Anderson-Werner, who was active in the Swedish Theatrical Society of Chicago, played the lead in *Syrsan* (*The Cricket*) on the Goodman stage. A few months later, the Goodman began supporting a series of events with the Polish Arts Club, hosting lectures, theatergoing parties, and meetings between January and March of 1927.[51] The group made a regular habit of having Polish reading events in meeting rooms at the Art Institute and then attending performances in the repertory season.[52] The connection between the two was so successful that the Goodman produced a Polish concert featuring a Chopin polonaise and gave a party in the foyer, and Stevens himself addressed the club with a lecture titled "The Theatre of Today and Tomorrow."[53] The relationship endured into the following season when the Polish choral group Filarety performed a grand jubilee concert on the Goodman stage in November 1927,[54] and the Polish Arts Club dramatics department had a "theatre party at the Goodman theatre" on January 28, 1928.[55]

The Goodman continued to develop their relationship with Chicago's immigrant and international communities into the early 1930s. In April 1932, the theater hosted "Dances of Spain and Mexico": a vocal recital performed by Milla Dominguez, and a dance recital performed by Clarita Martin. Dominguez had been an opera star in her native Mexico City but moved to Chicago with her husband, the vice-consul for Mexico in Chicago, and boasted of having learned to speak (and sing in) fluent English.[56] The program was sponsored by "a group of about twenty ladies of foreign Consuls resident in Chicago, the international relations committee and the heads of a dozen artistical and educational organizations," and the guest of honor was Dr. J. M. Puig Casauranc, the Mexican ambassador to the United States.[57] This production is an interesting case because it shows the desire for immigrants to assimilate into American life while keeping their homeland talents, a desire all the more pronounced after the United States dramatically restricted immigration due to the Johnson-Reed Act of 1924. Furthermore, like the Kanellos performances six years earlier, this production made an association between foreign national heritage—be it Greek or Mexican—the arts, and high society.

Producing immigrant theater at the Goodman portrayed the theater, the Art Institute, and the city of Chicago as cosmopolitan. Journalist

Virginia Dale of the *Chicago Daily Journal* wrote that "these various players of various nativity who come occasionally to our lakeside bring with them a welcome diversity to the theater. Hebrew, Chinese, French and German languages and fashions of production and presentation come with the people of these tongues, and each in his own way augments the internationalism of the stage."[58] In this way, the theater school and the repertory company could claim to be not only a world-class theater, but a worldly addition to Chicago culture, a place where audiences could learn about other peoples and cultures by attending a theater production. According to an article in the *Chicago Daily News*, the Goodman's support filled a gap in the city's art scene: the article said the theater lent "their support to enterprises which would otherwise be impracticable for Chicago, [it] is a happy omen. Possibly now for the first time since Maurice Browne's Little theater [*sic*] closed, people who are interested in the classical and the experimental drama and the dance will have somewhere to go."[59] As the reviewer notes, this is evidence of the major shift that the Goodman created in the Chicago arts scene in the 1920s. While Browne, Aldis, Gerstenburg, and others had created Little Theatre work in different spaces dedicated to the project, none were as high profile, centrally located, or attached to such a reputable institution as the new Goodman Theatre was. The Goodman made the makeshift institutional. This was Kenneth Sawyer Goodman's dream. And one that legitimized immigrant theater traditions and neighborhood theater. As patrician members of the Art Institute could see, the performances of Greek or Italian or Jewish immigrants onstage in serious dramatic projects exemplified the cultural gifts of immigrants rather than evidence of "inferior" cultures degrading the nation. In an era marked by national Americanization campaigns, theater featuring immigrants onstage at the Goodman was a revolutionary gesture of inclusion.

Play Competitions and Exhibitions

The Goodman also provided space for annual play competitions wherein many immigrant, community, and Little Theatre artists appeared on the Art Institute stage. The Drama League of Chicago began the yearly tournament of plays in 1927. The competition was meant to "show to the city the Little Theatre activities that are being carried on [in Chicago] and . . . encourage the formation of more groups and the enlargement of the scope of activities of both old and new circles."[60] For four days, sixteen theater groups performed at the Vic Theatre on the city's North Side, and the four finalists competed at the Goodman on May 15, 1927. By 1929, the Goodman was hosting the whole tournament and continued to do so until 1933. Winners earned a cash prize and the Drama League Cup, and many went on to have robust productions. The winner of the 1928 tournament, Northwestern University's Town and Gown Players' presentation of *The Undercurrent*, toured on the Orpheum circuit,[61] and the 1931 winner, *If Booth Had Missed* (which revised history to have President Lincoln survive Booth's assassination attempt and face the difficulty of Reconstruction and an ultimate impeachment) had a Broadway production the following winter.[62]

The competition evolved to have a bracket consisting of amateur Little Theatres and one consisting of area high school productions.[63] The three best Little Theatre plays and the best high school play competed against one another in the final round for the cup, although there was also a special High School Cup for the drama group that got to the final.[64] Among the various community groups, such as the Bell Telephone Players and Austin Community Players, many settlement houses entered the competition, including the Hull-House Players and the Northwestern University Settlement House players. The Institute Players of the Jewish People's Institute also entered the tournament beginning in 1930, and the group took the prize each year between 1930 and 1932.[65] The group's first entry was an original play by Elma Ehrlich Levinger titled *The Tenth Man*,[66] set in the interior of a synagogue in a little Galician village a hundred years earlier at sunset on Yom Kippur.[67] Along with winning the cup, the Institute Players got a contract to play the show at the Palace Theatre, a Chicago vaudeville theater.[68]

In addition to hosting this annual Little Theatre and high school play tournament, the Goodman also hosted a religious drama contest beginning in 1930. The competition was arranged by the Chicago Council of Religious Education, and dozens of churches around the city participated.[69] Similar to the Little Theatre tournament, the religious theater competition presented the three finalists from church theater groups after the trial of the North, West, and South Side plays in the weeks leading up the championship at the Goodman.[70] Although the plays and players in this tournament did not get professional contracts, bookings, or tours, by 1934, the tournament evolved into a massive pageant play produced at the Goodman with 250 actors.[71] The show, titled *Judas Iscariot*, premiered at the Goodman Theatre on June 4, 1934, as part of the offering of the second summer of the Century of Progress Exposition.[72] The organizers hoped to popularize religious drama by offering this enormous show to playgoers.

In hosting both of these sets of tournaments, the Goodman invited amateur actors onto their stage, but did so in a way that helped further the theater's mission: for the Little Theatre tournament, the Goodman offered their stage and resources for a few nights to a week in order to find original plays suitable for Little Theatres such as the Goodman to present. As most of the winners of the tournament went on to have professional productions, the competition upheld the Goodman's mission to produce new plays. Additionally, in both the Little Theatre and the religious drama competitions, the Goodman exposed its audiences to the many smaller, community theaters already operating in the city. This move could have helped increase audience at settlement house theater events, which in turn showcased immigrant community talent. Furthermore, hosting the Institute Players of the Jewish People's Institute brought together three significant branches of American theater: the Yiddish theater, the Little Theatre, and the burgeoning regional theater. That the production went on to play in New York crystalizes the impact that the Goodman had on uplifting smaller community groups and making them into legitimate, commercially viable theater groups.

The End of an Era

While the Goodman benefited culturally and artistically from developing new, community-based and ethnic art theater, these productions did not keep the theater from debt. Despite the robust programming—from their own repertory and student companies, from the benefits they hosted, and from community and ethnic theater groups—the Goodman was running a $35,000 deficit within the first five years.[73] The Art Institute's board of directors blamed Stevens for producing "unappealing plays in productions of less than adequate quality."[74] Stevens resigned, and the board hired celebrity actors in hit shows for the 1930–1931 season to increase Goodman's entertainment value.[75] Still, the season failed, and the Art Institute discontinued producing professional theater for the next twenty-six years (the drama school continued producing student work). Finances aside, however, the work the Goodman produced between 1925 and 1933 brought new audiences into their spaces, helped develop new plays and the Little Theatre movement, and made ethnic theater part of Chicago's downtown theater scene.

The Goodman Today

From roughly the 1930s to the 1970s, the Goodman functioned primarily as a theater school, but in the late 1960s, it was reorganized into a professional regional theater. It is within this context that the Goodman has persisted in revitalizing its original mission within this larger professional theater context. For example, the Goodman began an annual Latino Theatre Festival in 1996 under the direction of Goodman Artistic Associate Henry Godinez.[76] For more than two decades, the Goodman has produced dozens of Latinx plays through the festival, exposing a hundred thousand Chicago theatergoers to Latinx plays.[77] Starting in 2017, the Goodman partnered with the not-for-profit Chicago Latino Theater Alliance (CLATA) to produce the Chicago International Latino Theater Festival. For the second annual version of this festival in 2018, the Goodman and CLATA hosted seven weeks of "Latino theater artists and companies from Chicago, the U.S. and Latin America in shows, panels and student performances at venues citywide."[78] In addition, the Goodman has used their second space—the Owen, in the theater complex opened in 2001—to host numerous productions from smaller and storefront theaters in Chicago.

Other theaters in Chicago have followed in Goodman's footsteps and use their spaces to promote smaller theaters' work. Martha Lavey, the long-time artistic director of Chicago theater giant Steppenwolf Theatre, stated early in her tenure her desire to "share [Steppenwolf's] wealth with the smaller itinerant companies in town."[79] The result has been Steppenwolf's Garage Rep (2009–2017) and its 1700 Theatre, both of which put smaller companies around Chicago in a Steppenwolf black box space, allowing them to reap the benefit of exposure to Steppenwolf's subscribers, access to Steppenwolf's production staff, and upgraded press coverage. TimeLine Theatre, a smaller but multi-decade theater company on the city's North Side, also began this practice in their 2018–2019 season, partnering with Firebrand Theatre in a coproduction of Jeanine Tesori and Tony Kushner's musical *Caroline, or Change*. In this arrangement, Firebrand Theatre, a newer and smaller theater company, had access to TimeLine's marketing department and resident artists to help provide added artistic and financial support for the project. Furthermore, it allowed TimeLine to add inclusiveness to their mission in production; TimeLine's mission is to produce stories inspired by history that connect to today's social and political issues, and Firebrand's mission is to empower women by expanding their opportunities on and off the stage.[80] The production also made a significant connection between up-and-coming Chicago director Lili-Anne Brown and TimeLine that is likely to result in Brown directing for TimeLine in the future.[81] And these examples are just a few of many.

These more recent examples show that Chicago has long had a practice of large theaters showcasing the talent of smaller theaters. As these many case studies make clear, even when these were win-win productions for both the groups onstage and the fledgling Goodman Theatre, the stakeholders' motivations ranged from utilitarianism to the creation of new revenue streams to attempts to educate audience and students. Goodman's choice to produce these types of shows so early in its founding demonstrates that partnerships between larger and smaller theater institutions are rarely clear-cut examples of the more privileged company reaching out to uplift marginalized groups. Reengaging with this erased history of one of the oldest and largest regional theaters in the country reveals a long-standing tradition of cross-cultural theater events, and provides a model for how arts institutions can engage with marginalized communities in ways that create mutual benefits.

Notes

1. By and large, the word "ethnic" was not used in the 1910s and 1920s in the United States. Instead, the lexicon for those we now consider "ethnic" was tied to immigrancy—so either "immigrant" or "nationality." I will use the term "immigrant theater" here to denote theater created by first-, second-, and third-generation immigrants still connected to their homeland heritage and theater practices while living in Chicago.

2. Dorothy Chansky, *Composing Ourselves: The Little Theatre Movement and the American Audience* (Carbondale: Southern Illinois University Press, 2004), 2.

3. Stuart J. Hecht, "Kenneth Sawyer Goodman: Bridging Chicago's Affluent and Artistic Networks," *Theatre History Studies* 13 (1993): 137.

4. Hecht, "Kenneth Sawyer Goodman," 137.

5. Ben Hecht was a prolific writer who wrote dozens of books, play, and screenplays. He is probably best known for his Broadway hit *The Front Page*. Mary Aldis was a playwright, poet, and general arts supporter who began the Lake Forest Players with her husband in the 1910s. Alice Gerstenberg was a playwright, actress, and Little Theatre pioneer. See Stuart J. Hecht's chapter and Shannon Epplett's chapter in this collection for more on these figures.

6. Hecht, "Kenneth Sawyer Goodman," 137.

7. Goodman's catalog of plays includes *Back of the Yards*, *A Game of Chess*, *Barbara*, *Dust of the Road*, *Masque*, *The Egg and the Hen* (coauthored with Ben Hecht), *The Wonder Hat* (coauthored with Ben Hecht), *Ephraim and the Winged Bear: A Christmas Eve Nightmare in One Act*, and *The Homecoming* (coauthored with Ben Hecht).

8. About the masque, see Carol Doty, "About the Masque," pts. 1 and 2, *Morton Arboretum Quarterly* 7, no. 1 (Spring 1971): 8; no. 2 (Summer 1971): 16; about the Cliff Dwellers and Goodman's interaction with Hull-House, see Hecht, "Kenneth Sawyer Goodman"; and about the Immigrant Protective League, see Kenneth Sawyer Goodman to Florence Griswold, September 15, 1915, Kenneth Sawyer Goodman Collection, Newberry Library, and "Immigrant League Pageant," note in the Kenneth Sawyer Goodman Collection, Newberry Library.

9. See Chansky's discussion of John Corbin and the Yiddish Theatre, *Composing Ourselves*, 53–54.

10. Kenneth Sawyer Goodman to Florence Griswold.

11. Kenneth Sawyer Goodman to Florence Griswold.

12. "Lieut. Goodman, Capt. Moffett's Senior Aid [*sic*], Dies," *Chicago Daily Tribune*, November 30, 1918; see also letters and other documents in the Goodman Family Collection at Newberry Library.

13. Laura Medgyesy, "Chicago's Goodman Theatre: The Transition from a Division of the Art Institute of Chicago to an Independent Regional Theatre" (MA thesis, American University, 1983), 19.

14. Medgyesy, "Chicago's Goodman Theatre," 19.

15. "Mary Aldis" exhibition pages for "The Greenwich Village Bookshop Door: A Portal to Bohemia, 1920–1925" (online exhibition), Harry Ransom Research Center for Humanities, University of Texas at Austin, https://norman.hrc.utexas.edu/bookshopdoor/signature.cfm?item=75#1.

16. Ann Lee, "The Kenneth Sawyer Goodman Memorial Stage," *The Drama* 16, no 1 (1925): 13–15.

17. Commemorative Memorial bound program book, 1925–26. Kenneth Sawyer Goodman Collection, Newberry Library.

18. Commemorative Memorial bound program book.

19. Each of the programs in the bound program book and several of those from the first five years of the theater have a paragraph explaining that people were welcome to rent the theater.

20. No Goodman records from these engagements exist.

21. For more, see Christina A. Ziegler-McPherson, *Americanization in the States: Immigrant Social Welfare Policy, Citizenship, and National Identity in the United States, 1908–1929* (Gainesville: University of Florida Press, 2010).

22. "Chicago Arts Alliance, Inc. Records, 1922–1929" (website page), New York Public Library Archives and Manuscripts, accessed November 7, 2018, http://archives.nypl.org/dan/19805.

23. "Chicago Arts Alliance, Inc. Records."

24. Not to be confused with Richard Brinsley Sheridan's eighteenth-century play of the same name.

25. "Allied Arts Gives Season Opening at Goodman Theater," *Chicago Daily Tribune*, November 9, 1925.

26. "Allied Arts Gives Season Opening."

27. "Chicago Arts Alliance, Inc. Records."

28. "Allied Arts Gives Season Opening."

29. "Club to Give Two Plays in Goodman Theater," *Chicago Daily Tribune*, April 13, 1926.

30. "News of the Chicago Women's Clubs: Blue Bird Club Holds Its Annual Spring Reunion," *Chicago Daily Tribune*, May 27, 1917, C5.

31. "Club to Give Two Plays."

32. Potter Palmer was a hotel magnate in Chicago who built the Palmer House, a famous downtown hotel. Gerstenberg was likely making a connection between her play and the donor class in the audience.

33. *When Chicago Was Young* program, Program Collection, Chicago History Museum Research Center.

34. Judith Cass, "'When Chicago Was Young' Opens Tonight, Benefits Olivet," *Chicago Daily Tribune*, November 7, 1932, 15.

35. For more analysis on the goals of theater at Hull-House, see Shannon Jackson, *Lines of Activity: Performance, Historiography, Hull-House Domesticity* (Ann Arbor: University of Michigan Press, 2004) and Stuart Joel Hecht, "Hull-House Theatre: An Analytical and Evaluative History" (PhD dissertation, Northwestern University, 1983).

36. Edith de Nancrede, "Dramatic Work at Hull House," *Neighborhood* 1, no. 1 (January 1928): 23–28.

37. Jane Addams, *Twenty Years and Hull-House with Autobiographical Notes* (New York: Macmillan, 1912), 394.

38. "New Playbills in the Chicago Theaters," *Chicago Daily Tribune*, April 18, 1926, E3.

39. Nancrede, "Dramatic Work at Hull House," 25.

40. I have surmised this from a survey of Marionette Player programs in the Hull-House Collection, Special Collections, Richard J. Daley Library, University of Illinois at Chicago.

41. "'Anna Christie' Author Blesses Hull-House Cast," *Chicago Daily News*, May 11, 1926.

42. "'Anna Christie' Author Blesses."

43. "'Anna Christie' Author Blesses."

44. Hull-House Theatre Collection, Hull-House Collection, Special Collections, Richard J. Daley Library, University of Illinois at Chicago.

45. "Classic Drama by Mr. and Mrs. Vassos Kanellos," *Saloniki-Greek Press*, April 10, 1926.

46. "The Goodman Theater," *Music News*, April 9, 1926.

47. "Classic Drama by Mr. and Mrs. Vassos Kanellos."

48. "The Goodman Theater," *Chicago Evening Post*, May 23, 1926.

49. "'Athanasius Diakos' Drama Produced at Hull House," *Greek Star*, March 17, 1905.

50. "Benefit Performance by Swedish Theatrical Society," *Svenska Kuriren*, November 11, 1926.

51. "Lecture on Modern Polish Literature," *Dziennik Zjednoczenia*, January 7, 1927.

52. "Study of Modern Polish Literature Is Begun by Members of Polish Arts Club," *Dziennik Zjednoczenia*, January 17, 1927.

53. "Polish Arts Club Bulletin," *Dziennik Zjednoczenia*, March 4, 1927.

54. "Concert of the Filarety," *Dziennik Zjednoczenia*, October 19, 1927.

55. "Literary Department Formed," *Dziennik Zjednoczenia*, January 25, 1928.

56. Article clipping from unknown newspaper in Scrapbook of Robert C. Jones, Chicago Foreign Language Press Survey, Newberry Library.

57. Edward Moore, "Spanish Songs and Dances Are Well Received: Charming Program Given at Goodman," *Chicago Daily Tribune*, April 23, 1932, 18.

58. Virginia Dale, "The Theaters," *Chicago Daily Journal*, May 21, 1926.

59. "Teutonic Players at Goodman," *Chicago Daily News*, May 21, 1926.

60. "Drama League Staging Play Tourney," *Chicago Daily Tribune*, May 1, 1927, I3.

61. "Drama Groups Rehearse for Play Tourney: North Side Clubs to Compete for League Cups," *Chicago Daily Tribune*, April 21, 1929, I6.

62. Burns Mantle, "'If Booth Had Missed' Takes New Slant on Lincoln Tragedy," *Chicago Daily Tribune*, February 14, 1932, F1.

63. Mantle, "If Booth Had Missed."

64. 1929 Chicago Play Tournament program, Program Collection, Chicago History Museum Research Center.

65. "Activities of Chicago Little Theater Folk," *Chicago Daily Tribune*, February 26, 1933, SC8.

66. Not to be confused with the Graham Greene novel or the Paddy Chayefsky play of the same name.

67. 1930 Chicago Play Tournament program, Goodman Collection, Special Collections, Chicago Public Library.

68. "Notes of the Theater," *Chicago Daily Tribune*, May 18, 1930, G6.

69. "Austin Church Players to See Title Tomorrow," *Chicago Daily Tribune*, March 8, 1931, H3.

70. "Religious Drama Fete at Goodman Tomorrow Night," *Chicago Daily Tribune*, March 8, 1931, J4.

71. John Evans, "Religious Play about Judas to Open Monday," *Chicago Daily Tribune*, June 2, 1934, 17.

72. Evans, "Religious Play about Judas." Also of note, Thomas Wood Stevens ended up directing the Globe Theatre players who put on Shakespeare plays at the Century of Progress Exposition.

73. Medgyesy, "Chicago's Goodman Theatre," 21.

74. Medgyesy, "Chicago's Goodman Theatre," 21.

75. Medgyesy, "Chicago's Goodman Theatre," 22.

76. And in fact, a show at the Goodman helped inspire the founding of Teatro Vista. See chapter 8.

77. Broadway World News Desk, "Goodman Theatre and the Chicago Latino Theatre Alliance (CLATA) Co-Present *Mendoza*," August 23, 2018, https://www.broadwayworld.com/chicago/article/Goodman-Theatre-And-The-Chicago-Latino-Theater-Alliance-CLATA-Co-Present-MENDOZA-20181001.

78. Broadway World News Desk, "Goodman Theatre and the Chicago Latino Theatre Alliance."

79. Justin Hayford, "At Steppenwolf's Garage Rep, Failure Can Spell Success," *Chicago Reader*, March 12, 2014, https://www.chicagoreader.com/chicago/steppenwolf-garage-rep-offloop-theater-showcase/Content?oid=12753527.

80. "Firebrand Theatre Presents Caroline or Change," Press Release.

81. Maren Robinson, TimeLine resident dramaturg, interview with author, November 16, 2018.

5

Theatrical Geographies of Segregation

Spatial Displacement in Theodore Ward's *Big White Fog*

Aaron Krall

BROOKS: I done let that black crank root me up once with his fool talk 'bout we goin' find freedom up here in the North. But he ain't goin' 'suade me again. I'se too old for another transplantin'.

—Theodore Ward, *Big White Fog*

Theodore Ward's 1938 play *Big White Fog* tells the story of the Masons, an African American family navigating racism, segregation, and their hopes and disappointments, in the wake of the Great Migration to the South Side of Chicago. The play follows Vic Mason and his family, as they make plans, pursue their dreams, and crash into the barriers that separate the Black Belt, the narrow stretch of land on the South Side that confined and segregated the Black migrants who settled in the city, from the opportunities that they believed to exist on the other side. It is a play about looking for freedom and failing to find it in the North, or anywhere else. The characters try out a wide variety of strategies—going to college, contributing to the Garvey movement,[1] finding dignity in work, investing in a home, working side hustles to leverage the housing shortage in the Black Belt—but none succeed. In the end, the family loses its home, and Vic is shot by the police when he resists being removed. His son, Lester, can only describe the crushing conditions his family faces from racism and discrimination as blocking out the ability to see any hope or possibility for change: "Seems like the world ain't nothing but a big white fog, and we can't see no light nowhere!"[2] The play has a bleak conclusion, but it works to represent and interrogate the struggles of Black families in the Chicago of the 1930s.

While the Masons' attempts to survive in the Black Belt lead directly to the play's tragic ending, the production history of *Big White Fog*'s debut is more complicated. The play was produced by the Chicago Negro Unit of the Federal Theatre Project (FTP), and through its inclusion in James V. Hatch's landmark 1974 anthology *Black Theatre USA*,[3] its role in the history of the FTP, and notable revival productions at the Guthrie in 1995 and the Almeida in 2007, it has been recognized as a significant contribution to twentieth-century American drama. Its original production, however, was troubled. FTP administrators initially supported the production of the play, but, cautious about its politics and pressured by African American community leaders who preferred more positive and uplifting representations of the community, they killed it. After a brief run of thirty-seven performances at the Great Northern Theatre in the Loop, the play was moved to the DuSable High School auditorium, a makeshift alternative venue, in the racially segregated South Side Black Belt. Pushed from the city's center to its periphery, the production closed in less than a week. Written, workshopped, and rehearsed on the South Side, the play was produced for a mixed-race audience downtown before being "sent home." As Rena Fraden explains in *Blueprints for a Black Federal Theatre, 1935–1939*, a debate around the location of the production was central to its history. African American cultural separatists like W. E. B. Du Bois argued that it "should be produced 'near us,' in a black neighborhood," while Ward and his allies on the political left wanted a Loop audience that joined "black leaders, left-wing liberals and communists, black and white."[4] The question about locations in the city was a question about audiences: Who should see the play, and what should the production accomplish?

This debate ultimately produced a play with no real home. The politics of a venue in the Loop—the city's established theater district, where white audiences were unaccustomed to seeing representations of Black characters—were untenable, and a run on the South Side proved impossible. In this way, the production history mirrors that of the Mason family. After trading the Jim Crow South for the industrial North, they found that white property owners, investors, and neighborhood associations made life in Chicago something less than a "promised land." Fading memories of the rural South, the reality of the segregated and unequal North, and the Garveyite promise of freedom in Africa divide the family. Compounding this spatial disorientation is the threat of literal homelessness—set against the economic crisis of the 1930s, the Masons are about to lose their home to foreclosure. *Big White Fog* represents a family looking for a permanent home in Chicago and failing. Its production suggests that makeshift theatrical spaces on the city's margins were precarious locations for ambitious but marginalized communities to tell their stories in the early twentieth century. This chapter reads Ward's play against the history of the Great Migration and Chicago's Black Belt and examines the ways it represents Black domestic space as tentative, unstable, and devalued. Then, moving from this analysis, it argues that the imagined spaces that provide the geographical and psychological landscape for the play—the remembered South, the possible future in Africa, and the urban South Side of Chicago—are mirrored in the debates about where the play should be produced and what it should accomplish for Black and white audiences.

"Sweet Home Chicago"

Big White Fog begins in August 1922 at the corner of Dearborn Street and Fifty-First Street. The Mason family's modest, but well-kept, living room is on the southern end of Chicago's Black Belt. Ward describes this space as "a large, congenial room, bearing the tell-marks of use polished by care, and indicating that people of means lived there."[5] The living room is well furnished, and it has a "commanding view" of the street below (181). Our attention is drawn to the objects that characterize the individuals that live here: "polished" furniture, a typewriter, and a Victrola. This is the home of a family that has recently established itself in Chicago after migrating from the rural South, and we see evidence of a family that is hopeful about its future in this Northern city. Although the Masons may not be "people of means," they are proud, educated, and ambitious. This home offers a way into Chicago's theatrical geography of segregation in the first half of the twentieth century. Ward's play engaged the racism that defined the social space of Chicago in the years between World War I and the civil rights movement by dramatizing the struggles in the wake of the Great Migration, exposing the housing crisis in Chicago's Black Belt, and confronting audiences with the devastating effects of segregation.

In this three-act "problem play" that spans ten years in the life of an African American family, the first two acts establish the relationships between the principal characters and develop a number of conflicts, which are ultimately resolved in the final act. Vic Mason, a Tuskegee-educated farmer and Garveyite leader, is the main character, and his story and his home on Fifty-First Street provide the dramatic arc and the setting of the action. His wife, Ella, is positioned in tension between her husband and her mother, Martha Brooks, who lives with the family and resents being uprooted and brought to Chicago. The Brooks family is rounded out by Juanita, Ella's sister, and her husband, Dan, a capitalist-oriented landlord whose exploitative business schemes work as a foil to Vic's Garveyite separatist idealism. The other major characters are Vic and Ella's children: Lester, a student turned Marxist revolutionary, and Wanda, an exploited shop girl. All of these characters are intimately connected by family bonds, but the social forces they confront ultimately destroy their relationships and their lives.

The play begins shortly after Vic and Ella move their extended family to Chicago because they were unable to make a living in Mississippi. Although he is an educated farmer, in Chicago Vic is only able to find work as a construction laborer. In response to this disappointment, Vic becomes a committed follower of Marcus Garvey and his plans to organize a return to Africa. Meanwhile, Lester receives tentative acceptance for a scholarship to study chemistry at Copeland Technical Institute, and his sister Wanda announces that she plans to quit school to work at the local drugstore and begin "to live" (283, 285). She has accepted Vic's critique of American society and argues that "there's nothing for us in this country" (285). Dan, Vic's brother-in-law, invests in real estate, renting inadequate kitchenettes to some of the thousands of African Americans who are also migrating to the North. Through the course of the play, all of these plans fail. The Garvey plan collapses, Lester is rejected when Copeland learns that he is Black, Wanda resorts to prostitution, and the kitchenette project goes bankrupt during the Great Depression. At the end of the play, the family is evicted from their home, and Vic is shot and killed by the police while resisting the eviction. In the world of *Big White Fog*, racialized segregation makes home impossible.

The Mason family's story is anchored in the history of the African American experience at the beginning of the twentieth century. In this moment, Chicago was more than a city; it was a promise, the hope for a better future. Beginning in 1915, approximately 5 million African Americans moved from the rural South to Northern cities to escape Jim Crow laws and the poverty of sharecropping, transforming those cities as well as the social identities of millions of African Americans.[6] Of those migrants, nearly 800,000 moved to Chicago in search of freedom and opportunity.[7] As Davarian L. Baldwin notes, "Chicago eventually became such a powerful symbol of prosperity and freedom that blues singer Robert Johnson literally relocated the city within the much older American mythos of the Western frontier, singing, 'Ooh, baby don't you want to go? / Back to the land of California, to my sweet home Chicago.'"[8] When migrants arrived in Chicago, however, they found a place with less freedom and fewer opportunities than Johnson's song promised. The characters' struggles in Ward's play reflect the realities of life in the Black Belt versus life in the South, which demonstrates the multiple geographies in the text and the production.

In "Race and Housing in Chicago," Roger Biles explains that between 1890 and 1915 alone, the Black population in Chicago grew from under 15,000 to over 50,000.[9] After World War I, the Black population in Chicago grew exponentially as Black migrants from the South, especially Mississippi, Louisiana, and Arkansas, rode the Illinois Central Railroad into the city. By 1920, 109,458 Blacks lived in Chicago, and one decade later the number was over 200,000 (32). As Robert Spinney argues in *City of Big Shoulders*, African Americans were drawn to Chicago for two reasons: to escape racial discrimination in the South and to make more money in the North. The financial opportunities in the North were clear. According to Spinney, in the South, "African Americans commonly earned $2 to $3 per week as tenant farmers or sharecroppers; in Chicago, working men in 1916 earned $2 to $2.50 per day."[10] Although employment discrimination existed in the North, there was a demand for cheap labor due to a decrease in European immigration and the demand for soldiers during World War I. African Americans quickly found work in the steel mills, meatpacking houses, and other unskilled-labor industries.

Although they could find better jobs in Chicago than in the rural South, African Americans still faced de facto discrimination, particularly in housing. The Black experience in Chicago in the first decades of the Great Migration was largely defined by racial segregation in the Black Belt. Biles offers an overview of the origin of this Black ghetto.[11] Although there was a Black population in Chicago since the city was incorporated, it was not until its numbers began to rise dramatically at the beginning of the twentieth century that "blacks found hostility where they had once encountered benign neglect."[12] Throughout the nineteenth century and into the first decades of the twentieth century, the city's Black population had lived in racially integrated neighborhoods. St. Clair Drake and Horace Cayton document this period and the increasing density of the Black Belt in their 1945 study *Black Metropolis*. They report that in 1910 "there were no communities in which Negroes were over 61 percent of the population."[13] Furthermore, "more than two-thirds of the Negroes lived in areas less than 50 percent Negro, and a third lived in areas less than 10 percent Negro" (176). These numbers paint a picture of a relatively racially integrated city.

As Biles explains, however, "the creation of a monolithic racial ghetto came at roughly the same time that Southern states erected Jim Crow barriers to integration."[14] By World War I, "a virtually all-black ghetto on the South Side had taken shape" (32). This original Black Belt was "shoehorned into a narrow slice of land between railroad yards on the west and Cottage Grove Avenue on the east," and it "extended southward from the central business district into the Woodlawn and Englewood neighborhoods below Thirty-ninth Street" (32). These early boundaries gradually expanded over the following decades, but they did not keep pace with the growing population, forcing increasing numbers of migrants into the narrow ghetto. By 1930, the Black Belt was fully consolidated though the discriminatory practices of neighborhood associations, realtors, and property owners, and the distribution of African American residents had changed radically. At this point, "90 percent were in districts of 50 percent or more Negro concentration" and "almost two-thirds (63.0 percent) lived where the concentration was from 90 to 99 percent Negro."[15] This rising density created housing shortages and established opportunities for exploitation by landlords and property owners who offered increasingly smaller and subdivided apartments and kitchenettes, generally decreasing the quality of life in the Black Belt.

The Great Migration is evoked throughout *Big White Fog*, and it provides the forward momentum that drives its action. Chief among the concerns of the African American community in Chicago was reconciling their current hardships and opportunities with those that were left behind in the South. All of the characters in *Big White Fog* are dealing with the transition to urban life, but Martha Brooks, the matriarch of the family and Vic's mother-in-law, personifies the longing for what has been lost. Throughout the play, she evokes the family's Southern origins and suggests that the move to Chicago was against her will. At numerous moments, Martha responds to Vic's Garveyite plans for another migration with a mix of scorn and pride. For instance, she insists, "I ain't no Affikan; I'm a Dupree! I was born in this country, and I'm going to die in it."[16] This is both a rejection of her Africanness and an assertion that she is where she belongs. Her need to defend her connection to America, though, emerges from spatial uncertainty. Although she firmly identifies as an American, Martha is also deeply skeptical of the family's Northern adventure: "I done let that black crank root me up once with his fool talk 'bout we goin' find freedom up here in the North. But he ain't goin' 'suade me again" (283). When her daughter Ella replies, "I guess you'd [. . .] rather be in Mississippi picking cotton," Martha responds, "Chicago's one thing but Africa's another" (283). She recognizes that conditions were untenable in the South and that moving to Chicago has had some advantages, but throughout the play her spatial unease is apparent.

This ambivalence about the migration to the North is shared by most members of the family. Ella is patient with Vic's political ideals, even when they compromise the family, but at a climactic moment in the middle of act 1, she expresses her suppressed frustration. When Vic suggests that things will improve when the family moves to Africa, she is furious: "I don't want to hear any explanations or promises either—I've had enough of them—'A stack of lies'—the whole world's a stack of lies! You brought me out of the South with one—You and your fine talk about freedom and giving the children a chance to be somebody!" (286). Here, Ella echoes Martha's dissatisfaction in the North, and she dismisses freedom and opportunity as a lie. The subtext, though, is that leaving the South might have been a mistake. While there were no opportunities there, at least there were no false expectations. If Ella is expressing nostalgia for the South, it is only because her current situation seems to be no better.

Despite the obvious pressure created by the rapidly growing population to expand the boundaries of the ghetto, the surrounding communities struggled to reinforce them. One of the primary tools for maintaining segregation in the Black Belt was the formation of neighborhood associations. Drake and Cayton explain that a post–World War I housing shortage led to stricter enforcement of the Black Belt's boundaries. Before World War I, Drake and Cayton contend, white communities adjacent to the Black Belt "had been willing to absorb a few Negros and then to relinquish the community to them as they become too numerous."[17] This process continued, gradually expanding the ghetto, until after 1915, when tens of thousands of Black migrants entered the city and were "interpreted as a 'mass invasion'" (177–78). In response, white neighborhood associations, "which had originally organized for neighborhood improvement, now began to focus their attention upon keeping out Negros" (178). This attention initially took the form of mass meetings, threatening articles and leaflets, and outright violence, including a wave of home bombings between 1917 and 1919 (178). During the period, "fifty-eight homes were bombed," resulting in two deaths, numerous injuries, and over $100,000 in damages (178), a staggering sum equivalent to over $1.5 million in current values.[18] Drake and Cayton are careful to note that the neighborhood associations "never admitted complicity in these bombings, and responsibility was never definitively placed by police," but the groups were clearly involved in agitating against Black families who moved into white neighborhoods.[19]

Ultimately, though, these means were unsuccessful, and Black families continued to challenge the boundaries of the Black Belt, mainly because it was too expensive. Because space was limited and the population was rising dramatically, landlords charged rents often twice as high as those outside the Black Belt (206). To combat the continued "invasion" of white neighborhoods, neighborhood associations turned to racially restrictive covenants to control the Black population. In "'Hemmed In': The Struggle against Racial Restrictive Covenants and Deed Restrictions in Post-WWII Chicago," Wendy Plotkin explains that "racially restrictive deed restrictions and covenants were legally enforceable provisions of deeds prohibiting owners from selling or leasing their residences to members of specific racial groups."[20] Although the U.S. Supreme Court found "municipally mandated racial zoning" to violate the equal rights protection clause of the Fourteenth Amendment in 1917, restrictive covenants were private contracts, and therefore upheld by the courts. This legal interpretation, upheld again in the 1926 Supreme Court *Corrigan v. Buckley* ruling, supported widespread use of the covenants in cities throughout the United States (39). It was not until 1948 in *Shelley v. Kraemer*, Plotkin notes, that the U.S. Supreme Court "ruled that courts could no longer enforce covenants" (40). Even then, however, neighborhood associations used intimidation and violence, as well as unofficial agreements to block African American home buyers and to limit the Black population to the Black Belt.

By restricting African Americans to the Black Belt, property owners and investors created opportunities to exploit the shortage of housing available to the growing population. *Big White Fog* suggests that it was not only white landlords who seized this opportunity. Vic's brother-in-law Dan recognizes the potential for profit in buying, subdividing, and renting apartments and kitchenettes. During a scene where Dan tries to recruit Vic for his kitchenette scheme, the two men debate the opportunities available in the North and their responsibility for the African Americans left behind in the South. First, though, we hear another claim of belonging in America. When Vic suggests that they share a common African heritage, Dan is appalled. He responds, "What *our?* My heritage is right here in America!"[21] Vic, though, immediately contests this spatial certainty: "What? A lynchrope?" (288). This response infuriates Dan, but it reveals a clear distinction about how they understand their position in America. It also leads to a discussion of the South. From Vic's mention of the lynchrope, Dan moves to argue that African Americans can escape discrimination in the South by moving to the North: "If those chumps down South haven't got sense enough to get out from under Mr. George, they ought to be strung up" (288). From Dan's perspective, discrimination—even racial violence—is what happens when one fails to seize the opportunities of American capitalism. He goes on to contend, "You can't do anything for people who don't care anything about themselves. You only stir up strife. Let them alone, I say, and try to get something out of them for yourself" (289). This is a clear statement of Dan's capitalist ideology, but it also articulates his view of the South—it is best left and forgotten. He belongs to America, but not the South.

For Vic, it is not so easy to leave the South behind. In a subsequent conversation between Vic and Dan, Vic shows how part of his Garveyite dream is to provide hope and opportunity for all African Americans, including those who have remained in the South. In response to Dan's continued arguments to join his entrepreneurial efforts, Vic claims that it is a limited and short-sighted venture. He exclaims, "Try offering your white man's method to the millions we got down South, (*shaking his finger*) living on corn bread and molasses and dying like flies from hook-worm and pellagra!" (295). The conditions of African Americans in the South are familiar, personal, and unacceptable. Dan offers his now familiar solution: "Let them come North! [. . .] Why can't they come North, like we did—There's plenty of room up here for everybody!" (295). For Vic, this is inadequate, and he turns the problems in

Chicago on his brother-in-law; he argues that living in overpriced and overcrowded kitchenettes in the segregated Black Belt is not freedom or opportunity. He even accuses Dan of exploiting the new arrivals in the city: "Well, there's one thing you can't deny: I'm against cutting my own brother's throat to get somewhere!" (295). In this scene, it is clear that Vic identifies with the Southern African Americans and that although he is currently in the North, he is not at home there.

In this scene, there is a clear sense of displacement, homelessness, as the characters struggle to feel grounded in the wake of the Great Migration. In *Big White Fog*, the home is often the site where characters struggle with the boundaries imposed by economic status, social inequality, political disenfranchisement, and moral obligations. As Una Chaudhuri argues in *Staging Place: The Geography of Modern Drama*, "The fully iconic, single set, middle-class living room of realism produced so closed and so *complete* a stage world that it supported the new and powerful fantasy of the stage not as a place to pretend in or to perform on but a place to *be*, a fully existential arena."[22] Indeed, Fraden notes that the sets for *Big White Fog* "were said to be so real that one felt as though one were walking into someone's living room."[23] The intended effect was to blur the line between performance space and social space, but it was also to make the setting function as a character. The worn-out furniture, inadequate lighting, sofas that double as beds, and overcrowded rooms reveal traces of poverty and an inability to establish a comfortable home. These sets, and the social inequality that they suggest, contribute to the geography of the play.

The set pieces also illustrate a family drama marked by spatial uncertainty, and characters who struggle with limited choices and occupy homes that are insecure, inadequate, and impossible to maintain. In "Housing the Black Body: Value, Domestic Space, and Segregation Narratives," GerShun Avilez theorizes "Black domestic space" by using U.S. Supreme Court cases that respond to restrictive covenants to develop a connection between mobility, housing, and citizenship. Most compellingly, he explains that the 1940 ruling in *Hansberry v. Lee*[24] establishes that these covenants are a restriction on both domestic space and civic identity. Avilez uses Gaston Bachelard's *Poetics of Space* to define "domestic spaces" as both "the family and the physical structures of home."[25] In this way, "domestic space" works to indicate and to connect social relationships and the walls and buildings that physically define the home. Avilez argues that "given the centrality of segregation to restrictive practices affecting citizenship, the relationship of

African Americans to places of residence and to domestic space in general is indicative of their relationship to legal structures" (135). By connecting segregation to citizenship, he contends that political and legal disenfranchisement is accompanied by an alienation from social relationships, like family, and the physical structures of home. Avilez concludes that this created the "conditions for African Americans to feel estranged from their domestic space" (135).

This estrangement is evident in the spatial disorientation in Ward's play, particularly the way that segregated domestic space is constructed as valueless. Avilez contends that the legal arguments mobilized to defend segregation render "Black-occupied spaces as 'valueless'" (136). This concept of "valuelessness" depends on an understanding of whiteness as a kind of property. To shape this understanding, Avilez depends on Cheryl J. Harris's definition of property as "expectations in tangible or intangible things that are valued and protected by law" (136). Although whiteness is "intangible," it is legally protected "because there is a value socially invested in Whiteness that is not similarly invested in Blackness" (136). That is, racially restrictive covenants worked to legally defend segregation because whiteness was understood to be a kind of property that was valued in the same ways as houses. While state and local governments were prohibited from legally imposing segregation, private actors were free to engage in segregationist practices. Because the Supreme Court refused to reject restrictive covenants until *Shelley v. Kraemer* in 1948, individuals and neighborhood associations formed and enforced restrictive covenants with the implicit backing of legal authority. As Avilez claims, this gave covenants "the force of law in restricting Black existence" (136). In this way, "Black domestic space not only comes to be seen as a threat to White spaces and to White assessments of 'value,' but such space also becomes aligned with 'valuelessness'" (137). Black domestic space is not valued or protected, so it is defined in contrast to white space by its lack of value, most notably in final scene of the play when the Masons' home is seized by the police as the result of foreclosure and Vic is fatally shot for resisting.[26]

The idea of Black domestic space as valueless disrupts bell hooks's notion of "homeplace" as a "safe place where Black people could affirm one another and by doing so heal many of the wounds inflicted by racist domination."[27] As Avilez notes, this situates "Black space as a site resistant to the effects of oppression" (136). He is quick to complicate this interior/exterior binary, though, by arguing that the "spatial realities of segregation construct Black domestic spaces and continuously encroach on families and the housing structures" (136). Specifically, the sense of valuelessness of Black domestic space created by segregation produces a condition of "'placelessness' for Black subjects or the displacement of the Black subject more generally attributable to belonging and security within the home" (136). This theory of Black domestic space demonstrates the effects of segregation in Chicago's Black Belt, and it provides a framework for reading the action that happens in the Masons' living room.

This conflict is most apparent in Vic's sense of displacement, which contributes to his Garveyite politics. If African Americans are out of place in both the South and the North, he argues, they should make a home in Africa. Although Ella patiently supports him, most of the time, and his children understand his commitment, Vic stands alone as a representative of the Black Nationalist desire for a place where a self-sufficient African American community can thrive without the constraints of white oppression. Throughout the play we see Vic expound on the possibility of an African American renewal in Africa. In a monologue that ends the first scene of the play, Vic offers Africa as a mother calling her children home:

> We'll soon be out of this rut and on our way to Africa. I can see her now, like a mother weeping for her lost children, calling to us, 'come home.' Soon, and it won't be long now. You're going to see the black man come out of the darkness of failure and into the light of achievement with the cloak of greatness about his shoulders.[28]

In this speech, and others like it, Vic employs poetic and visionary language to project a place where he can feel at home. Indeed, it is this hope that motivates his character throughout most of the play.

Vic's poetic revelry, however, is balanced by a kind of pragmatism. The second act begins with Vic writing a paper to present at a Garveyite conference in Harlem. He is proposing an agrarian cooperative be established in Africa as an alternative to the hostile conditions in the South and the futility of industrial work in the North. As the scene opens, he is dictating his talk to Wanda, who sits at a table typing. He dictates, "Therefore, we must of necessity conclude that by relying on the Nine tried and proven principles of the English Producers-and-Consumers-Cooperatives [. . .] we shall eventually be able to build an agrarian cooperative economy" (293). Although this plan is only suggested, we hear traces of Vic's Tuskegee education in the ways he works to translate his dreams into plans. While it must be noted that Ward presents the Garveyite officers, who are little more than props for Vic's speeches, as somewhat buffoonish in their costumes and pomp, Vic's sincerity is compelling, as is his weariness with dealing with prejudice in America. The dream of Africa stands as a hope for the future, but it is also a way of psychologically escaping from the lack of opportunity in Chicago.

Aside from Vic's agricultural plans, though, the references to Africa are largely abstract, mythic images rather than the specific and vivid depictions of life in the South. In fact, for all of the other characters in the play, Africa is usually little more than the name of a place. And when it is evoked by other members of the family, it is rarely in positive terms. For Ella, Juanita, and Dan, who see themselves as American, Africa is no utopia. Instead, it is described with terms that evoke a savage, if unfamiliar, place. When Ella finally loses her patience with Vic at the end of act 2 and effectively ends their marriage, she tells him, "Get out or stay! Or better still, go on to Africa. Maybe you'll find the company of your own kind in the jungle!" (308). This image of Africa as "the jungle" stands in sharp contrast to Vic's imagined geography; where he sees hope and freedom, Ella admits to seeing no place where she could live. Throughout the play, the language of the jungle is suggested, particularly in references to Marcus Garvey. Both Juanita and Dan refer to him as a "monkey-chaser" (282, 290). While obviously intended to disparage Garvey, this language also works to characterize Africa as a place imagined to be uncivilized, uninhabitable, primitive, and foolish. Like the South, Africa is always present in the minds of the characters in *Big White Fog* as contested terrain.

If these absent places constantly intrude in the Masons' living room, they stand in uncomfortable tension with the place that exists outside its walls: the urban North and Chicago. The city works as an unseen character throughout the play. The members of the Mason family exit to the street for work, shopping, and entertainment, and the stage directions note noises of the street from the widows, but the action of the play happens in the family home. Chicago, then, like Africa and the South, is represented in the play's dialogue. This representation largely appears in two ways: the challenges the city presents and the opportunities, however limited, that it offers. The obstacles presented by the North begin with the house itself. The house is a tentative foothold in Chicago, but one that slips away at the end of the play. Owning a home is certainly a positive opportunity for the Mason family, but at Fifty-First and Dearborn the house is squarely in the segregated Black Belt of Chicago, which serves as a constant reminder of the limits to the freedom of the North.

Staging the Black Belt

While the action of *Big White Fog* happens at Fifty-First Street and Dearborn Avenue, the geography of the play's production is the story of a five-mile journey up State Street from the Black Belt into the Loop—and back. After a series of readings, workshops, tryouts, and rehearsals on the South Side, the play debuted at the Great Northern Theatre at the corner of Jackson Boulevard and Dearborn in Chicago's downtown business district (called the Loop due to the elevated train loop of the city's transit system), where it played for a short but well-attended run of two months. And then the production was abruptly moved back to the South Side into the auditorium of the newly constructed DuSable High School at Forty-Ninth Street and Wabash Avenue, two blocks away from the play's fictional setting, where the production closed in less than one week. As the action of the play unfolds in the Masons' living room on the pages of Ward's script and on stages in the Loop and the South Side, the spatial disorientation experienced by the characters and the production overlap and intersect in revealing ways.

The displacement represented in the play is rooted in the history of the Great Migration and Theodore Ward's biography. Although the play is not autobiographical, it reflects Ward's experiences of Chicago, and it provides a platform from which he critiques his urban experience and the boundaries that shape it. Ward, an African American playwright born in Thibodaux, Louisiana, in 1902, left home in 1915 and traveled the United States "working as a bootblack and a hotel bellboy."[29] As Fraden observes, his "journey from the South to the North mirrors those of thousands of blacks" during the Great Migration, including the Mason family of *Big White Fog* (117). Ward participated in this migration, but he was able to get a college degree and avoid the industrial labor that most Black migrants sought. After studying at the University of Utah and the University of Wisconsin, he moved to Chicago to teach for the Lincoln Center Players, a local arts organization that staged performances at the Abraham Lincoln Center (700 East Oakwood Boulevard) in the Black Belt's Oakland neighborhood. There, he met

Richard Wright and joined the South Side Writers' Club, a literary and intellectual group with an interracial membership and leftist politics.[30] As Fraden explains, the South Side of Chicago housed a vibrant and thriving African American culture. In the 1920s, the neighborhood was teeming with churches, social clubs, political organizations, theaters, dance clubs, and African American newspapers.[31] It was a place where a young African American writer could experiment and find considerable success. It was in this milieu that Ward developed the ambivalence about political movements and social change that underlie his play. It was also here that he became intimately familiar with racial segregation and the unequal geography of the city.

In this context, Ward was recruited to write a play for the Chicago Negro Unit of the Federal Theatre Project in 1937. As John Frick argues in his history of the Federal Theatre Project, by the early 1930s theater faced the dual challenges of attracting audiences during the Great Depression and competing with the growing film industry.[32] In New York City alone, the results were devastating: most of the theaters were closed, and more than twenty-five thousand theater professionals were unemployed (225). These circumstances were mirrored in all of the arts in cities and small towns throughout the United States. To put artists back to work and to provide the public access to art during the Great Depression, the Roosevelt administration established arts programs as a part of the Works Progress Administration, including the Federal Theatre Project, which produced over eight hundred plays between 1935 and 1938 and employed tens of thousands of theater workers. Hallie Flanagan, a white director and scholar of modern European theater, oversaw the project.[33] Flanagan supervised the development of "Negro Units" in major cities across the country that employed African American writers, directors, actors, and designers to produce theater for the African American community, providing opportunities for African American theater professionals, who often struggled to find work in a white-dominated industry. The Chicago Federal Theatre Project was directed by Harry Minturn, a white director and producer with experience in vaudeville; Shirley Graham, a Black director who would later marry W. E. B. Du Bois, was responsible for the Chicago Negro Unit.

Ward used the opportunity presented by the Federal Theatre Project to offer a critique of the very segregationist policies that made the Negro Units necessary. Unsurprisingly, his play was controversial from the beginning, both within the Federal Theatre Project and in the South Side community. Although it had support from the South Side artistic community, Minturn and Graham believed that the play was too political, and that its representation of the complex struggles of residents of the Black Belt would divide members of the African American community who wanted to project positive images to outside audiences. This conflict over space and representation is embedded in the structure of its story. *Big White Fog* has three imagined spaces that provide the geographical tension for the play: the remembered South, the possible future in Africa, and the urban South Side of Chicago where the Mason family fights to make a home. The tensions between these spaces suggest that this fight will not end well. Rather than a destination, Chicago is positioned as only one stop on a long migration—reaching back to the origins of the African diaspora in slavery and the transatlantic crossing. For the Masons, though, the more immediate sense of origin is in Mississippi.

When the FTP received Ward's play in 1937, Minturn believed that the script had merit, but was cautious about its politics and suggested that a South Side venue for a production might be most appropriate (Fraden, 121). He passed the script to Graham and asked her to explore potential audiences for the play (121). This led to a staged reading at a South Side YWCA in January 1938 and two performances at the International House at the University of Chicago on February 17 and 18 (122). Graham reported mixed responses: while the virtually all-Black audiences appreciated the performances, they were concerned about how the African American community was represented. Consequently, Graham and Minturn became reluctant to stage the play at all. Ward was a strong advocate for a production though, and he insisted on a Loop venue. After an impasse that lasted over a month, Minturn agreed to book the play into the Great Northern Theatre in the Loop. Little evidence exists about why Graham's objections were overruled, but Fraden suggests that "Chicago city administration brought pressure on the WPA" to fill the theater (128).

The play opened at the Great Northern Theatre on April 7, 1938. The theater, which opened in 1896 as part of an addition to the Great Northern Hotel designed by Daniel H. Burnham, was part of a vibrant turn-of-the-century theater scene in Chicago's Loop. According to Konrad Schiecke's history of Chicago's downtown theaters, the opulent theater had 1,400 seats "upholstered in crimson," an eighty-five-foot-wide stage, and a lobby "paved with mosaics" and with walls and ceilings of marble.[34] Its ownership and programming changed several times during the first decades of the twentieth century, including over a decade of Shubert ownership. The Great Northern hosted productions ranging from theater and musicals to vaudeville and movies, until it closed in the wake of the Great Depression. It was dormant for several years before the Federal Theatre Project reopened the venue as "Federal Theatre No. 1" in 1936 (73). The theater was used in this capacity for several projects by the Chicago Negro Unit, as well as for successful runs by the main branch of the FTP, including an acclaimed production of Ibsen's *An Enemy of the People* (73).[35]

Despite the initial controversy, it appeared that staging *Big White Fog* in the Loop was the right decision. As Fraden explains, the production "played in Chicago between April 7 and May 30, altogether for 37 performances."[36] The audiences were mixed, consisting of middle- and upper-class whites from the North Side, as well as a wide spectrum of African Americans from the Black Belt, who traveled to the Loop to see and support the production. Contemporary observers described "enthusiastic" audiences and "favorable press reviews" (128). Charles Collins in the *Chicago Daily Tribune*, for example, found the play to be an "intelligent use of racial material from the point of view of the American Negro."[37] Although he notes that the "play runs to discussion more than to incident," Collins concludes that "its picture of life in a self-respecting Negro home on the south side is rich with realistic detail." The play was a success, if a modest one, and was expected to extend its run at the Great Northern. At the end of May, however, Minturn moved the play to the South Side. There is no consensus about why this decision was made. While Ward suspected Minturn of sabotaging the production, historians including Melissa Barton suggest that the play was moved to the South Side because it "was not attracting a black audience."[38] In any case, in June 1938 the play migrated to the newly constructed auditorium at DuSable High School in the Black Belt on Forty-Ninth Street, only blocks away from the fictional Mason family home.

This South Side venue may have appeared to be an appropriate setting for bringing Black theater to Black audiences. DuSable High School opened in 1935 at 4934 South Wabash Avenue to accommodate the growing population of African Americans migrating from the South and settling in Chicago's Black Belt during the Great Migration. According to a report on the building's designation as a Chicago Landmark, it was necessary to relieve overcrowding at other neighborhood high schools. The report explains that "during the late 1920s, the Chicago Board of Education was increasingly criticized by the black community for not providing the same quality of school facilities available in other, predominately white neighborhoods."[39] Construction began in 1931, but was left unfinished for several years during the financial crisis of the Great Depression. The building was eventually completed with federal stimulus funding through the Public Works Administration (10). Designed by Paul Gerhardt Sr., the architect for the Chicago Board of Education, the school fits within a style known as "PWA Moderne," a subdued art deco style common in public works buildings from the 1930s that features bold lines but modest ornamentation. The school fills an entire city block and includes two assembly halls. The larger space, a 2,200-seat auditorium, was used for *Big White Fog* as well as local performances, including musical revues and jazz concerts featuring school alumni Nat "King" Cole and Dinah Washington (10, 20). In short, it is an impressive building with a theater suitable for large-scale productions, but it was designed for students and community events, not professional theater.

Although there is some debate about why the production failed in its new home at DuSable High School, it is clear that there was no audience for the play on the South Side. With minimal ticket sales, "the play closed in a matter of days."[40] While African Americans would travel to the Loop to see Ward's play, they were uninterested in seeing this kind of theater in the Black Belt. Like the Mason family, the production could not make a reliable home inside or outside of the Black Belt. Its temporary venue in the Loop suggests that challenging the racial boundaries of the city was possible, but that these efforts were contingent and unstable. At the same time, it also could not survive within the confines of the segregated South Side. In this way, the production mirrors both the opportunities that were available to and limitations that were enforced on the African American community. Its eviction from the Loop left the play itself, like the Mason family it represents, first in a tentative South Side home, and then homeless. This concern about home is also reflected in Fraden's reading of the ways that audiences interpreted the play as a representation of an urban, African American family. She focuses on African American community leaders, who were offended by the idea that the Masons were a typical Black family. A representative of the NAACP, for instance, was "preoccupied with how the play would be interpreted by the white community" and argued that the play emphasized "the worst phases of Negro life" (126). He thought it would be more appropriate to stage positive or "uplifting" representations of the African American community.[41]

In this way, Black audiences evaluated *Big White Fog* both on its merits as a theatrical text and on the "authenticity" of its representation of the Black community. As Fraden notes, much of the debate was over what the play was attempting to represent. Production designers wondered "whether this family was primarily constituted by their difference from or similarity to white families of the same class."[42] Furthermore, it was not clear whether the play was depicting a Black family or "the whole Negro race," "the essence of all Negro homes" (124). Hal Kopel, the set designer, wanted "to distinguish blacks from whites by talking about the whole Negro race and yet at the same time to insist that one race is not *really* different from another" (125). This was complicated by a desire on the part of middle-class Blacks to avoid "being lumped into what they considered a 'typical' portrait of the African American citizen, especially one that depicted them as losers and second-class citizens" (125). There was a question of identity and also of self-presentation. Black leaders, who were working toward greater rights and freedoms, did not want to showcase a struggling Black family for white audiences in fear that it could compromise their efforts, a concern that contributed to the play's premature closure in the Loop (126). All of this debate centered on the appearance, and the meaning, of the Black family home, a space that was viewed as threatening to whiteness and devalued by segregation.

This, then, is the best explanation for the play's short run on the South Side. The representation of Black domestic space mattered when it was being displayed for mixed audiences outside of the Black Belt. As Fraden argues, the Black "audience was not attracted to the idea of a separate theater; they *wanted* to go downtown and sit with an interracial audience" (133). Based on my reading of the play and its historical context, this seems like an obvious point. The African American community, which was segregated in the Black Belt on the South Side, was looking for opportunities to push against those boundaries. They wanted a reason to go downtown. Although only temporarily, the Mason family had the opportunity to "live" outside of the Black Belt, an opportunity that was denied the community they were meant to represent. When displaced from the Great Northern and relocated to the "makeshift" space of the DuSable High School auditorium, the production no longer served this purpose. Life in Chicago's Black Belt was often makeshift enough, leaving audiences looking for ways out. It is possible, then, to read in this theatrical migration a kind of spatial liberation—one that was fleeting, but that suggested the possibility of escaping the geography of segregation. If this is the case, it is not surprising that there was an enthusiastic audience for the play at the Great Northern Theatre, but not on Chicago's South Side.

Notes

Epigraph: Theodore Ward, *Big White Fog*, in *Black Theater, U.S.A.: Forty-Five Plays by Black Americans, 1847–1974*, ed. James V. Hatch (New York: Free Press, 1974), 283.

1. Marcus Garvey (1887–1940) was the controversial leader of a Black separatist movement that advocated a return to Africa. For a detailed biography, see Colin Grant, *Negro with a Hat: The Rise and Fall of Marcus Garvey* (New York: Oxford University Press, 2008).
2. Ward, *Big White Fog*, 292.
3. James V. Hatch, ed., *Black Theater, U.S.A.: Forty-Five Plays by Black Americans, 1847–1974* (New York: Free Press, 1974).
4. Rena Fraden, *Blueprints for a Black Federal Theatre, 1935–1939* (Cambridge: Cambridge University Press, 1996), 120.
5. Ward, *Big White Fog*, 181.
6. Alferdteen Harrison, ed., *Black Exodus: The Great Migration from the American South* (Jackson: University Press of Mississippi, 1991), vii.
7. Roger Biles, "Race and Housing in Chicago," *Journal of the Illinois State Historical Society* 94, no. 1 (2001): 32.
8. Davarian L. Baldwin, *Chicago's New Negroes: Modernity, the Great Migration, and Black Urban Life* (Chapel Hill: University of North Carolina Press, 2007), 14.
9. Biles, "Race and Housing in Chicago," 32.
10. Robert G. Spinney, *City of Big Shoulders: A History of Chicago* (DeKalb: Northern Illinois University Press, 2000), 168.
11. Mitchell Duneier, *Ghetto: The Invention of a Place, the History of an Idea* (New York: Farrar, Straus and Giroux, 2016). Mitchell Duneier provides an important contribution to this literature, tracing the origins of the term "ghetto" to the Jewish quarters of the European cities of the sixteenth century, connecting this history to its current usage, and arguing for the enduring value of the concept in explaining segregation and spatial discrimination.
12. Biles, "Race and Housing in Chicago," 32.
13. St. Clair Drake and Horace R. Cayton, *Black Metropolis: A Study of Negro Life in a Northern City*, rev. ed. (Chicago: University of Chicago Press, 1993), 176.

14. Biles, "Race and Housing in Chicago," 31–32.

15. Drake and Cayton, *Black Metropolis*, 176.

16. Ward, *Big White Fog*, 283.

17. Drake and Cayton, *Black Metropolis*, 178.

18. "CPI Inflation Calculator," Bureau of Labor Statistics, United States Department of Labor, accessed March 27, 2019, https://www.bls.gov/data/inflation_calculator.htm.

19. Drake and Cayton, *Black Metropolis*, 179.

20. Wendy Plotkin, "'Hemmed In': The Struggle against Racial Restrictive Covenants and Deed Restrictions in Post-WWII Chicago," *Journal of the Illinois State Historical Society* 94, no. 1 (2001): 39.

21. Ward, *Big White Fog*, 288.

22. Una Chaudhuri, *Staging Place: The Geography of Modern Drama* (Ann Arbor: University of Michigan Press, 1995), 10.

23. Fraden, *Blueprints for a Black Federal Theatre*, 91.

24. This is the well-known U.S. Supreme Court case in which the playwright Lorraine Hansberry's father mounted a legal challenge to restrictive racial covenants; it served as inspiration for *A Raisin in the Sun*.

25. GerShun Avilez, "Housing the Black Body: Value, Domestic Space, and Segregation Narratives," *African American Review* 42, no. 1 (2008): 136.

26. Ward, *Big White Fog*, 318.

27. Avilez, "Housing the Black Body," 136.

28. Ward, *Big White Fog*, 286.

29. Fraden, *Blueprints for a Black Federal Theatre*, 116.

30. Bill V. Mullen, *Popular Fronts: Chicago and African American Cultural Politics, 1935–46* (Urbana: University of Illinois Press, 1999), 16.

31. Fraden, *Blueprints for a Black Federal Theatre*, 111.

32. John Frick, "A Changing Theater: New York and Beyond" in *The Cambridge History of American Theater: Volume II, 1870–1945*, eds. Don B. Wilmeth and Christopher Bigsby (Cambridge: Cambridge University Press, 1999), 224.

33. Fraden, *Blueprints for a Black Federal Theatre*, 4.

34. Konrad Schiecke, *Downtown Chicago's Historic Movie Theatres* (Jefferson, NC: McFarland, 2011), 72.

35. The Great Northern Theatre closed in 1959 and was demolished in 1961. The location is currently occupied by the Dirksen Federal Building.

36. Fraden, *Blueprints for a Black Federal Theatre*, 128.

37. Charles Collins, "Drama Depicts Family Life of Chicago Negro: 'Big White Fog,'" *Chicago Daily Tribune*, April 8, 1938, 16.

38. Melissa Barton, "'Speaking a Mutual Language': The Negro People's Theatre in Chicago," *TDR: The Drama Review* 54, no. 3 (2010): 57.

39. "Landmark Designation Report: DuSable High School," City of Chicago Commission on Chicago Landmarks, accessed September 29, 2018, http://www.cityofchicago.org/content/dam/city/depts/dcd/Zoning%20Application/ExhibADuSablFinalReport.pdf, 9–10.

40. Fraden, *Blueprints for a Black Federal Theatre*, 131.

41. Debates about the purpose of Black art and the extent to which it should work to improve the lives of African Americans were a regular feature of intellectual and political life in this period, exemplified by the dialogue between Alain Locke and W. E. B. Du Bois. In this case, Du Bois's belief that art should uplift the community carried much weight in discussions of whether or where *Big White Fog* should be produced. For a history of the discourse of community uplift, see, for example, Kevin K. Gaines, *Uplifting the Race: Black Leadership, Politics, and Culture in the Twentieth Century*, 2nd ed. (Chapel Hill: University of North Carolina Press, 1996).

42. Fraden, *Blueprints for a Black Federal Theatre*, 124.

6

Lincoln Avenue and the Off-Loop Scene

Urban Renewal and the Early Years of the Chicago Storefront Movement

Cat Gleason

Theater has blossomed in spaces outside the city's commercial center throughout Chicago's history. Yet it was not until 1969, when the Body Politic Theatre and the Kingston Mines Theatre opened on the Near North Side, that the term "Off-Loop" became associated with Chicago's homegrown, noncommercial, and independent theater. Soon after those spaces opened, journalists declared Lincoln Avenue a new hotspot for theater, heralding a growing Off-Loop arts and counterculture scene. The founders of the Body Politic Theatre and the Kingston Mines Theatre built on this, carefully positioning themselves as "Off-Loop" theaters—oppositional, independent, and experimental sites operating outside Chicago's downtown theater district.[1] Many historians and practitioners of Chicago theater trace the roots of Chicago's contemporary theatrical legacy to the late 1960s and early 1970s at the Body Politic Theatre and the Kingston Mines Theatre on Lincoln Avenue.[2] Indeed, the dust jacket of the only published narrative that covers Chicago theater from its first performances in the mid-nineteenth century to the twenty-first century, Richard Christiansen's *A Theatre of Our Own*, sports a photograph of the 1969 production of *The Serpent* at the Kingston Mines Theatre. Here Christiansen metonymically substitutes the artistic production of a Lincoln Avenue theater for the whole of

Chicago theater activity from its very inception.[3] Furthermore, many theater companies that currently make up the core of Chicago's mainstream theater practitioners gesture toward ideas of authenticity and homegrown-ness by claiming origins as Off-Loop, marginal, or grassroots theaters.[4]

The Kingston Mines Theatre company members and artistic director June Pyskacek created a theater space from a former trolley barn on the 2300 block of Lincoln Avenue.[5] Voluminous and drafty, the space had a large open floor well suited for changing stage configurations on a whim, with benches and carpet pieces defining the stage. The Kingston Mines Theatre housed just one theater space and resident company, but they also played host to other companies in their later years.[6] A block south, the Reverend James Shiflett and the other founders of the Body Politic Theatre found a two-story property with four storefronts. The first floor held a bar and a slicing machine company, and upstairs a bowling alley traversed all four storefronts.[7] The Body Politic Theatre folks transformed the building, fashioning three theaters (only two at their opening), a rehearsal room, and offices out of the space.[8] In the fall of 1969 the press heralded the opening of the two venues, and the combination of positive critical responses and early box office successes helped brand the work of these Lincoln Avenue theater artists as new, energetic, and Off-Loop.

From the vantage point of fifty years later, Chicago's early Off-Loop theater is vital and influential, yet the research reveals an origin story intertwined with societal and cultural forces outside the theater community. The buildings that housed these venues had been slated for clearance by the City of Chicago in the *Lincoln Park General Renewal Plan* released to the public in 1963.[9] This plan, developed jointly between the City of Chicago's Department of Urban Development and a local homeowners association, the Lincoln Park Conservation Association, sought to transform Lincoln Park from a neighborhood spotted with low-income, dilapidated housing into a middle-class community with stable home values.[10] Driven by civic economic imperatives and racial bias, urban renewal as a federal and local practice in Chicago included a fraught history of wholesale land clearance and the displacement of low-income and minority communities.[11] Lincoln Park housed people of diverse income levels and cultural backgrounds, all of whom had different relationships with the idea of urban renewal as well as differing ideas about community and home.[12]

Furthermore, by 1969, the Old Town counterculture scene located in the southeastern sector of the Lincoln Park area had spread north and west to the blocks surrounding the two new theater venues.[13] This shift brought increased political activity into the area, along with a host of cultural and social performances designed to change the nature of the neighborhood. Finally, local churches, as a part of an overall thrust in ecumenical urban outreach, designed social programs that used the arts to create a more stable and spiritual community.[14] These competing, complex, and complementary social performances, engaged in improving the material and cultural environment, fostered the growth of the Lincoln Park neighborhood. The influence of all these diverse entities played an important role in the actual and figurative beginnings of Chicago's Off-Loop theater movement.

The micropolitics of neighborhoods and the way social conditions foster arts and activist organizations demonstrate that although origin myths often smooth over the many-faceted realities of how theaters and theater communities come to be, the story can be told in a way that accounts for more variables. Gilles Deleuze and Félix Guattari's ideas in *A Thousand Plateaus*—about how human systems work rhizomatically rather than in neat phylogenic pathways—support an argument that entertains the validity of historical narratives tracing transverse connections between social constructs such as the political environment, cultural mores about art and activism, and the changing built environment, suggesting an "anti-genealogy" instead of neat family trees with clear causal lines of descent.[15] Furthermore, as Sue Ellen Case reminds us in her critique of narrativity, history can be told from multiple perspectives—beginning and ending in many loci and resisting the reductive forces of origin narratives by including "contiguities, microstrategies, and heterogeneous agents."[16] This sort of inquiry leads to the assertion that the histories of these two theaters are profoundly intertwined with issues of race, inequality, and the urban renewal of the Lincoln Park neighborhood. Because of the social and cultural forces at work in Lincoln Park in the late 1960s, and the Body Politic and the Kingston Mines Theatres' ability to position themselves between the forces of urban renewal and community resistance, they came through a turbulent period by assisting in the change of Chicago's strict fire codes while setting a new standard for what would become known as Off-Loop theater—reclaimed adapted spaces, new and experimental work, and audiences drawn from around the city.

Starting the Lincoln Avenue Theater Scene

Before the opening of the Body Politic Theatre and the Kingston Mines Theatre, June Pyskacek, Paul Sills, and James Shiflett, the practitioners who founded the theaters housed in the Body Politic Theatre and the Kingston Mines Theatre, were all a part of an ecumenical arts outreach program at the Wellington Avenue Church. The Wellington Avenue Church had joined with several urban ecumenical organizations in Chicago committed to addressing urban ethnic, housing, and civil rights issues. Furthermore, they sponsored a drama program as a part of this urban mission to "humanize the city."[17] The Chicago City Players, a group of variously trained and untrained actors and directors (including associate director Pyskacek), produced theater in the church complex's Baird Hall. Meanwhile, Reverend Shiflett started the Community Arts Foundation as an arts outreach organization for the Chicago City Missionary Society. In 1965 the leadership of the Wellington Avenue Church brought in the Community Arts Foundation to manage their drama programs, with Shiflett and Sills thereby joining Pyskacek. Shiflett and Sills never intended to stay at the Wellington Avenue Church; their intent was to find a new space of their own for their various art programs. Their exodus would spur Pyskacek's, and she would leave the Chicago City Players to form the Kingston Mines Theatre in 1969.

The three founders brought a variety of skills and experience to Lincoln Avenue to start the Off-Loop theater community. Paul Sills, who had learned Chicago-style improvisation at the knee of his mother, Viola Spolin, and honed his directing skills in Old Town at the Playwrights Theatre Club (1953–1955),[18] came to the Body Politic Theatre fresh from starting the hugely successful Second City improv company and after turning down an offer to run a cabaret at the Yale School of Drama.[19] Shiflett, who had met Sills in Sills's Theatre Games classes, brought organizational skills and a set of valuable neighborhood connections. Pyskacek brought her training from the Goodman School of Drama and experience from directing happenings and new plays in the Chicago area, as well as a knack for networking and a penchant for the experimental that more than once garnered the Kingston Mines Theatre the opportunity to offer Chicago premieres of important Off Off Broadway plays.[20]

Pyskacek's move from the Wellington Avenue Church complex was abrupt and prompted by Sills and Shiflett's move to their new space.

According to Pyskacek, she procured a grant from the National Endowment for the Arts for a production she planned to direct for the Chicago City Players. She invited Shiflett and Sills to her home to discuss the use of the funds, but they told her that the money would be better spent supporting Sills and Shiflett's new community arts center project.[21] Pyskacek does not hold a grudge about this choice but said that when it happened, she felt betrayed.[22] Nevertheless, she immediately moved on to her own project. While rehearsing Jean-Claude van Itallie's *The Serpent* in a borrowed space, she heard from a friend about an old trolley barn on Lincoln Avenue available to rent.[23] She had just been paid for a summer class, so she used the money to convert the space at 2356 North Lincoln Avenue into a theater space and adjoining coffee shop. Likely vacant since the late 1950s, when the City of Chicago discontinued trolley service on city streets,[24] the whitewashed brick building held a capacious single space that the company used well. Larry Hart, one of the original members of the company, recalls the space:

> It was an incredible space. It was a cement ground floor with two big sliding barn doors that opened out on the alley. There was no ceiling for three stories. . . . We didn't have any seating; we had these big iron pilings for people to sit on and carpet pieces on the cement floor . . . just a big open space.[25]

Although the space worked well for the cutting-edge productions the Kingston Mines Theatre favored, no one would call this converted building a renewed or even a rehabilitated theater—although critics were quick to comment on its cleanliness. For four years, Pyskacek and her group of artists brought folks to Lincoln Avenue for new plays and Chicago interpretations of new imports from Off Off Broadway.[26]

Pyskacek's New York connections allowed her to produce not only *The Serpent* within a year of its premiere in Europe, but also Megan Terry's *The People vs. Ranchman* and Maria Irene Fornes's *Promenade*, with Fornes coming to Chicago to work with the company.[27] Critic Marilynn Preston said the Kingston Mines Theatre was "building a wide following by presenting some of the best contemporary authors and established experimental shows that needed doing and weren't being done [in Chicago]."[28] With a scenic design by Rick Paul, their 1969 production of *The Serpent* featured a giant psychedelic backdrop painted in a batik-like floral pattern that seemed to reach up at least two stories. The audience sat on carpet squares on three sides of the carpeted playing space while pendant lights hung from above and a lighting tree supplied front light. Actors wore solid-colored daily wear—jeans, T-shirts, and sheath dresses—as they performed "The Doctor," an early scene where a woman is held up by three actors in a supine position as if for an autopsy.[29] Since *The Serpent* relied on the physicality of the actors to communicate the story, this choice of an open playing space made sense, yet the selection of this play as the Kingston Mines Theatre's first may have also reflected the tight funds of a new company. By the time they produced *The People vs. Ranchman* the next summer, they committed to a much more significant design that made good use of the space. The space was doomed from the start, however, because the city and the local neighborhood association had agreed to cede this land to the hospital across the street prior to Pyskacek's residency.

One block south and in the same fall that Pyskacek opened the Kingston Mines Theatre, Sills and Shiflett secured a two-story, twenty-thousand-square-foot property at 2257–63 North Lincoln Avenue[30] for their new community arts center run by the Community Arts Foundation. The first floor housed the U.S. Slicing Machine Company and Oxford's Pub, and the Monte Carlo Bowling Alley occupied the second floor. The Community Arts Foundation convinced an anonymous board member to sign for an $80,000 loan, and the organization purchased the building.[31] The Community Arts Foundation planned to run a variety of arts programs from converted second-floor office space and use the rest of the building to create theaters to rent.[32] Sills and Shiflett carved three theaters out of the space: the 150-seat first-floor Center Theatre, the 200-seat Upstairs Theatre, and the 75-seat Little Theatre.[33] The ceilings in all of the spaces were very low—only about ten and a half feet to the lighting grid—making it hard to light the stages and to use platforming.[34] They only managed to convert the two larger theaters for their 1969 opening, and Paul Sills's Story Theater became the first-floor tenant with William Russo's Free Theatre renting part of the second floor, constituting the first generation of resident theaters in the Body Politic Theatre complex.

The first production at Body Politic Theatre was Story Theater's *Ovid's Metamorphoses: Love Lives of the Gods*, an evening of short stories derived from Ovid's classic text about the Roman gods. Performed in the style of "story theater," a new form developed by Sills, it "adapt[ed] stories, fables and fairytales for adults."[35] Relying on pantomime, these plays tell stories accompanied by music but without a narrator, having the actors narrate while in character using a rapidly shifting cinematic style.[36] *Metamorphoses* lacked scenic elements and used actors' bodies and voices to create the environment, a unique physicality that relied on the idea of transformation developed in relationship to Viola Spolin's theater games.[37] Sills used Spolin's transformation exercises to develop a method of staging that transitioned seamlessly between location, character, and action. In the downstairs theater, several low risers supported the audience space surrounding the shallow thrust of the five-hundred-square-foot playing space bordered by three walls and a single upstage entrance.[38] William Leonard of the *Chicago Tribune* remarked, "The imagery is beautifully effective. Jove hurling thunderbolts . . . goddesses swimming underwater . . .—these and several other flights of fancy work stunningly in this technique."[39]

Lincoln Park Geography: Race, Blight, and Urban Renewal

In many ways, the story of urban renewal in Chicago is the story of Richard J. Daley's early years in the mayor's office. His election in 1955, during the height of the post-WWII housing and industry boom in the United States, positioned him at the forefront of what many considered a national crisis regarding the twin problems of urban blight and white flight threatening American cities economically. Moreover, the federally subsidized move of industry and workers to the suburbs left urban industrial areas abandoned. Over the course of his administration, Daley oversaw a flood of federal renewal money—clearing whole neighborhoods of low-income housing and building block after block of public housing. Consequently, this process of urban renewal, embroiled in issues of race and class, often polarized communities between the "haves" and "have-nots." In this struggle, Daley usually positioned himself as the leader of the "haves."[40] Over time, as racism forced many African Americans out of mixed neighborhoods and into public housing, the practice of "urban renewal" became known as "urban removal," or worse yet "Negro removal," and public housing became a wholly African American locus in the city of Chicago.[41]

During the mid-century, Americans renamed the "slums" of the early part of the twentieth century as "blight." Urban leaders and city planners applied this metaphor to the problems found in the low-income areas of the inner city: failed or evacuated business areas, aging housing stock, overcrowded conditions, poverty, and a general lack of order. This disease metaphor highlighted a strategy of removal for the purpose of halting contagion.[42] Moreover, juxtaposing the idea of "white flight" with blight corresponds to the Western ideology of correlating white with purity and desirability and darkness with death, disease, and contamination.[43] In this way, white flight signified the need for "healthy" white people to leave the diseased, unhealthy, and racially "dark" city. Consequently, this set of metaphors could mask common knowledge about the "causes" of blight without naming the racial biases that caused white flight. Social performances of civic boosterism were thereby untainted by charges of racism when renewal programs were perceived as simply battling "blight."

Because of the negative connotations attached to the word "renewal," "conservation" became the new watchword of the continued fight against blight. The 1953 federal Community Conservation Act exemplified this thrust by strengthening cities' power of eminent domain, and as Roger Biles reports in his text, this spurred on Chicago's Land Clearance Commission to assemble the nation's most ambitious set of urban renewal plans (13). Through the establishment of "conservation areas," cities could use strategic zoning laws and selective enforcement to force the sale of properties to the city and bring about an "unprecedented opportunity to rebuild major parts of the city."[44]

By 1969, most individuals in Lincoln Park had joined one or more neighborhood groups organized by ideological, economic, racial, or ethnic affiliation in order to shape or change the course of renewal in the neighborhood.[45] These groups aligned with geographies in the neighborhood. For example, lying in the south-to-southwest section of the neighborhood, and just to the west of the Old Town Triangle, the African American section of the Lincoln Park community barely had a toehold into the neighborhood. Michael Ducey points out in his study that the first of the Lincoln Park homeowners' associations, the Old Town Triangle Association, was likely formed in 1948 to push back against the threat of the overcrowded and encroaching Black community just south of the neighborhood.[46] The rest of the neighborhood was divided among several ethnicities. In Lincoln Park, there was notable overlap and mingling between the different white communities, and, to some degree, with the Puerto Rican population, but the Black population lived exclusively in the southwest sector in nearly complete segregation. Puerto Ricans in Lincoln Park occupied a figuratively and literally liminal space between the Black and white

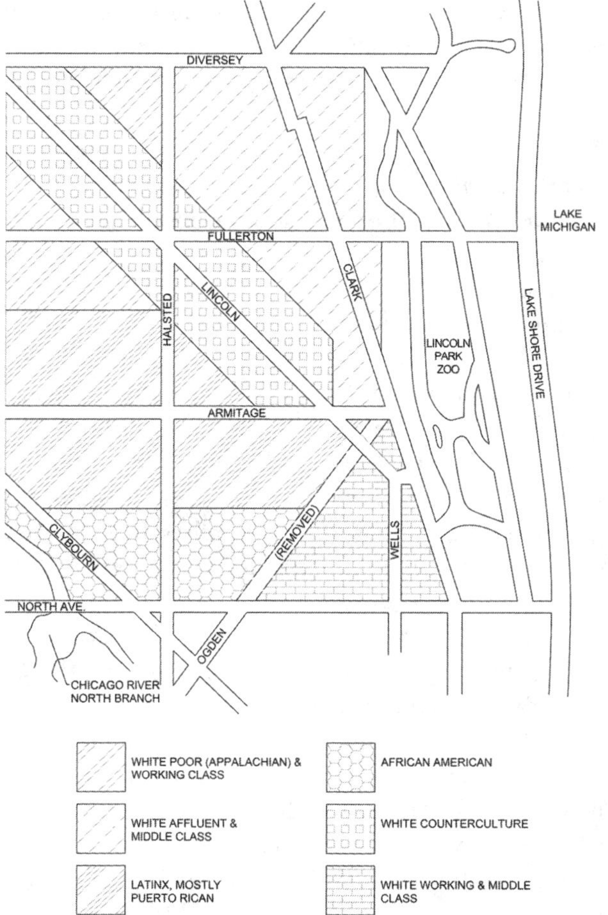

Ethnic and racial divisions within the Lincoln Park neighborhood, circa 1965–1970. Map by Brad M. Carlson. Sources: Adapted from information and maps in Paula Angle, *City in a Garden: Homes in the Lincoln Park Community* (Chicago: Lincoln Park Conservation Association, 1963), front matter; James J. Dalton, "The Politics of Community," 70–73; Michael H. Ducey, *Sunday Morning: Aspects of Urban Ritual*, 14–24; and Ana Y. Ramos-Zayas, *National Performances*, 48.

communities. Concentrated in the southwestern sector of the neighborhood just north of the African American community, Puerto Ricans mixed with the African American community as well as with the poorer sections of the white community.[47]

The majority of Lincoln Park's population was white, with only 1.5 percent African American and 3.2 percent "other races."[48] The white population can be divided into three groups based on income, political tendencies, and geography. Poor and working-class whites lived north and west in conditions much like the poor Blacks and Puerto Ricans—ramshackle wood-frame tenements that were overcrowded and poorly maintained.[49] Affluent whites lived in new and old high-rises and overlapped into the more moderate-income areas of Old Town. Today, we would call this final group "liberal whites." Concentrated in the area of Old Town within the Lincoln Park community, but also sprinkled about in the other white areas of Lincoln Park, these middle-class, white-collar workers and professionals with families lived in rehabilitated two-flats or single-family homes. The city's urban renewal plans benefited this demographic group most as the focus of conservation plans.

In late 1950s and 1960s, the two blocks where the two theaters would make their homes appeared to be part of the problem. The 2200 block of Lincoln alternated between bars, light industry, old residences, abandoned storefronts, and a hardware store. A block north, the trolley barn that would become the Kingston Mines Theatre stood empty across from Children's Memorial Hospital. Consequently, the 1963 *Lincoln Park General Renewal Plan* marked the 2200 and 2300 blocks of Lincoln Avenue as blighted and in need of renewal. As a part of the plan, the city planned closure of a portion of Lincoln Avenue to create a pedestrian mall.[50] Called a "conservation" project from its inception, the Lincoln Park project was a model of the city working closely with neighborhood organizations. This cooperative method did not preclude the objections of community members, but it did make it harder for community activists to fight the city because their neighbors had worked with the city to make the plan. By 1966, the first stage of the project was moving forward, and the city was buying and clearing land throughout the project area.

As the reality of the plan set in and the city started relocating residents, people began to protest what they saw as the destruction of their neighborhood.[51] Soon it became clear that displaced people did not return. As the project moved forward, residents saw the Lincoln Park Conservation Association less as a citizen organization and more as a cover for the city and landowners to achieve the removal of low-income people from Lincoln Park. Authors such as Michael H. Ducey and James J. Dalton remember the deep wounds in the community marked by the empty lots or block after block of clearance on both sides of a street. Activists in the neighborhood demanded that the destruction and removal stop.

In a series of public meetings regarding the renewal plan in 1969 (the same year the two theaters opened), proceedings were often disrupted by protesters and sometimes devolved into altercations. The dual goals of diversity and democracy rather than a "nice neighborhood" drove the work of the many dissenting neighborhood organizations. Groups such as the Neighborhood Commons Corporation, Concerned Citizens Survival Front, North Side Cooperative Ministry, Young Lords Organization, Young Patriots, Welfare Working Mothers of Wicker Park, and Black, Active, and Determined banded together in a Poor People's Coalition and worked together to fight for a voice in the change happening in their neighborhood.[52] These groups and the Body Politic Theatre's parent ecumenical organization felt that diversity should be celebrated and not "managed."

By the time the Body Politic Theatre and the Kingston Mines Theatre opened in the fall of 1969, they were joining a stretch of Lincoln Avenue already transforming into an arts and counterculture scene. A dance company and several local artists had taken up residence in several storefronts along the block. Across the street from the Body Politic Theatre, the Wise Fools Pub opened their doors for jazz and blues entertainment, and the Bakery offered fine dining.[53] In the years that followed, with the transformation of one square block of razed housing into a public park (Oz Park) and the completion of construction of other clearance areas, most of the community started to view the 2200 and 2300 blocks of Lincoln Avenue as an asset.

Shiflett, through his work as the director of the Community Arts Foundation, and Sills, as a board member of the North Side Cooperative Ministry, an ecumenical umbrella renewal organization of which Community Arts Foundation was a member, positioned themselves between the establishment powers and the oppositional community groups in the Lincoln Park community. They included in their early plans an intent to work closely with the Mayor's Commission on Economic and Cultural Development as well as other established local educational arts organizations, demonstrating their willingness to work within the structure of the establishment.[54] As early as 1965, Community Arts

Foundation documents claim both the city's urban renewal program and the existing programs of the North Side Cooperative Ministry as assets in their developing arts center program in Lincoln Park. On the other hand, Community Arts Foundation organizers also stated, "We have healthy contact with a segment of the Black militants from the near north community and they are sympathetic to our program,"[55] indicating the Community Arts Foundation's alignment with radical social justice organizations such as the Black Panther Party or Black, Active, and Determined. Moreover, Chicago police arrested Shiflett when he refused to comply with an ordinance about showing films, which he celebrated in the Community Arts Foundation's newsletter, demonstrating his—and by extension the Community Arts Foundation's—ease with Shiflett ending up on the "wrong side of the law."[56] Thus, Shiflett presented his organization as a grassroots or community organization with strong connections to the many disparate factions in the Lincoln Park community.

Activist organizations who fought for a diverse housing landscape won many battles, but they lost the war as Lincoln Park continued to change. The success of this economic upswing is in part because of the success of these two theaters. Lincoln Park became a more attractive place to live for middle-class white people, and although the process took a long time, Lincoln Park became a premier location for young urban professionals to settle by the 1980s. Managing the linkage between arts development and urban renewal has always been challenging, and those that started these companies found this relationship fraught with ideological and financial challenges.

Lincoln Avenue Theater—Beyond the First Year

Within the first year of the Body Politic Theatre's existence, Sills left for New York with his Story Theater, and Russo's Free Theatre moved on to their own space. Shiflett's Dream Theater, and a new company led by director Stuart Gordon, the Organic Theater, together initiated the next generation of Body Politic Theatre theaters. Dream Theatre used Story Theater techniques of merging the role of narrator and actor to present dreams as dramatic events. They used the newly completed downstairs studio space, the Little Theatre, which was the closest to a true storefront space in the building with its long narrow room, bench seating, and a tiny stage filling the east end of the space. Their first performance used minimal scenic elements such as small platforms on casters and abstract projected backdrops. They completed the environment with lighting used to create visual separation and live music.[57] The Organic started with communally authored adaptations of well-known texts like *The Odyssey* and *Candide*.[58]

In 1971 the Organic opened *Warp!* in the downstairs Center Theatre. Penned by Bury St. Edmund and Gordon, this eventual trilogy of comic-book-style sci-fi adventures ran in sold-out rep for a full year and could have run longer.[59] *Warp!* strove to achieve a complete sci-fi world using "traditional theatre tools: lighting, smoke and costuming, with a few large operating props and set pieces." Ralph Willingham argued that *Warp!*'s success depended on its "playful spirit" in the "execution of audience collaboration in theatrical illusion."[60] For example, in episode three, there was a clever use of puppets and a dragon arm that helped the audience believe that two of the characters had been chased by a giant dragon.

The Organic transferred the show to New York in 1973, but it failed there, which illustrates the importance of these converted spaces in the Chicago theater community. The Organic originally intended to bring *Warp!* to an Off Broadway theater, but as there was not an available space, they moved into the 1100-seat Ambassador Theatre. *Warp!*'s kitsch and humor were scaled for the cramped quarters and intimacy of the downstairs theater in the Body Politic Theatre, which didn't read in the Ambassador.[61] Further, Terry Curtis Fox argues that their Broadway budget had caused them to trade wine-opener ray guns for "real" ones, and the absurd nuance of *Warp!* disappeared, causing the show to lose its charm.[62]

For the theaters on Lincoln Avenue, 1971 was a banner year, with *Warp*! changing the Body Politic Theatre's fortunes and a new show at Kingston Mines Theatre. Pyskacek's company was enjoying moderate success with its early experimental Off Off Broadway imports, but they also decided to take a chance on a production that did not fit their usual style. Company members Jim Jacobs and Warren Casey came up with an idea for a 1950s musical titled *Grease*, which would become the Kingston Mines Theatre's biggest success, even while it was an anomaly in their repertory. Based on Jacobs's time at Taft High School on the Northwest Side, this rock 'n' roll musical brought audiences from all over the city and the suburbs to Lincoln Avenue for nine months.[63]

In contrast to *Warp!*'s ill-fated New York transfer, *Grease* would triumph on Broadway, becoming the longest-running Broadway musical of its time. The Kingston Mines Theatre folks did not bring *Grease* to Broadway; it was optioned by a pair of Broadway producers who added songs, dance, and commercial "polish." Thus, it lost its Chicago authenticity and grit. This caused Gary Houston (one of the original cast members) to write a scathing article at the advent of *Grease's* "triumphant" return to Chicago from New York City, though the production still ran thirty-three weeks in the Loop. He points out that the original production did not lack polish because the Chicago actors were incapable of it, but because they were purposefully trying to capture an era that they saw as awkward and tacky.[64]

Lincoln Avenue Fights City Hall

Despite these successes and Shiflett's efforts to position the Body Politic Theatre as an ally to all parts of the Lincoln Park community, the Lincoln Avenue theaters, especially the Body Politic Theatre, often found themselves in adversarial relationships with the city, the police, and their neighbors. Start-up Chicago theaters often ran afoul of the law and struggled to keep their doors open in the face of regular shutdowns due to strict fire and building codes. The legacy of the Great Chicago Fire of 1871 and a fire where 602 people died at the Iroquois Theater in 1903 ensured that Chicago's fire and building ordinances for theaters were the strictest in the country.[65] Ironically, Chicago's codes prior to the Iroquois fire were already strict; unfortunately, they were not followed. According to Nat Brandt's *Death Trap: The Iroquois Fire of 1903*, even though sprinklers were a part of code at the time, not one theater in Chicago had installed one. Moreover, only one of the many fire regulations was followed in the newly opened Iroquois Theater. The primary change following the fire was that inspections were more likely to happen and be enforced.[66]

Chicago's building and fire code challenged start-up theater companies because they were written for large proscenium houses, often applying to auditoriums that could hold a thousand or more patrons.[67] For theater artists in the latter half of the twentieth century converting spaces that would seat fewer than two hundred people in flexible configurations, the law rarely applied in a reasonable or cost-effective way. For example, according to the ordinances adjusted after the Iroquois fire, "legal theatres" maintained a proscenium stage with "hydraulic fire curtains fed by twenty-six-inch water pipes."[68] In other words, this law required the ability to separate completely the audience from the stage in seconds using an expensive fire curtain system. Hence, noncommercial theaters with limited resources constantly fought to remain open in the face of inspection. Because small theaters found this investment impossible or impractical, most early companies did what they could to avoid notice by local political bosses and police. Residents of Chicago were long aware of corruption in city management and took pride in understanding the "rules" of doing business; Chicagoans understood that city inspectors needed to be bought.[69] If theater companies could not afford the bribes or refused to pay, they found themselves in a battle with the city administration.

Small theaters who followed the "rules" still might find themselves closing their doors in the face of code violations. For example, even though the Playwrights Theatre Club in Old Town, a self-described group of "beatniks" who produced socially conscious plays such as Brecht's *Caucasian Chalk Circle*, followed the "rules" and greased the palms of sanitation, ventilation, and electrical inspectors, the city closed their theater in 1955 due to fire code violations. They protested in the courts, trying to get the ordinance amended, but the newly elected mayor, Richard J. Daley, did not see fit to get behind a change in the law.[70] This sort of city response was representative of the sort of struggles low-budget artists faced.

Because of the Body Politic Theatre's and the Kingston Mines Theatre's roles in changing in the code, they are considered important in the origin of the Off-Loop theater movement.[71] According to Shiflett, between 1970 and 1973 the Body Politic Theatre consistently fought to stay open. If neighbors complained about 6:00 a.m. trash pickups at the theater, the city inspectors would come running, handing out multiple citations and code violations.[72] At the heart of the Body Politic Theatre's battle with the city stood its insistence that the Body Politic Theatre was a community center, not a theater. Bringing the Body Politic Theatre up to code would take $500,000. After appeal, the zoning board ruled against the Body Politic Theatre in 1971.[73] In 1972, theater critic and advocate of Off-Loop theater Glenna Syse wrote an open letter to the city, published in the *Chicago Sun-Times*, that advocated for the easing of city ordinances. Syse argued that zoning disputes and harassment of theater companies by city inspectors threatened the existence of companies and called for "reasonable flexibility in official attitudes."[74]

Many other newspapers and critics picked up the story, and the lore about the Off-Loop theater's fight with Chicago's "boss" eventually grew to legendary status.[75] News reports of the time state that the mayor called Reverend Jim Shiflett of the Body Politic Theatre and other community theater leaders to his office in late 1973 to discuss the issue. Following the impassioned pleas of the spokespeople, Daley announced, "If these people can make their theaters safe, I want a solution found to the problem."[76] Because of the efforts of the Lincoln Avenue theaters, the city created a new code category named "theatrical community centers."[77] Shiflett and others, with the aid of the media, had made it possible for small theaters to continue operation and the scope of Off-Loop theater to expand. However, small theaters and the city government remained at loggerheads in some cases. Indeed, the same news report that reported the theaters' victories estimated the Kingston Mines Theatre would have to raise $300,000 to meet even the relaxed code, forcing them to close their doors in 1973.

Defining Chicago's Off-Loop Theater

Half a century later, early Off-Loop theater looms large in the city's theater history, but the theater critics of the time struggled to define the nature of the artistic product on Lincoln Avenue while these theaters were in their infancy. These critics found the issue of amateurism a part of this confusion. The same plays and companies would show up in the same newspaper listed in two different event calendars. The *Chicago Tribune* lists "Swinging Things This Weekend," which included professional opera, the Chicago Symphony Orchestra, and a touring show at the Blackstone Theatre staring Hume Cronin along with the Body Politic Theatre's and Kingston Mines Theatre's first performances of their opening seasons: Paul Sills's Story Theater *Metamorphoses* and *The Serpent*, respectively. One month later, the *Chicago Tribune* included the Story Theater production under a listing of "Neighborhood Performances," which included myriad community theater productions from such organizations as the Des Plaines Theatre Guild and the theater department of one of the two-year city colleges. This might have been because the people running the Body Politic Theatre and Kingston Mines Theatre were unabashed promoters (and the evidence suggests this). But in Chicago, where before 1969 there was no resident professional repertory,[78] and very few Equity houses, Chicago's thriving newspaper industry considered everything fair game for listing as worthwhile entertainment.[79]

Moreover, according to Kathleen Sills's study of Chicago theater in the 1950s and 1960s, critics and audiences had no category for independent small theater at that time. Commercial houses had touring shows, and churches, parks, and schools had community theater, but this new type of not-for profit company doing noncommercial theater was a rare animal. The Playwrights Theatre Club did it in the 1950s, as did the Hull-House Theatre under the direction of Bob Sickinger in the late 1950s and 1960s, but somehow audiences and news sources did not gain enough understanding of what "Off-Loop" theater might be until the so-called explosion of the 1970s.

Actors' Equity helped to resolve this confusion about Off-Loop theater as neither fish nor fowl. In 1971, Actors' Equity offered special consideration for the work being done in Chicago by creating—for the first time in any market—a special contract for Chicago companies. Named the Contract for Off-Loop Theatres (COLT), this tiered contract instituted flexibility regarding the size of house and the pay the actor would receive.[80] Hence, the national organization of actors recognized this special category of theaters in Chicago two years before the city changed the code to allow their legal operation and two years before the Chicago theater honors, the Joseph Jefferson Awards, recognized the work done in these theaters.

Lincoln Avenue Theater's Legacy

The complex story of Kingston Mines and Body Politic Theatres shows how Lincoln Park, once set on the trajectory of renewal, bypassed anyone's expectations. It is currently one of the most affluent neighborhoods in the city, with few (if any) properties that would be targeted by the neighborhood association for clearance.[81] Many of the anchor institutions have remained and thrived—DePaul University, Children's Memorial Hospital, and the public high school (then Waller, now Lincoln Park High School, one of the best in the city). Theater continues in Baird Hall at the Wellington Avenue Church, but Kingston Mines Theatre and Body Politic Theatre as producing organizations are gone. While the Kingston Mines Theatre closed its doors as a theater in 1973, the café space became one of the premiere blues clubs in Chicago and retained the name. The hospital across the street took possession of the lot to build a parking garage in 1982, and the blues club would remain in the neighborhood on Halsted Street.[82]

The story of the Body Politic Theatre building is much more complicated. Shiflett stayed on until 1979, when he passed on the leadership. The building went through a number of ownership changes including the Body Politic name leaving the building when the company folded in 1981.[83] The building's current occupant, the Greenhouse Theatre Center, operates as an incubator and rental spaces for many Chicago theater companies, continuing the spirit of the Body Politic Theatre through a "residency program, which offers a reduced rate to local storefront companies."[84] Theater continues to flourish on Lincoln Avenue with the Victory Gardens' conversion of the Biograph Theater to a multi-theater space, and in the neighborhood with Steppenwolf building their permanent home on Halsted and expanding it in 2019. Are these theaters Off-Loop? With the expansion of the Loop theater district and the many Broadway in Chicago offerings, they are certainly not Broadway-style houses, but they are established institutions, and you would have to go much farther from the Loop to find a theater that embodies that early Off-Loop spirit.

Notes

1. This chapter draws, in part, from my dissertation: Catherine H. Gleason, "Mapping the Lincoln Park Nexus: The Origin of the Chicago Off-Loop Theatre Movement" (PhD diss., University of Wisconsin, 2010).

2. See for example Richard Christiansen, *A Theatre of Our Own: A History and a Memoir of 1001 Nights in Chicago* (Evanston, IL: Northwestern University Press, 2004), 150–51, and Chris Jones, *Bigger, Brighter, Louder: 150 Years of Chicago Theatre as Seen by Chicago Theatre Tribune Critics* (Chicago: University of Chicago Press, 2013), 214–15. See also Stuart J. Hecht's work regarding Bob Sickinger's Hull-House Theatres of the early to mid-1960s that laid the groundwork for the Lincoln Avenue scene: Stuart J. Hecht, "Staging the Avant-Garde," *Chicago History*, Spring–Summer 17, nos. 1–2 (1988): 46–61.

3. Christiansen, *Theatre of Our Own*.

4. The most prominent of these would be The Second City and Steppenwolf. See "Over 50 Years of Funny," The Second City, accessed October 30, 2018, https://www.secondcity.com/history/, and "About Us," Steppenwolf, accessed October 30, 2018, https://www.steppenwolf.org/About-Us.

5. Chicago uses a grid system to number addresses, with each block increasing 100 in the cardinal directions. Lincoln Avenue is an angle

street, and like other North Side angle streets, it counts upward 100 each northward block.

6. In 1971, for example, Godzilla Rainbow Troupe brought their successful *Whores of Babylon* over from the Body Politic to continue their run as a late-night show alongside the Kingston Mines' regular shows. Godzilla Rainbow staged their next two shows at Kingston Mines. Finding Guide, Godzilla Rainbow Troupe, Chicago Theatre Collection, Harold Washington Library, Chicago. accessed May 19, 2019, https://www.chipublib.org/fa-godzilla-rainbow-troupe.

7. In my tours of the property, guides cannot help but point out the traces of the bowling alley that remain behind the seating and on the walls.

8. Community Arts Foundation, "History of the Community Arts Foundation," Body Politic Theatre Papers, box 1, folder 24, Chicago Theatre Collection, Harold Washington Library, Chicago.

9. Chicago Department of Urban Renewal, *Lincoln Park General Renewal Plan*, 1962, Municipal Collection, Harold Washington Library, Chicago.

10. For the purposes of this study, "Lincoln Park" will indicate the geographical area of the Lincoln Park Community Area, which also conforms to the neighborhood United States Census Tract. Additionally, it is useful to keep in mind that the phrase "Lincoln Park" can be used by Chicago natives to indicate an actual park adjoining the census tract, a smaller neighborhood within the census tract whose social boundaries have shifted over the years, as well as the entire area of the census tract. Amanda Seligman, "Community Areas," Electronic Encyclopedia of Chicago, Chicago Historical Society, 2005, date accessed July 4, 2010, http://www.encyclopedia.chicagohistory.org/pages/319.html.

11. See Jane Jacobs, *The Death and Life of Great American Cities* (New York: Random House, 1961), and P. J. Madgwick, "The Politics of Urban Renewal," *American Studies* 5, no. 3 (1971): 265–80 for contemporaneous critiques of urban renewal in the American context. See also Roger Biles, *Richard J. Daley: Politics, Race, and the Governing of Chicago* (DeKalb: Northern Illinois University Press, 1995), and Adam Cohen and Elizabeth Taylor, *American Pharaoh: Mayor Richard J. Daley, His Battle for Chicago and the Nation* (New York: Fast Back Bay, 2000), for the history of urban renewal in Chicago's political context.

12. See James J. Dalton, "The Politics of Community Problem Solving: The Lincoln Park Findings" (Chicago Regional Hospital Study, Working Paper, July 1971) Lincoln Park Conservation Association papers, Lincoln Park Neighborhood Collection, DePaul University Library Digital

Collection, accessed May 20, 2010; Michael H. Ducey, *Sunday Morning: Aspects of Urban Ritual* (New York: Free Press, 1977); and Daniel Kay Hertz, *The Battle of Lincoln Park* (Cleveland: Belt Publishing, 2018).

13. Chicago's counterculture of the late 1960s and early 1970s had three locations. One was on the South Side in the area near the University of Chicago. Another centered on the northernmost part of the city near Evanston and the campus of Northwestern University. The third was in the neighborhood of Old Town. This scene grew up in the 1910s around a center for free speech and radicalism known as Bughouse Square (a slang name for Washington Square Park) and the Dill Pickle Club (a bar and speakeasy) located in the southeast section of Old Town. "A Brief History of the Dill Pickle Club," *Frontier to Heartland*, a publication of the Newberry Library. https://publications.newberry.org/frontiertoheartland/exhibits/show/perspectives/dillpickle/briefhistory.

14. Nearly every religious organization in the area took part in the ecumenical and social justice outreach movement of the time. The Body Politic Theatre was started by the Community Arts Foundation, an ecumenical arts organization, and June Pyskacek also worked for that organization. For more on the religious aspects of this discussion not included here, see Gleason, "Mapping the Lincoln Park Nexus," chapter 2. See also Ducey, *Sunday Morning*, and Terry McCabe, "Onstage at the Creation: The Role of the Clergy in the Early Off-Loop Theatre Movement," *New England Journal of Theatre* 58 (2012): 133–46.

15. Gilles Deleuze and Félix Guattari, *A Thousand Plateaus: Capitalism and Schizophrenia*, trans. Brian Massumi (Minneapolis: University of Minnesota Press, 1987), 10–11.

16. Sue Ellen Case, "Theory / History / Revolution," in *Critical Theory and Performance*, ed. Janelle G. Reinelt and Joseph R. Roach (Ann Arbor: University of Michigan Press, 1992), 427.

17. Chicago City Players, *Chicago City Players—Newsletter*, October 1965, Body Politic Theatre Papers, box 4, folder 9, Chicago Theatre Collection, Harold Washington Library, Chicago.

18. See Janet Coleman, *The Compass* (New York: Knopf, 1990), for a full accounting of Sills's early years.

19. Paul Sills, "Letter from Chicago," *Yale—Theatre* 1, no. 2 (1967): 51.

20. In this author's interview with June Pyskacek, Pyskacek took pains to point out that Shiflett had little training in theater. She also argued that Richard Christiansen had misrepresented her own professionalism in his volume, *A Theatre of Our Own*. Pyskacek stated: "I had a real theater background you know, I had an MFA in directing. I mean I never get credit for

this, like I'm some little girl off the streets who happened into a theater and put on some shows."

21. Kathleen Sills, "Inside Track to the Future: Chicago Theatre 1950–1971" (PhD diss., Tufts University, 2001), 76, accessed through Proquest Dissertations and Theses; June Pyskacek, phone interview with the author, May 12, 2011.

22. Pyskacek, interview.

23. Kathleen Sills, "Inside Track," 174.

24. Kevin Zolkiewicz, "A Brief History of Chicago Surface Lines," accessed October 2, 2010, https://www.chicagobus.org/history.

25. Kathleen Sills, "Inside Track," 174–75.

26. Pyskacek made regular trips to New York at this time and hosted New York theater artists in her home on a regular basis. Pyskacek, interview.

27. Gary Houston, "Her Plays Create a World Filled with Beauty and Wisdom," *Chicago Sun-Times*, October 8, 1972.

28. Marilynn Preston, "Homegrown Theatre Blooming Here," *Now—Chicago Today*, March 26, 1972, Body Politic Theatre Papers, Chicago Theatre Collection, Harold Washington Library, Chicago.

29. Christiansen, *Theatre of Our Own* dust jacket, and Jean-Claude van Itallie, *The Serpent, America Hurrah and Other Plays* (New York: Grove Press, 2001), 126.

30. The property was one building with at least three addresses. The pub on the north end of the property has always used 2263. Generally, the Community Arts Foundation and the Body Politic Theatre used 2261. When Victory Gardens purchased half of the building in 1981, they used 2257 as their address. Phillips, "Theatrical Tapestry," 9–10.

31. Some sources claim that Mike Nichols—formerly of Second City fame and who by this time had garnered great success directing *The Graduate*—had donated the seed money, but neither Sills nor Shiflett have directly corroborated this; see, for example, McCabe, "Onstage at the Creation," 140.

32. Community Arts Foundation, "History," 9.

33. Richard Christiansen, "Body Politic Unveils Big Plans for Expansion," *Chicago Daily News*, April 12, 1974.

34. Christopher Ash, Ground Plan, VG Greenhouse Downstairs Studio, June 27, 2008, in author's possession.

35. Mary Daniels, "The Gods Are Only Human," *Chicago Tribune*, October 24, 1969. Sills continued to develop, produce, and teach the Story Theater form at his school and theater in Door County, Wisconsin, and at the New Actors Workshop in New York City until his death in 2008.

36. Paul Sills, introduction to *The Blue Light and Other Stories* in *Paul Sills' Story Theater: Four Shows*, by Paul Sills (New York: Applause, 2000), 13.

37. Laurie Ann Gruhn, "Interview: Paul Sills Reflects on Story Theatre," Story Theater, Paul Sills' Wisconsin Theater Game Center (website), accessed September 4, 2009, https://www.paulsills.com/biography/interview-paul-sills-reflects/.

38. Ash, Ground Plan.

39. William Leonard, "The Body Politic Exciting, Maybe Revolutionary," *Chicago Tribune*, April 19, 1970.

40. Jon C. Teaford, *Rough Road to Renaissance: Urban Revitalization in America, 1940–1985* (Baltimore: Johns Hopkins University Press, 1990), 12–25; Biles, *Richard J. Daley*, 4.

41. Author and activist James Baldwin used the phrase "Negro removal," quoted in Biles, *Richard J. Daley*, 51; Madgwick, "The Politics of Urban Renewal," 265.

42. Cohen and Taylor, *American Pharaoh*, 221–33.

43. See Biles, *Richard J. Daley*, 10, about race-fueled housing riots from the 1940s onward that became a part of what city dwellers "knew" about the problems of urban blight. This is not to say that the housing problems did not exist or that the riots did not happen, but it is important to note that these issues became a part of the received wisdom white people held about urban blight in the mid-twentieth century.

44. Chicago Department of Urban Renewal, *A Preliminary Study: Preserving the Architectural Character of a Neighborhood* (Chicago: City of Chicago, Department of Urban Renewal, 1964), 1–5, Municipal Collection, Harold Washington Library, Chicago.

45. Dalton, "Politics of Community Problem Solving."

46. Ducey, *Sunday Morning*, 17–18.

47. Ana Y. Ramos-Zayas, *National Performances: The Politics of Class, Race and Space in Puerto Rican Chicago* (Chicago: University of Chicago Press, 2003), 48.

48. Amanda Seligman, "Lincoln Park," Electronic Encyclopedia of Chicago, Chicago Historical Society, 2005, accessed July 4, 2010, http://www.encyclopedia.chicagohistory.org/pages/746.html.

49. *American Revolution* 2, directed by Howard Alk (1969; Chicago: Facets Video, 2007), DVD.

50. Chicago Department of Urban Renewal, *Lincoln Park General Renewal Plan*.

51. Joy Baim, "Renewal to Bring Parks, Heartaches." *Chicago Tribune*, November 27, 1966.

52. Dalton, "Politics of Community Problem Solving," 6.

53. Community Arts Foundation, "A Proposal for the Establishment of a Center for the Arts and Communication Fields Sponsored by the Church," December 9, 1965, 3–4, Body Politic Theatre Papers, box 1a, folder 5, Chicago Theatre Collection, Harold Washington Library, Chicago.

54. Community Arts Foundation, "History," 1–2.

55. Community Arts Foundation, "Proposal," 3.

56. "Film and City Ordinance," *Community Arts Foundation Newsletter*, August [c1967], North Side Cooperative Ministries Collection, Richard J. Daley Library, University of Illinois at Chicago.

57. "Dream Theatre," Body Politic Theatre Papers, box 7, folder 36, Chicago Theatre Collection, Harold Washington Library, Chicago.

58. Finding Guide, "Programs of the Community Arts Foundation: A History," Body Politic Theatre Papers, Chicago Theatre Collection, Harold Washington Library, Chicago.

59. Richard Christiansen, "'*Warp!*' Wending Its Way Back to Town for a Slam-Bang Reprise," *Chicago Tribune*, August 5, 1979.

60. Ralph Willingham, *Science Fiction and the Theatre* (New York: Greenwood Press, 1994), 62–63.

61. Willingham, *Science Fiction*, 64.

62. Terry Curtis Fox, "*WARP* Bombs in Gotham," *Chicago Reader*, February 13, 1973.

63. "*Grease* Ends Run in Chicago," *Chicago Defender*, March 30, 1974.

64. Gary Houston, "Did We Need New York to Tell Us That *Grease* Is Worth Seeing?," Body Politic Theatre Papers, box 1, folder 14, Chicago Theatre Collection, Harold Washington Library, Chicago.

65. Elder complies a number of relevant building and fire codes for small converted theaters and states, "Chicago is well known for its tough building and fire codes and for strict enforcement." Eldon Elder, *Will It Make a Theatre?: Find, Renovate, and Finance the Non-Traditional Performance Space* (New York: Alliance of Resident Theatres, 1993), 207.

66. Nat Brandt, *Death Trap: The Iroquois Fire of 1903* (Carbondale: Southern Illinois University, 2003), 106, 139–42.

67. Brandt, *Death Trap*. Chapter headings throughout the book excerpt sections of the Chicago municipal code regarding fire safety.

68. Coleman, *Compass*, 80.

69. Alan Erhrenhalt, *The Lost City: Discovering the Forgotten Virtues of Community in the Chicago of the 1950s* (New York: Basic Books, 1995), 48.

70. Coleman, *Compass*, 81.

71. See Christiansen, *Theatre of Our Own*; Kathleen Sills, "Inside Track"; and Sharon Phillips, "A Theatrical Tapestry," in *Resetting the Stage: Theatre beyond the Loop, 1960–1990* (Chicago: Special Collections Department of the Chicago Public Library, 1990), 7–10.

72. Linda Winer, "Body Politic's Friendly Giant and a Miracle on Lincoln Av.," *Chicago Tribune*, August 20, 1972. Theaters that preceded the Body Politic Theatre and the Kingston Mines Theatre either closed due to code violations or were left alone because they were considered community theatres and apparently exempted.

73. Les Bridges, article title unknown, *After Dark* (magazine), [c.1973], Body Politic Theatre Papers, box 5, folder 2, Chicago Theatre Collection, Harold Washington Library, Chicago.

74. "Aldermen to Hear Theatre Groups' Grievances," *Chicago Sun-Times*, November 21, 1972.

75. Mayor Richard J. Daley was often referred to as the city's "boss." Mike Royko's best seller chronicles this aspect of this tenure. Mike Royko, *Boss* (New York: E. P. Dutton, 1971).

76. Bridges, article title unknown.

77. Bridges, article title unknown. It is important to note that there are many such stories about Daley, some of them apocryphal, as this one may be. The change in code remains but the exact mechanics of the decision may not be known.

78. The Goodman changed from a school into a professional theater in 1969, and it was by no means certain that they would succeed at that time, "Our History," Goodman Theatre, accessed October 30, 2018, https://www.goodmantheatre.org/About/Our-History/.

79. At the time of this study, three major dailies published in Chicago: the *Chicago Tribune*, the *Chicago Daily News*, and the *Chicago Sun-Times*.

80. In 1983, it became the Chicago Area Theatre (CAT) contract, and it continues into the twenty-first century with modifications. "1970s, Fate and Fortune," Actors' Equity Association, accessed October 30, 2018, https://www.actorsequity.org/timeline/timeline_1970.html.

81. According to Real Group Real Estate the median selling price of a single-family home in Lincoln Park in early 2019 was $1.6 million dollars. "What Are the Current Real Estate Market Conditions in Lincoln Park?," accessed March 22, 2019, https://www.realgroupre.com/blog/187-current-real-estate-conditions-in-lincoln-park.html. For a comparison of Lincoln Park to other Chicago communities, see the zip code 60614 in "Rich Blocks Poor Blocks," accessed March 22, 2019, https://richblockspoorblocks.com/.

82. Patrick Murfin, "Doc Pellegrino—Radical Icon, Blues Impresario of Kingston Mines," accessed October 30, 2018, http://patrickmurfin.blogspot.com/2018/05/doc-pellegrinoradical-icon-blues.html.

83. Phillips, "Theatrical Tapestry," 10.

84. "About Us," Greenhouse Theater Center, accessed October 30, 2018, https://www.greenhousetheater.org/about-us.

7

Object Permanence

ImprovOlympic and the Legitimacy of Improv in Chicago

Travis Stern

ImprovOlympic (later known as iO, 1981–present) changed the shape and expectations of improvisation in Chicago by making its performance commercially available while asserting the place of improv as an art. Though frequently used as a tool to create other, often scripted, content, improvisation as performance is suited to making a place for itself. It fits restrictions placed on it due to time, location, or subject, and it can expand to incorporate the vagaries of its audience's desires. "Improv" as it is being used here refers to one of the types of improvised performance that emerged in the twentieth century in the United States. The term has become as associated with Chicago as deep-dish pizza or machine politics in large part because of ImprovOlympic's success in presenting the form to audiences and performers. Their success prompted the long-established and renowned Chicago comedy theater The Second City to alter their own improvisation training and performance.

How ImprovOlympic managed to claim space in Chicago in its trajectory from itinerant theater to major institution reflects the impermanence of improv as a form. As an inherently makeshift theatrical form, improvisation didn't attain stability as a performance form until the incorporation of the repeatable structure of the Harold in the 1980s. Looking at the comedy theater world in Chicago that ImprovOlympic entered into and how they defined themselves against it, we can see that their itinerant nature and the impermanent nature of improvisation itself worked against their efforts to establish "improv" as a performance art form until the opening of their longtime home on Clark Street in Wrigleyville. Once in a permanent location, they were able to use the same markers scripted theaters have long used to proclaim the legitimacy of improv as an art form.

Improv's Makeshift Nature

One of the ways "improv" distinguishes itself as a form of improvisation is by making the audience aware that the group is spontaneously generating the content with no planning—that everything is being made up on the spot. The structure of the performance, however, is predetermined and often explicitly stated to the audience by telling them the name of the form they are performing, such as a Harold or a Deconstruction. Part of the art of improv is making the audience aware of the art. It usually designates a time frame for the performance but not a prescribed or predetermined ending. By foregrounding craft and coordination, improv asserts that presenting the act of creation is as much a legitimate performance as something labored over for weeks.

Improv often takes two forms: short form or long form. Short-form improv consists of game-style, improvised bits without a connection that links individual games together, as seen on the British and American television program *Whose Line Is It Anyway?* or on ComedySportz theater stages. These short-form performances have a competition framework, though the stakes of winning or losing are either very low or nonexistent. The winner is determined through audience recognition—either laughter or applause—reflected in a points system that may be comically inclined itself.[1] The framework geared toward nonsense reinforces the playing aspect of the form: a good time is the goal.

ImprovOlympic specializes in long-form improv, which is narrative based with a through line linking elements together through character or theme. The result is a collage-type story with several narrative threads that interweave by the end of the performance though they all began from the same audience-suggested stimulus. Long form's framework is collaborative storytelling rather than a competition, so that the end of the piece, however absurd or removed from its beginning, is traceable back to that single audience interaction. While the aim of both long form and short form is primarily comedic, and both audiences and performers often assume a comedic orientation for the performance, long form presents itself as something worthy of analysis and critique. The choices made by performers, although spontaneous, are not without purpose and meaning and create something more than the sum of their parts.

Improvisation for performance seems to occupy a space between comedic scripted theater and stand-up comedy, and improv's two types of forms—short form and long form—are allied either with one end of the spectrum or the other. Differences obviously exist in the scripted or unscripted nature of these entertainments. Though stand-up comedians may include improvisations as part of their act, whether through interactions with the audience or in other ways, their act is predominantly scripted and set, while improv performers spontaneously generate their content. Short-form improv, featuring clearly structured and defined games with a premise often directly explained to the audience such as in Party Quirks, where performers enter the scene with a predetermined trait that another player decodes to the delight of the audience, is closer to stand-up comedy as an enactment of a situation that would be primarily narrated by a stand-up comedian. Both stand-up and short form specialize in presenting jokes or other thought-provoking entertainment packaged as jokes. While certain jokes or bits may recur as callbacks, typically for both stand-up and short form there is no narrative being presented that ties the entire presentation together.

Long-form improv more closely resembles comedic scripted theater. Here multiple performers create a narrative presented as a series of scenes that tie together through theme, story, or character and lead to an ending that seems to be a natural culmination of the story. The purpose of both long form and comedic scripted theater may be to make the audience laugh, but through the development of humorous situations and reactions to events by the characters rather than through the performer's sequential presentation of jokes or a set of material. Both stand-up and short form are relatively overt in their acknowledgment of and presentation for an audience. By contrast, long form and scripted theater are more oriented toward the illusionistic creation of a world that is regarded by the audience—but not foregrounded—as being presented directly to them. This allows the possibility of critical analysis of that world and its process of creation as understood on its own terms rather than by its direct impact on an audience.

As a type, improv acknowledges the makeshift conditions of its performance by foregrounding each performance as uniquely created for its moment, location, and audience. To highlight the immediacy and temporary nature of the situation, performers engage audience members to influence the performance directly in a limited way by eliciting some information from the audience as a stimulus for the performance, whether it is a character trait or a detail from someone's life. Though the gimmick used to compel audience interaction varies widely, the incorporation of an audience suggestion used only once for this performance and not again establishes a temporary community made only by those present that dissipates when the performance does. The incorporated interaction, often framed as a suggestion, creates for this makeshift performance community what improviser and scholar Matt Fotis has talked of as being the same as an inside joke, where the performance itself depends on the implication of being temporary and specialized.[2] The audience's active participation in the performance ensures its creation only for this specific audience. The form or style may be replicable, but the discrete elements of that performance itself, such as the story, cannot be, as they always fit that particular situation.

Though improvisation's makeshift nature can be advantageous, that nature also permits its dismissal as artistic performance due to the assumption that no craft or artistic skill is required for its production.[3] Though long form creates a world similar to scripted theater, there is no script remaining after the performance to analyze. The variety of possible performance venues for improv—from bars, nightclubs, and restaurants to black box and storefront theaters—provides a kind of visual reinforcement of improv's relegation to entertainment rather than its consideration as an art form. Without a defined space, improv in a way remains immaterial and trivial.

Improvisation in Chicago

Much of what became recognizable as Chicago improv grew from the idea that children like to play games. From this simple idea, Viola Spolin influenced several generations of performers. Neva Boyd introduced Spolin to games as a teaching technique at Jane Addams's Hull-House, which served as both a refuge and point of assimilation for children from immigrant families.[4] The games were vital in helping build a sense of community among those experiencing isolation from the rest of society. Spolin later used games as the basis of her work as a teacher and supervisor of creative dramatics for adults with the Works Progress Administration Recreation Project in Chicago beginning in

1939 and for children and young adults at Hull-House. Under Spolin, the children used the games and other storytelling techniques they had learned as well as audience suggestions to create the spontaneous stories they performed for the community.[5] These games, later developed and published in various volumes aimed at different groups, not only sparked creativity but also promoted a sense of inclusivity, acceptance, and community as seen in the first sentences of the opening chapter of Spolin's *Improvisation for the Theatre*: "Everyone can act. Everyone can improvise."[6]

A direct line exists from Spolin's teaching to the next major step in the development of improv in Chicago through her son, Paul Sills. While working near the University of Chicago in the early 1950s, David Shepherd prompted Sills, then a student at the university, to teach his mother's techniques to develop the improvisational skills of a group of actors Shepherd had gathered to present scenario plays. After a month of workshops with both Sills and Spolin, the Compass Players debuted with a cabaret setting in the Compass Tavern on Fifty-Fifth Street in July 1955.[7] Five nights a week the group would present a unique, daily, forty-minute-long scenario play rehearsed earlier that day. At its conclusion, the group would present several shorter pieces and end with an extemporaneously staged reading of that day's newspaper. After a short while, the strain of the rehearsal process led to running the scenarios beyond the single day. Eventually the group gave up on the scenario form altogether in favor of the improvised shorter pieces.[8] While Shepherd believed improvisation would be best suited to facilitate the creation of longer plays, he accepted its use in performance for paying audiences because he wasn't able to find the plays he wanted to produce otherwise. Shepherd opened another Compass theater in St. Louis based on the same premise, but both venues eventually closed in 1957.[9] Sills remained interested in continuing presentations of the shorter pieces, both improvised and scripted, to audiences but in a revue format.

On December 16, 1959, Paul Sills, Howard Alk, and Bernie Sahlins opened The Second City's doors for the first time. Located at 1842 North Wells Street in the city's Old Town neighborhood (see chapter 6), The Second City continued the work of the now-defunct Compass Players in a slightly different, more polished, and much more commercially viable way. To avoid the stringent theater regulations in the city, the audience sat at cabaret-style tables where the crowd of up to 125 ate and drank before and during the performance, creating a much more social than theatrical atmosphere.[10] Taking the name "Second City" from an A. J. Liebling article in the *New Yorker*, the company has always used a specifically Chicago lens on its presentation of society. From the beginning, the primary performance form was a two-act satirical revue that included dialogue scenes, musical numbers, and parodies, predominantly scripted with occasional improvised moments taken from audience suggestions. Like the Compass Players, the Second City cast honed their improvisational skills in workshops run by Viola Spolin; however, the cast's improvisations for audiences were relegated largely to an end-of-night, after-show piece five times a week.[11]

From its beginning The Second City never charged audiences to watch improvisation only, though people regularly arrived near the end of the scripted revue specifically to watch the after-show improv performance. The implication that purely improvised performances aren't worth paying for extended to the playing of the improv piece itself. After asking the crowd for a variety of suggestions, the performers would then retreat backstage to gather costumes and props and strategize how they would piece together some of the new suggestions with other pieces and bits they were workshopping to be written down and integrated into the revue show at a later time.[12] These improvised afterpieces resembled the old scenario format used at the Compass but were much more extemporaneously performed as there was no real rehearsal, only planning. The audience was watching improvisation but not improv.

The Second City gained near-immediate recognition in Chicago, and in August 1967, they moved to a new location in Piper's Alley at 1616 North Wells that sat 350. The massive success of several alums on NBC's *Saturday Night Live* brought greater national recognition beginning in 1975. Chicago then became a destination for performers from around the country with hopes of becoming famous. With the addition of a touring company, a de facto training center run by Jo Forsburg called the Players Workshop to teach games, and the opening of a second location in Toronto, The Second City had effectively established and exported an identifiably Chicago brand of humor. This included both the revue form, built through a series of improvisations but performed from a script for audiences, and classic sketches from the theater's history revived and played by current cast members. The latter was the primary responsibility of the touring company until the opening of The Second City e.t.c. next door in 1982. Presenting a mix of the past with potential for the new, The Second City had become such a recognizable franchise that *Time* magazine proclaimed them the "capital of comedy" in 1985.[13] Due in part to The Second City's appeal and success, as well as the frequent renewal of performers in the limited number of players needed for a revue cast, there was a proliferation of trained comedic performers in Chicago who had no opportunities with the company but were still compelled to perform. Through the 1980s, performers and groups had to carve out space for themselves outside the establishment of The Second City.

ImprovOlympic Appears

One of the companies to emerge in The Second City's wake used another David Shepherd idea: to organize teams of people from various backgrounds to compete against each other in improvisation matches with the hope of creating a kind of international improvisational Olympics. Having read about his idea, young improviser and entrepreneur Charna Halpern sought out Shepherd with an idea of how to produce these competitions in Chicago regularly, and they created ImprovOlympic in 1981. Held at Jo Forsburg's Players Workshop, where Halpern had trained previously, the initial competitions had a team of trained improvisers compete against an assembled group of untrained amateurs in a series of ten improv games, with the audience choosing the winner at the end of the competition.[14] The assembled teams consisted of people who had previously attended a show and were grouped based on their profession, so teams of doctors, police officers, lawyers, rabbis, etc. were formed, which gave each competition a popular rather than professional theater feel and filled the seats with family members, friends, and coworkers to support the amateurs and be awed by the experts.[15] In a way that harkened back to Spolin's work at Hull-House, friendly, community-enabling competition was the focus of the performance rather than improvisation, which was merely the vehicle to achieve it.

Halpern, however, wanted to go beyond this community-building orientation to focus on the performance capabilities of improvisation instead. She admitted the ten short games–based format lost its appeal for her after about a year, despite the success of the presentations' competitive aspect. In 1983, after David Shepherd left the project, Halpern asked former Compass member and former Second City director Del Close to do some workshops for her performers, who had become increasingly reliant on reproducing the same bits that had gotten laughs in previous performances. Based on their shared belief that improvisation itself could be a viable performance form that wasn't reliant on the creation of jokes or skits, Close quickly convinced Halpern to shut down the game orientation of the competitions.[16]

Del Close had recently left The Second City due to creative differences with managing partner and producer Bernie Sahlins.[17] The two held a long-running, sometimes good-natured debate on the purpose of improvisation that, after the split, became a significant difference between The Second City and ImprovOlympic. From his position as both businessman and producer, Sahlins was understandably concerned with the onstage, commercial product saleable to tourists and locals alike, and to that extent he viewed improvisation as a means to achieve The Second City's recognizable finished comedy product. Close fervently believed improvisation was its own end, and that it was indeed an art unto itself. Ultimately, Close's perspective on improvisation would become the foundation of improv as a legitimized art form.

Enabled by Halpern and no longer restrained by The Second City's training and performance formats, Close developed his theories and teachings on improvisational theater and performance at ImprovOlympic, often in contrast to The Second City's renowned practices. The early pages of Close and Halpern's 1993 "manual of improvisation," *Truth in Comedy*, defines his style against the Second City approach, stating, "Real improvisation is more than just a garnish, thrown like parsley onto a prepared stand-up comedy routine. Nor is it just a tool used to manufacture prepared scenes."[18] The book further lays out Close's and, by extension, ImprovOlympic's philosophy that sought to legitimize improv as an art form for performance through their signature long-form improv called "the Harold."

When originally developed by Close, the Harold's only purpose was to foster process, eschewing any sense of product for audience. Halpern describes the "nascent form" of the Harold as "a little too large and chaotic for the stage. The trick would be preserving the chaos on stage while at the same time making it comprehensible."[19] Early Harolds could consist of a twenty- to thirty-scene barrage over a given topic, presenting what Second City performer and early Harold participant Tim Kazurinsky later admitted to be "more than you ever knew—or possibly wanted to know—about the selected topic."[20] Upon his association with ImprovOlympic in 1983, Close modified the Harold with Halpern's game Time-Dash, a three-part scene where situations emerge through spans of time, forming a theatricalized, manageable merger of process and product, yet staying true to the original intent of its creator. This alteration for the sake of practicality to fit the competition framework ImprovOlympic had been presenting illustrates not only the form's flexibility but also enabled long form to be a viable presentation for audiences. This is the form of the basic Harold that became and remains the basis of instruction and performance at ImprovOlympic.

Simply described, the Harold utilizes, ideally, six to seven actors and takes a limitless number of formats, but usually consists of a template pattern of three basic elements: scenes (involving two to four players), games (usually involving the full group), and one-person monologues. Beginning with an audience-inspired theme or suggestion, the company personalizes that theme in the opening game, which illustrates connections among the players rather than quick wit or competition. The players follow with a first round of scenes (three seems to be the standard number) stemming from the suggestion, which is followed by another game. The scenes reappear a second time for further development. Another game follows, and then the scenes return a third and final time (not all scenes may reappear). The Harold can end with one scene or with a game, and the entire process usually takes approximately thirty-five minutes.[21] Additional details and variations to this template increase its complexity to create a multitude of performance possibilities to suit whatever story is being told in that specific performance. This structure allows for building a story strong enough to be engaging while still only existing for this performance.

With the Harold as its base, ImprovOlympic found a way to create consistency for fully improvised performances without depending on repeatable bits or rehashing previously played situations. The form emphasizes artistry and craft by being repeatable without replicating the content. While the process of spontaneous creation had always had appeal for audiences, the Harold ensured that even occasional bad performances were due to less-than-able performers rather than the style of performance itself.

Integrating Close's philosophy into the already established ImprovOlympic structure required a shift in focus. As a result they presented no performances for three months. After Close's arrival in 1983, while ImprovOlympic continued to present their performances in various locations around the city as a competition between teams, they no longer consisted of ten improv games and no longer had an audience team on stage. Instead, two teams each performed a Harold inspired by audience suggestion, and the audience then rated them one through six in four categories: intelligence, theme, structure, and teamwork. Rather than the rapid-fire delivery of jokes, which had led to repetition and familiar patterns by performers, Close wanted a slower form of comedy that would draw in the audience.[22] The new style gave more onstage opportunities to improvisers, but it also required a new kind of training for performers that would be different from The Second City's games-oriented improvisation workshops—a training that was available only through ImprovOlympic.

Using the Harold form as the means for the teams' competition resulted in a focus on process rather than product, which eventually made even the competition aspect of each performance superfluous. By the end of the 1980s, ImprovOlympic eliminated the last remnants of competition, as audiences no longer picked winners. The performances retained the same structure for the most part, with two Harold teams each performing for around thirty-five to forty minutes apiece and then both teams appearing on stage together at the end for an additional piece, bringing the total running time usually to between seventy-five and ninety minutes. Groups still existed as teams even beyond the use of competition because of the sense of ensemble required to promote the group mind. Some teams lasted longer than others as Halpern and Close removed and added performers to teams at their discretion, at times dismantling teams to make new ones.[23]

One team known as the Family, originally the Victim's Family, became a favorite of Close's to use in further experiments with the Harold and long-form improvisation in general. By using the Family to play with time and pacing deviating from the slow comedy, Close created a faster form of the Harold called the Spineless Harold. Other forms followed, including the Movie, the Check-in Deconstruction, and the Horror or Expressionistic Horror, featured across two specially produced ImprovOlympic productions using the Family, *Three Mad Rituals* and *Dynamite Fun Nest*. Later, ImprovOlympic would feature other variations on the Harold form, but in each, the performers were encouraged to eschew the quick jokes in favor of a complex narrative.[24] By having a template structure that performances can adhere to or deviate from, improv assures audiences of a base-level standard for the presentations, akin to a night of scripted theater or stand-up, even though the content is never repeated.

Impermanence and Itinerancy

While many other Chicago theaters emerged and rose to prominence after The Second City's opening and on through the 1990s, none were devoted to presenting improv as its own performance form. As these theaters moved from basements to storefronts to their own dedicated spaces, the style of theater they presented—whether gritty realism or theatricalized fantasy—was tied to scripted performances that produced artifacts of their production: photos and newspaper reviews that promised audiences what they would see if attending, as well as the scripts themselves that allowed the potential of a revival in a new space, even if it never materialized. Groups specializing in improvisation as performance—where lack of repeatability is a selling point—leave little trace behind other than stories and memories of what occurred on stage. Even newspaper reviews could comment only on what had been presented that night and would not be seen again. Though the nature of improvisation makes moving performance sites easier to manage for performances, it creates additional difficulties in trying to maintain a lasting presence, as can be seen in ImprovOlympic's itinerant nature in the late 1980s and 1990s. Even as the performances of improv became stabilized, the presentations of it remained in flux.

ImprovOlympic most frequently played at CrossCurrents at 3206 North Wilton during the 1980s, both before and after its shift in focus toward Close's artistic philosophy. The century-old building had been the home of the Swedish Community Center, and the cabaret's artistic director Thom Goodman believed that CrossCurrents was continuing the legacy of being a cultural center for the Lakeview neighborhood. ImprovOlympic was not the only entertainment the venue provided. The space had hosted a variety of performances, from the "standard North Side club fare" (as the *Tribune* noted) and a jazz series to a reunion of the beat poets Allen Ginsberg, William Burroughs, and Gregory Corso and productions by Remains Theatre and Steppenwolf Theatre. The *Tribune* wrote that the venue served a pivotal role in the revitalization of the Belmont / Lakeview Central area as an entertainment location.[25] Around two hundred audience members filled the space for the finals of an intercollegiate Harold competition at the end of 1985.[26]

The perils of not having control over their performance space became clear to ImprovOlympic the next year. Goodman envisioned CrossCurrents becoming an incubator for a variety of artistic groups where he would provide not only the performance space but also organizational and administrative support in the form of reduced rent for office space, shared goods and services, and a management structure that would encourage tenant organizations to graduate after a period of time. Operating with other investors under the name Corporation for Cultural Reinvestment, Goodman planned to renovate the club's second floor to put office space alongside the new eighty-five-seat second-floor theater. The group New Age Vaudeville inaugurated the new space and became the first resident group in CrossCurrents' history. However, Goodman asserted that he didn't want to have ten theater groups as tenants, preferring to diversify his nonprofit clientele through a grant-like process.[27] Exactly one year after sharing those grand plans, CrossCurrents closed its doors on a Saturday at the stroke of midnight as the liquor license expired. Goodman then locked the doors to all tenants the following Monday as the insurance lapsed. The building itself was in foreclosure, and the corporation that owned the building and the club, Chicago Cooperative Productions, Inc., was almost half a million dollars in debt. Attorney Rick Darby took over controlling interest from Goodman earlier in the year and hoped to acquire a short-term insurance policy to keep some tenants in place. Goodman admitted that while the bar and restaurant maintained themselves, the second-story facilities lagged behind. Before the shutdown, the phone company disconnected the office phones, and a dance troupe renting the upstairs performance space left when the building's heat was shut off. Restoration occurred only when tenants like ImprovOlympic began paying utilities in lieu of paying their rent. Darby was able to keep two tenants temporarily, but Halpern, who had just paid a $900 utility bill the previous week, moved ImprovOlympic to the Ivanhoe Theater.[28]

Upon their departure, ImprovOlympic began the process of finding a new, long-term home, which ultimately took several years. The Ivanhoe Theater at 750 West Wellington Avenue in the Lakeview neighborhood hosted them for the remainder of 1987 and into the next year. General Manager Jim Pappas announced plans to enclose the venue's small courtyard to create a two-hundred-seat cabaret space called Camelot that would open in the spring and could possibly serve as the new home for ImprovOlympic or some other comedy-based revue show.[29] By the end of the next January, however, ImprovOlympic had left the Ivanhoe and was performing in the music room at Orphans, a bar at 2462 North Lincoln Avenue. The bar, which had been open since 1969, had taken its name from the abandoned feeling that patrons at the far end of the unusually long counter got as new people arrived at the near end. Just as with the Ivanhoe, ImprovOlympic's short run at Orphans was not the end of their itinerancy.[30] For a group attempting to present a unique improvised form in a city dominated by The Second City's continued success, the inability to establish even a permanent residency in one of the city's many entertainment venues implied that improv might be unsuitable as a stand-alone performance.

The next stop was a restaurant and bar known as At the Tracks, located at 325 North Jefferson. Owner Carl Berman turned a run-down warehouse into a nightclub primarily because of the scenic view that included the John Hancock Center and the Merchandise Mart. Though the building was on a dead-end block that abuts several rail tracks—hence the name—Berman increased visibility by painting the building bright yellow.[31] For about a year from late 1988, ImprovOlympic played mostly Saturdays and Tuesdays in the West Loop location, which was much farther south than they had previously appeared. Aware of where she had built her audience, Halpern returned to the CrossCurrents space on Wilton when an opportunity arose. Now a blues club run by James Cotton called Cotton Chicago, the space reopened on July 1, 1988, to serve as a home base of sorts for the Grammy-nominated musician to return to when not touring the United States and Europe. With a slightly revamped main room that now sat 175, it was a natural fit for ImprovOlympic to return to fill some of the entertainment slots. Beginning on January 11, 1989, ImprovOlympic presented Harolds on Wednesdays at the blues club while still playing at At the Tracks on several other nights during the week. A Friday night party on July 7, 1989, began a promised permanent, exclusive return to the space for an open run. Approximately a month later though, the building was once again in foreclosure, and by mid-August 1989, ImprovOlympic was again looking for a regular place to perform.[32]

Returning to the CrossCurrents space under the newly reconstituted Cotton Chicago name would have been incredibly important for Halpern and the ImprovOlympic brand regardless of how unstable the situation may have been. The location, however changed, would have seemed familiar to patrons and performers alike. In less than two years, the company had played in three different locations around the city. Though performances had exposure to new audiences, it became more difficult to build and maintain an audience base—especially since The Second City was celebrating icon status with thirty years at the same location.

As a comedy theater, The Second City had legitimacy through longevity and performed stability. Both were put on display as famous scenes from the archives would be remounted with the current generation of performers taking over the roles of those who had moved on to other, more nationally recognized things. ImprovOlympic's itinerancy implied that Sahlins was right—that audiences didn't want to see improvisation as performance, and that improv remained dismissible as an art form. It existed on the margins of theatrical performance like magicians, comedians, ventriloquists, and others who had acts performable on demand. The work of the improvisers could be dismissed as a parlor trick.

ImprovOlympic remained in a shadow of The Second City that was hard to escape. For part of 1989 and 1990, the group played in Italian restaurants. The first was Ciao Restaurante at 1516 North Wells, near The Second City's longtime home. The restaurant had regularly hosted magicians as entertainment for diners and had previously offered patrons a free entrée if they stomped grapes barefoot in a vat for sixty seconds.[33] Then in June 1990, ImprovOlympic began performing at a new Papa Milano restaurant at 1970 North Lincoln Avenue. Branching out from their original location at State and Oak, the restaurant took over the spot that had housed McMahon's, owned by former Chicago Bears quarterback Jim McMahon. The basement room, with a separate entrance and once designated the VIP room, became an entertainment space seating 150 and showing Harold performances four times a week. Before the end of the year, Papa Milano's owner arranged to host the performances by the members of the Harold team Blue Velveeta exclusively rather than all of the ImprovOlympic teams. To distinguish themselves from ImprovOlympic, they now called themselves the Comedy Underground featuring Blue Velveeta. This parting from both the space and one of its teams was less than fully amicable, and ImprovOlympic was again searching for a performance location for its shows.[34]

Even after years of performances, ImprovOlympic still did not have geographical stability, and Halpern again engaged multiple venues in order to have some control in case another unplanned, but likely anticipated, departure arose. One venue was at the Wrigleyside bar at 3527 North Clark Street in the upstairs Shuman Theater built by another improv group, Ed. The other venue that ImprovOlympic occupied was a small fifty-seat theater at 1218 West Belmont Avenue across the street from the Theatre Building. Unlike their previous locations, this space fulfilled a variety of functions. Because the location was near to both Halpern's and Close's apartments, it served as a convenient space for classes and workshops. The smaller space allowed Close to experiment a bit more with his forms as performances without taking away any of the performance slots at Wrigleyside. The venue hosted the Family, Close's primary experimental group, and their run of experimental Harold forms in their show *Dynamite Fun Nest*, as well as other shows by other ImprovOlympic-associated groups such as Great Exploitations and the Upright Citizens Brigade. Just as important, for the first time Halpern could advertise their performance location as the ImprovOlympic Theater rather than being tied to the name of a bar or restaurant.[35]

The frequent changes in performance location that ImprovOlympic experienced affected this improvisational company differently than such changes affected groups doing scripted, realistic theater. With scripted theater, audiences have a stable text to return to after the performance to revive their memories of the choices made by the production. In realistic theater, production photographs provide a sense of visual elements such as setting, properties, or costumes that again evoke memories of the production. Improvisation doesn't leave these remnants. There is no script for an audience to consult, and photographs of improvised performances tend to reveal less meaning without the context of a script to correlate with the depicted moment or action. These pictures tend to feature performers in everyday clothing with mimed properties and surrounded by a location established through spoken decor rather than physical scenery. For improv, the primary markers of the past are memory and stories, which do have a currency for improv teachers and performers, but must be refreshed in an audience's mind to create a sense of lasting permanence, which is crucial in building an audience base.

Without a permanent location, ImprovOlympic lacks a visible history for audiences to consume. The physical location in the city may have changed between the times an audience member attended a production. In this way, there is no consistency in arriving at the location or seeing the building itself to spark memory and storytelling for audience members. Combined with rotating performers and spontaneously created performances, nearly all the elements of a production may be different for a spectator except for the name of the group.

Additionally, for an itinerant company, the decor of their performance locale doesn't speak to a sense of history for the group. There are no pictures of notable previous productions or past performers in the entryway or lobby as there would be for a company with a permanent home like The Second City. Even if images and photographs of productions have less capability to evoke specific memories, their presence as decor serve an important role in branding and marketing as an assertion of general history and longevity.

A falling out with the landlord of the Belmont space led Halpern to conclude she must have her own permanent space. Her cousin, Steve Schultz, had bought the old Swedish American club building at 3541 North Clark two spots down from the Wrigleyside bar with plans to turn it into a parking lot for nearby Wrigley Field. Halpern was able to convince him to let her rent the space, and she immediately invested in a renovation that cost three times the initial estimate of $30,000. The inability of a building contractor to secure a building permit and the reluctance of the previous tenants to relinquish their liquor license further complicated the venue's opening. Despite all the issues, ImprovOlympic Theater and Cabaret opened the Clark Street location as scheduled in March 1995. The venue held two performances spaces: a sixty-seat cabaret on the main floor eventually named after the team the Family, and a ninety-nine-seat theater on the second floor named the Del Close Theater from the start.[36]

In this new space, Halpern took advantage of what she had not had before: the relics of history. The building was painted black with a giant, unmissable, imperfect white spiral as adornment. Pictures of previous teams and famous alums lined the wall of the ramp leading down to the Family Cabaret. The bars, frequented by audience members and performers alike, helped pay for the space. The red seats for the Del Close Theater had come from the old Chicago Stadium and borrowed a sense of Chicago history as part of the decor. A prominently displayed urn containing Close's ashes after his death in 1999 sat at an altar—featuring pictures of him throughout his life and his various awards—in the theater space that bore his name. Close had informed Halpern that he wanted his ashes in the theater so that he could "still affect the work."[37] With this permanent space, ImprovOlympic attained the same stability for presenting improv as an art form that having a repeatable structure like the Harold did for improv as performance.

ImprovOlympic faced other issues in its quest for legitimacy that were provoked by others' uncertainty about what was being presented by the group. The ill-defined place of improv led in part to the legal issues for ImprovOlympic over their name that partly served to position the work they did against a broader field of entertainment and provided spaces for them to assert their legitimacy. In 1988, as a Chicago location of Budd Friedman's stand-up comedy clubs called the Improv was about to open, Friedman's lawyer sent a cease and desist letter to Halpern demanding a name change to anything that did not include the words "improv" or "improvisation," since both terms were trademarked and registered to Friedman. Noting the differences between stand-up and improv, several local media outlets like the alternative weekly newspaper the *Chicago Reader* came to Halpern's and ImprovOlympic's defense. The *Reader* quotes Chicago copyright attorney Tom Leavens saying he saw no path to victory for a potential lawsuit against Halpern because she had used the name for a long time and the term itself had a cultural resonance in Chicago that would be akin to someone trying to claim exclusive rights to the term "deep-dish." Walter Gertz, the local franchisee of Friedman's club, declared that he had no problem with the ImprovOlympic name and expressed to the newspaper that he was afraid the backlash would harm his business. A full lawsuit never materialized, but the event served as evidence of two things: that improv was closely associated with comedy and humor to the point that Friedman believed he had to assert some legal authority to protect his investment, and that Chicago valued improv as a cultural institution clearly distinguishable as its own separate performance form. As the *Reader* put it: "Real improvisation, a great Chicago tradition, is our business."[38]

An issue over the other half of ImprovOlympic's name had a different result, however. Shepherd's original conception of the competition format and the coming together of people from different walks of life led him to see the endeavor as an Olympiad, which led to the name. He and Halpern originally differed on its spelling. Shepherd preferred two words and ending with an "s" or sometimes even an "x" to denote the games and process of competition, while Halpern preferred one word ending with a "c," which became predominant after Shepherd's departure. As the group began garnering attention beyond Chicago, initially from a 1985 *New York Times* article and subsequent interest by actor and producer Michael Douglas that led to the name appearing regularly in *Variety*, the United States Olympic Committee sent a first cease and desist letter to protect their trademark in 1987. While their challenge was even more unfounded than Friedman's challenge to the name, Halpern at first asserted she would sell the name to them for $2 million. However, as the threats were renewed periodically, Halpern briefly changed the name of the company to ImprovOlympia around the time the competitive aspects of the performances were removed. The name returned to ImprovOlympic in the mid-1990s and remained so until around the time of the group's twenty-fifth anniversary in 2005, when they officially shortened the name to iO. Despite having admitted that she was never really fond of the name ImprovOlympic, Halpern clearly understood the power and recognizability of the brand associated with what she and Close had created. Without a consistently stable location, that ImprovOlympic name was often the only marker for audiences to use to find their unique kind of comedic performance. As the name changed to iO, a new sign noted that the company was established in 1981 and clearly identified the theater as presenting "Chicago's Best Improv Comedy."[39]

The uncertainty of the presentation itself was felt by both audiences and critics and required some acclimation to see the form the way ImprovOlympic wanted them to. Both David Shepherd and Del Close frequently expressed a desire to have audiences react actively to performances like fans at a sporting event rather than sit passively like those at a realist theater piece. At the same time, audiences who were used to the rapid-fire-joke pace of improv games also had to get used to the slower pace of the Harold. Close believed audiences would respond favorably to the intellectual-emotional moves of the performers on the stage, which would evoke laughter and perhaps a different kind of response. One of Halpern's most frequently told anecdotes is of an audience member so moved by the importance placed on a pantomimed basketball shot by one performer that he leapt on stage and tipped in the shot. Rather than kick him out, Halpern offered him a spot in one of her classes.[40]

The more the audience understood the form, the better they would be as an audience to the form. The *Chicago Reader* was very important in helping to spread the successes and shortcomings of the form by frequently running reviews of long-form productions, particularly those at ImprovOlympic. For example, a review of *By Accident* noted the performers' impressive technique even while critiquing them as offering little that was "profound or memorable."[41] A negative review of *Frank Booth in the Blue Velvet Lounge* by critic Lawrence Bommer that called the dialogue lame, the energy low, and the pacing slow perhaps levied its most damning critique with the statement that "the *Frank Booth* improv artists seemed to be waiting for punch lines that never arrived."[42] The review prompted letters to the editor by several improvisers advocating for a more nuanced review process for fully improvised long-form productions since the playing and process of the ensemble should be critiqued rather than the night's performance, an important distinction for anyone attending who might be expecting a series of jokes. While the letters may not have swayed a critic's opinion, they served to encourage multiple views and further consideration of performances of a form that would never be the same twice.[43] This shift in debate toward *how* improv should be performed for audiences rather than *whether* it should be performed marks an acceptance of improv as a legitimate art form worthy of critique and examination.

Another sign that ImprovOlympic had made a mark on Chicago entertainment was that other groups began using it as an influence. Throughout the 1980s, comic performers who trained at The Second City, but were not working there, often mounted their own sketch revue shows in that model. By the end of the 1980s, however, these performances regularly integrated elements of long-form improvisation, and when those elements were absent, reviewers noted it. ImprovOlympic itself became a target for performers spoofing the local scene. In the mid-1990s, both the *Chicago Reader* and the *Chicago Tribune* noted that long-form improvisation had not only gained wide acceptance locally, but it had replaced the Second City–style revue show as the most produced form in the city.[44] It had become the dominant form of improvisation in the city that others now had to make their own space around. The Second City's revue shows began to be constructed using the tools that performers had honed at ImprovOlympic.

Redevelopment of the area around Wrigley Field, led by Cubs' ownership, eventually pushed Halpern and ImprovOlympic/iO out of Wrigleyville to a new permanent location in Lincoln Park in 2014. The forty-thousand-foot building at 1501 North Kingsbury, a former furniture warehouse, cost Halpern approximately $7 million to buy and renovate. Each of the four theater spaces in the building featured the presentation of long-form improv to audiences. The largest space, the Mission Theater, seating 225 and run by improv duo T. J. Jagodowski and Dave Pasquesi, was the only one not fully under Halpern's control. The Chris Farley Cabaret and the Jason Chin Harold Cabaret, both named in memory of beloved alums, sat 80 and 100 respectively. The Del Close Theater remained the main space for iO, seating 170 and still holding the urn with Close's ashes. The four spaces could each hold performances simultaneously and not be disturbed by each other or by patrons at the central bar.[45] Unlike the previous locations, this space fit the art form of improv rather than improv fitting into the space.

Coda

Having a permanent performance location, however, meant that iO could no longer use the impression of impermanence as an excuse not to confront both acute and chronic issues faced by other theater companies with their own spaces. On March 14, 2020, as part of the steps taken to prevent spread of the novel coronavirus COVID-19, iO announced through email and social media that it was closing the Kingsbury theaters and suspending all classes and performances until March 30 following guidance from the City of Chicago and the Centers for Disease Control and Prevention.[46] The announcement followed an attempt to stay open as long as possible with extra precautions in place.[47] On March 21, iO's initial planned closure was extended indefinitely in compliance with the stay-at-home orders of the State of Illinois and Chicago local government.

Without income from performances or classes, iO felt the weight of the financial obligations of maintaining their own permanent space. Several times, Halpern posted pleas to government officials for financial relief on her personal Facebook page. One complicating issue was that the federal government had declared COVID-19 a national emergency; had they declared it a national disaster, additional funding would have been available to Halpern and iO. Of more immediate concern to Halpern was the lack of property tax relief from Cook County.[48] While the county approved a temporary waiver of late payments, they still expected property owners to pay property tax bills in full regardless of any lost income.[49]

As the COVID pandemic exasperated iO's financial ills, it brought into sharper focus other long-standing issues within the theater, and some of the practices established as an itinerant group showed how unsustainable they were for a permanent theater. Steven Plock, an iO staff member and performer, set up a GoFundMe crowdfunding page to help offset money lost by iO staff including "our piano players, our techs, servers, hosts, bartenders, not to mention our teachers, box office staff, our kitchen staff, food runners, training center, and janitorial staff."[50] Noticeably absent from the list were performers. With most revenue coming through alcohol sales and classes from the training center rather than ticket sales, iO had long maintained a business model where performers were not paid for their work onstage even back to the beginning of the theater.[51] This created a long-standing tension between the theater and many of the performers, who desired the time on stage to craft and display their skills, but who also felt that their labor was worthy of remuneration and was being exploited to support the money-making aspects of the theater.

On top of the performers' general feeling of exploitation, the events of spring 2020 brought often-dismissed complaints of further inequity and injustice in the theater to the fore. During the nationwide calls to dismantle systemic racism in the United States following the death of Minneapolis man George Floyd at police hands on May 25, 2020, Olivia Jackson began a Change.org petition with signees pledging to withhold their performing labor from iO until Halpern acknowledged and apologized for the institutionalized racism at the theater, decentralized the decision-making process to distribute power, hired an outside diversity and inclusion coordinator, and committed to a revised and decolonized curriculum.[52] The petition was presented to the theater on June 9, 2020, in a meeting with three iO administrators who verbally agreed to prioritize and carry out the action steps. The next day Halpern emailed a letter of apology, which was also posted to iO's Facebook page, acknowledging and apologizing for having "not been engaged or active enough in supporting the BIPOC and LGBTQIA+ members of our community" as well as for not reacting more effectively to previous criticism and calls for change.[53] Halpern's letter further acknowledged that some reforms would not be possible until the business could return, while also asking for patience and noting that "the future of iO is fragile." On June 17, 2020, the iO Comedy Network team Free Street Parking, the only all-BIPOC team associated with iO, sent the theater a letter supporting the original Change.org petition and further identifying needed changes, including further transparency and the investigation of sexual misconduct and assault.[54] That day, David Razowsky posted a screenshot of Halpern's emailed reply to the team that did not address any of the team's specific concerns but restated the financial difficulties the theater was under and that it was unlikely that iO would reopen its doors. She wrote, "I can't continue the struggle to stay open."[55] The next day newspapers in Chicago and nationwide reported that iO would be closing permanently.[56]

In October 2020, the iO Theater was officially listed for sale as a banner hung on the side of the Kingsbury building. The notice came just days after The Second City had announced it was also for sale. Arranged by Compass Commercial, the building's list price was set for just under $13 million and described as "turn-key" and ready to go as a theater space. The sale price also included the iO brand itself, with

Halpern's hopes that someone would continue the work of the theater.[57] Some potential buyers were interested more in the location than the theater space, so at the time of this writing, it remains possible that the iO brand could return to the earlier itinerant model and resume presenting performances and offering classes in a variety of spaces across Chicago. In whatever way the brand moves forward, iO has an opportunity and an obligation to correct previous practices established in itinerancy and address the concerns of performers of color, members of the LGBTQIA+ community, and survivors of sexual misconduct. Whether iO returns to the itinerant model or reestablishes a permanent location, its continued survival requires reconciliation between the work of the theater and the people of the community who made it.

Notes

1. Consider the phrase uttered by hosts at the beginning of episodes of the American version of *Whose Line Is It Anyway?*: "The show where everything is made up and the points don't matter."

2. Matt Fotis, interview with author, March 2018.

3. Indeed, those who are expert improvisers make this appear to be the case.

4. Janet Coleman, *The Compass: The Improvisational Theatre That Revolutionized American Comedy* (Chicago: University of Chicago Press, 1991), 29; Dorothy Andries, "A Look at Viola Spolin—'High Priestess of Improv,'" *Chicago Sun-Times*, March 29, 2013.

5. Viola Spolin, *Improvisation for the Theater*, 3rd ed. (Evanston: Northwestern University Press, 1999), xlvii–xlvix; Coleman, *Compass*, 30–31.

6. Spolin, *Improvisation*, 3.

7. Coleman, *Compass*, 101.

8. Coleman, *Compass*, 103–4, 150.

9. Sheldon Patinkin, *The Second City: Backstage at the World's Greatest Comedy Theater* (Naperville, IL: Sourcebooks, 2000), 17, 20; Jeffrey Sweet, *Something Wonderful Right Away* (New York: Limelight, 1987), xxvii–xxviii.

10. Stuart J. Hecht, interview by Megan E. Geigner, January 28, 2019.

11. Patinkin, *Second City*, 26–27, 32–33.

12. Anne Libera, *The Second City Almanac of Improvisation* (Evanston, IL: Northwestern University Press, 2004), 150–51.

13. Patinkin, *Second City*, 74, 110, 140, 144.

14. Founded in 1971, the Players Workshop served as an affiliated but unofficially recognized training facility for aspiring Second City performers until the opening of The Second City's own training center in 1985.

15. Matt Fotis, *Long Form Improvisation and American Comedy* (New York: Palgrave Macmillan, 2014), 54–55; Rob Kozlowski, *The Art of Chicago Improv* (Portsmouth: Heinemann, 2002), 24–25.

16. Charna Halpern, *Art by Committee* (Colorado Springs: Meriwether, 2006), 103–4.

17. According to Sahlins, a contributing factor in the decision rested in the fact that Close "was seldom a finisher. Basic ideas: brilliant. Nitty gritty of the scenes: not so brilliant." Bernard Sahlins, *Days and Nights at The Second City* (Chicago: Ivan R. Dee, 2001), 101.

18. Charna Halpern, Del Close, and Kim "Howard" Johnson, *Truth in Comedy: The Manual of Improvisation* (Colorado Springs: Meriwether, 1993), 13.

19. Halpern et al., *Truth in Comedy*, 3.

20. Halpern et al., *Truth in Comedy*, 20.

21. Halpern et al., *Truth in Comedy*, 133.

22. Rick Kogan, "Competing for Laughs, 'Harold' Fills House," *Chicago Tribune*, August 16, 1985; David Prescott, "Slowdown Takes Improv One Step Beyond," *Chicago Tribune*, September 28, 1984; Deanna Isaacs, "What's in a Name?," *Chicago Reader*, July 7, 2005.

23. Albert Williams, "Comic Abandon," *Chicago Reader*, August 25, 1988; Albert Williams, "ImprovOlympic," *Chicago Reader*, December 10, 1987; Tom Valeo, "ImprovOlympic," *Chicago Reader*, July 12, 1990; Jack Helbig, "ImprovOlympia / Blue Velveeta," *Chicago Reader*, March 19, 1992.

24. Kim "Howard" Johnson, *The Funniest One in the Room: The Lives and Legends of Del Close* (Chicago: Chicago Review Press, 2008), 319, 332–33; Mary Shen Barnidge, "Night of the Mutant Harolds," *Chicago Reader*, April 25, 1996; Adam Langer, "Dynamite Fun Nest and ImprovOlympic," *Chicago Reader*, March 17, 1994; Fotis, *Long Form*, 72–78.

25. Deborah Lee Wood, "Patrons Sing Blues—Folk and Jazz, Too," *Chicago Tribune*, June 6, 1984.

26. E. R. Shipp, "A Competitive 'Sport,' Harold, Takes the Stage," *New York Times*, December 2, 1985.

27. Rick Kogan, "CrossCurrents Takes on a New Challenge," *Chicago Tribune*, October 31, 1986.

28. Michael Miner, "The Troubles," *Chicago Reader*, November 5, 1987; Michael Miner, "CrossCurrents Still Afloat," *Chicago Reader*, November 19, 1987.

29. Sid Smith, "Stage Notes," *Chicago Tribune*, November 26, 1987.

30. Wood, "Patrons Sing Blues"; Rick Kogan, "Fairmont Patrons Can Stay Put for Whyte," *Chicago Tribune*, January 29, 1988.

31. Steve Dale, "At the Tracks Has Steam Up with Food, Fun," *Chicago Tribune*, October 7, 1988; Albert Williams, "Comic Abandon."

32. Chris Heim, "Another House of Blues," *Chicago Tribune*, October 13, 1988; Rick Kogan, "Cook a Glorious Voice, Grand Show," *Chicago Tribune*, June 29, 1988; Judy Hevrdejs, "When Julie Wilson Sings, She's in Heaven," *Chicago Tribune*, July 7, 1989; O'Malley & Gratteau, "Inc.," *Chicago Tribune*, January 6, 1989; O'Malley & Gratteau, "Inc.," *Chicago Tribune*, August 9, 1989; Rick Kogan, "Two Joints That Swung in the Night," *Chicago Tribune*, August 13, 1989.

33. "Inc.," *Chicago Tribune*, September 17, 1985; Allan Johnson, "Looking for Laughs?," *Chicago Tribune*, May 11, 1990; Phyllis Magida, "Presto: Fun Can Be Pulled Out of a Hat," *Chicago Tribune*, April 4, 1986.

34. Rick Kogan, "Playing the Adventurous Improv Tune," *Chicago Tribune*, June 10, 1990; Fotis, *Long Form*, 63–64; Johnson, *Funniest One in the Room*, 316.

35. Johnson, *Funniest One in the Room*, 318; Fotis, *Long Form*, 72, 77, 185n65.

36. Scott Markwell, "Comedy Mother," *Chicago Reader*, August 10, 1995; Allan Johnson, "Olympic Heroes," *Chicago Reader*, July 29, 2001; Isaacs, "What's in a Name?"

37. "Charna Halpern's Final Tour of the Original Improv Olympic IO Theatre," YouTube, https://www.youtube.com/watch?v=_rFCxY1BUtI.

38. Michael Miner, "Annals of Crime: Chicagoans Steal 'Improv'!," *Chicago Reader*, June 23, 1988; Fotis, *Long Form*, 62.

39. Rick Kogan, "Improv Is Flowing into the Mainstream," *Chicago Tribune*, February 15, 1987; Amy E. Seham, *Whose Improv Is it Anyway?* (Jackson: University Press of Mississippi, 2001), 231n6; Isaacs, "What's in a Name?"

40. Sid Smith, "Funny Business," *Chicago Tribune*, April 9, 1995; Prescott, "Slowdown Takes Improv One Step Beyond"; Halpern et al., *Truth in Comedy*, 10; Ron Grossman, "To Win This Game, Hit Crowd with a Schtick," *Chicago Tribune*, November 22, 1985.

41. Adam Langer, "By Accident," *Chicago Reader*, August 7, 1995; Helbig, "ImprovOlympia / Blue Velveeta."

42. Lawrence Bommer, "Frank Booth in the Blue Velvet Lounge," *Chicago Reader*, October 26, 1995.

43. Robert Burke, "Predisposed Oracle of Contempt," *Chicago Reader*, November 16, 1995; Rich Talarico, "Understanding Improv," *Chicago Reader*, November 23, 1995.

44. Diana Spinrad, "Laugh, Inc.," *Chicago Reader*, August 3, 1989; Jack Helbig, "The Third Rail Comedy Hour," *Chicago Reader*, September 7, 1989; Robert Wolf, "When It Comes to Improvisation, There's a New Game in Town," *Chicago Tribune*, February 23, 1986; Tom Valeo, "Happy Happy Good Show," *Chicago Reader*, July 14, 1988; Jack Helbig, "Theatre," *Chicago Reader*, April 14, 1994; Smith, "Funny Business."

45. Nina Metz, "Inside the New iO, Where Fey, Poehler Got Their Start," *Chicago Tribune*, August 1, 2014; Chris Jones, "iO's Move Is More Than a New Address," *Chicago Tribune*, July 20, 2014; Brianna Wellen, "iO Makes a Big Move into Founder Charna Halpern's 'Dream Theater,'" *Chicago Reader*, August 13, 2014.

46. Mass email, https://mailchi.mp/ioimprov/covid-19-update-from-the-io-theater-6b5w7ntjsz, and linked to iO's Twitter and Facebook accounts.

47. Mass email, https://mailchi.mp/ioimprov/covid-19-update-from-the-io-theater, and linked to iO's Twitter and Facebook accounts.

48. Charna Halpern Facebook page, March 16, March 26, April 4, May 9, 2020.

49. A. D. Quig, "Cook County Passes COVID Property Tax Relief," *Crain's Chicago Business*, May 21, 2020, https://www.chicagobusiness.com/government/cook-county-passes-covid-property-tax-relief.

50. "Support the iO Theater Staff," https://www.gofundme.com/f/support-the-io-theater-staff. Created March 15, 2020, by Steven Plock. The effort did achieve its $30,000 goal.

51. Nina Metz, "What's Your Take: Comedians Working for Free at iO," *Chicago Tribune*, February 21, 2013.

52. Olivia Jackson, "I Will Not Perform at iO until Until [*sic*] the Following Demands Are Met," Change.org, https://www.change.org/p/io-chicago-i-will-not-perform-at-io-until-until-the-following-demands-are-met. The petition had 2,559 signatures when it was closed.

53. Olivia Jackson, "Response from Charna Halpern, Owner and Founder of iO," petition update, https://www.change.org/p/io-chicago-i-will-not-perform-at-io-until-until-the-following-demands-are-met/u/26936317.

54. Free Street Parking, Facebook, June 17, 2020, https://www.facebook.com/freestreetparkingcomedy/photos/rpp.316587925654687/597830017530475/?type=3&theater.

55. David Razowsky, Facebook, June 17, 2020, https://www.facebook.com/photo.php?fbid=10158487050758770&set=a.74158523769&type=3&theater.

56. Melena Ryzik, "Chicago Comedy Institution iO Theater Is Closing," *New York Times*, June 18, 2020; Doug George, "Chicago's iO Theater Is Shutting Down Permanently," *Chicago Tribune*, June 18, 2020; Megh Wright, "Chicago Comedy Institution iO Theater to Shut Down Permanently," *Vulture*, June 18, 2020; Miriam Di Nunzio and Darel Jevens, "Chicago's iO Theater Owner Says Comedy Hub Will Not Reopen," *Chicago Sun-Times*, June 18, 2020; Zach Long, "iO Theater Is Closing Permanently, Due to 'Financial Issues,'" *Timeout*, June 18, 2020.

57. Miriam Di Nunzio, "Chicago's iO Theater for Sale," *Chicago Sun-Times*, October 9, 2020; Chris Jones, "iO Theater of Chicago Is for Sale, a Sad Week for Chicago Comedy," *Chicago Tribune*, October 9, 2020.

Part 3 theater locations. Map created by Kelsey Rydland, Northwestern University Libraries, Geospatial and Data Services.

Part 3

Centering the Decentered, Itinerant, Civic, and Home

Jasmine Jamillah Mahmoud

On a frigid Chicago evening in November 2017, I found myself sitting in a folding chair, crammed among fifty audience members in a narrow venue facing Ashland Avenue. There, eight performers moved within that narrow venue—and at times onto the exterior street—by standing on tables, blowing up balloons, and telling stories of their experiences as Latinx Chicagoans. This was a production of *Meet Juan(ito) Doe*, conceived of by Ricardo Gamboa and codirected by Ana Velazquez; a Free Street production, it was staged in Chicago's South Side Back of the Yards neighborhood in a former refrigerator repair shop, in a venue called the Storyfront. That name—a play on the "storefront" theater so central to Chicago's makeshift aesthetics—and the venue's South Side location suggest the importance of centering stories, lives, and embodiments of those otherwise decentered by dominant Chicago theater practices.

The spatial story of this production frames much of the makeshift Chicago theater and performance in the late twentieth century and early twenty-first century that follows in chapters 8 through 10. Often, work in this period was (and still is) staged within brazenly repurposed spaces as purposely itinerant productions in Chicago neighborhoods and geographies not known for theater in dominant (or racially white) spheres; this work often centered stories of minoritized populations and variously multilingual people. The chapters in this, the closing section of *Makeshift Chicago Stages*, capture this spatial and racial presence of Chicago theater, and do so through an ethnographic lens.

In "Reclaiming Space: An Oral History of Teatro Vista," Laura A. Lodewyck chronicles the lifespan of the Chicago theater company devoted to staging Latinx voices. Spanish for "theater with a view," Teatro Vista was founded by Edward Torres and Henry Godinez in 1990. Lodewyck's chapter documents the theater's purposely itinerant work, with productions "mounted across non-theatrical spaces such as the Edgewater Presbyterian Church and the former Mexican Fine Arts Center Museum [now the National Museum of Mexican Art], to partnerships with companies with established traditional theater spaces." Crucially, she argues that for Teatro Vista, itinerancy is an opportunity, rather than a detriment. She particularly focuses on the aesthetics of productions—including ensemble member Sandra Delgado's *La Havana Madrid*—as well as on the meanings made by putting Latinx stories on makeshift stages through the city of Chicago.

LaRonika Marie Thomas's chapter also centers the spatial with an exploration of the work of Theaster Gates, the Chicago-born Black artist and urbanist known for using social practice techniques to animate spaces. In "Temple-Swapping in the City: The Spatial Imaginary and Performances of Place-Making in the Work of Theaster Gates," Thomas shows how, contradistinctively to techniques used by Teatro Vista, Gates purchased many of the Chicago spaces in which he staged performances, including a home in the South Side's Grand Crossing neighborhood and a former bank that he bought from the City of Chicago for one dollar. In these venues, Gates staged intentional interactions and performances that practiced different repertories within racially segregated and dispossessed neighborhood spaces. Using Gates's investment in real estate and performances in mostly Black neighborhoods, Thomas argues for his work through her concept of civic dramaturgy as "performing identity through changes to and impacts on the built environment, along with a method of analyzing and contextualizing those performances to better understand the multiple modes of identity expression that make up . . . Chicago." Her particular focus on Gates's term "temple-swapping" reveals how Gates staged makeshift performances to expand and confound zoned notions of residential, religious, and commercial space in a way that reimagined aesthetic, racial, and spatial relationships.

In my chapter, I center the spatial techniques of the Chicago Home Theater Festival (CHTF). Founded in Chicago in 2012 by Chicago-based theater artists Irina Zadov, Laley Lippard, and Blake Russell, CHTF first staged a monthlong festival of productions in 2013 in

Participants in the 2016 Chicago Home Theater Festival walk across the street in the Grand Crossing neighborhood on the city's South Side. Photograph by eedahahm. Courtesy of the photographer and the Chicago Home Theater Festival.

private homes in neighborhoods across Chicago. My chapter features interviews with two of the founders—Zadov and Lippard—as well as two producers central to how the festival grew across its five-year lifespace in Chicago: Aymar Jean Christian and Meida McNeal. McNeal, for example, worked to extend the annual festival's productions into public parks, expanding how the CHTF centered the private home space to reimagine theater's public. For the founders and producers, the home space allowed for freedom to stage works without regard to institutional confines, but rather with regard to a home's real and imagined relationships, people, and aesthetics. Through the makeshift space of the home, CHTF interrelated performers, audiences, geographies, and relationships often not apparent or available on more traditional stages.

Each chapter in this section relies on ethnographic methods, including observation, performance documentation, and interviews with Chicago theater makers, as the central way of collecting and interpreting data. As a section these chapters suggest that a closer understanding of makeshift practices comes from documenting and interpreting the voices of practitioners. Thomas not only interviewed Gates, but her chapter also analyzes other interviews Gates has given, and she includes close ethnographic documentation of his artistic and spatial work. Lodewyck collected oral histories from Teatro Vista's cofounders

Edward Torres and Henry Godinez as well as other figures central to the theater's work and understanding of Chicago Latinx theater, including Sandra Marquez, Nilda Hernandez, Ricardo Gutiérrez, Myrna Salazar, Eddie Martinez, and Carlos Tortolero. Her chapter focuses on many of these voices to archive their stories as central to what has often been decentered in Chicago theater history. For example, Lodewyck interviews Sandra Delgado, whose play *La Havana Madrid*, about a Chicago-based Latinx nightclub, relied upon interviews for its script and was produced by Teatro Vista during the 2016–2019 seasons at various venues including a nightclub-lit space. This work, Lodewyck reveals, staged an immersive experience by taking place in the setting named in the script. Participant observation also extends this section's ethnographic methods. My own experience attending a CHTF production in Humboldt Park—walking from the Chicago Transit Authority (CTA) station with a guide who grew up in the neighborhood, sitting on the couches of the hosts who lived in the venue, and experiencing the multi-genre performances—directly influenced how I chose to interview the festival's founders and producers. These ethnographic methods, as this section attests, capture the multi-voiced and multi-experienced meanings made by these practices.

Crucially, this section highlights "makeshift" through a needed focus on racially and ethnically minoritized theater makers, who are often decentered in Chicago history. Much of the history Lodewyck presents reveals how Teatro Vista, as an itinerant theater company, had to counter existing stereotypes, exclusions, and quotas given to Latinx artists and companies. Lodewyck suggests that by vigorously staging shows across traditional and nontraditional venues in Chicago, Teatro Vista imbued the racially diverse city with a truer representation of the plurality of Latinx experiences and imaginations. Similarly, by centering Theaster Gates's spatial technique of purchasing Chicago property in disrepair to make performance, Thomas suggests that Gates's social practice included subverting the century-old racist spatial logics such as restrictive covenants and redlining that prevented and dispossessed Black homeowners. Part of Gates's makeshift theater practices included a performative critique of structurally racist forces that prevent Black homeownership. The founders and producers of the Chicago Home Theater Festival specifically curated performances in homes whose neighborhoods were often outside of traditional theater geographies, in order to subvert, even temporarily, the intense hyper-racial segregation in Chicago. The space of the home invited embodiments across racially segregated lines.

Chicago—the racially hyper-segregated city where "urban ethnography" was codified in the 1920s, the city on the make and of the makeshift—provided the fabric for this work and for our analysis of this work. This closing section differs from much of this volume with its ethnographic methods and often presentist focus on the last thirty years of Chicago theater. But it also coheres with the longer genealogy of Chicago using makeshift spaces to represent and reimagine performance in the city.

8

Reclaiming Space

An Oral History of Teatro Vista

Laura A. Lodewyck

As Michael McKinnie writes, following David Harvey and Michel de Certeau, "space does not simply exist but has to be made through social practice."[1] McKinnie posits that one of the assumptions of a materialist geography is that space does not function merely as a "pre-existing context" for performance, but is built into meaningful existence through the dialectic of place with performance.[2] This meaning is acknowledged as fundamentally temporal; spaces are made and remade, dependent upon complex interactions in particular moments. Though performances across Chicago have endowed theatrical architecture and geographies with significance, a theatrical site does not typically hold lasting evidence of itinerant companies' work. While spaces across Chicagoland are filled with the memories of such companies' histories, the theaters are not named for their work. The physical structures where foundational performances occurred may not exist in the same form and may be publicly disconnected from this past. These places alone typically do not materially recall itinerant productions; their legacy may be manifested largely in the stories of those who lived them.

Likewise, not much academic work has been published about the Latinx theater communities specific to Chicago, despite their thriving presence and expansive history.[3] Demographically, the census category of "Hispanic" is categorized as the largest minority in Chicago, reaching almost a third of the 2.7 million population as of 2017.[4] That which has been written, such as José Castro Urioste's 2013 article in *Latin American Theatre Review*, notes the idea of underrepresentation as reflected in the performance itself: "The main characteristic of the latest performances by the Latino theater groups of Chicago is the portrayal of a self whose voice is denied. At the same time, this self insists on being heard in order to demonstrate his/her existence."[5] Urioste's point is compelling: such existence should be uncontested. As the stories here represent, Latinx artists and community members are an ever-present but often under-recognized force of Chicago and its artistic life.

Itinerant Latinx companies can therefore be said to be twice erased. Physical manifestation is not communicated through the relative permanence of architectural structure, and the accounts of such organizations are not widely documented.[6] This chapter seeks to reclaim a part of such foundational twenty-first-century histories through a focus on Chicago-based Teatro Vista, who leveraged its early days as a company in itinerancy to make space for work throughout the city. Against the narrative of marginalization—and building on and with traditions of other Chicago Latinx companies—Teatro Vista asserted not only the need to share Latinx talent and vision, but the right to claim ownership as part of Chicago's theatrical culture, geographies, and history. In this chapter, I document a part of the city's theatrical legacy in tracing some moments relevant to Teatro Vista's making of space, both literal and metaphorical. I relay the company's movement from a meeting of artists in 1989 to a formal ensemble in 1991 to a now well-established company that functions as a leader in Chicago theater. After charting origins across various spaces in the 1990s, this chapter closes with an account of a twenty-first-century Teatro Vista performance that deliberately considers both the aesthetic creation of space and the reclamation of histories from within Chicago's landscape,[7] entitled *La Havana Madrid*.

The accounts that follow are from the earliest days of the company, as well as from representative moments across Teatro Vista's timeline. From productions in community venues to those at Teatro Vista's residency in the Richard Christiansen Theater at Victory Gardens, these histories come from the words of those who lived them.[8] In collecting some of the artists' narratives regarding moments where "spaces" were created across these years, I rely on oral history as a model. Oral histories promote the words of those present, who best speak for themselves. Though much more could be said of the company's rich decades-long history, these particular stories are included due to their direct relation to space. By space, I refer to physical investment within the geography of the city, but also symbolic space as part of Chicago's theatrical story, as well as material contributions to the city's canon of creative work. This chapter also serves to document ongoing moments in Teatro Vista's chronology, record their ensemble history, and evidence several important productions in the company's record, including a full production history that includes theater sites.

As these stories demonstrate, from its inception in 1990, Teatro Vista rebelled against practices that excluded artists of Latinx heritage while they simultaneously celebrated shared cultural histories and the innovation of their members. Over the years, the ensemble and its leadership understood the particular opportunities that the Chicago theatrical community provided. These artists embraced a wide geographical collection of creative relationships, as members of both the Latinx and the larger Chicago theater communities, and in doing so claimed space for their artistic voices. Here, I follow how Teatro Vista developed and advanced an artistic mission that did not simply draw on its partnerships and locations throughout the city, but helped shape Chicago theatrical culture from within.[9]

While Teatro Vista is a critical site of Latinx performance production in Chicago, it is certainly not the only local theater committed to Latinidad. Teatro Vista exists within a broader genealogy of Latinx Chicago theater, and there are significant voices, histories, and companies that also demand reclaiming and recognition. Such instrumental forces in Chicago theater history include Aguijón Theater,[10] the longest standing Latinx theater company in Chicago, founded in 1989 and committed to Spanish-language and bilingual works; Urban-Theater Company,[11] dedicated to the Humboldt Park community and the works of Chicago Latinx artists, who announced the celebration of their Quinceañera in 2020; and Latino Chicago Theatre,[12] a company which predated the other organizations in its founding in 1979, and was eventually shuttered after a catastrophic fire in their space. This particular detailing of Chicago's theater history does not focus on these founders' and members' stories, though they are also remarkable accounts and are foundational to any Chicago Latinx narrative of theater. In the confines of this chapter, I show how Teatro Vista's histories animated spaces—geographical, communal, cultural, and aesthetic—that were filled and served by their often-itinerant work, and in doing so cocreated the artistic life of Chicago theater. These productions were mounted in non-theatrical spaces such as the Edgewater Presbyterian Church and the former Mexican Fine Arts Center Museum, and through partnerships with companies with established, traditional theater spaces such as Lifeline Theatre, Goodman Theatre, Next Theatre, Oak Park Festival Theatre, Apple Tree Theatre, Steppenwolf Theatre, and Victory Gardens Theater.

1989–1991: Partnerships and First Productions

Depending on whom you ask, Teatro Vista was born for a variety of reasons. "Culturally, we [Latinx theater artists] were marginalized,"[13] says founding member Henry Godinez, a resident artistic associate at Goodman Theatre and professor of theater at Northwestern University. Latino Chicago Theatre had been established since 1979. In the early 1990s, Godinez recalled Teatro Vista receiving questions from fellow theater artists and producers as to why "another" Latinx company was necessary. As Godinez pointed out, this was in contrast to majority white theaters: in the 1970s, no one had asked the directors of Steppenwolf why Chicago needed another white theater company. Godinez recollected reviews for a show that he directed at the Goodman, Luis Alfaro's *Straight as a Line*, which questioned why a Latino playwright was writing about British characters. As Godinez recalls, "It was so revealing."

Teatro Vista emerged from a meeting of artists in this context. "It all started when Eddie [Torres] and I were in a production together in 1989, in a play called *The Rover*," Godinez said. "Eddie was fresh out of Roosevelt [University] and was in the ensemble, and I was playing one of the leads." Godinez played the leading character Belvile alongside the "wonderful Mexican actor" Ramiro Carrillo as Don Pedro. Torres and Godinez noted that, at the time, they observed that it was rare to see three Latinx actors together in that context. "I had never seen three Latinx actors in a production that wasn't 'a Latino play,'" Godinez recalled. Director Kyle Donnelly had chosen to stage John Barton's adaptation of Aphra Behn's seventeenth-century work, which in Barton's interpretation was set in a Spanish colony in South America. This deliberate staging provided a concept that called for actors of color, and specifically, Latinx actors.

Edward Torres is an accomplished director (some notable works include the world premiere and subsequent Off Broadway productions of Pulitzer Prize finalist *The Elaborate Entrance of Chad Deity* and the world premiere of *La Canción*), actor (most recently, as of this writing, appearing in the world premiere of *Downstate*, a coproduction of

Steppenwolf and the National Theatre of Great Britain, performing in the fall of 2018 and the spring of 2019), and a 2013 3Arts Artist Award winner. Torres recalled being cast in the Goodman's production of *The Rover* and meeting Godinez: "It was shocking to me, trying to figure this out as a kid from the South Side," because he "saw this Latin actor playing the lead role amongst other actors."[14] Torres began discussing the possibility of reading Latinx plays with Godinez, citing the absence of these works in production. Torres elaborated on their move toward this collaboration:

> There is so much work, and history and culture, that one or two [theater companies] is never a good idea to be the sole proprietors of that. I started Teatro Vista also because I wasn't getting any traction auditioning for "regular" theaters in Chicago, which was very hard to do. I wasn't an MFA actor. . . . That was the time where there was a lot of tension in Chicago about cross-cultural casting, or what they liked to call "colorblind" casting. All those issues affected me. That pushed me to say, let me just do this, because it seems to be what the tradition in Chicago is: if you cannot find a place, then you build it for yourself, and make it happen. And that's that blue-collar, Chicago-working-class ethic, you know?

Torres was speaking to an array of issues affecting Latinx artists: the fact that Latinx heritage is not a monolithic culture, nor one that can be contained within a single company; the difficulty of breaking into a professional career as an actor, particularly if opportunities are gatekept by institutions that arbitrarily prefer specific credentials; the issues around casting, namely the limited roles afforded to non-white performers; and the mainstream questioning of casting practices and the possibilities that such emerging conversations opened, despite still-problematic casting philosophies. Moreover, Torres categorized the creation of a new theater company as a uniquely "Chicago" act, steeped in labor. The work that Torres and others noted across the years may have been joyous and rewarding, but it was still a significant and sustained effort. Notably, every individual interviewed here expressed the importance of acknowledging numerous figures who have contributed to Teatro Vista's achievements across the years.

Around the time of the 1989 production of *The Rover*, Torres and Godinez arranged an early reading of Eduardo Machado's *Broken Eggs*, a show that later became one of Teatro Vista's inaugural productions. The play features a Cuban American family nostalgic for the homeland they fled, and follows their reflection on this loss as they prepare for a comically elaborate high-society wedding in Los Angeles. Torres described their choice of the play:

> Henry said, "This is something that might be fun. It's funny, it can include most of the company, and we can cast it however we want." . . . It had more women characters than most. . . . It was big enough to include as many actors as we had in the ensemble. And that was one of the first times that we used an actress of color that wasn't Latin to be in the show. . . . I like to think we were ahead of our time. . . . [The play was] having to do with family dynamics, and the fact that this kid was gay, but hadn't come out. We also had a man playing the grandmother. The play was set during a wedding—and a lot of issues come out at weddings!

The play selection speaks to factors important to the early company: representation of Latinx stories and authors onstage; utilization of the full company, along with progressive casting and attention to issues of gender and sexuality; and the joy of entertaining audiences with heightened comedic situations. This is consistent with Torres's recounting of another main impulse for the creation of the company: "We were impassioned with the idea of storytelling and theater." Such stories demanded inclusion not simply in order to rectify their absence, but because of the expressive value they added. The play also addressed a hunger in audiences and artists to experience this work. As Godinez emphasized of this initial reading of *Broken Eggs*, simply put, "The reading was really popular."[15] This reception encouraged Torres and Godinez to further continue their mission and to mount full performances.

Along the way, the group transitioned from a loose collective of performers to a formal company. Godinez explained that the need was straightforward: "Basically, it was a group of actors that wanted to see our culture represented and wanted to do plays about our cultures." From that moment, Teatro Vista was committed to defining Latinx culture broadly, and from the early years has represented a wide spectrum of Latinx cultures. Godinez specified, for instance, "Mexican, Dominican, Colombian, Argentine, Afro-Caribbean . . . this is what made us different, and this became our go-to answer as to 'why another Latino

The cast of *Broken Eggs* at the Greenview Arts Center, 1991. Standing: Maricela Ochoa, Margie Oquendo, Jenna Ford Jackson, Edward Torres, and Noah Navar. Seated: Marilynn Dodds Frank, Juan Carlos Seda, and Gustavo Mellado. Written by Eduardo Machado; directed by Henry Godinez; costumes by Sraa Davidson; lighting design by John Imburgia and Dana Low; scene design by Rob Martin. Photographer unknown. Courtesy of Edward Torres and Ricardo Gutiérrez.

company.'" Torres originally was also a member of Latino Chicago Theatre, a company that was helmed by Juan Ramirez and started through a grant earned by Victory Gardens Theater's Dennis Začek. Začek, who served as artistic director of Victory Gardens for over thirty years, received the $94,000 grant from CBS for a "Hispanic-themed production,"[16] and this grew into Latino Chicago Theatre. Torres recalled that Latino Chicago was supportive of the formation of a new company, in that Latino Chicago felt that "we can't carry the banner by ourselves."[17] Torres stated that the two companies worked to similar ends (sometimes literally, as with an unofficial coproduction of Migdalia Cruz's *Lolita de Lares* that he directed with Latino Chicago Theatre in 1995) but branched out in different forms of storytelling:

> Being an ensemble member of Latino Chicago, and then creating Teatro Vista, those things were kind of in sync already. So by the time Teatro Vista got its full start . . . [the Latino Chicago company members] were doing work that was more devised at that point. . . . I believe that part of the genesis of Teatro Vista came out of Latino Chicago . . . especially at that time when writers were starting to write lot of new work. . . . We were taking the mantle on of trying to produce newer Latino work from them.[18]

This meant that Teatro Vista was invested in finding and reading plays. After coming together with Godinez on the initial reading of *Broken Eggs*, Torres said that the group of actor friends would simply "get together and have readings in an apartment and have food."[19] Community was as important as the art. Torres joked, "We always would call ourselves theater with an appetite, not just Teatro Vista [theater with a view]." As Torres recalled, "there were not really a lot of opportunities for Latinos to do work that represented themselves onstage," and these script readings highlighted the opportunities of plays not being produced.

Teatro Vista's first official productions happened in tandem, in 1991: a full production of their earlier reading of Machado's *Broken Eggs* in October at the Greenview Arts Center in Rogers Park, and *The Crossing* by Hugo Salcedo in January at the Mexican Fine Arts Center Museum (now called the National Museum of Mexican Art) in Pilsen. Torres had reached out to his former high school teacher and the museum's founder, Carlos Tortolero, about producing Latinx plays. At the end of their conversation, Tortolero offered $10,000 to produce a play in the museum's space. Torres explains that Tortolero's contribution "pushed me to say, hey, we need to start." As Tortolero was interested in mounting a Mexican play for the museum, Godinez and Torres found another "really wonderful" play in *The Crossing*, based on the 1987 real-life deaths of over two dozen Mexican men who suffocated in a railroad boxcar attempting to immigrate to the United States, and they selected it to produce at the museum.

Today's National Museum of Mexican Art has a history of supporting the performing arts, as well as social justice and community concerns. Tortolero stated: "We actually did more performing arts than visual arts, believe it or not! We always wanted to be that. We wanted to be free and in the neighborhood—we didn't want to be elitist."[20] Once Tortolero hosted over two hundred women, most of them over fifty years old, who never had a mammogram before, and had a health education event showing them how to complete breast self-exams. "We got a text saying, 'Museums don't do that!'" Tortolero laughed, "but that's how [the] backwards museums are." It had always been important to Tortolero to use space in a way that benefited community and the arts. In 1994, he began two festivals: the annual Del Corazón Festival, which was discontinued in 2010 due to funding; and the Sor Juana Festival, which extended into its twenty-fifth year as of 2019. As Tortolero emphasized, educating and involving audiences across the diverse work of the museum has always been central to its mission. The seventeenth-century nun and self-educated scholar Sor Juana Inés de la Cruz is a particularly important historical and cultural figure. "Every child should hear about her," Tortolero stated. The Sor Juana Festival features plays, music, film screenings, book readings, and other relevant cultural events. The 2019 festival, for instance, included a "Selena Tribute" dance party.

Tortolero also personally facilitated a number of companies through the support of the museum. Torres noted of Tortolero, "He's a very important person for the Latino theater history in Chicago."[21] As Tortolero relayed: "Teatro Vista and Aguijón were both born here in the 1990s. In 1990 we let them keep the box office, and we paid them . . . the more groups the better. . . . I can't believe how many we've launched."[22] Godinez and Torres both express gratitude for the furtherance of their work, particularly in these critical early years. Godinez marveled that "all of our partner organizations [across the years] were really super supportive."[23]

The Mexican Fine Arts Center Museum and the Greenview Arts Center provided different kinds of support particular to the creation of space in Teatro Vista's early productions. As materialist analysis of space posits, place is connected to both political and economic ends, though it cannot be interpreted merely in economic terms.[24] However, the practical realities of space are ones that shaped their work. Torres explained:

> The museum was like a proscenium lecture hall. We couldn't do anything with the wood, we couldn't nail the wood. You couldn't do all the things you wanted to do. We didn't have a lot of theater lights . . . they had a few, and what used to be a really good system, but would be antiquated now . . . they had a few lights there, and a light booth that was really part of their storage facility. . . . They funded that production. They gave us ten thousand dollars to start that show, which was very generous. But they didn't know a lot about [theater production] scheduling, so we had to educate each other—we didn't know a lot about the museum and the building facility, right? So you could only be there for a certain period of time before the alarm system came off. We had to pay the guard extra to help us stay a little later. And Carlos was great about all of that. And then we had to schedule things in conjunction with events at the Mexican Fine Arts [museum], hoping that we could also build an audience through them.[25]

Torres elaborated that the flexibility of the large proscenium-type space at the museum was later used for innovative purposes. The limits of the space, in this case, helped inspire creative choices:

> We did another show there called *Santos & Santos* [by Octavio Solis], which had fifteen people in the cast. . . . Because it was a museum, it wasn't theater seating. It was more like bleacher seating. And [the museum] actually then got bleachers that you could put seats on . . . and you could move it around anywhere you wanted. So at some point, the Mexican Arts started to get really creative about how they would do it. They started to do theater festivals [the Del Corazón Festival and the Sor Juana Festival]. They would do stuff in an alley [seating arrangement]. They would use that proscenium stage where you could set

> people on that stage, or where you could look down on it—but you still couldn't nail anything! . . . And they started to figure out creative ways, as time went on, to utilize that space in a very, very funky, cool kind of way.

These extended accounts of the physical space that hosted Teatro Vista's initial production mark the location as one of dynamic and exciting possibilities but also one that presented practical challenges due to the atypical features of the stage structure and the institutional business model. As Torres noted with humor, there were clear technical and design limitations due to the permanent architecture of the museum that prohibited damage to the space, which was not designed for theatrical use. Performance schedules proved out of sync with traditional business hours, even requiring improvised arrangements with security personnel.

However, a partnership with a venue not already dedicated to performance meant the potential to expand theatrical audiences in works such as the museum's festivals. The adaptability of the space in terms of seating arrangements brought inventive aesthetics and helped invite creative spatial possibilities, in the tradition of Chicago's revamped "storefront" spaces. As Torres mentioned, the openness of the museum space also meant the ability to accommodate larger casts like that of the fifteen-person *Santos & Santos*. That is a relatively sizable cast within the tradition of itinerant Chicago companies, which often mount smaller productions in response to material conditions such as intimate storefront theater space.

A few months later, Teatro Vista staged the full production of *Broken Eggs* in a very different space, at the Greenview Arts Center. Godinez notes that the company was "interested in bridging the gaps between communities, between ourselves as Latinx artists and actors . . . and also bridg[ing] the gap between Latino and non-Latino audiences."[26] In other words, they wanted non-Latinx audiences to experience their work. It was for this reason that Teatro Vista purposefully headed north to the Greenview Arts Center in the 6400 block of Devon Avenue in Rogers Park. "We were interested in exploring and representing who we were as multicultural Americans," Godinez explained. This site was more of a traditional theater space, per Torres:

> Of course, the difference between a space that you rent, and a space that is a museum—they are completely different spaces,

> and two different things. There was also an aesthetic [difference] as well. The museum had this big proscenium space. . . . And then the Greenview Arts Center was a more of a [conventional] theater, but again, had its own limitation, because you have owners who run the space who are trying to figure out what they want to do with the space.[27]

While the museum ostensibly connected to existing audiences of the Latinx community in Pilsen, as well as patrons of the museum invested in Mexican American culture, the architecture of the space required more flexibility in physically mounting the aesthetic vision of the show. The Greenview Arts Center, however, was prefabricated as a structured theatrical space. As Torres noted, "All we did was put the play up. We had postcards, and we distributed the postcards—old-school style, you know, put up a bunch of theater signs—everybody get your family and friends to come." As a rental space, however, Greenview necessitated outreach to the local community, and scheduling had to be managed around other companies' bookings as well. Torres frames Teatro Vista's experiences at both sites as an exciting but labor-intensive time of learning and an era of navigating production logistics for a young company.

These material considerations are just a few of the sheer practical issues to oversee when a production space is externally managed. Despite this, the founders approached itinerancy as an opportunity, to the extent that they were able. Godinez feels that their itinerancy led to many coproduction partnerships, highlighting their work with "all kinds of people" across the city.[28] In their first few years, Teatro Vista worked with Goodman Theatre in their former space downtown, Lifeline Theatre and Next Theatre in Evanston, New American Theater in Rockford, and notably, with future theatrical home Victory Gardens Theater. Godinez reflected, "We felt that really, being itinerant was kind of useful in our desire to share our work with all people." On another facet of collaboration, Torres explained that his part in the founding of Teatro Vista is also indebted to his work with Latino Chicago Theatre. Torres notes that Latino Chicago "is extremely important in the history of Chicago when you are talking about space, and when you are talking about the first real Latino theater company in the city that started to produce plays in English for a Latin American audience."[29]

According to Torres, Latino Chicago Theatre was "revolutionary in having an actual space that they had to refurbish themselves, and in that we had to build that space out."[30] It was a firehouse at 1625 North Damen Avenue in the area of Wicker Park and Bucktown, sadly destroyed in a fire a few years later, in 1997. Torres continued:

> When I auditioned for Latino Chicago, and I became a member, they had just acquired a firehouse. They acquired the firehouse for a dollar to the city through some sort of TIF program. But before that, they were housed in a bomb shelter, which was under North Avenue and Milwaukee, the five-points corner over on the North Side. . . . They were in that neighborhood at the time where it was not gentrified. It was still very much Latin, Puerto Rican. . . . But just like the Steppenwolf space used to be on Halsted further north, they had a small space right across from the famous actor bar called the Gaslight.[31] . . . And they also had the bomb shelter under the street in Chicago, which is, I think, very unique. I don't know too many theater companies that can have an office and space in a bomb shelter under North Avenue. We had great parties, I can tell you that!—that being in late eighties, early nineties, of course.

Godinez agrees that Latino Chicago had "a space that was pretty awesome, that old firehouse—on Damen, near the heart of Bucktown. Now it would be worth a fortune."[32] Founding Latino Chicago Theatre member Nilda Hernandez recalled the path to obtaining the space as more fraught. Latino Chicago was given the bomb shelter by local building owners, and they knew early on that they wanted to transition their company to the firehouse space. Hernandez spoke at length about the material and moral support provided by local businesses, including banks that allowed use of their parking lots, and bars like the Border Line Tap (now the Wicker Park Tap) that encouraged Latino Chicago's settling in the area. Hernandez said:

> Our goal was to get the firehouse. That was our goal. . . . We had the support of some of the neighboring businesses. . . . The Northside Café—which was based on the North Side of Chicago—knew that we were there, and they were so intrigued that they moved into the neighborhood. They literally brought the Northside Café to the Damen area, because they wanted to be a part of this culture.[33]

Hernandez's account demonstrates that Latino Chicago's establishment helped motivate the cultural investment at the time. Latino Chicago's presence invited others to become a part of an arts presence in the neighborhood.

However, obtaining the firehouse was not as simple as completing a TIF program process from the city. Hernandez recalled:

> Juan [Ramirez, Latino Chicago's artistic director] happened to walk in [to the firehouse], and found out that it was being used as storage. You know, it wasn't really anything. Somebody was running a private ambulance company there, also. But it was supposed to be a part of the city. So we went to this community meeting, and they would not even [listen]—we sat down, and you might think they'd say, "OK, we'll listen to what you'll have to say," but our story never came up. So we just literally stood up, all of us, at that community meeting, and Juan would not stop talking. You know, he was very upset. . . . He was very vocal. He was like, "This is what we wanted to talk about. You told us to write on these scribbly papers of yours, and what you wanted—" And Mayor Washington just said . . . "We're going to set up a meeting." And we did. We went to his office . . . and we voiced what we wanted to do: build a theater there. And there was a time [for not-for-profits] when the city . . . basically said, "Here, you can have the theater. And all you have to do, after a certain amount of years, is pay $35,000, and have it." It's like we were renting it for a dollar a year. And right away, Juan said whoever was in there had to leave. . . . And so [Mayor Washington] said come the following week and pick up the keys. And I went. I went downtown to pick up the keys. And of course they were giving me a hard time. They were like, "Oh, we're looking for it." And I was on the phone with Juan, and I said, "Juan, this is crazy. I'm not leaving here." The guy comes out, and he goes, "OK, well, why don't you come back in couple of days," and I said, "No." I said, "Mayor Washington said the key would be ready. I'm here for the key. If you cannot give me the key, then let's go talk to the mayor." And he knew. The guy knew I was not budging. . . . So finally, of course, the key appeared.

Power does not easily cede space. Further, since the late 1980s, existing families were pushed farther west and north by rising property prices, and by the implication that they no longer had any authority of ownership to the area. By the time of Latino Chicago's catastrophic fire in 1997, the neighborhood was becoming rapidly populated with a white "hipster" demographic. In the spring of 1994, for instance, the famed graffiti on Abco Building Supply in Wicker Park, which read "Yuppies Out—The Natives Are Hostile," was erased; in February, the "white-tablecloth" restaurant Papa Jin's window was smashed, with "Keep Warm—Burn Out the Rich" painted outside. Other graffiti in the area read, "Stop the War on the Poor" and "Yuppies Afuera" ["Yuppies Outside"].[34] In one heartbreaking account of the spontaneous fire that destroyed the firehouse, *Chicago Reader* relays:

> "Nobody called this in," the chief said. He pointed at Con Fusion's floor-to-ceiling windows. Patrons sat watching the action, enjoying a perverse dinner theater. "The people in this restaurant, they shoulda been able to see something. I don't know. Turns out somebody was passing by and saw the fire. They walked into the firehouse up the street and told them." When Raul Jaimes, an actor and light technician, heard this, he turned red and faced the restaurant, unleashing a torrent of profanity in Spanish on the unsuspecting diners. Someone put a calming hand on his arm. A huge bear of a firefighter approached the group, his helmet and greatcoat well worn. He had once served at this firehouse. "It broke my heart," he said. "When I got here, I went right up to where my old locker was." [Latino Chicago company member Michelle] Banks smiled. "We never took the names of the firemen off the lockers."

With this story comes the end of an era of a Latinx company essential to the theatrical legacy of Teatro Vista and the wider Chicago community. It is poignant in its account of belonging, ownership, and recognition of history. Latino Chicago—who, by all accounts, went to great lengths to clean and redesign the firehouse—notably did not feel that the previous inhabitants' names should be erased from their place in the building's history. Today, that once-abandoned firehouse obtained by Latino Chicago Theatre for a pittance (though not without a notable bureaucratic struggle) would indeed "be worth a fortune," in Godinez's words. At the time, the communities in these areas supported the early theatrical work created in these spaces, sometimes explicitly in the case of the financial sponsorship of Tortolero's Mexican Fine Arts Center

Museum in Pilsen, or in the investment of businesses near Latino Chicago's firehouse in Bucktown. Teatro Vista's early itinerant spaces and the legacy of Latino Chicago's firehouse illustrate the power and relevance of both geographical and aesthetic ownership. Itinerancy, while a real and material challenge, provided Teatro Vista the opportunity to experiment with production in very different spaces while fulfilling their mission to make space for Latinx stories.

1997–1998: Transitions and Beyond

When Godinez left Teatro Vista in 1997, Torres took the mantle of artistic director. He was joined in 1998 by Sandra Marquez as associate artistic director, and she managed many of the day-to-day operations throughout her eight years in the role. Marquez is a noteworthy theatrical artist: the first Latinx member of Steppenwolf Theatre as of 2016, as well as the first self-identified Latina to play a lead role in a Steppenwolf Theatre production (Sonia in 2006's *Sonia Flew*, by Melinda Lopez).

Though not associated with Teatro Vista's founding, Marquez was a key figure during her tenure, and her contributions were essential to the company's longevity and continued success. Marquez recalled that, in the mid to late 1990s, the company "became more of an ensemble collective."[35] She clarified that Teatro Vista focuses on Latinx stories, but has never been a Latinx-only company. She further specified: "We have always been inclusive in terms of our ensemble members." Marquez credited several company members in these early days of the ensemble: Sabrina duArte, who was "a big part of the company . . . she did a lot of the heavy lifting early on in the company's history," and who has since passed away; Deb Davis, an emeritus ensemble member who was instrumental in the company's development, and who, among other things, headed the play-reading committee for thoughtful and strategic season selection; Diana Pando, who Marquez emphasizes worked incredibly hard in a large role as managing director; current ensemble member Charín Alvarez, a prominent Chicago theater, film, and television performer, who as of this writing most recently closed the 2019 production of Isaac Gomez's *La Ruta* at Steppenwolf; Juan Villa, a now Los Angeles–based actor, director, and playwright, author of *Don Chipotle*, *Empanada for a Dream*, and *Finding Pancho*; and Sandra Delgado, an accomplished actress and playwright, author of

La Havana Madrid and *Hundreds and Hundreds of Stars*, among other works. Though these individuals are a critical part of the company's advancement and history, Marquez underscored that many others also contributed over the years.

During the late 1990s and early 2000s, Teatro Vista continued to define itself as a company, mounting works in venues across Chicagoland, often in collaboration: again in Pilsen at the Mexican Fine Arts Center Museum for *The Sins of Sor Juana*; across the North and Near North Sides at Theater on the Lake and with Steppenwolf at their Studio Theatre (both in Lincoln Park); with Victory Gardens in their Studio Theatre at its former location just southeast of their current location at the Biograph in Lakeview; with the now shuttered American Theater Company at their former warehouse space in North Center, adjacent to Roscoe Village; downtown at the Goodman's Albert Theatre as part of the Latino Theatre Festival; in nearby suburbs at the Oak Park Festival Theatre and at the since-closed Apple Tree Theatre in Highland Park; and in several productions at the Chopin Theatre, in the 1500 block of Division Street in Wicker Park. Marquez recalls the Chopin space, in particular, as advancing the company's collaborative spirit:

> We used to work there a lot, because it was affordable, and it felt very homey. We all felt very at home there for a number of years. It was tricky, though, because of the parking situation! . . . I have some very good memories of working there. It feels like a very "Chicago story," because that is a theater where a lot of companies have worked. . . . Sometimes I still do miss the feeling of what it used to be like, at the Chopin. It's a quirky place, you know. . . . I remember that once we were having problems with the light board, and Ziggy [Zygmunt Dyrkacz], who owns the Chopin, wasn't around, but his thirteen-year-old son was home. They lived above the theater. I went upstairs, and I got Chris to come downstairs, and he knew how to fix the light board. I just have fond memories of that. Something about it . . . all of us together making it happen. We wanted to make the show good, and we were working so hard, and doing all kinds of things to get the show up. I think probably the production that stands out in my mind is a play called *Icarus* by Edwin Sánchez. It was at the Chopin. It was . . . sort of a typical proscenium style, though it's not really a proscenium theater. I just remember it was, I think, five people in the cast, and

> four of them were company members. I just remember having the sense of—I finally really belonged to this group of people. It may not have been the most memorable show in the world, but everyone was just so committed to making it happen. And I think it was one of the first ones that we all chose together. So it felt like this committed group effort.

As Marquez's reflections illustrate, these itinerant years were not simply moments of nascence or uncertainty, but experiences that provided genuine occasions for collaboration and community building. Part of the joy and value of the work did not stem simply from the creation of theater that fulfilled the mission of Teatro Vista, but from working to build something together from the ground up. This is not to say that there were not practical challenges, or that having a facility was not desirable; prior to the residency at Victory Gardens beginning in 2013, the company attempted to get a permanent home on three different occasions, but the arrangements fell through for various reasons.[36] In the interim, however, Teatro Vista did not accept that long-term residency was a prerequisite to success.

Teatro Vista achieved many milestones in these itinerant years. Tanya Saracho's 2009 *Our Lady of the Underpass*, inspired by visitors to the Kennedy Expressway underpass on Fullerton Avenue, where many believed the image of the Virgin Mary had appeared in a road-salt stain, played to sold-out houses. It was one of the first of Teatro Vista's productions that was moved to another theater in the next season, from the Greenhouse Theater Center on Lincoln Avenue in Lakeview to Berwyn Cultural Center in Berwyn Township. *Our Lady* was a uniquely Chicago production, focusing on a local phenomenon that had received national attention. The ensemble piece, directed by Sandra Marquez, dramatized the complex experiences and identities behind faith (or nonbelief) in a contemporary miracle. *The Elaborate Entrance of Chad Deity* opened as the 2009 world premiere of Kristoffer Diaz's award-winning play. Directed by Edward Torres, the production played to rave reviews at Victory Gardens' Biograph. It surpassed historic ticket sales at Victory Gardens, and Diaz's script became a Pulitzer Prize finalist in 2010. The production later moved to Off Broadway and to Los Angeles. Torres recalled *The Elaborate Entrance of Chad Deity* as a landmark production:

> It marked one of the many key moments in our production history. . . . It broke box office records and received critical

A scene from *The Sins of Sor Juana*, in the space at the former Mexican Fine Arts Center Museum (now called the National Museum of Mexican Art), 2004. Left to right: Sandra Marquez, Stephanie Diaz, Carmen Severino, Emilio G. Robles, Eddie Martinez, and Deb Davis. Written by Karen Zacarías; directed by Edward Torres; costume design by Christine Pascual; set and lighting design by Brian Sidney Bembridge; sound design by Mikhail Fiksel. Photograph by Brian Sidney Bembridge. Courtesy of Edward Torres.

> acclaim. It was one of the few productions that made the front page of the *Chicago Tribune*. . . . *Chad Deity* strengthened the idea that it is important to give Latinx or playwrights of color their perspective on America. This opportunity to share their story and be heard is at the core of our mission.[37]

Throughout this itinerancy, Teatro Vista was solidifying its place on the local and national stage and breaking new barriers in terms of popular reception, artistic achievement, and Latinx representation.

Still, the nature of itinerancy itself may contribute to companies' historiographical erasure. As part of its logistical reality, itinerancy can denote a lack of security or permanence, and absence of a physical space may also inhibit opportunities. Cofounder of the Chicago Latino Theatre Alliance (CLATA)[38] Myrna Salazar, who helped launch the

Kamal Angelo Boulden in *The Elaborate Entrance of Chad Deity*, coproduced with Victory Gardens at the Victory Gardens Biograph Theater, 2009. Written by Kristoffer Diaz; directed by Edward Torres; sound design by Mikhail Fiksel; scenic design by Brian Sidney Bembridge; lighting design by Jesse Klung; costume design by Christine Pascual; prop design by D. J. Reed; video projections by John Boesche. Photograph by Brian Sidney Bembridge. Courtesy of Edward Torres.

careers of numerous actors as a former talent agent (she mentions early relationships with Justina Machado, Raúl Esparza, Aimee Garcia, and Carlos Sanz), and who is herself a character portrayed in Teatro Vista's *La Havana Madrid*, said that she is focused on acquiring a space for Chicago artists: "What is needed . . . is we do not have a Latino theater complex that can house several theaters."[39] Salazar cited the Los Angeles Theatre Center, a five-story structure and former bank that now holds five theaters within the complex—including "black boxes and an amazing atrium"—which has allowed them to host two Latinx theater festivals and plan a third "global theater festival":

> My main push is to talk with our elected officials to get the support of the county, the city, and the state . . . to support our initiative in regards to identifying land, or a building, in order to come up with a Latino theater complex that can serve as an incubator, a storage space . . . and stages for younger

> companies, to larger multidisciplinary works. . . . There are 1.9 million of us in the greater metropolitan area. In our quest to continue identifying new audiences, we need to sustain and support that.

Salazar goes on to point out that many houses of existing companies, such as Aguijón Theater and UrbanTheater Company, can seat maybe fifty to sixty-five maximum, depending on the configuration. There does not exist a large-scale location where there may be a "convening of the minds," as Salazar described it. Beyond the practical challenges of itinerancy for any individual company, Salazar identified some fundamental advantages to large, structured space in a long-term location: community building, artistic development, and the enhancement of national and international networks.

Geographies remain essential to the mission of community building, and a source of tension regarding the presumed value and visibility of theaters of color. Ivan Vega, cofounder and executive director of UrbanTheater Company, adds that their company is one of the few Latinx companies with their own space, Café Teatro Batey Urbano in Humboldt Park.[40] Vega says that he and Salazar have discussed a central large-scale venue, and UrbanTheater would "be more than happy to perform at the future venue, but the work has to always point back to our community. . . . We have a space and a community we serve."[41] Vega states that they are "working from a lens of decolonizing the theater," and as such, "aren't seeking to take their performances downtown or to Lincoln Park." As downtown Chicago and North Side neighborhoods such as Lincoln Park are broadly known for wealthy, white demographics, these areas are more central to traditional white narratives of Chicago theater's cultural capital, an assumption which Vega and UrbanTheater push against. As Vega states, location alone doesn't presume to make the work "better."

The question of Chicago theater companies' perceived value, community location, and social mission came to a head in the summer of 2020. In the midst of the transformative momentum of the Black Lives Matter protests, and within a national conversation regarding a pandemic that disproportionately claimed Black, indigenous, and Latinx lives, the call to #OpenYourLobby urged theaters to operate as a resource to activists. In the wake of protests over Victory Gardens' decision to board up the theater building during Black Lives Matter demonstrations, and following a controversial search for the position of artistic director, Victory Gardens' Erica Daniels resigned.[42] In response to #OpenYourLobby, UrbanTheater Artistic Director Miranda Gonzáles penned an article critiquing the erasure of companies that are located in, and serve, historically Latinx and Black communities:

> Our audiences raised us. Many of our neighbors have worked assembly lines with our grandparents, gone to school with our parents, and have had their children taught by our artists. Closing our doors would be turning our backs on our family. We are and have always been in service to them. UTC has been a donation center many times over, a press conference room, a polling place for numerous elections, a place for healers to gather, a screening location, and so much more. We've had an open-door policy since occupying a permanent space in between the Puerto Rican flags on Division Street. By partnering with our nonprofit neighbors, like El Rescate, Vida/SIDA, the Honeycomb Network, and the Puerto Rican Cultural Center, we are able to provide accessible theater productions to our residents. We are and will continue to be a theater based in our community.[43]

Just as location can falsely denote value, so may a site's permanence. While the practicalities of itinerancy present challenges and may limit the larger collaborative ventures that Salazar mentions, itinerancy does not signify lack of accomplishment or expertise. Teatro Vista has rivaled any distinguished company in terms of achievement, both in the distinctions of individual performers and in the company's artistic innovations and long record of recognitions. As of this writing, Teatro Vista has garnered numerous awards and grants[44] from such organizations as the League of Chicago Theatres, Broadway World Chicago, the MacArthur Foundation, the Paul M. Angell Family Foundation, and the Joyce Foundation. The company's work has been continually acknowledged across the past decade with Joseph Jefferson "Jeff" Awards and nominations,[45] a long-standing and well-recognized credit for citywide theater talent. In 2018, the newly launched Chicago-based Alliance of Latinx Theatre Artists (ALTA) Awards honored Teatro Vista for artistic distinction in production, ensemble, choreography, musical direction, and costume and scenic design, and again in 2019 with awards for sound design and stage management alongside nearly a dozen nominations across the company.[46] Also in 2019, the ALTAs named ensemble member and longtime former Associate Artistic Director Sandra Marquez the winner of the Migdalia Cruz Mentorship Award for her work with Teatro Vista and beyond.

In contrast to the perception of itinerancy as a characteristic of less-established theater companies, Teatro Vista took advantage of a variety of spaces. They used traditional proscenium and flexible studio-type stages at the Goodman, Steppenwolf, and Chopin theaters, warehouse space at American Theater Company, and the Prairie-style structure of Theater on the Lake in order to thrive in ways that were both by supported by and beneficial to the organizations in these partnerships. With its residency at Victory Gardens Biograph Theater since the fall of 2013, Teatro Vista now has a facility in a historic Chicago building[47] and a proud partnership with a renowned theater in Chicago's Lakeview neighborhood. The company's work across disparate spaces builds a rich and varied history that is not secondary in status to a permanent home. This mission continued in the 2019–2020 season with the midwest premiere of Evelina Fernández's *Hope: Part II of a Mexican Trilogy* at the Den Theatre, and was set to progress with the world premiere of Marvin Quijada's *The Dream King* at Victory Gardens Theater and José Cruz González's *American Mariachi* in association with the Goodman Theatre at Goodman's Albert Theatre, but both were postponed due to the COVID-19 pandemic.

2013: Victory Gardens Residency Begins

Teatro Vista's break from itinerancy occurred with their 2013–2014 season, when the noted actor and director Ricardo Gutiérrez became executive artistic director as Torres stepped down after many years as artistic director. Gutiérrez negotiated with Victory Gardens to set Teatro Vista's residency in a second space opened within the theater in 2010: the Richard Christiansen Theater. The initial production of *White Tie Ball* by Martín Zimmerman,[48] directed by Torres, is a piece that powerfully interrogates the intersections of race, class, colorism, and family relationships across power and politics.[49] Zimmerman recalls smaller audiences in the transition to both a new space and the expiration of a grant that funded a previous marketing director, and recounts "great admiration" for the artists:

> I was very happy with how it turned out, in terms of artistically and the production. And I felt like the reception was good. It

> was an interesting sort of pivot point in the history of the company, in the sense of it was the first piece in residence at Victory Gardens. . . . I think for me, the salient thing for the experience, other than the sort of broader context of what does it mean to be a part of a company—entering a company at a pivot point, in its relationship with other institutions—I think for me the most salient memory of the process is the meaning of just purely being in collaboration with other artists, regardless of what the public is there to see, and to me, coming back to see the end of the run, to see how rewarding for them the act of just doing the play—the act of doing it—was the reward itself. I think, for me, this is a good summation of my experience of the play. . . . I think that's a part of the DNA of Chicago, even from the settlement houses on: the act of working on the thing to create community.

Later in the season, 2014's production of *A View from the Bridge* is notable for disrupting presumptions about Latinx representation and the white American theater canon. Gutiérrez, who directed the piece, underscored that it was Teatro Vista's first production with an all-Latinx cast in roles not specified as Latinx by the playwright. Sandra Marquez won a Jeff Award for Best Supporting Actress for her role as Beatrice, and in doing so became the first Latina to win a Jeff Award for best actress. Marquez stated,

> *A View from the Bridge* was particularly satisfying. . . . I think for so long that mainstream theater just hasn't associated Latinx actors with an Arthur Miller play. And because [the Teatro Vista ensemble members] have such a variety of backgrounds and facility with language—not everybody in the company is bilingual—there is still often an assumption that we can only do things that have "Latino names" in the cast of characters. And so, to be able to do something like *A View from the Bridge*—which from my point of view is a no-brainer, that we are able to do that—it seems surprising, I think, to some people, or novel to some people. It was a great opportunity for the cast to be able to show a wider variety of capabilities that I think maybe some people don't typically allow themselves to see.[50]

Until retiring in 2021, Gutiérrez led Teatro Vista with Managing and Development Director Sylvia Lopez. In addition to Teatro Vista's

Ayssette Munoz, Tommy Rivera-Vega, Ramón Camín, Sandra Marquez, and Eddie Diaz in *A View from the Bridge* at Victory Gardens Biograph, Richard Christiansen Theater, 2014. Directed by Ricardo Gutiérrez; set design by Regina García; costume design by Christine Pascual; sound design by Christopher Kriz; lighting design by Brian Hoehne. Photograph by Joel Maisonet. Courtesy of Joel Maisonet.

professional artistic recognitions, its status and contribution to the Chicago community is widely acknowledged. Gutiérrez and Lopez were named in the "50 Leaders of Chicago's Theater, Dance, Opera and Comedy Culture" by long-standing Chicago cultural publication and online outlet *Newcity*. The company has also been honored by the League of Chicago Theatres with an Artistic Leadership Award, and commended as a top "Chicago Cultural Leader" by the Arts & Business Council of Chicago. Both *Newcity* and Chicago's arm of the global magazine publication *Time Out* named *La Havana Madrid* on the "Best of" lists for 2017.

These aforementioned accolades signify that Teatro Vista has a profile to rival any professional theater company in Chicago. Teatro Vista currently boasts ensemble members who are regular national presences on television, such as actors Max Arciniega (*Better Call Saul*), Desmín Borges (*You're the Worst*), Ivonne Coll (*Jane the Virgin*), and Joe Minoso (*Chicago Fire*), as well as writers Martín Zimmerman (*Ozark*, *Narcos*) and Kristoffer Diaz (*GLOW*, Fox's *Rent*). The company's list of roughly two dozen current ensemble members showcases many familiar names with impressive résumés and continually emerging work, and a full ensemble history includes more still.[51] Gutiérrez mentioned one consequence of Teatro Vista's members' success: the company's performers are in such demand that they often quickly transition to unionizing with Equity membership status, which Teatro Vista wholeheartedly supports. However, this situation also presents Teatro Vista with a logistical challenge regarding contractual obligations and costs, as it is typical for theaters to budget a certain number of non-Equity actors in a production season. This reality speaks to the wide appeal of Teatro Vista's contributions to Chicago and to the country's artistic community.

Gutiérrez highlighted Teatro Vista's most recent evolution: the investment in the creative writing skills of the company. One of the company's goals is to continue to develop playwriting expertise and ensemble-generated work. Gutiérrez envisions a future season of all-original work—not necessarily devised, but entirely written by the company. Gutiérrez recounted:

> A few years ago I encouraged the ensemble to bring me ideas they had for projects—in particular, ideas that focused on their creative writing skills. We wanted to foster ensemble-written projects and bring them to our stage. *La Havana Madrid*, by Sandra Delgado, is the first play to come out of this initiative. A goal is to have an entire season of ensemble-written plays.[52]

As Gutiérrez indicated, this mission lives in *La Havana Madrid*, directed by ensemble member Cheryl Lynn Bruce and featuring live music by Carpacho y Su Súper Combo. *La Havana Madrid* was first staged in partnership with Steppenwolf at their 1700 Theatre in April and May 2017, then with community partner the Miracle Center in Logan Square in June 2017, and then at the Goodman Theatre's Owen stage in July through August of 2017. It was later remounted at the Den Theatre in Wicker Park in the summer of 2019 with Collaboraction Theatre, with *La Havana* being the third coproduction between the companies. Though the play is just one moment in Teatro Vista's long history, the production is particularly significant when considering space, both symbolic and physical.

La Havana Madrid is intimately connected with the Latinx histories and geographies of Chicago. Delgado originally set out to write a play

Sandra Delgado with Carpacho y Su Súper Combo in *La Havana Madrid* at the Den Theatre, 2019. Written by Sandra Delgado; directed by Cheryl Lynn Bruce; music direction by Yendrys Cespedes; scene design by Ashley Woods; costume design by Elsa Hiltner; lighting design by Heather Sparling; sound design by Robert Hornbostel; sound engineering by Rae Segbawu; projections and video design by Liviu Pasare; choreography by Wilfredo Rivera. Photograph by Joel Maisonet. Courtesy of Joel Maisonet.

about her parents' early days in the city after arriving from Colombia. The piece was born from a story that Delgado's father told her about a Latinx nightclub that used to exist on Belmont and Sheffield Avenues. Delgado relayed, "I know that whole stretch of Belmont, from Ashland to the lake, like the back of my hand. . . . I have memories, like walking all the way down Belmont to the beach with my aunts in the summertime . . . in my earliest recollections, which would be like late seventies, there was never a Latinx presence that I could remember. At all."[53] Delgado began to research, but couldn't find anything about the club in traditional sources on the internet, at the library, or in existing music volumes—even, she says, in "a book that was literally called *Chicago Music History of the 1960s* . . . and in two-hundred-something pages, there was not one Latinx musician." Delgado realized that this was a story that needed to be told, and that if she had been intrigued by this largely forgotten history, others would be, too. Though she had originally intended to write a play about her parents, she realized that "no, the play is this *place*. And I could immediately see it, and hear it."

Delgado's account of the production, in her words, is a narrative about space and place that gives fullness to the way that theater has both addressed and reclaimed a Latinx Chicago and the individuals who call or called it home. *La Havana Madrid* is an immersive theatrical and musical piece based on interviews with Chicagoans, particularly Caribbean Latinx, including a homesick Cuban exile, Colombian newlyweds chronicling their young love, and a Puerto Rican teen, Carlos, who discovers a profound talent for photography. *La Havana Madrid*'s production life extended across venues at Steppenwolf, the Goodman, the Miracle Center, and the Den. Delgado, who both wrote and performed in the piece, told me:

> It was really important for me that the first production of *La Havana Madrid* took place in the neighborhood that some of these people inhabited, in this sort of reclamation of the space. Steppenwolf had just opened up this cabaret space. . . . Luckily, the stars aligned, and here was a theater in Lincoln Park that already had the cabaret seating . . .
>
> Carlos [Flores, a well-known photographer and music historian who grew up in Lincoln Park when it was a Puerto Rican neighborhood, and one of Delgado's first interviewees that inspired a piece in the play] comes on opening night. . . . And it was also beautiful, because I asked him for permission to use some of his photography of the neighborhood and his family to incorporate into the piece, which he graciously did. And we're walking down Halsted Street after the show, just the two of us . . . and he gets tears in his eyes and he goes, "I haven't walked down these streets for forty years. I haven't walked down Halsted in forty years." Basically, saying his family had to move away from the neighborhood. And we both started crying.
>
> And the thing is that this was happening all the time . . . because Lincoln Park specifically was very Puerto Rican, I would say it *was* a Puerto Rican neighborhood. That strip of Armitage, between Halsted and Racine, was like a little downtown. There are pictures that Carlos has taken where they are all Puerto Rican businesses: record stores and little sandwich shops, and Young Lord headquarters, and little bodegas, all that kind of stuff. . . .

My favorite thing about the show was talking to people afterwards. I wouldn't even get out of costume. We would end the show, and I would come off the stage and I would just talk to people. . . . I knew that with *La Havana Madrid* I wanted to create a show that multiple generations of a Latinx family could enjoy together, and I knew for me that I wanted it be this reclamation of land, in a way. But that part, I wasn't expecting . . . people saying, "We haven't been here in decades!" Because there is that invisible line now. Lincoln Park is *Lincoln Park*. . . . And there was something so satisfying to have all these people coming back, and to be having a drink at the bar, and taking photos with the band, and people my age who had come to the show with their partner or friends, and then they'd say they'd have to come back with their kids, or "I have to bring my parents to this!" . . . People were coming to the show four or five times. And they followed it from Steppenwolf, to the Miracle Center . . . And then, to bring it to the Goodman . . .

There was this woman who reached out to us. . . . She emailed Teatro Vista, and Ricardo forwarded me the email. It was this woman saying, "Hi, I live in Florida with my mom, and my parents met at La Havana Madrid at a New Year's Eve party. Here is a photo of them from that night. They ended up getting married and were together for many, many, many years. My father passed away and my mom is suffering from Parkinson's." . . . [We got them tickets and] they sat at one of the front tables. And the daughter told us that the Parkinson's had affected her mother's ability to speak, so she didn't really talk at lot. . . . I start singing "Sabor a Mí." And the woman starts *singing along*. And I almost lost it. . . . If you are someone who doesn't know "Sabor a Mí," and that's not in your history, but you see and hear the person next to you—or a couple you see holding hands and singing it—that does something to you. That is real. That is real energy.

As Delgado's account relates, *La Havana Madrid* resonates with what is lost and reclaimed. It physically brings generations of inhabitants back to a place they once called home. It validates and amplifies underrepresented stories that make up the fabric of the city. Beyond simple nostalgia, it reactivates a present moment of shared cultural experience in the communal moment of performance, while introducing its power to new generations and audiences in the geographical place where these events once played. Though I have given extended attention to *La Havana Madrid* here due to its Chicago-centric focus on place, the piece is but one original production in Teatro Vista's history. Teatro Vista has hosted an incredible number of new works, including eighteen world premieres—from Kristoffer Diaz's Pulitzer Prize–nominated *The Elaborate Entrance of Chad Deity*, to MacArthur award winner Luis Alfaro's *Electricidad*, to acclaimed resident playwrights' pieces, such as Candido Tirado's *Fishmen* and Martín Zimmerman's *White Tie Ball*. As Marquez noted of the evolution of the company throughout the years:

> Most of our company members are Equity, and everybody is pretty much working, somewhere. So the need is less about getting ourselves acting gigs, but more about fostering theater artists in other capacities. So opportunities to produce, direct, write . . . I think that's the company's place now. It is to look at what the company members have to offer, and ask how we help develop those skills within the company.[54]

Teatro Vista's focus has long addressed both the immediate and long-term strategic needs of the Latinx community, from the initial productions of *Broken Eggs* and *The Crossing* to the newest work in development with Teatro Vista's members. Across the memories of these early productions and artistic relationships, there were a constellation of factors important to these artists, among them: storytelling, cultural unity and representation, concerns of actor-audience and theater-community relationships, and ideas about what could practically be accomplished in the space given its structure and possibilities.

Teatro Vista's expansive work across the Chicago area, as chronicled in the production history at the close of this chapter, demonstrates the continued and active inclusion of numerous neighborhoods and audiences. They have also deeply invested in local resources: the company has cultivated talented artists in their ensemble and artistic associates, and under Gutiérrez's leadership, members are proactively encouraged to build their own storytelling capacities and theatrical careers. Teatro Vista builds artistically resonant partnerships across the multitude of theater companies named throughout, as well as with significant cultural institutions like the National Museum of Mexican Art. In their work, Teatro Vista also magnifies local and cultural histories, and gives representation to Chicago narratives such as the pilgrimage to the miraculous

Virgin Mary image dramatized in Saracho's *Our Lady of the Underpass*. And as *La Havana Madrid* illustrates, Chicago's Latinx presence animated the streets and structures of the city in ways that may now be hidden, but demand to be seen. By including their voices here, I hope to make space for their stories in Chicago's theatrical testimony, following the ways that Teatro Vista continues to make space for Latinx artists and histories across the geography and communities of the city of Chicago.

History of Teatro Vista's Productions and Spaces

1991 Season

The Crossing by Hugo Salcedo at the Mexican Fine Arts Center Museum (now called the National Museum of Mexican Art), 1852 West 19th Street.

Broken Eggs by Eduardo Machado at the Greenview Arts Center, 6418 North Greenview Avenue (now the location of the Leather Archives and Museum).

1991–1992 Season

The Show Host by Rodolfo Santana, coproduced with Victory Gardens Theater at Victory Gardens Studio Theater, former location at 2257 North Lincoln Avenue.

La Nona by Roberto M. Cossa at the UIC Theater, 1044 West Harrison Street.

1992–1993 Season

Pain of the Macho by Rick Najera, coproduced with Goodman Theatre at the Goodman Studio Theatre, former location at 200 South Columbus Drive.

1993–1994 Season

D'Ambrosio by Romulus Linney at Edgewater Presbyterian Church, 1020 West Bryn Mawr Avenue.

Grapes of Wrath adapted by Frank Galati, coproduced with New American Theater at the New American Theater, 118 North Main Street, Rockford, IL.

1994–1995 Season

Cloud Tectonics by José Rivera, coproduced with the Goodman Theatre at Goodman Studio Theatre, former location at 200 South Columbus Drive.

1995–1996 Season

Journey of the Sparrows by Meryl Friedman, coproduced with Lifeline Theatre at Lifeline Theatre Family Mainstage, 6912 North Glenwood Avenue.

Santos and Santos by Octavio Solis at the Mexican Fine Arts Center Museum (now called the National Museum of Mexican Art), 1852 West Nineteenth Street.

1996–1997 Season

El Paso Blue by Octavio Solis, coproduced with Next Theatre Company at Noyes Cultural Arts Center, 927 Noyes Avenue, Evanston, IL. (Next Theatre closed in 2014.)

Broken Eggs by Eduardo Machado, Chicago Theatres on the Air at DoubleTree Guest Suites, 198 East Delaware Place (recorded live for later broadcast on WFMT-FM 98.7).

Santos and Santos by Octavio Solis at the annual Del Corazon Festival presented by the Mexican Fine Arts Center Museum (now called the National Museum of Mexican Art), 1852 West Nineteenth Street.

1997–1998 Season

The Adventures of Don Quixote adapted by Dale Calandra, in collaboration with the Oak Park Festival Theatre at Oak Park Festival Theatre in Austin Gardens, Forest Avenue at Lake Street, Oak Park, IL.

The Boiler Room by Ruben C. Gonzalez, in collaboration with Steppenwolf Theatre at Steppenwolf Studio Theatre, 1650 North Halsted Street.

1998–1999 Season

The Show Host by Rodolfo Santana at Theater on the Lake, 2401 North Lake Shore Drive.

Aurora's Motive by Jamie Pachino at the Chopin Theatre, 1543 West Division Street.

1999–2000 Season

Aurora's Motive by Jamie Pachino at Theater on the Lake, 2401 North Lake Shore Drive.

2001–2002 Season

Black Butterfly Jaguar Girl, Piñata Woman and Other Superhero Girls Like Me by Luis Alfaro at the Chicago Historical Society as part of the Chicago Humanities Festival at Walter Payton College Prep, 1034 North Wells Street.

Icarus by Edwin Sánchez at the Chopin Theatre, 1543 West Division Street.

2002–2003 Season

Anna in the Tropics by Nilo Cruz at Victory Gardens Studio Theater, former location at 2257 North Lincoln Avenue.

Sueños, Vampiros y Bebés by Teatro Vista ensemble at the Chopin Theatre, 1543 West Division Street.

2003–2004 Season

The Sins of Sor Juana by Karen Zacarías, coproduced with the Mexican Fine Arts Center Museum at the Mexican Fine Arts Center Museum (now called the National Museum of Mexican Art), 1852 West 19th Street.

Two Sisters and a Piano by Nilo Cruz, coproduced with Apple Tree Theatre at Apple Tree Theatre, 595 Elm Place, Highland Park, IL. (Apple Tree Theatre closed in 2009.)

Electricidad by Luis Alfaro, in the Goodman's Latino Theatre Festival at Goodman's Albert Theatre, 170 North Dearborn Avenue.

2004–2005 Season

Breakfast, Lunch and Dinner by Luis Alfaro at the Chopin Theatre, 1543 West Division.

Living Out by Lisa Loomer, collaboration with the American Theater Company at the American Theater Company, 1909 West Byron. (American Theater Company closed in 2018.)

2005–2006 Season

Elliot: A Soldier's Fugue by Quiara Alegría Hudes, coproduced with Rivendell Theatre at Steppenwolf Theatre Garage, 1650 North Halsted Street.

Another Part of the House by Migdalia Cruz at the Chopin Theatre, 1543 West Division Street.

Blind Mouth Singing by Jorge Ignacio Cortiñas at the Chopin Theatre, 1543 West Division Street.

2006–2007 Season

La Posada Magica: The Magical Journey by Octavio Solis, concert-style reading featuring local students and ensemble at Little Village Lawndale High School, 3120 South Kostner Avenue.

A Park in Our House by Nilo Cruz, coproduced with Victory Gardens Theater at Victory Gardens Biograph Theater, 2433 North Lincoln Avenue.

Massacre: Sing to Your Children by José Rivera, coproduced with the Goodman Theater at Goodman's Owen Theatre, 170 North Dearborn Avenue.

2007–2008 Season

La Posada Magica: The Magical Journey by Octavio Solis, concert-style reading featuring local students and ensemble at Little Village Lawndale High School, 3120 South Kostner Avenue.

Dreamlandia by Octavio Solis at Victory Gardens Greenhouse, 2257 North Lincoln Avenue.

2008–2009 Season

The Elaborate Entrance of Chad Deity by Kristoffer Diaz, coproduced with Victory Gardens at the Victory Gardens Biograph Theater, 2433 North Lincoln Avenue.

El Grito del Bronx by Migdalia Cruz, coproduced with Collaboraction and the Goodman Theatre at Goodman's Owen Theatre, 170 North Dearborn Street.

Our Lady of the Underpass by Tanya Saracho at the Greenhouse Theater Center, 2257 North Lincoln Avenue.

2009–2010 Season

26 Miles by Quiara Alegría Hudes, collaboration with Rivendell Theatre Ensemble at the Chicago Dramatists Theater, 1105 West Chicago Avenue.

Our Lady of the Underpass by Tanya Saracho at the 16th Street Theater, Berwyn Cultural Center, 6420 Sixteenth Street, Berwyn, IL.

2010–2011 Season

Freedom, NY by Jennifer Barclay at Theater Wit, 1229 West Belmont Avenue.

El Nogalar by Tanya Saracho, coproduced with the Goodman Theatre at Goodman's Owen Theatre, 170 North Dearborn Avenue.

2011–2012 Season

Momma's Boyz by Cándido Tirado at Chicago Dramatists Theater, 1105 West Chicago Avenue.

Fish Men by Cándido Tirado, coproduced with the Goodman Theatre at Goodman's Owen Theatre, 170 North Dearborn Street.

Yo Solo Festival of Latino Solo Shows coproduced with Collaboraction at Collaboraction Theatre Company, Flat Iron Arts Building, 1579 North Milwaukee Avenue.

2012–2013 Season

I Put the Fear of Mexico in 'Em by Matthew Paul Olmos at Chicago Dramatists, 1105 West Chicago Avenue.

Empanada for a Dream by Juan Francisco Villa, coproduced with 16th Street Theater, Berwyn Cultural Center, 6420 Sixteenth Street, Berwyn, IL.

The Happiest Song Plays Last by Quiara Alegría Hudes, coproduced with the Goodman Theatre at Goodman's Owen Theatre, 170 North Dearborn Street.

2013–2014 Season

White Tie Ball by Martín Zimmerman at Victory Gardens Biograph, Richard Christiansen Theater (opened as second space in the Biograph in 2010), 2433 North Lincoln Avenue.

A View From The Bridge by Arthur Miller at Victory Gardens Biograph, Richard Christiansen Theater, 2433 North Lincoln Avenue.

2014–2015 Season

Tamer of Horses by William Mastrosimone at Victory Gardens Biograph, Richard Christiansen Theater, 2433 North Lincoln Avenue.

The Upstairs Concierge by Kristoffer Diaz, co-commissioned by Teatro Vista, produced by the Goodman Theatre at Goodman's Owen Theatre, 170 North Dearborn Street.

Between You, Me & the Lampshade by Raúl Castillo at Victory Gardens Biograph, Richard Christiansen Theater, 2433 North Lincoln Avenue.

2015–2016 Season

My Mañana Comes by Elizabeth Irwin at Victory Gardens Biograph, Richard Christiansen Theater, 2433 North Lincoln Avenue.

Where Did We Sit on the Bus? by Brian Quijada at the Storefront Theater, 66 East Randolph Street.

In the Time of the Butterflies by Caridad Svich at Victory Gardens Biograph, Richard Christiansen Theater, 2433 North Lincoln Avenue.

2016–2017 Season

Parachute Men by Mando Alvarado at Victory Gardens Biograph, Richard Christiansen Theater, 2433 North Lincoln Avenue.

The Wolf at the End of the Block by Ike Holter at Victory Gardens Biograph, Richard Christiansen Theater, 2433 North Lincoln Avenue.

La Havana Madrid by Sandra Delgado at Steppenwolf's 1700 Theatre, 1700 North Halsted Street, and at the Miracle Center, 2311 North Pulaski Rd.

2017–2018 Season

La Havana Madrid by Sandra Delgado, coproduced with the Goodman Theatre at Goodman's Owen Theatre, 170 North Dearborn Street.

Fade by Tanya Saracho, coproduced with Victory Gardens at Victory Gardens Biograph, Richard Christiansen Theater, 2433 North Lincoln Avenue.

The Madres by Stephanie Alison Walker at Victory Gardens Biograph, Richard Christiansen Theater, 2433 North Lincoln Avenue.

2018–2019 Season

American Jornalero by Ed Cardona Jr. at Victory Gardens Biograph, Richard Christiansen Theater, 2433 North Lincoln Avenue.

The Abuelas by Stephanie Alison Walker at Victory Gardens Biograph, Richard Christiansen Theater, 2433 North Lincoln Avenue.

La Havana Madrid by Sandra Delgado at the Den Theatre, Heath Mainstage, 1331 North Milwaukee Avenue.

2019–2020 Season

Hope: Part II of a Mexican Trilogy by Evelina Fernández at the Den Theatre, 1331 North Milwaukee Avenue.

The Dream King by Marvin Quijada at Victory Gardens Biograph, Richard Christiansen Theater, 2433 North Lincoln Avenue.

American Mariachi by José Cruz González, coproduced with the Goodman Theatre at Goodman's Albert Theatre, 170 North Dearborn Avenue.

Notes

1. Michael McKinnie, *City Stages: Theatre and Urban Space in a Global City* (Toronto: University of Toronto Press, 2007), 5.

2. McKinnie, *City Stages*, 13.

3. I use the term "Latinx" throughout, though it is not without its complications and backlash. Latinx is intended to be a gender-inclusive term, rather than a presumed "neutral" male term that enforces a masculine/feminine binary. The terminology continues to rapidly evolve (from Latina/o to Latin@ to Latinx) in dialectic with the argument about what the "x" may serve to erase: colonial histories, indigenous roots, or the accessibility

of the Spanish language itself. For this reason, Latino/a/x is used interchangeably across this piece in quotations and citations, acknowledging the functionally overlapping usages across timelines and contexts. More recently, some argue that "Latine" is preferential over "Latinx" because of its facilitation with language (in substituting "e" for "o/a") but it remains a term that has not yet taken hold across institutional titles and cultural organizations. Authority of any singular term is not settled, nor is it claimed here. For a broad overview of the use of terminology, see "Mapping and Recontextualizing the Term *Latinx*" in *Critical Readings on Latinos and Education* (New York: Routledge, 2019). For the development of terms across the field of theater and performance studies, see Patricia Herrera's "Building Latinidad, Silencing Queerness: Culture Class's *Nuyorican Stories*," *Theatre Topics* 27, no. 1 (March 2017) within the *Theatre Topics* Special Issue on Latinx Performance; and Anne García-Romero's introduction to *The Fornes Frame* (Tucson: The University of Arizona Press, 2016). For scholarship on controversies and challenges to "Latinx," see "What's in an 'x'? An Exchange about the Politics of 'Latinx,'" in *Chiricú Journal: Latina/o Literatures, Arts, and Cultures* 1, no. 2 (Spring 2017). Notably, though it is the current accepted term of academia, it has at this point not been adopted as quickly in larger culture, as chronicled in Concepción de León's "Another Hot Take on the Term 'Latinx,'" *New York Times*, November 21, 2018, https://www.nytimes.com/2018/11/21/style/latinx-queer-gender-nonconforming.html and Giancarlo Sopo's "Progressives, Hispanics Are Not 'Latinx.' Stop Trying to Anglicize Our Spanish Language," *USA Today*, October 28, 2019 https://www.usatoday.com/story/opinion/2019/10/25/latinx-race-progressives-hispanic-latinos-column/4082760002/.

4. Jacqueline Serrato, "Mexicans and 'Hispanics' Now the Largest Minority in Chicago," *Hoy*, October 13, 2017, https://www.chicagotribune.com/hoy/ct-mexicans-and-hispanics-largest-minority-in-chicago-20171013-story.html. Latinx communities, besides growing in number, have expanded past the south and northwest areas of the city, where they were pushed out from valuable lakeshore real estate through rising property rates. Neighborhoods traditionally known as Latinx, such as Logan Square and Pilsen, are now documented as losing tens of thousands of individuals identified as "Hispanic." In 2017, the University of Illinois at Chicago and the Metropolitan Family Services cited the communities with the highest Latinx populations as Belmont Cragin, Little Village, Gage Park, Brighton Park, Logan Square, Humboldt Park, West Lawn, Pilsen & Heart of Chicago, Chicago Lawn, Irving Park, Albany Park, and Back of the Yards (José Miguel Acosta-Córdova, *The Latino Neighborhoods Report:*

Issues and Prospects for Chicago, Institute for Research on Race and Public Policy, Great Cities Institute, University of Illinois at Chicago, October 11, 2017, https://greatcities.uic.edu/wp-content/uploads/2017/10/Latino-Neighborhoods-Report-v2.3.pdf).

5. José Castro Urioste, "Negotiating Spaces: Latino Theater in Chicago," *Latin American Theatre Review* 46, no. 2, (Spring 2013): 199. Additionally, another overview of Teatro Vista is featured among a variety of other companies in 2019's *Ensemble: An Oral History of Chicago Theater* by Mark Larson (Midway Publishing), as well as in Priscilla M. Paige's "Charting the Terrain of Latina/o/x Theater in Chicago" (PhD diss., University of Massachusetts Amherst, 2018).

6. Noe Montez writes of "scholarship as activism" and the "Wikiturgy Project" through the Latinx Theatre Commons (LTC), which sought to grant students of color authorship and to diversify the site of Wikipedia, while promoting Latinx theater artists ("Decolonizing Wikipedia through Advocacy and Activism," *Theatre Topics* 27, no. 1 [2017]: E1–E9). LTC's *El Fuego* initiative also seeks to document and critically engage Latinx work, as well as support the production and dissemination of new plays (https://howlround.com/el-fuego-fueling-american-theatre-latinx-plays). Trevor Boffone's 50 Playwrights Project also highlights Latinx work in the American theater (https://50playwrights.org).

7. Though this chapter explores the relatively recent histories of Chicago's geographies, its populations, and the idea of ownership and reclamation, it is essential to acknowledge what the American Indian Center of Chicago writes for the 2019 *Chicago Architecture Biennial*: "Chicago is part of the traditional homelands of the Council of the Three Fires: the Odawa, Ojibwe, and Potawatomi nations. Many other tribes—such as the Miami, Ho-Chunk, Sac, and Fox—also called this area home. Located at the intersection of several great waterways, the land naturally became a site of travel and healing for many tribes. Today, Chicago is still a place that calls people from diverse backgrounds to live and gather. American Indians continue to live in the region, and Chicago is home to the country's third-largest urban American Indian community, which still practices its heritage and traditions, including care for the land and waterways. Despite the numerous changes the city has experienced, its American Indian and architecture communities both see the importance of the land and of this place, which has always been hospitable to many different backgrounds and perspective" (American Indian Center of Chicago, "Land Acknowledgement," *Chicago Architecture Biennial*, accessed February 26, 2021, https://chicagoarchitecturebiennial.org/about/land_acknowledgement).

8. I am very grateful to the many people who took the time to speak with me for this chapter, including Sandra Delgado, Henry Godinez, Ricardo Gutiérrez, Nilda Hernandez, Sandra Marquez, Myrna Salazar, Edward Torres, Carlos Tortolero, Ivan Vega, and Martín Zimmerman. Even if I were able to include all their words in this particular history, their great generosity and contributions to the artistic community in Chicago could not possibly be contained here (along with other notable individuals with whom I was not able to connect with at this time). The interview excerpts may be lightly edited for clarity. I am also thankful to this volume's tireless and patient editors, Megan E. Geigner, Stuart J. Hecht, and Jasmine Jamillah Mahmoud; to North Central College students Marissa Olavarria and Carter Rose Sherman for their research assistance; and to John Warrick for feedback and perspective.

9. As the author, I acknowledge that I have worked with Teatro Vista in an artistic and grant development capacity, though I have endeavored to focus on others' voices here. This is their story.

10. Aguijón began as the Spanish-language arm of Latino Chicago Theatre. It was founded by current co–Artistic Director Rosario Vargas, and codirected by Marcela Muñoz since 2008. Muñoz, a member of the company since 1992, also serves as executive director of Aguijón and is an ensemble member of Teatro Vista. Aguijón, located at 2707 North Laramie Avenue, has a mission "dedicated to creating exciting and meaningful theatrical experiences through the cultural exploration, discussion and performance of high-quality Spanish-language and bilingual works" ("Mission," Aguijón Theater, http://aguijontheater.org/mission/).

11. Ivan Vega says of UrbanTheater's initiatives, "The most important thing for us is community. We aren't just a theater company working in a Puerto Rican community. We are a theater company that's fully rooted within the fabric of Humboldt Park. . . . The work that we do as a company aligns with the issues that are happening in the community. We are just really fully invested within the community, and working hand in hand." In terms of production, "Since there is a Chicago Skyline, which is our logo, [the plays that we produce] have to be reflective of Chicago and of our community." Vega says this is taking root even more fully since their thirteenth season, when the administrative team (Vega, along with Artistic Director Miranda Gonzáles and Company Manager Antonio Bruno) began deliberately commissioning local work, because "it has to be Chicago work. It has to be written by a Chicago native playwright. . . . It's like I've always said, you know, we can do plays forever; we have enough plays. But are

we going do plays that our community can identify with, and can come onstage, and come to our theater, and say, 'That's my story. That's me. I can relate to that' ?" (Vega, in discussion with the author, November 2019).

12. Latino Chicago Theatre was founded to find a forum for Latinx theater. "We did what we wanted to do," recounted company member Nilda Hernandez of Latino Chicago Theatre. "We definitely believed in Latino theater itself . . . We wore many hats. Many, many hats. And we developed pieces in that firehouse, and we did a lot of readings of new works . . . There's nothing in there that I can say I'm not proud of. I was very proud of everything that we did there. Especially, you know, we had one kid come in to us, and say hey, I don't want to be out on the streets . . . Every time I go home—he lived in Humboldt Park—I mean, I grew up in Humboldt Park . . . and he's like, I go home, and I look like my brother, who's a gang banger, and they're always chasing me, they're always doing something to me. And we told him, hey come on, join us. He performed, but he also did box office, whatever to help build the sets . . . To this day, right now, I'm still in touch with him, and he's a proud dad . . . And because of that he wasn't being chased, no longer worried if he was going to make it home or not. There's a lot to be had with what we wanted to do when we said we didn't want to go into the theater district. We wanted to be in the community" (Hernandez, in discussion with the author, April 2019).

13. Godinez, in discussion with the author, December 2018.

14. Torres, in discussion with the author, December 2018.

15. Godinez, in discussion with the author, December 2018.

16. Achy Obejas, "Theatre Troupes Taking Their Place on Center Stage," *Chicago Tribune*, September 16, 1992, https://www.chicagotribune.com/news/ct-xpm-1992-09-16-9203240632-story.html.

17. Torres, in discussion with the author, December 2018.

18. Torres, in discussion with the author, April 2019.

19. Torres, in discussion with the author, December 2018.

20. Tortolero, in discussion with the author, April 2019.

21. Torres, in discussion with the author, December 2018.

22. Tortolero, in discussion with the author, April 2019.

23. Godinez, in discussion with the author, December 2018.

24. McKinnie, *City Stages*, 13.

25. Torres, in discussion with the author, December 2018.

26. Godinez, in discussion with the author, December 2018.

27. Torres, in discussion with the author, December 2018.

28. Godinez, in discussion with the author, December 2018.

29. Torres, in discussion with the author, December 2018. In this context, Torres also credited Aguijón as "the Spanish-language component of Chicago Latino."

30. Torres, in discussion with the author, December 2018.

31. Located at 2858 North Halsted, the Gaslight was "a neighborhood joint that catered to many of those working in nearby theaters. . . . Back then, you could hang out at the Gaslight after Steppenwolf performances and chat with the likes of Gary Sinise, Laurie Metcalf, Joan Allen, and William L. Peterson who came for a burger or grilled cheese" (Sean Parnell, "Gaslight Corner," Chicago Bar Project, https://www.chibarproject.com/Memoriam/GaslightCorner/GaslightCorner.htm).

32. Godinez, in discussion with the author, December 2018.

33. Hernandez, in discussion with the author, April 2019.

34. Jeff Huebner, "The Panic in Wicker Park," *Chicago Reader*, August 25, 1994, https://www.chicagoreader.com/chicago/the-panic-in-wicker-park/Content?oid=885350.

35. Marquez, in discussion with the author, April 2019.

36. Torres cited a brief residency at the Goodman Theatre in the early 1990s, at the former location at 200 Columbus Drive, though the precise dates are not documented. Torres also recalls a later non-continuous Goodman Residency, at the Owen Theatre at Goodman's current Dearborn location, that incorporated one play a year for three years: 2011, *El Nogalar*; 2012, *Fish Men*; and 2013, *The Happiest Song Plays Last* (Torres, email to the author, May 2019).

37. Torres, email to the author, May 2019.

38. CLATA, founded in 2016, "works to showcase existing and new thought-provoking U.S. Latino playwrights, actors and directors primarily in Chicago, along with national and international counterparts. CLATA strives to preserve cultural heritage and serve as a conduit to promote and identify new and exciting works" ("Mission," Chicago Latino Theater Alliance, https://www.clata.org/about). CLATA also runs *Destinos*, an annual Chicago International Latino Theater Festival. CLATA is slated to move the Fourth Chicago International Latino Theater Festival to the fall of 2021 due to the COVID-19 pandemic, and mounted a single-night drive-in performance of *Destinos al Aire* at Pilsen's Chitown Movies in September 2020.

39. Salazar, in discussion with the author, April 2019.

40. The description of the space on UrbanTheater's website states, in part: "The history and legacy of Batey remains vibrant and alive within the walls of our Humboldt Park storefront. We wouldn't be where we're at without Batey and their collective who've deeply inspired us since day

one. That space to us is sacred and special as it is to many others in our community. Who is Batey Urbano? The name Batey (pronounced bah-tay) is a Taino word, which means a sacred place for special events. Founded in 2002, Batey Urbano was a space for critical expression through spoken word, poetry, dancing, music, painting, and writing. This was achieved by fusing cultural expression and technology as means of organizing in creative ways . . . the work builds on the human and social capital of our community to develop youth leadership in our many programs and projects" ("Café Teatro Batey Urbano," UrbanTheater Company, May 2, 2019, https://urbantheaterchicago.org/hello-world/).

41. Vega, in conversation with the author, June 2020.

42. In May 2020, Victory Gardens Theater's Playwrights Ensemble resigned, protesting the search process for the new artistic director, following Chay Yew's planned exit. Over sixty artists had previously signed a letter sent to Victory Gardens' board of directors, requesting a transparent search for a new artistic director. When Erica Daniels was internally promoted from executive director to a dual role as artistic director, under the title executive artistic director, the Playwrights Ensemble (Luis Alfaro, Marcus Gardley, Ike Holter, Samuel D. Hunter, Naomi Iizuka, Tanya Saracho, and Laura Schellhardt) resigned "as a unified collective" ("Letter from the Playwrights of Victory Gardens Theater," *Medium*, May 22, 2020, https://medium.com/@ofvictorygardensplaywrights/letter-from-the-playwrights-of-victory-gardens-theater-fcbd3e1d1840). Following Daniels's resignation and board chair Steve Miller's stepping down (though he remained on the board), Victory Gardens announced plans for new leadership. Roxanna Conner served as acting managing director until April 2021, when Ken-Matt Martin began as the next artistic director, following a nationwide search emphasized as open. The theater also announced a new Diversity and Inclusion Committee on the board, led by Jaime Viteri (newsletter email from Victory Gardens Theater, "An Update on Theater Leadership and Next Steps," June 22, 2020).

43. Gonzales writes, "Because UrbanTheater has not been given the same value by the institutions that are committed to Eurocentric ideology, our contributions to the ecology of theater are overlooked. It is a cycle of value that is perpetuated through academia, the press, and the regional theaters themselves that make BIPOC artists reject the learning or support of BIPOC theaters, in lieu of investing in the regional ecosystem" ("It Takes More Than #OpenYourLobby to Address Racism in American Theatre," *Chicago Reader*, June 16, 2020, https://www.chicagoreader.com/chicago/beyond-openyourlobby-supporting-urbantheater-bipoc-theaters/Content?oid=80701587).

44. Teatro Vista's work is supported by several funding agencies: the MacArthur Foundation, the Paul M. Angell Family Foundation and the Angell Foundation, the Chicago Department of Cultural Affairs and Special Events (DCASE), the Gaylord and Dorothy Donnelly Foundation, the Alphawood Foundation Chicago, the Saints, the Shubert Foundation, the Bloomberg Philanthropies, the Joyce Foundation, the Bayless Family Foundation, the Illinois Arts Council, Art Works Vidal and Associates, and the Chicago Community Trust.

45. Awarded Best Production, Best New Work (Kristoffer Diaz), Best Director (Edward Torres), Best Actor in a Principal Role (Desmín Borges), Best Fight Choreography (David Woolley), all for *The Elaborate Entrance of Chad Deity*, 2010; Best Actress (Sandra Marquez) in *A View From the Bridge*, 2014; Solo Artist and Sound Design (both for Brian Quijada) for *Where Did We Sit on the Bus?*, 2016; and various Jeff nominations for *El Grito Dex Bronx*, 2009; *Our Lady of the Underpass*, 2009; *26 Miles*, 2011; *Fishmen*, 2012; *Empanada for a Dream*, 2013; *In the Time of the Butterflies* and *Where Did We Sit on the Bus?*, 2016; and *Parachute Men* and *The Wolf at the End of the Block*, 2017.

46. 2018 ALTA Awards: Outstanding Production, Outstanding Ensemble, Outstanding Choreography, and Outstanding Musical Direction for *La Havana Madrid*; Outstanding Costume Design for *The Madres* (Uriel Gómez); and Outstanding Scenic Design (Regina García) for *Fade*. 2019 ALTA Awards: Outstanding Sound Design for *Hope: Part II of a Mexican Trilogy* (Giselle Castro) and Outstanding Stage Management (tied with Vanessa Garcia Productions' Carolina Cormack Orellana for *La Carne Asada 2: The Seasoning*) for *Hope: Part II of a Mexican Trilogy* (Alden Vasquez).

47. The Biograph Theater is a Chicago landmark in the North Side neighborhood of Lincoln Park. It is famed for being the movie theater outside which John Dillinger was pursued and shot by the FBI in 1934. The building was renovated to house Victory Gardens Theater in 2006.

48. Zimmerman recounts of the play: "I believe I started writing in what would have been my first or second year of grad school, so right after Obama was inaugurated—so that was a very poignant question, for me, about what does it mean to be a symbolic first leader? What are the tricky ways of navigating that, and the political traps of that? Also, what does it mean to be a symbolic first leader who has different cultural backgrounds on different sides of the family, which I also have. . . . I'm not Mexican American, but my own relationship with my brother [is similar]—in the sense that we look very, very different, even though we have the same

parents. What does that mean about how people treat us, and how we are received. . . . So I think all of those things were converging" (Zimmerman, in conversation with the author, June 26, 2020).

49. The concept of intersectionality is indebted to Kimberlé Crenshaw, "Demarginalizing the Intersection of Race and Sex: A Black Feminist Critique of Antidiscrimination Doctrine, Black Feminist Theory and Antiracist Politics," *University of Chicago Legal Forum* 1989, no. 1, article 8 (1989): 139–67.

50. Sandra Marquez, in discussion with the author, February 2019.

51. Teatro Vista's ensemble member history includes, in alphabetical order: Charín Alvarez, Max Arciniega, Desmín Borges, Cheryl Lynn Bruce, Rámon Camín, Andrew Carrillo (founding member, former member), Ivonne Coll, Lauri Dahl, Deb Davis (emeritus member), Sandra Delgado, Anthony Diaz-Perez (former member), Sabrina duArte (founding member, deceased), Liza Fernandez, Khanisha Foster, Henry Godinez (founding member, former member), Isaac Gomez, Cruz Gonzalez-Cadel, Ricardo Gutiérrez, Jenna Ford Jackson (founding member, former member), Erick Juarez, Juan Luco (founding member, deceased), Jon Lyon, Sandra Marquez, Eddie Martinez, J. Salome Martinez, Gustavo Mellado (founding member, emeritus member), Joe Minoso, Ayssette Muñoz, Marcela Muñoz (former member), Christina Nieves, Maricela Ochoa (founding member, deceased), Marvin Quijada, Luis Antonio Ramos (former member), Tommy Rivera-Vega, Gabriel Ruiz, Tony Sancho, Nate Santana, Tanya Saracho (former member), Juan Carlos Seda (founding member, former member), Cecilia Suárez, and Edward Torres (founding member). As of this writing, current artistic associates include: Jennifer Aparicio (stage manager and production manager), Rinska Carrasco-Prestinary (actor and director), Steve Casillas (actor), Ilana Faust (actor), Carlo Lorenzo Garcia (actor), Nancy García Loza (playwright), Uriel Gómez (costume designer), Kristin Leahey (dramaturg), Gabi Mayorga (actor), Yunuen Pardo (actor), and Jessie Prez (actor). Resident playwrights include Kristoffer Diaz, Cándido Tirado, and Martín Zimmerman. Designers include Brian Sidney Bembridge, Mikhail Fiksel, Regina García, Jesse Klug, and Christine Pascual.

52. Gutiérrez, in discussion with the author, December 2018.

53. Delgado, in discussion with the author, April 2019.

54. Marquez, in discussion with the author, April 2019.

9

Temple-Swapping in the City

The Spatial Imaginary and Performances of Place-Making in the Work of Theaster Gates

LaRonika Marie Thomas

In a short video promoting the 2012 Art Basel in Miami, the curator and museum director Jeffrey Deitch interviews Chicago artist Theaster Gates, whose work is included in that year's exhibition. In the video, Gates states, "My art practice is to ask hard questions about why systems fail. Like if there's a desire that I have to see a library in my neighborhood, instead of being mad at a government for not having a library, what would be required to build one? So in some ways my body becomes accountable to that process." Gates continues: "'Art' isn't the word that I lead with; I think maybe 'belief' is the word that I lead with. I believe in places, I believe in people, I believe in the value of material things. And one way that I express belief is through the creation of art objects or art experiences or performances. You know, that all of those things are really vehicles by which I express my belief."[1]

Accountability. Belief. Systems. Bodies. Value. Process. These words have complex spatial meanings and implications, and they show up time and again in discussions with and about Theaster Gates and his multifaceted body of work. These words impact the work Gates makes, not only in a studio but also along the streets and in the neighborhoods of Chicago. I would argue that Gates's work, in inverting the public and the private, the domestic and the civic, in swapping temples, turns doors into bridges and argues that our personal definitions of home carry with them very public and material consequences for a city.

Gates, an American artist with a rapidly growing international presence, has developed a unique practice as a social artist working in Chicago and beyond, and he and his work have been profiled in the *New Yorker*, the *New York Times*, the *Guardian*, *Smithsonian Magazine*, *ArtForum*, and *Art in America*, among others, as well as in a monograph titled *Theaster Gates* published by Phaidon. His work includes a robust studio practice, with pieces in museums and galleries around the world, including the National Gallery of Art, the Whitney Biennial, Art Basel, the Walker Art Center, the Museum of Contemporary Art Chicago, Palais de Tokyo, Gagosian Paris, and White Cube London, as well as an increasingly complex series of real estate developments on the South Side of Chicago and in St. Louis and Omaha. In these pieces, Gates pursues a much larger conceptual and social project that involves pulling back the layers of meaning in space and place as they are experienced in Chicago in the twentieth and twenty-first centuries, especially in regard to performances of urban planning and the multiple meanings of home. Gates's work engages in a complicated choreography of public and private, domestic and civic, bringing elements of each into the other to highlight tensions and incongruities in the way we make our homes, our neighborhoods, and our cities. Gates uses elements we traditionally consider to be tools of domestic life—plates, sinks, even houses themselves—to begin conversations with his audience about what home means to them, and what it could mean to all of us. In creating these public domestic spaces, so to speak, Gates is complicating spatial imaginaries—making visible what is seemingly invisible and practicing domestic place-making in the public arena.

Although Gates's work is not theater, it is both theatrical and performative in the way it problematizes spatial imaginaries playing with notions of domestic and civic life in Chicago and is an important example of civic dramaturgy. In brief, I conceptualize civic dramaturgy as a process of performing identity through changes to and impacts on the built environment, along with a method of analyzing and contextualizing those performances to better understand the multiple modes of identity expression that make up a specific place, in this case the city of Chicago. In this chapter, I argue that utilizing the theory of civic dramaturgy to understand his work can give us a better sense of the effects of Gates's work on the "stage" of Chicago. In the case of Gates's work, this civic dramaturgy is one of what he calls "temple-swapping," and it involves a negotiation of domestic and civic objects and spaces, inverting and reimagining their uses and purposes for a variety of audiences, in order to challenge notions of the spatial imaginary, in particular how this imaginary relates to concepts of race. I explore these concepts through an examination of Gates's work, research into his past exhibitions and performances, and magazine and newspaper coverage of Gates, in addition to my own visits to his work and to the Stony Island Arts Bank and two phone interviews with the artist. This unpacking of Gates's art practice helps us understand the ways Chicago's growth has changed in the late twentieth and early twenty-first century as industrial sectors have given way to service industries, tourism, and cultural production, as well as how Chicagoans have utilized performances of urban planning, and how those performances carry implications for concepts like "the arts as a tool for urban renewal," "creative placemaking," and "artwashing."[2]

Theaster Gates's art is of particular note in discussions about race and the built environment because his work is both divergent from other interventions in public space that frequently separate studio artist practice and bureaucratic planning efforts (like public art sculptures or programs that temporarily rent vacant city buildings to artists at a reduced rate as a way to spur private investment), while also being part of a rich tradition of artists and scholars who reconsider definitions of public and private and question in theory and practice the intersection and tensions of urban design and social justice, such as Rick Lowe and George Maciunas. Gates's work interrogates the concepts of the "racialization of space"[3] and the "spatialization of race," or what George Lipsitz writes of when he states that

> the lived experience of race has a spatial dimension, and the lived experience of space has a racial dimension. People of different races in the United States are relegated to different physical locations by housing and lending discrimination, by school district boundaries, by policing practices, by zoning regulations, and by the design of transit systems. The racial demography of the places where people live, work, play, shop, and travel exposes them to a socially-shared system of exclusion and inclusion.

And so Gates's work helps us understand the role of contemporary visual and performance artists in the creation of cultural spaces here in the United States and beyond, and it also helps us uncover a "logic of urban space," which, as the architectural historian and professor

Dianne Harris states so nicely, "though not elided with a rhetoric of 'natural,' is nonetheless designed to appear inevitable."[4] Rather, this illusion of the "organic," a disputed term in performance theory as well as in other critical discourses, may unpack the ways in which we construct, navigate, and produce spaces. Cultural spaces are of particular interest both for Gates and for the topics covered within this chapter, as these spaces can often seem to be geographic frontiers in deconstructing inequality, while also holding a conservative function of enforcing the status quo.

In many ways, Gates has made Chicago, his hometown, a place of experimentation with the idea of "home," whether contemplating the West Side of Chicago, where he grew up; the many in-between spaces in Chicago he had to cross to get from one home to another; the South Side, where the need for a studio space led him to transformed homes and public spaces; or the city itself as a whole. His work creates an audience and asks them to consider not only his home and their homes but also the homes of others and the very definition of "home." When is one "at home"? How far beyond the walls of a house do the barriers of a "home" extend? Gates's work asks these questions while also highlighting how questions of spaces (both civic and domestic) and race are entangled and how these concepts relate to issues of value, ownership, bodies, and accountability. As this chapter will lay out, Gates is intimately aware of the ways some spaces of the city, because of the bodies that occupy these spaces (poor bodies, Black bodies, "deviant" bodies), are devalued by the hegemonic forces of the city and the ways value is simultaneously placed upon some people and places as those people are working to craft value for themselves in those places. Gates's civic dramaturgy highlights questions of the value of objects, places, and people for his audience and is the core of his practice, as is the "temple-swapping" of bringing objects from his neighborhood into museum and gallery spaces and bringing the aesthetic of those museum and gallery spaces to his neighborhood.

Relational Aesthetics and Social Studio Practice

Theaster Gates's work is bound up with his biography. Gates was born in Chicago in 1973 and grew up in Garfield Park, on the city's West Side. He is the youngest of nine children—and the only boy. Gates's father worked as a roofer; his mother wanted Gates to be a scientist or a preacher. He attended church regularly as a kid and sang in the youth choir, experiences that inform much of his performance work. As a high school student, Gates gained admission to Lane Tech, a selective-enrollment magnet school on Chicago's North Side. Just as thousands of Chicago Public School students do today, Gates traversed multiple neighborhoods in the city to go from home to school, moving between the so-called Black spaces and white spaces of Chicago—spaces that are both physical and imagined, which is what Lipsitz notes as the physical implications of these types of racialized boundaries. As Gates puts it in an interview with *Chicago* magazine, "I have walked in two worlds since fifth grade. I had a better understanding of both because I was moving between them."[5] He was walking in and out of a variety of doors in Chicago, crossing spatial imaginaries as well as geographic boundaries.

Gates holds a bachelor's degree in urban planning and ceramics from Iowa State University, and a multidisciplinary master's degree in urban planning, religion, and sculpture. He spent four months in Japan in the late 1990s on a ceramics residency and, beginning in 1999, worked for the Chicago Transit Authority (CTA) as their art planner, a position that included the charge to place more public art in CTA stations. Since 2014, he has been a professor of visual arts and the director of the Arts and Public Life program at the University of Chicago, having arrived at the university in an administrative capacity in 2006. His studio practice gained traction when he moved from working primarily as a sculptor and ceramicist to expanding his work to include performance and event-making projects.

His first solo art show, titled *Plate Convergence*, was in 2007 at the Hyde Park Art Center on Chicago's South Side. This early work displays the importance of performance and domesticity as spatial disruption in his work. *Plate Convergence* was an installation piece: a dinner party hosted by the center where friends and strangers dined with each other and conversed, eating off plates Gates crafted for the event and which were later exhibited in the gallery. Hence the attendees both ate dinner and performed the rituals of sharing a meal in a public space. Gates explained that the plates and the dinner event were in reference to Shoji Yamaguchi, a Japanese ceramist with whom Gates had studied ceramics for some months and who lived in the American South, married to an African American woman who was a civil rights worker. A timeline labeled "The Yamaguchi Narrative" lined one long hallway in the space, with clay objects along the opposite wall, crafting a story for the audience and inviting them to perform a kind of contemplative walk that married object, narrative, and bodies. Clay shards, pottery dishes, and fragments of larger works littered multiple rooms, hallways, and stairwells, interspersed with video dedicated to the craft of ceramics. The dinner was meant to carry on the legacy of the couple's work in the civil rights movement and in the art world, since they had passed in a car accident several years earlier. But what the diners did not realize was that the story's premise was fictional—there is no Shoji Yamaguchi. Theaster Gates played the trickster for his first major art show and, in doing so, not only asked strangers to dine together and talk about civil rights and issues of food and eating and family and home, but also asked them, in the reveal of the lie, to consider why it took a fictional premise to get them in the room together, why this conversation about seemingly banal topics of everyday life needed a high-concept entry point, and how they might dream up better ways of being neighbors in Chicago in the twenty-first century. Gates's subsequent work would continue to draw on these themes and consider the ways in which domestic objects are implicated in public processes.[6]

Gates is highly conscious of the spaces he inhabits in museums and galleries as an installation and performance artist. For Gates, this consideration must also extend outside of those walls, those "white" spaces, into the city. The entire city carries a potency, in that the space may be manipulated and transformed—this potential allows him to ask questions about systems and about belief. Gates is conscious of institutional doors and walls. Georg Simmel, in his essay "Spatial and Urban Culture," looks at two basic structures of the built environment—bridges and doors—and considers their meaning. In regard to doors, he writes,

> The human being who first erected a hut, like the first road-builder, revealed the specifically human capacity over against nature, in so far as he or she cut a portion out of the continuity and infinity of space and arranged this into a particular unity in accordance with a single meaning. A piece of space was thereby brought together and separated from the whole remaining world.[7]

For Simmel, doors both cut off space that had been continuous and provide a way to move from one section of that space to another. This may be a good interpretation of the difference between space and place. Cultural institutions create and exist within built spaces that contain doors, marking themselves as separate from the world outside—in the case of this analysis, from the rest of the city of Chicago and its populace. But the success and the continued existence of the institution as a separate entity depends upon the flow of people, capital, and ideas through those doors. Those who run these institutions are continually concerned with getting people in the door of the museum or gallery or theater, or with how the institution wants to open its doors to everyone in the community. As audiences, we travel to the arts and culture created and located in proximity to our homes, and, mostly, we travel to and into a building set aside for that specific purpose. However, an open door may be empty of meaning unless an invitation to enter is extended. In engaging in "temple-swapping," Gates breaks the reverence for the physical spaces of both the museum and the church, signaling a symbolic opening of the doors of both spaces, as the tension that arises from the multiple kinds of labor momentarily coexisting in the museum works to create a third contested space.

In 2006, the University of Chicago's Cultural Policy Center released the study "Mapping Cultural Participation in Chicago," a first of its kind, which looked at the demographics of households across Chicago and mapped how and where they participated in cultural activity throughout the city. Their findings, summarized in their executive report, were not surprising to anyone working in Chicago cultural institutions. They found that "participation in Chicago's largest arts and cultural organizations is highest in predominantly white, high-income areas of the metropolitan area," that "there are also many predominantly white areas, regardless of income, that are not significantly engaged with Chicago's largest arts organizations," that "the socioeconomic attributes of a neighborhood are the most important predictors of the density of arts participation," and, finally, that "even after we account for a neighborhood's socioeconomic characteristics, its ethnic composition still is a predictor of participation in the area's largest art organizations."[8]

The study's findings prompt further questions about arts and cultural institutions and their audiences. Are the differences in participation due to economics? Perhaps wealthier households have more leisure time and money to spend on these activities. Perhaps the programming at these institutions left non-white audiences feeling uninterested in the institutions—perhaps these audiences were not being spoken to by the venues' events. The maps within the study certainly show that participation, especially at smaller arts and cultural organizations in the city, tends to happen close to home—if you live on the North Side, you are much more likely to attend a cultural event on the North Side, rather than venture to the city's South Side. Cultural consumption in Chicago is a neighborhood affair.[9]

To take the work of the cultural institution out of its walls, therefore, also has significant meaning for both the institution and the city in which it resides, in that as the populace is audience, there is the opportunity for new audiences to be exposed to the work and, significantly, to influence the kind of work coming from the institution. Or in the case of Gates's work, to bring into those public spaces the kinds of domestic objects and performances that are usually found in more private spaces activates a tension between what is on either side of the institutional door. Henri Lefebvre, whose paradigm-shifting and oft-quoted idea that social practices produce social (and in particular, for our concern, urban) space, also notes, "If there is production of a city, and social relations in the city, it is a production and reproduction of human beings, rather than a production of objects."[10] However, Gates's work suggests that a reorganization of objects that creates a different kind of encounter between human beings can produce a new place within the same space.

Leaving those walls and doors behind for the city streets changes the bodies of the performer, audience, and passersby—their interaction with each other and the possibility for change. Removing the door removes a method of gatekeeping for the meaning produced by the theater performance. To reiterate, Gates's work, in inverting the public and the private, the domestic and the civic, in swapping temples, turns doors into bridges and argues that our personal definitions of home carry with them very public and material consequences for a city.

No One Cared about the Neighborhood I Lived In

The Chicago neighborhoods of East Garfield Park and West Garfield Park, located approximately halfway between downtown and the upscale suburb of Oak Park, are prime examples of the results of the problems of urban divestment and the large-scale migration of white residents that increased after World War II in cities across the United States. The neighborhood demographics changed from predominantly white to predominantly African American over the course of about twenty years, from the 1930s to the 1950s. By the 1950s the construction of the Eisenhower Expressway[11] cut through the southern portion of the neighborhoods, displacing many residents, and the racial and spatial strategies of restrictive covenants and redlining eviscerated communities.[12] And when, in the 1970s, many suburban neighborhoods began to lessen restrictions on homeownership by non-whites, middle-class African American families also fled the city's increasing poverty and violence, leaving the neighborhoods and further destabilizing the area's economy.[13]

Growing up in the 1970s and 1980s, Gates was aware of the intersections between race and space in his neighborhood. In an interview I conducted with Gates, he spoke of his childhood, and of being affected by the neighborhood blight he saw around him:

> I think I grew up understanding that the policy of the day was that if prostitution or drug distribution was happening in a building, that the city would put that building on a demolition list and the building would be torn down. And I watched my neighborhood get "unhoused" because of this very, very basic policy. That the solution to the kind of black epidemics of deviance were [*sic*] to simply take spaces away. I knew that there was this onerous demolition list from the time that I was like ten. And that even the mini mansions in our neighborhood—that's what we called them—even these gorgeous brick yellow buildings—even in these mini mansions, that if deviance happened in them, the solutions wouldn't be to try to address the issues of prostitution or issues of the economy, the issue would be to simply take the building away. In addition to that, it was a moment when the last of the non-blacks who had property on the West Side of Chicago were trying to get out of their properties, and so there was a fair amount of arson that was black-faced on the surface but then it was actually working to the credit of some of these other folks that had property that they wanted insurance on. For a ten-year-old, or a twelve-year-old, it just looked like no one cared about the neighborhood I lived in. And that no good thing could happen.[14]

What Gates observed as a child—that his community was being "unhoused" by forces outside of it because that community was not valued—is an example of how attuned he was and is to the spatial imaginaries of the city. And this awareness is at the core of his civic dramaturgy. As an adult, Gates has cultivated a belief in places in order to combat the notion that no one cared—and to try to fix or circumvent the broken systems he sees. Gates continues to walk in two worlds, but his walks are performances of urban planning, and they are an attempt to close the gap between those two worlds and correct this "un-housing" of the predominantly African American neighborhoods of Chicago.

For Gates, space itself becomes the means of performance. What is a museum if one does not recognize the people making the art or visiting its halls? What is a home, even a gorgeous "mini mansion," if it can be destroyed so that a stranger can make a profit? What is a neglected bank if no one is investing in the neighborhood around it? These questions float through Gates's work. In this way, he inherits the tradition of contemporary artists living in lofts in New York in the 1960s and 1970s. Just as Fluxus founder George Maciunas eventually became known as the father of SoHo through his purchase and renovation of buildings in lower Manhattan, Gates may eventually be known as the founder of a renegotiation of space on the South Side of Chicago. Even if this does not become the case, Gates and those who call the South Side home will need to negotiate the changes he and his projects may cause in their lives.

Producing Space on South Dorchester

As a potter working in Chicago, Gates faced a very practical problem familiar to many artists—he needed a kiln and a space to make his work. He could no longer afford to rent kiln space and studio time. He needed a house, and he wanted it to be near his work at the University of Chicago. These problems are not unique to Gates; the city zoning ordinances that housing developers and renovators are subjected to create endless obstacles for artists to navigate as they make work and build their careers. To solve his problem, Gates purchased a house in 2006 on South Dorchester, in the aptly named Grand Crossing neighborhood, approximately two miles south of the university; the neighborhood, like Garfield Park, was unusually violent and lacking investment. In 2007, he began to renovate the previously boarded-up house, using many recycled and repurposed materials—an act that recalls Gates's belief in the potency of materials—and eventually he bought the house next door, too. These two houses together are now called the Dorchester Projects, and they are both an ongoing development project and a live-work space for Gates. Until Gates renovated and opened the Stony Island Arts Bank, a new gallery and archive on the South Side set in a former savings and loan that Gates purchased from the city for one dollar, these houses served in part as a space for the archives Gates continues to foster. The first house, called the Listening Project, housed the archive of records from Dr. Wax, a culturally significant record store on the South Side of Chicago known for supporting local artists, that was donated to Gates when the legendary Chicago record store closed its doors. The second house, the Archive House, held other archive collections that Gates has acquired, including a collection of sixty thousand glass lantern slides from the University of Chicago that required Gates to reinforce the floor of the house in order to hold the slides.[15] As the Rebuild Foundation's website notes, it is significant that "world-class" archives have found a home on the South Side of Chicago, highlighting issues of archival access throughout the city.[16] All these collections—as well as the library from Johnson Publishing, the publisher of *Ebony* and *Jet* magazines; the vast vinyl collection of Frankie Knuckles, aka "The Godfather of House Music"; and the Edward J. Williams Collection of "negrobilia"—have since been moved to the Stony Island Arts Bank building.

In 2011 Gates received one of the first round of grants (worth $125,000) issued by the NEA's new program, ArtPlace, in order to develop a third property near the first two. ArtPlace is a public-private partnership between the NEA, other government agencies, foundations, and banks, and is dedicated to creative place-making or, as they put it, "projects in which art plays an intentional and integrated role in place-based community planning and development."[17] The award to Gates was for a new phase of the Dorchester Projects called Black Cinema House, a community home serving film artists of color as well as the local community. Black Cinema House is a venue for screening African American films, for discussion, and for community classes and workshops. Instead of "un-housing" the neighborhood, Gates is quite literally rebuilding it.

Since moving to the neighborhood in 2006, Gates has regularly hosted domestic-oriented community dinners and gatherings at the Dorchester Projects—this time bringing civic discourse into these domestic settings. Interns and staff work to archive the many collections first stored in the homes and now located at the Stony Island Arts Bank. These initial projects spurred Gates to create the Rebuild Foundation in 2011; this organization dedicated to "artist-led and

Dorchester Art + Housing Collaborative at 1456 East Seventieth Street. Photograph by LaRonika Marie Thomas. Courtesy of the author.

culture-initiated development"[18] now has a staff of six and operates in three cities. In 2013, Gates purchased an entire block of housing—a former public housing project—near the Dorchester Projects, and he is working with a private development corporation to turn that into thirty-two two- and three-bedroom townhomes, along with an arts center.

The development of these spaces, as well as the activity occurring within them—meetings, meals, the sharing of ideas and works of art—required embodied action, and in this way they are performances. Indeed, Gates's refurbishing of the spaces is a kind of performance, one that he has leaned into by, in turn, taking some of the actions of home building and repair into the museum and gallery space. These actions work upon the space, producing it, and the space also works upon the bodies. Accounts of the gatherings at the Dorchester Projects, especially the initial gatherings (and I think it is important to note that reception of these participatory performances has changed over time as the Dorchester Projects have become more familiar to a wider audience, and more of a destination to experience), include descriptions of

Interior of Stony Island Arts Bank with an exhibition of Glenn Ligon's *A Small Band*. Photograph by LaRonika Marie Thomas. Courtesy of the author.

how the participants were at first physically uncomfortable and unsure of how to relate to the space. Many white attendees at these first events were unfamiliar with the neighborhood, or at least only familiar with it from a distance, evoking the white and Black spatial imaginaries that cover Chicago and influence the movement of bodies across the city. Food and music—rituals of domestic place-making—helped to break down that discomfort. These rituals evoked communitas, Victor Turner's term for the equal sharing as a community in an event, as people let go of an expectation for the gathering and instead allowed themselves to come together to experience something both new and familiar at the same time.

According to a 2013 article by Cassie Burke and Elly Fishman in *Chicago* magazine, "Gates calculates that he has poured $20 million into the South Side of Chicago over the past five years—a figure that includes his own spending on not just buildings but also a small army of architects, contractors, artisans, and administrators—plus grants, city and state redevelopment funds, and private donations."[19] The 2015 opening of the Stony Island Arts Bank, the newest and most public space from the Rebuild Foundation, was a remodel of a neglected bank that the city was preparing to tear down, and was financed in part by offering engraved marble "bank bonds" for $1,000 each to arts patrons. These efforts qualify him as a major developer on the South Side of Chicago. When philanthropists approach Gates to ask about helping in the developments, he often sends them to his gallery representative, where they can buy the art objects he has crafted for his exhibitions (shoeshine stands, dinner plates, etc.) so that he can, in turn, use that money to further these development projects. Theaster Gates is quickly becoming Theaster Gates, Inc.

So, what is going on here? While Gates is part of a rich history of artists challenging the development of their city, he has also gained global attention and notoriety for his work in a way that others have not. Gates sees both his gallery work and his development work as one and the same thing. If we want to understand how he is reconciling these two worlds, a return to the concepts of the Black spatial imaginary and the white spatial imaginary may allow us to reconsider the processes at work.

Lipsitz asserts that space as we think of it in the United States is marked by these two imaginaries. He writes:

> A white spatial imaginary, based on exclusivity and augmented exchange value, functions as a central mechanism for skewing opportunities and life chances in the United States across racial lines. Whiteness, as used here, is an analytic category that refers to the structured advantages that accrue to whites because of past and present discrimination. Not all people who are white consciously embrace the white spatial imaginary, and not all whites profit equally from their whiteness, but all whites benefit from the association of whiteness with privilege and the neighborhood effects of spaces defined by their racial demography.[20]

For the purpose of this chapter, I take this to mean that the dominant, white paradigm for the value of particular places in Chicago—a house in Grand Crossing, an empty, decaying bank, the roof of a closed church—is based on the money that can be made from it. Additionally, that money, or exchange value, is attached to the white supremacist structures that have been constructed in terms of race in this country.

Lipsitz further asserts that "communities of color, especially black communities, have developed a counter-spatial imaginary based on sociability and augmented use value. Blackness here, like whiteness, is not reducible to an embodied identity. Not all blacks consciously embrace the black spatial imaginary, even though all blacks are subjected to it."[21] Lipsitz argues that the only way to unmark these spaces is, first, to address directly the systems that prevent people of color from accumulating wealth that can be passed down from one generation to the next and, second, to privilege a separate spatial imaginary that favors use value over exchange value. So a decaying bank (and the land beneath it) may have an exchange value of one dollar to the city of Chicago if it remains a decaying bank, but it may be worth more—or at least the land might—without the bank. Gates's proposition to the city is not just that he purchase the bank from the city for a dollar, but that in adding use value through the building's renovation and transformation into a cultural institution attractive to visitors both from and outside of the neighborhood, he can ultimately raise the exchange value of that place and, in doing so, increase the exchange value of the surrounding buildings in the neighborhood.

These spatial imaginaries encompass both private and public space; they affect the arrangements of the built environments of our cities, neighborhoods, and houses, the laws governing these spaces, and the language we use to talk about these spaces. The white spatial imaginary, because it is the privileged imaginary, "hides in plain sight,"[22] as Dianne Harris says, and gives space the illusion of naturalized order. Gates's performances of development intervene in both the white and Black spatial imaginaries through the use of his material interventions in the gallery and in the street. His work reveals the mechanisms of both imaginaries and calls for their erasure.

I asked Gates about how the Dorchester neighborhood has changed since he moved to the area and began to fix up these houses and bring attention and visitors to the area. He says it hasn't changed much materially, but the difference now is that people know each other. He knows that he can call Mr. Johnson on his block to ask about the kids who are hanging out watching the cops, because Mr. Johnson is watching the kids; people do not feel so isolated anymore.[23]

During an interview with Lilly Wei for *Art in America* magazine, Gates talked about eventually leaving Grand Crossing. He said, "This part of my practice is about the politics of staying. I believe in the place, and I'm invested in it. But it's fine for my neighborhood to change around me. It would even be fine if in five years, maybe because of me, the whole thing is lily-white. . . . Gentrification won't need my approval or disapproval. But 6901 and 6916 South Dorchester were available because of policies that moved people out and other people in. . . . If it is the politics of staying, then you invite black people back."[24]

When I mentioned this interview to Gates, he made the point that while his neighborhood may look all-Black from the ground level, very few of the residences there were owned by the people who lived in them. Instead, large tracts of housing and land are owned by private portfolios as investments. So, in that way, his neighborhood of Black homes was already white. Why should he blame a Black family for, say, cashing in and selling a property in a so-called gentrifying neighborhood, and taking that money and living comfortably in the suburbs? As he put it in his talk at the Maryland Institute College of Art in February 2012: "And you call it gentrification. Who you mad at?"[25]

These statements are part of Gates's politics of staying. Gates, like Lipsitz, believes that you can have a material effect on a neighborhood by highlighting both the white and the Black spatial imaginary—by drawing attention to it and shining a light on the tensions between the two, and on their connections to use value and exchange value. But he is careful to point out how exchange value can be manipulated to serve use value. In this way he disrupts the white spatial imaginary. And Gates's work highlights the significance of an artist's individual agency while working within larger systems. The existing system (renting a kiln space and living somewhere else, making his pots, selling them at fairs) was not working, so he disrupted the system by buying the house he could afford and renovating it. That work not only allows Gates his studio practice but becomes a part of it.

How might artists make real, material changes to both their practices and the cities in which they live and work? Gates offers us an example in Chicago that starts with the personal, the private, and the domestic concerns of individuals as they navigate their homes, their churches, and their neighborhoods. He then crafts what we might call an inversion of sorts—taking those spaces into the public eye, and swapping the temples of the private and the civic in order to highlight problematic racial relationships in and between both. In a way, Gates is asking how we match our idea of home to our material circumstances.

Gates's work also carries implications for addressing Michael McKinnie's notion of the "civic transnational," or the political subjectivity created by the state, culture, and performance. City power structures are acutely aware that the arts can be *used* as fuel to power their economic engines. As Gates's projects become larger and their influence—especially on the South Side of Chicago—grows, the city will come calling. Indeed, it already has—with development dollars, with a seat on the advisory committee for the second Chicago Cultural Plan, with relationships and partnerships and conversations about the renewal of Grand Crossing. What does a politics of staying look like on a regional, national, or global scale? How are all of our bodies held accountable to these systems?

Performances of disruption can create echoes on a larger scale, but they also threaten to be swallowed whole by global capitalism. Speaking at a conference in Pittsburgh in April 2015, Rick Lowe, an artist whose work has also ventured into the sphere of urban planning, spoke about the risks in this kind of work of becoming, essentially, a tour guide into lower-income neighborhoods for developers. I confess that as I visit Grand Crossing to get a firsthand sense of Gates's buildings and to take in the collections at the Stony Island Arts Bank, I have worried that I am nothing more than a sort of gentrification tourist—taking in the sights of change with no real stake in the consequences of that change. But that is the point. My body—every body—is implicated in these processes of urban planning and imaginary crossings that create the pieces of space, stitched together, that form the city.

Given that, as Lefebvre has written, all space is produced, it is not enough to say that "time will tell" how these kinds of performances, events, and projects that highlight how we position the importance of labor and home and neighborhood will ultimately effect Gates's neighbors. Gates's intent, though he is fine with the neighborhood changing, is clearly to have a material effect on the residents of Grand Crossing and of Chicago. Will his foundation be able to leverage the power they have built in order to follow through on that change? From an anecdotal perspective, Gates's projects have not (yet?) spurred either an increase in housing costs or a rush of development money into the neighborhood.[26] And in the summer of 2015, some community members became publicly upset with Gates when he proposed to some members of the board of the DuSable Museum of African American History (where Gates also served as a trustee) a partnership between the museum and the University of Chicago (where Gates is employed as a professor and program director)—specifically, having the university take over some of the museum's educational programs. As outlined in the *Chicago Tribune*, when news of Gates's proposal leaked to the public, an activist coalition known as the Concerned Committee for the Support of Independent Black Cultural Institutions issued a statement that read, "This proposal . . . will result in a radical reconceptualization of the ideas, cultural focus, historical knowledge, and critical black direction of the DuSable Museum. . . . The defining ideas of Dr. Margaret Burroughs and other cofounders of the DuSable Museum are being disregarded and set aside for 'new thought' and a 'major conceptual shift.'"[27] Locals also came out in force to a meeting organized by the group.

The proposal was ultimately rejected, and this particular controversy seems to have been short-lived, in part because Gates stepped down from the board in 2018, but it is a powerful example of the ongoing tension on the South Side of Chicago between two symbolically powerful institutions—one (DuSable) considered a "Black" space and the other (the university) considered an ever-encroaching "white" space. Gates continues to travel between "white" and "Black" spaces in Chicago. Additionally, Gates and the organizations he has built are not themselves immune from accusations of racialized spatial violence; in 2017 former employees of the Rebuild Foundation took over the organization's Twitter account and detailed, in a long series of tweets, how the institution had "created a toxic and hostile work environment disproportionately affecting Black workers."[28] This controversy seems to have disappeared from the media, but I would be surprised if at least the tension resulting from this conflict did not still exist for those former employees, as well as for the current employees and leaders at the Rebuild Foundation.

In our interview, Gates mentioned wanting to materially compensate his neighbors (our aforementioned theoretical Mr. Johnson) for the invisible work they already do to make their neighborhood a community, which it already was before Gates bought his first building there. It is unclear if this has yet happened or if it is part of the future development plans for the neighborhood. How many guests can fit at the dinner table before it becomes impossible to nourish them all? Where does a home end and a city begin?

Notes

1. "Jeffrey Deitch and Theaster Gates: I Believe in Places," last modified January 13, 2012, https://www.youtube.com/watch?v=m34aIZG-_JM.

2. "Artwashing" is a term that has gained popularity since anti-gentrification protestors in L.A. began using it a few years ago. However,

I originally encountered the term in 2012 in an article on a problematic news blog about pro-Israeli graffiti in Palestine, which is the earliest use of the term I could find. Nonetheless, it refers to the use of art and artists to cover up processes of gentrification, neoliberal late-stage-capitalist urban development projects, and the like. Much like greenwashing uses the hype of environmentalism as a feel-good tactic in place of actual sound environmental policy, artwashing uses art projects in place of actual community investment.

3. George Lipsitz, "The Racialization of Space and the Spatialization of Race: Theorizing the Hidden Architecture of Landscape," *Landscape Journal* 26, no.1 (2007): 12. Lipsitz continues his analysis: "These interconnections among race, place, and power in the United States have a long history. They stem from concrete policies and practices: Indian removal in the age of westward expansion; restrictive covenants during the industrial era; and urban renewal and urban restructuring in the late industrial and early post-industrial periods. Yet these policies also emanate from shared cultural ideals and moral geographies based on a romance with pure spaces. This romance fuels allegiances to defensive localism and hostile privatism. Having a better understanding of differential space, of the roles played by exclusion, exchange value, and use value in determining the racial meanings of places, can help landscape architects and other professionals whose work shapes the built environments to ameliorate the racialization of space and the spatialization of race" (12).

4. Dianne Harris, "Seeing the Invisible: Reexamining Race and Vernacular Architecture," *Perspectives in Vernacular Architecture* 13, no. 2 (2006/2007): 100.

5. Cassie Walker Burke and Elly Fishman, "Theaster Gates: The Rise of an Unconventional Art Star," *Chicago*, May 7, 2103, accessed May 22, 2013, http://www.chicagomag.com/Chicago-Magazine/June-2013/Theaster-Gates-The-Rise-of-an-Unconventional-Art-Star/.

6. Gates also had a significant exhibit at the Milwaukee Art Museum in 2010 that put the work of Dave the Potter, an enslaved man living in the nineteenth century who signed and wrote on his ceramic pots, into conversation with the American craft movement and the current issues facing immigrant and blue-collar labor in the United States by creating work with the laborers at the local Kohler factory. I do not analyze this exhibit here since it did not happen in Chicago.

7. Georg Simmel, "Spatial and Urban Culture," in *Simmel on Culture*, ed. David Frisby and Mike Featherstone (London: Sage Publications, 1997), 172.

8. Robert LaLonde et al., *Mapping Cultural Participation in Chicago* (Chicago: Cultural Policy Center at the University of Chicago, 2006). The study notes that it was driven by data volunteered by the institutions in response to an invitation from the study organizers. The organizers invited participation from "all registered not-for-profit arts, culture, and humanities organizations in the Chicago metropolitan area in Illinois. These 467 organizations received a written invitation but were not marked for extensive follow-up. Only 33 responded" (20).

9. Since Chicago is described as a city of neighborhoods, this is not entirely surprising. One of the largest efforts of the first cultural plan of Chicago was to conduct a large number of town hall meetings in various neighborhoods—neighborhood pride is a material phenomenon in Chicago, and often the cultural landscape has been framed as city center offerings (large institutions) against neighborhood venues (smaller, and somehow more authentic, institutions). Aldermen fight for money and recognition of their wards in return for supporting larger citywide efforts.

10. Henri Lefebvre, "The Specificity of the City," in *Writings on Cities*, trans. and ed. Eleonore Kofman and Elizabeth Lebas (Malden, MA: Blackwell Publishing, 2006), 101.

11. The first Mayor Daley, as many histories of the expressway detail, approved the construction of the highway through these neighborhoods purposefully, in order to discourage Black families from integrating traditionally white neighborhoods, including the mayor's own neighborhood of Bridgeport.

12. WBEZ has a detailed exploration of the ways in which the expressway changed the Garfield Park neighborhood and decimated the communities located in that part of Chicago. It can be found at https://interactive.wbez.org/curiouscity/eisenhower/.

13. Amanda Seligman, "East Garfield Park," *Electronic Encyclopedia of Chicago*, http://www.encyclopedia.chicagohistory.org/pages/404.html.

14. Theaster Gates, in discussion with the author, November 15, 2012.

15. Since these archives have moved to the Stony Island Arts Bank, my understanding is that the Dorchester Projects are used for visiting artist housing and as event spaces.

16. "Dorchester Projects," Rebuild Foundation, accessed October 15, 2014, https://rebuild-foundation.squarespace.com/dorchester-projects/.

17. "Introduction," ArtPlace America, accessed August 1, 2015, http://www.artplaceamerica.org/about/introduction. The introduction continues: "In everything we do and support, arts and culture work to help achieve a place-based change, which means that it is the community development

interventions that are creative, not necessarily the outcomes. In creative placemaking, 'creative' is an adverb describing the making, not an adjective describing the place. Successful creative placemaking projects are not measured by how many new arts centers, galleries, or cultural districts are built. Rather, their success is measured in the ways artists, formal and informal arts spaces, and creative interventions have contributed toward community outcomes."

18. Rebuild Foundation, accessed October 15, 2014, http://rebuild-foundation.squarespace.com/.

19. Burke and Fishman, "Theaster Gates."

20. Lipsitz, "Racialization of Space," 13–14.

21. Lipsitz, "Racialization of Space," 13–14.

22. Harris, "Seeing the Invisible," 99.

23. Theaster Gates, in discussion with the author, November 15, 2012.

24. Lilly Wei, "Theaster Gates," *Art in America* (December 2011): 126.

25. "Theaster Gates—February 8, 2012," MICAMultimedia, last modified April 5, 2012, https://www.youtube.com/watch?v=fwGqhqml87o.

26. This differs from the concerns over housing costs due to the new 606 Line (a public park akin to New York City's High Line) currently being discussed in the Humboldt Park neighborhood of Chicago. You can see the *Chicago Tribune* for coverage on this issue, specifically: http://www.chicagotribune.com/news/local/politics/ct-emanuel-606-housing-met-20150811-story.html#page=1.

27. "DuSable Museum Proposal from U. of C. Professor Gets Heated Response," *Chicago Tribune*, July 20, 2015.

28. Rebuild Foundation Twitter account, September 21, 2017.

10

Staging Private Homes and the Transformations of Public Lives

The Chicago Home Theater Festival

Jasmine Jamillah Mahmoud

in conversation with Irina Zadov, Laley Lippard, Aymar Jean Christian, and Meida McNeal

A public transit ride began this theater performance. After traveling on the CTA from my home in Edgewater to the Chicago Transit Authority's Western Blue Line stop, I connected with a crowd of ten mostly strangers assembled outside the station near the intersection of Western and Milwaukee Avenues. There, a young woman named Alexis Smyser met us, and led us west—by foot—toward Humboldt Park, the largely Puerto Rican neighborhood on the Near West Side named for its eponymous 207-acre public park and known for its lush boathouse and vibrant festivals, including the Puerto Rican Festival.

Demographics often center descriptions of Humboldt Park; the neighborhood of fifty-five thousand residents was, in 2013, about 28 percent Puerto Rican (among 50 percent Hispanic/Latinx) as well as 23 percent Black, and 23 percent white. The tour—which took place May 11, 2015—narrated a more personal Humboldt Park. Raised here, our guide (of Puerto Rican descent) shared her stories about growing up and the schools she attended, and the histories of corner stores we passed, one once owned by her family. She shared insights about imminent neighborhood changes, including gentrification from mostly white artists. At one moment, she pointed up at another change: the

Bloomingdale Line. Opened in the late nineteenth century, this elevated rail line once saw regular commuter and freight train traffic. After it was abandoned in 2001, grass and trees overgrew the old train tracks, and it became an unofficial park for walkers, runners, and bikers. A month after this tour, on June 5, 2015, the Bloomingdale Line officially reopened as the 606, "a multiuse recreational trail and park."

Our guide eventually led us to a three-story house, where brick covered the first floor and wood siding wrapped the upper two floors. Days earlier, I had purchased a ten-dollar ticket online. At the home's front door, event organizers checked my name and ushered me inside the home's living room, where our group of ten who had come from the optional walking tour ballooned into thirty attendees for the main performance. This event was sold out, we were told, and we had to get physically close to accommodate all. I squeezed next to others on a large sectional sofa, while others sat on the floor.

Our hosts were Wil Ruggiero and J. Gibran Villalobos, Latinx artists and curators. After they introduced themselves from the kitchen island, which connected to their home's living room, and gave their history in the neighborhood as new-ish residents, they offered us food. Then the performances began. While kneeling on the living room floor, Fatimah Asghar performed a poem linking her Pakistani heritage to United States militarism. Rae Langes, a queer performance artist, walked around the living room floor while performing about a road trip through the U.S. South and encounters with police. Performances also included experimental music from Zo/Ra, a Black queer artist collective, and dance by Donnell Williams, which moved into the bathroom.

Without lighting plots, fire exits, and risers, most private homes are ill-suited to staging professional theater productions. Yet from nineteenth-century French salons to early twentieth-century antilynching plays staged in African American living rooms to the International Home Theater Festival founded by artist Philip Huang in San Francisco in 2010, homes have long been a site of theater.

Inspired by Huang and founded in 2012 by theater director Laley Lippard, theater actor Blake Russell, and community organizer Irina Zadov, the Chicago Home Theater Festival (CHTF) staged performances annually in private homes and public parks in twenty-five distinct Chicago neighborhoods including Austin, East Garfield Park, Rogers Park, Pilsen, and Albany Park. My experience was typical of many evenings: a resident's neighborhood tour, a food-framed welcome by hosts, and then an evening of five ten- to fifteen-minute performances often including dance, theater, and poetry. Attendees often sat on couches and the floor, and artists performed in living rooms, kitchens, basements, and bathtubs.

This chapter centers the history and practices of the founders and producers of the Chicago Home Theater Festival, which produced five twenty-day annual festivals from 2012 to 2017. According to its website, the festival launched "with an intention to disrupt historically entrenched race and class divides and continues to re-imagine safety and accessibility." By using private homes and public parks, the organizers drew upon "arts . . . at the heart of Chicago's labor, immigration, civil rights, and other movements for justice and liberation" and aimed to "transform the cultural landscape of Chicago by creating spaces that honor marginalized groups and amplify their narratives and struggles." They also wrote: "We choose to work in homes because we believe that art done and experienced in private, intimate spaces can transform how we relate to each other in our public lives."[1]

What follows are interviews I conducted with cofounders Zadov and Lippard, as well as with leading artistic producers Aymar Jean Christian and Meida McNeal. Each interview, edited for space and clarity, seeks to archive the festival, including its people, artists, homes, and neighborhoods. In considering how home as theater *is and is not* makeshift, each interview reveals how the curated space of the home brought diverse people together; confronted, even temporarily, Chicago's hyperracial segregation; and transformed private space and public lives.

Irina Zadov

Irina Zadov (she/they) is an artist, educator, and cultural organizer. They are a queer post-Soviet Jewish immigrant and settler living on the unceded territories of the Three Fires Confederacy: Ojibwe, Odawa, and Potawatomi. Their practice explores the liminal space between the individual and the collective, diasporic community and chosen family, the home and the state. Irina aims to co-create joyful, healing, and liberatory spaces by, for, and with Black, Indigenous, and People of Color, immigrants, young people, and LGBTQIA+ communities. They are currently a senior program specialist at the Chicago Park District. They are a cofounder and co-executive producer of the Chicago Home Theater Festival, which they love with all their heart.

I'd love to hear about your background, and how you got into the arts and theater.

IRINA ZADOV: My background is that I'm an artist, an educator, and a cultural organizer. I was born in Minsk, Belarus, in the former Soviet Union. I came to the so-called U.S. or Turtle Island when I was seven. I got into the arts initially through visual arts. And then, in graduate school, I went to SAIC[2] here in Chicago, and I studied arts education. My thesis work was at Cabrini-Green, one of the largest public housing complexes in Chicago that was being demolished at the time, and I did work with young people around memory, trauma, and archiving their history. In addition to chronicling this transition in the young people's lives, I was interested in understanding the mechanisms of displacement, urban renewal, segregation, the race and class dynamics that impact how cities are shaped, who is welcomed, who is pushed out, and why.

After I finished my graduate work in Chicago, I moved to the Bay Area. I worked with Lex Leifheit at SOMArts[3] Cultural Center. We developed a monthly event series that brought together artists and chefs, and opened up a storytelling potluck. We would host a monthly open mic, and think about how breaking bread is this really generous act of evoking memory and history, specifically in the South of Market neighborhood where a lot of folks [were] experiencing homelessness and a lot of artists lived in, and where the violent impacts of gentrification were all around us.

In 2011, I went back to Belarus and I did a project with my partner at the time, Abraham Epton, called "Open Feast." That's where I became aware of Belarus Free Theater, a really big influence on my involvement with the Home Theater Festival, this very radical performance art group in Belarus who worked in opposition to the government, a dictatorship. Part of their work was critiquing the current state in a way that didn't jeopardize the artists and the audiences. A lot of that was very much about being underground. In order to go to a performance, you would meet at an unmarked intersection. Then someone would take you in silence to a home, where the performance would take place, because oftentimes KGB members would show up to these performances and take down names of who was there. It really was a very dangerous pursuit. Being witness to that made me think about the ways in which performance in home spaces can be politically subversive and community building at the same time.

When I was living in the Bay Area, I had a friend, a performance artist named Philip Huang, who was the founder of the International

Home Theater Festival, and he and I were involved in something called SQUART (Spontaneous Queer Arts), and out of that emerged his idea to reclaim performance spaces and bringing them into home spaces. His motto was "fuck institutions." We don't need them. We don't need to apply for grants. Artists should produce their own work, in their own homes, and get the proceeds directly. We don't need the middleman. That's really how I've come to this work.

How did you found Chicago Home Theater Festival?
After I finished my work in Open Feast in Belarus, we actually did a residency in The Hague, intentionally spending time in a place that dealt with state violence and genocide, and thinking about what does justice look like? Coming back to Chicago, I found myself really looking for community, and Philip connected me to Blake Russell, one of the cofounders. We started talking about this idea. What would it mean to bring the International Home Theater Festival to Chicago because initially the platform was very decentralized, very open-ended. It was just a Google form. Anyone in the world could fill it out and house it in their home. Part of what we were interested in is how not to reproduce the culture that was already happening in Chicago, which was one of hyper-segregation. How do we intentionally curate in ways that disrupt that?

I met Laley [Lippard] shortly thereafter. Within the next few months, we just started planning what became the first year of Chicago Home Theater Festival.

This was 2012 when you started planning, is that right? What was Chicago like at the time? I know that Rahm Emanuel was elected mayor in 2011.
There was a very intentional plan to reimagine the city as something very outward facing, something for tourists. Millennium Park[4] was built at that time. The cultural plan[5] was rolled out at that time. A lot of poor people of color were being pushed out. I could just see that systematically happening.

My entry back into Chicago was through the Jane Addams Hull-House Museum. I started working there in January of 2012. By virtue of being in that space, I became very involved with folks like Mariame Kaba (a monumental community organizer and abolitionist), We Charge Genocide, and groups working on police and prison abolition, looking at the intersection of feminism, antiracism, and antiwar movements during the Progressive Era during the turn of the twentieth century. Taking this work that was the woman's domain of home economics into the public sphere. I believe they called it "municipal housekeeping."[6] How do we take this idea that when women were relegated to the sphere of maintaining a home, what does it mean to maintain a city? That was really the lens through which I was reintroduced back to Chicago, [it] was in these organizing spaces. It was also in 2012 that Rahm Emanuel closed fifty Chicago public schools in Black and Brown neighborhoods. It was Rekia Boyd, [and later] Ferguson, Mike Brown, Black Lives Matter, and the Movement for Black Lives.

I think my experience of Chicago at the time was definitely as someone who had just moved back after being away for a few years, and I was becoming aware of the formation of these intersecting movements as I began learning more about the movement history of Chicago. Specifically, labor history, immigration history, looking at the history of redlining, housing segregation, and race riots. And then just being thrown into the middle of all of these organizations doing really powerful work. That created the foundation from which I was able to approach the social and political aspects of organizing the Chicago Home Theater Festival.

What was the initial process like of selecting homes, neighborhoods, and artists and curating those together?

The platform that Philip Huang put together was literally just a Google form that anyone could fill out. When Blake and Laley and I started working on it, we wanted to be a little bit more intentional and think about how we are creating in a way that doesn't reinforce the status quo. I think in the first year, it was put together really quickly, to be honest. We probably did it in four months' time and we had twenty homes. I think it was a very DIY[7] process.

It was so exciting and so energetic, and we were building on a long history of performance art happening in homes and home galleries and art in co-ops and collectives, so I think it was very ripe for that energy.

Over the years, we were really intentional about continuing to bring in more people of color, more gender nonconforming and trans people, more people with disabilities at every level of leadership, and really thinking about, as we decide which neighborhoods we want to be in, how are we not reinforcing if this was already a neighborhood that already has a lot of theaters. It doesn't really make sense for us to be here. Like, how are we intentionally holding space in parts of the city

Angel Bat Dawid performs in a DIY home space hosted by Amina Ross in Little Village, 2017. Photograph by eedahahm. Courtesy of the photographer and the Chicago Home Theater Festival.

that are structurally disinvested in by the city, and are really rich with arts and culture.

By year two, we created a curatorial committee and expanded our festival producers to include about fifteen artists who were all people of color with deep roots in very specific neighborhoods and specific arts practices. So we worked with folks like Maria Gaspar, who has a long history of doing socially engaged art in Little Village around Cook County Jail. We worked with NIC Kay, who's a gender nonconforming performance artist who helped us make connections with folks like Chances Dances and Sky Cubacub, folks doing work in non-binary, disability rights advocacy.

When did you start using parks? How did the use of parks compare and contrast with the use of homes?

We began working with the Chicago Park District when we became aware of the Night Out in the Parks program. When we applied and received funding, I was really thinking about how our parks are an extension of the home and one that is bridging the public-private domain, so thinking specifically about parks in neighborhoods where we didn't have homes. Or parks that maybe were intersecting points for a number of different communities.

Working in the parks changed the festival. The parks are also very different. We had a performance in the Garfield Park Conservatory, which is a very fancy park space. It's beautiful and lovely but it doesn't have a backyard vibe. It's palatial. But that was a cool venue, and a lot of our artists had never been there, and it was definitely more of an international reach because it's more of a tourist destination.

We also worked in places like Hamilton Park in Englewood, which is a very, very neighborhood-based park and it's partnered with a TRACE program (Teens Reimagine Art, Community, and Environment) from the Chicago Park District, and those young people conducted the tour of the space. We had Free Street Theater, a youth performance group, perform there. I think it was a really beautiful intersection of folks who grew up in that community and folks who were there for the first time. We had a lot of young dancers, ages 5 through 18, from the neighborhood, whose parents and grandparents came to support them. And then folks who had never been there before.

Working in parks allowed us to have a broader reach, and a more in-depth relationship to the space that people already have a relationship to. Parks are places where communities have barbecues and family reunions and picnics and soccer games. It felt really nice . . . and also, because we got funding from the Chicago Park District, all of those events were free to the public, which was another way to make the performances accessible to folks.

I am really interested in some of your inspiration being "fuck institutions." In running Chicago Home Theater Festival, did you interact with any of those laws or cultural policies that a lot bigger arts institutions have to wade through?

We would definitely open up every night with "fuck institutions," and also, we did apply for funding. We were really committed to paying artists and organizers, and we did everything we could to do that with integrity, so we did get funding from funders like the Propeller Fund, and the Chicago Park District and Meadows, but because we never [became] a 501(c)(3) we also didn't really have access to larger foundations and larger institutions.

We also partnered with multiple cultural institutions, so we had an opening at the Hyde Park Art Center. We had an opening at the Museum of Contemporary Art [MCA]. There were other cultural institutions that we partnered with over the years, and if anything, I think it challenged them. For example, when we were at the MCA, Faheem Majeed, who's one of our hosts, had built a structure at the MCA and invited us to program it. Part of that meant that we were really committed to accessibility. For him, he hadn't built a ramp for his structure, so that was something that he added on.

We had young people of color who were coming to the event and felt like they were being harassed by security at the MCA and that started years' worth of conversations and training at the MCA that their director of education let me know about.

One of the biggest challenges and growth edges for us over the years was working with artists with disabilities, and really thinking through the very real structural challenges there are to institutions and private homes in the city. Most of them are not wheelchair accessible. Working with folks like Carrie Kaufman, who worked for Access Living and was a host, curator, and adviser for years. What do multiple entry points look like? How do we make sure that we have ASL interpreters? How do we make sure that we have wheelchair access? How do we think about harm that happens in our spaces? How do we address interactions that might happen between audience members when we have the spirit of radical generosity, people are opening up their homes? What happens when a boundary is crossed? How do we, as an organization, address that? So I think those were definitely points of learning and growth for us over the years—how to continuously expand our understanding of what access, and equity, and inclusion really mean.

What unique meanings were made by staging this work in homes versus in traditional theaters?

We were in homes, neighborhoods, communities that have really specific histories. I think the home as a site for art-making is integral to the practice of most artists. That tends to be people's first studio space. Most of us have childhood memories of making art at home, performing in our homes. And that act of opening up a home to a stranger [and] really having to address the biases and the fears that people bring with them when they enter a new neighborhood and a new home and really confronting those head-on. Thinking about what it means to travel to a neighborhood. What does it mean to be a stranger and how does that idea come from the imagination of a voyager or a colonizer and what does it mean when all of these people travel to a neighborhood they've never been to before?

How are they impacting that community? How is it impacting gentrification and displacement? Are they just there to consume culture and then leave, or are they somehow contributing to it? So I think the home as a venue opened up a lot of really important questions for us in terms of how do we continue to build sustained relationships with communities. So the festival isn't just a spectacle that happens for twenty days in May but how is it a yearlong commitment to organizing with communities, to really investing in communities, to putting our bodies in front of the harm that is being done to these communities that we're invested in?

What are some of your most memorable performance and spaces?
Leah Gipson's home in Austin was one that crystallized something very powerful because she brought up this conversation around [cultural] voyeurism. avery r. young, a performer who's been with us from the beginning, talked about how there's something very intentional in the festival about lifting up the people who actually live in these communities and making sure that our performers include people from that neighborhood. Oftentimes we'll invite someone who has lived in the neighborhood for thirty, forty, fifty years to co-facilitate a tour with someone who just moved into that community.

Part of what I really loved about that night is the layers of nuance. YEPP's[8] performance project that centers trans people of color and trans youths experiencing homelessness addressed the idea of home that really acknowledged that home isn't always a safe space. How do we shift a very romantic notion of home as a sanctuary when oftentimes it's not something that everyone has access to?

Another night that was really memorable was, I believe it was in 2014 or '15, at Jason Howard's home in Pilsen. It was a three-home tour of Pilsen and at the second home there was a performer who appeared naked and wrapped himself in plastic and proceeded to butcher a live fish, the guts of which splashed over everyone in the room and produced a really intense smell and no one was prepared for this. This was early in the festival where we didn't [have] a process or a set of agreements that artists consented to around harm and safety within the contents of their work. We just really trusted our host to pick artists that they vouched for and that was a really violent night, you know?

There were people who were vegan who left and really felt violated and felt like the performance wasn't consensual. They weren't ready for that—they didn't know they were going into it and it opened up a lot of conversations about censorship and what it means to perform in non-traditional venues and how obviously this wouldn't have happened in a theater or in a museum and that's maybe a good thing. So I felt like that performance was something that we've come back to over the years, both as producers and artists and audience members. It's one that I think shifted our approach to thinking about how do we care for our audiences without silencing artists? What is that tension of creating a space that is both free and safe?

The last performance of the entire festival in 2017 was a performance in my home, and my partner, Michael Aguilar, and [we] lived in an apartment complex. One of the reasons we wanted to host is that it's wheelchair accessible, there are elevators, which as I mentioned is not something that can be said for most housing in Chicago.

He and I are both immigrants and our families experienced state violence and trauma, as well as resilience and resistance. What was special to me about that performance is everybody who participated, including the producers and the artists, were all immigrants and refugees.

We used this theme of migration and displacement and border crossing. We utilized the entire building. We had performances in elevators and staircases and throughout multiple levels of the building. One of the performers was a musician who crossed the border from Mexico to the U.S. a total of four times, three of which he was detained. He's a classical guitarist and he performed in a very tiny room at the top of the building which reminded him of the cell that he was in when he was incarcerated at the border. He played his guitar and he talked about how memories of music and playing the guitar through his imagination is what kept him alive during his internment. His art practice was his connection to wanting to be alive. Feeling like there's hope.

How does the concept of makeshift resonate with the spaces used by Chicago Home Theater Festival, especially given the festival's work in more "permanent" institutions?

We definitely did partner with multiple permanent, as you say, institutions. For the most part those experiences were really positive because most homes are pretty small. Especially for something like an opening or closing, larger institutions allowed us to have more accessibility, but I think the intimacy and the history of a home just doesn't translate to a museum or a gallery or a theater.

Although it was lovely to be in spaces that were wheelchair accessible and could hold one hundred, two hundred people, some of the magic that we feel in living rooms and kitchens and basements and rooftops—it's hard to translate that to a more formal institution even if it's the same performers.

In terms of the idea of makeshift, we partnered with Joshua Kent, who's a performance artist who lives in an intentional housing community in Uptown for people experiencing homelessness and substance abuse. The transient nature of the home, and the Catholic charity that's been operating it for over a hundred years, lent itself to work around just very raw ideas. It was a very sacred space. Sometimes the residents would participate, sometimes they wouldn't, but just knowing that we were entering into this space that was about love and service and transformation and trauma I think shifted the energy. It wasn't necessarily the kind of thing that you want to hashtag, you know? I think it opened up people's hearts in a way that maybe a different type of home wouldn't. We were careful to curate performances that would be respectful of the space, its residents, and the mission of the home. Our intention was to create vulnerability, intimacy, and trust.

So I think it's always a negotiation and a true collaboration, and most of our hosts we've worked with over the years, they often come to us with ideas about what they want and more often than not we really want to provide that for them because they're the ones that are generously offering their space. I hope that speaks to the makeshift.

I guess what I want to say about makeshift is there's a range of homes in which the families who have lived there have lived there a really long time and are deeply rooted in a community which I wouldn't exactly call makeshift. It's a very stable and secure and permanent place that people have committed to for decades. And then there are also homes that are apartments that people are renting and maybe have only been in for a year and are still trying to figure out what it means for them to live in that neighborhood. I think part of hosting performances helps them think about what their role is within their own community. We always really encourage our hosts to invite their neighbors and to not think of this as just a venue but to really think of it as an opportunity to build and invest in where you're living in, who you're living with, and even though your neighbors may not be people who would come to a performance per se or wouldn't buy theater tickets, you're inviting them to your home as a neighbor and that is a different kind of trust vulnerability and that's something that I think is really important to us.

That's great. I appreciate your articulating around what is and isn't makeshift. So my closing questions are about legacy. Looking back, how did the festival change over time?

The festival has become more intentional. The first year Blake and Laley and I had just met each other. We were all relatively new to Chicago and we had these really beautiful intentions but we didn't have the infrastructure. Over the years we've worked in partnership with Aymar and Meida and Carrie [Kaufman] and Bill [Ayers] and Faheem [Majeed], all the folks who have really contributed to the festival to make it something that reflects our collective wisdom, and really practically that's meant a lot more spreadsheets and better grant writing and budgeting and a marketing plan and partnerships with media and press.

The last year that we did it we were written up in every major newspaper, we sold out every single night, we were able to pay our artists more than we ever have. So in many ways it grew up. In a way it did become an institution. But the spirit of building intentional relationships across lines of difference and the intentionality around knowing your neighbor and expanding who we consider to be "our people" and who we continue to care about and whose humanity we're invested in I think has really stayed foundational and grown over time.

What did or does the Chicago Home Theater Festival mean for the city of Chicago?

I think that it's been really successful in Chicago because it builds on such a deep history of organizing, of activism, of collaborative and ensemble-based arts practices of people creating everything from settlement houses to artists collective, to co-ops, to DIY venues and things like Freedom Square. I think Chicago is a place where people intentionally build the reality they want to see all the time, and we have been very privileged to do this work in a time where there's just such a strong need for that. People are so hungry to create intentional spaces where they can be their full selves and they can be really valued for who they are.

Laley Lippard

Laley Lippard (she/her) is a director, creative producer, and educator committed to championing anti-oppressive work across disciplines, developing new plays, and creating performances that disrupt injustice.

Lippard has directed and collaborated with Steppenwolf Theatre Company, The Kennedy Center for the Performing Arts, O'Neill Theatre Center, Guthrie Theater, Round House Theatre, Alliance Theatre, Cleveland Play House, American Theater Company, Magic Theatre, American Conservatory Theater, Court Theatre, and Virginia Stage Company, among others. World premieres include Matt Pelfry's *Pure Shock Value*, Eric Coble's *These Mortal Hosts*, and the National New Play Network's Rolling World Premiere of David Valdes's *The Mermaid Hour*. Additional work includes Ronan Noone's *The Smuggler*, Inda Craig-Galván's *Welcome to Matteson!*, Lucy Prebble's *The Effect*, and George Brant's *Grounded*. Lippard has taught, workshopped, and directed at Stanford University, Northwestern University, Hampshire College, and in the Case Western Reserve MFA Acting program. Lippard is a member of the National Directors Fellowship, a partnership between the O'Neill Theater Center, National New Plays Network, Stage Directors and Choreographers Society (SDC), and the Kennedy Center. She is a member of the Lincoln Center Theater Directors Lab and an associate member of the SDC and holds an MFA in directing from Northwestern University. Co-creating the Chicago Home Theater Festival as cofounder and co-executive producer for five years is still one of the most profound organizing projects of her life.

When did you come to Chicago?

LALEY LIPPARD: Growing up as a Quaker, I had an early introduction to social justice work, service, and the faith-based idea of radical hospitality and egalitarian structures. Following graduation, having studied theater and world religion with a focus on ritual and myth-making through the performative arts, I left DC and moved to California for a directing and dramaturgy apprenticeship. San Francisco's art scene was full of cross-collaborative performance, house shows, pop-up performances, and experimentations at the intersection of video, dance, and performance. I lived in a Hayes Valley home full of artists where we had weekend house shows; a revolving cast of musicians, painters, and poets for parties and salons; and created some truly incredible work together. It was a wildly experimental and limitless time in my creative life.

But, my lines of inquiry began to shift back towards the institution of theater, and specifically, training as a stage director, and I pursued a masters in directing at Northwestern University with mentors like Anna D. Shapiro, Mary Zimmerman, and Michael Rohd among other exceptional faculty. Michael Rohd, artistic director of Sojourn Theater and a foundational thinker and practitioner of community-based performance work, had a huge effect on the praxis of CHTF. It was Michael who suggested many of the first artists, including Meida McNeal.

Tell me about founding Chicago Home Theater Festival.
In 2012, I met Irina at a Halloween party, during a time when I had been thinking about my work in San Francisco and was seeking a space to engage at the intersection of experimental performance and civic practice. She talked about the Home Theater Festival and her time in the Bay Area—there were so many value-based and intuitive connections and resonances. When she mentioned wanting to start the Home Theater Festival in Chicago, I was immediately on board to envision and shape with her.

The first year felt like a canvassing of the art and performance scene in Chicago. Irina, Blake, and I had different circles, perspectives, and passions that fed off one another and kept us searching for a deeper core value even as we expanded the festival's programming. There was such magical chemistry.

Once the festival started, we were deeply engaged in the flexibility and energy of the single night's ephemeral experience. It was truly emergent. Blake, Irina, and I would stay out until the early hours of the morning after each night of the festival, discussing our purpose and how we might pivot for impact and deeper engagement.

My training as a director really spurred an inquiry about the containing framework of the festival itself, the internal process of asking questions to realize a time-based event, the structure of an evening that takes an audience on an emotional journey, and bringing in my interest and suspicion of ritual—of gathering around the fire to tell our stories. Who was invited to that fire? Who was not there and why?

That first year, the audience took to and treated the festival like water—it nourished something, fed something.

How did your experience directing theater influence how you approached the festival?
My work as a director is to help craft an event through a moment-by-moment shaping of the viewer's experience, especially in the transitions of one performance or part of the night into the next. The transitions were key, and we wanted to make them feel inevitable and effortless. As a director, I am also a steward of and in service to an artist's vision, so I

think in a 360 and multisensory way about the wish of the artist within the event as a whole—as each is a time-based narrative where an "act" is not necessarily in direct conversation with another. I was endlessly curious about the curation of an evening, the order of the events, and the flavor of the transitions—and how we kept the community engaged with one another throughout. That inquiry led to artistic producers having an overall "theme" for the night with a series of questions guiding the programming. For example, in 2017 at the park district in Englewood, producers framed the night: "What does it mean to come from a demonized neighborhood?"

A big, overarching question I would always ask myself as a director was, on a given night, "When does the Home Theater Festival start, when does it end?" That added to and expanded how we pre-cared for and cared after artists, neighbors, and audiences. It influenced how we guided folks to the events, what ticketing format we used, how we crafted the first meeting of audiences at a public transportation stop, what the rhythms of the night were, how each aspect of the festival was like an act of a play.

Directly and most practically, my experience as a director led Blake and me to curate Chicagoans to create short plays specifically for a home and/or neighborhood. For instance, Zayd Dohrn's "'Cause You Know You Got Soul" about Michelle and Barack Obama's first date, that I staged on Bill Ayers's front stoop, three blocks from the actual site of the date—which was a good-natured but revealing fight about the film *Do the Right Thing*. Another was Joel Kim Booster's play for the West Loop exploring the neighborhood's devastating gentrification through a morning-after conversation in the kitchen between two male lovers as we perched on barstools, sat cross-legged on the linoleum, and spied in on a lovers' quarrel. That evening was followed by the surprise, real wedding ritual between the hosts with the CHTF audience as witness.

You said that people treated the festival "like water"; they didn't realize how much they needed it. How did the festival respond to a need in the Chicago theater scene?

Looking back, I feel struck by the simple act of intimacy—sitting "too" close together with people you just met, or being radically welcomed into a stranger's home, a neighbor's bathroom, a friend's bedroom to witness deeply engaged art about identity, rage, lust, loneliness, loss. Asking for the salt across a stranger's knee, belly laughing on a hardwood floor, being splashed by the bathwater in a too-tight tiled room, a hyper-intimate one-on-one healing ritual in the basement. The "water" we were all so thirsty for was a space of connection, a disruption in rote assumptions about the person next to you, a momentary bridge built through art and conversation. Even as the festival sought to disrupt injustice, center marginalized communities, reclaim domestic space as a public forum for decrying oppression—the water was the recognition of our shared humanity. The still point at the center of every night was a call out to a group of strangers that said, "You and me. You and me. You and me."

What was the process of curating the festival like? How did you select the homes, the neighborhoods, the artists?

Each year we adapted. We understood more. We took in more research. We talked to neighbors and artists and community leaders and activists about what our goals were, what their needs and wishes were—we stopped being the decision makers and the drivers of the programming. We listened deeply to our network, and we were able to immediately adjust and reflect more clearly the values of the artists, neighbors, and audiences. The life and curation of the festival was not in our hands, but shared among a larger community.

Our language, our mission and organizing tagline that first year was "Get out of your comfort zone," but by the second year, we realized that statement [enabled] racism, ableism, and classism. Then, we started to decenter ourselves as decision makers, and we invited artistic producers to curate individual nights. Before that, the curation had been a mix of applications, previous relationships, hosts' suggestions, former audience members, and referrals. By the fifth year, we were all branching out and wanted to create artistic maps based on the idea of oral histories of the neighborhoods. This led to the zine that we created in 2017 in partnership with City Bureau and Andrea Hart, *Sixty Inches From Center and Tempestt Hazel*, and the Chicago Park District as a documentation of, record of, artistic legacy of, and celebration of the arts and culture that existed, and had been thriving, in the neighborhoods.

What are some of your most important and interesting memories from the festival?

In 2015, we had our opening at MCA as part of Faheem Majeed's exhibit. Spoken word artist Frankiem Mitchell's excoriation of the recent killing of Black people by the police left the past-capacity group chanting together in unison, a play presented by the Illinois Caucus of Adolescent Health included listing the names of Black men and women murdered that year, and the evening ended with the performance duo In the Spirit forging a healing drum circle.

There was a conversation at Humboldt Park similar to the one in Lakeview the year before in 2015 or 2016, about identity—specifically as it relates to who gets to tell whose story, and more importantly, who truly understands the story of a "homeland," especially on colonized, stolen land. In our discussion, a white woman was challenged about her knowledge of her people's effect in relationship to the erasure and destruction of ancestral knowledge in the Black community at the hands of white people. The white woman took a lot of emotional space in the room, breaking down into tears in defense that she knew all about her ancestors and their country of origin, not grasping that the implication of reference to lineage was the story of white oppression and our enslavement of Black people. There was a moment that the room began to shift toward caretaking for this woman, when a Black artist said, "I don't have time for white tears." The room rung with the call-in. The conversation went on, with bravery and boundary, and for just a short amount of time, that tiny living room became a community forum for very basic, spontaneous anti-racist practice among strangers at very different stages of the work.

There is an image of Black trans artist Darling Shear[9] dancing in secular ceremonial body worship in front of this huge Catholic church that is burned into my mind from South Shore at Faheem Majeed and LaShana Jackson's home. The tour had revealed a rapidly changing neighborhood that went from being Jewish to African American to white and back again, with the church at the center—we had entered that church during the tour and heard breathtaking music. The echo of the music, the story of displacement, and the history of silencing and oppression by the Catholic Church, even as it was one of the biggest patrons of the arts—all of that. That history and the contemporary resonance of the South Shore neighborhood being played, danced out. Even now it's hard to put into words.

[The play] *White Rabbit, Red Rabbit* at Ayers's[10] home, in the top floor room with folks piled onto beds, couches, pillowed floor. The playwright Nassim Soleimanpour was under house arrest in Iran. He wrote the play in order to be released, to find freedom from his home, and to warn of the poisonous effect of an oppressive regime. The play requires audience interaction, and the performer is reading the script for the first time, cold in front of the audience. One of the members of the audience came up at the end, where there's a possibility that the reader is going to be poisoned—grabs the glass of "poisoned" water and pours it out. Stopping the ending. It was a radical act, a performative act maybe, but important practice to disrupting injustice.

I was struck by how the neighborhood tour effected a different consciousness as I engaged with the artists. How did you come up with this format of first the tour of the neighborhood, next the introduction to the host and the home, then the meal, and finally the performances and talkback?
The development of the different ingredients of each night of the festival corresponds to deep human needs as we build relationships: to be nurtured, to be engaged creatively, to know our people, to have brave space to know the stranger, to be in conversation, and to better the lives of those we feel connected to. It's about creating empathy. The ingredients emerged, though each was a solution to a problem and/or a creative answer to a need in the festival.

The sharing of a meal by the host became a way to introduce their familial culture and story, and the meal became more than just breaking bread, transforming into a way of passing on a family's legacy, a homemaker's cultural identity, a lineage of nurturing cumulating throughout generations.

Specifically with the tour, the seed of it was about when and how the neighborhood could be a participant in the evening. We had begun conversations around oral histories, preserving the stories and cultural narrative of the neighborhood. So, our conversation became, "The home doesn't exist separately from the neighborhood. How is the neighborhood part of the performance?" How can we foster greater and greater circles of concern? How can empathy be created within a framework of gentrification and displacement?

What meanings were made by the homes and the parks that you used? How did that dialogue with the work that you were producing?
I remember one night discussing blood family versus chosen family, and that what we were hoping was to create—even if for a moment—the world we wanted to see, a dream of what home could be. If the home becomes a space of performance, disrupting injustice, breaking

bread, then it's also a site of forging of intimacy. Every single object, energy, memory . . . the architecture, the choices of the homeowner and host of art, of furniture, paint color, the legacy and history of what's happened on that land becomes part of the artistic, social, and political event.

For some, it was a reminder of oppression, colonization, domination, and supremacy. I think the more that the festival was about awakening each other to the piercing truth of a moment and the layered conversation of the space, relationships, and stories around them, it just reinforced that it's harmful to walk through the world riding on nurtured and natured assumptions or unexamined internalized racist and supremacist paradigms.

I'm curious about the ways in which you think the spaces that Chicago Home Theater Festival used could be considered to be makeshift?
What America sells as a capitalist society—the American Dream—if you have a house that means . . . fill that in with a cis, hetero, patriarchal concept of belonging and worth.

But the culture of the home, in general, has been a meeting place. We didn't come up with the salon idea. The Home Theater Festival is only a sentence in the larger story and conversation of what it means to gather together in a place of comfort over a meal perhaps, to brainstorm for change, to dream of the rebellion, to enact social care for a neighborhood, to do art, to read plays, to speak poetry, to sing songs, to find one another. The home is meant for chosen family, and the idealistic human dream for self-actualization in tandem with group liberation.

We reclaimed the makeshift purpose of the home, and why we make spaces for our human brothers, sisters, and cousins. The concept of the makeshift invitation to build a home for a moment—just the moment—acknowledges the ephemeral nature of it all, and the creative potential, too.

What were some of the most memorable spaces that you used, and why were those spaces memorable?
I was really invested in understanding how we could incorporate and partner with alternative homes like prisons, safehouses, and shelters.

The St. Francis Hospitality House truly embodied a concept we were in conversation with—radical hospitality. One performance group interviewed many of the people who lived there, then incorporated the history

Performance at Eco Collective with host Mykele Deville curated by Isaac Gomez and Nancy García Loza in Pilsen, 2017. Photograph by eedahahm. Courtesy of the photographer and the Chicago Home Theater Festival.

of the building and its residents—it was a wholehearted experience to hear the echoes of the people who had built the home over time.

There is the Eco Village home and collective of artists hosted by Mykele Deville, produced by Nancy García Loza and Isaac Gomez. They asked, "In the context of gentrification and change in Pilsen over the years pushing out more and more people of color, what does radical nourishment look like?"

There was the mixed-income artist community in 2016—Dorchester Artist and Housing Collaborative in Grand Crossing. At that event, Barak adé Soleil did a series of movements about breaking apart the concept of artistic organizations "inviting" folks of color "to the table" at predominantly white institutions.

In 2015, we were invited to I Grow Chicago in Englewood. It's a home that was dedicated to the community, a community space, but built in a home. It has a kitchen, with wings and lemonade in the refrigerator. There's a backyard that is all our backyard. That was a beautiful night, open to the public, teaming with an intergenerational, intercultural audience.

How do you feel that the Chicago Home Theater Festival and your use of space dialogue with the more traditional theater scene and art scene in Chicago?
Organizations have three powerful resources: venue capital, intellectual capital, and artistic capital. We were in dialogue about traditional notions of access to that capital, and the oppressive structures that defined who got the keys to that cultural power. When the artist was at the center of the event and in independent, creative relationship to venue capital, with a free and liberated relationship to space, the art was still profound, moving, revelatory. The grandeur of the building did not matter, the artist's training didn't matter, the budget of the performance didn't matter. Traditional notions of "excellence" and "value" are flimsy.

We were also interrogating the traditional arts administration model. Who holds the power? Who makes the decisions? How do we dismantle that oppressive structure? As more producers and core collaborators joined, and artists began driving the events—that dialogue revealed how successful it was to decenter the idea of a "core" leadership. I was applying Quaker egalitarian modes, and in a way, we were moving back towards Philip's original model.

What does the Chicago Home Theater Festival mean for the city of Chicago?
The festival exemplified the tenacity, vision, creative genius, community building power, and restorative impact of the arts and the artists of Chicago. The festival told the story of Chicago as a segregated one, yes, but it revealed a city of peace builders, of social justice warriors, of intersectional communities fighting for justice and liberation from a spectrum of obstacles—from redistricting and gentrification to dismantling white supremacy at a national level through hyper-local organizing. It has meant lifelong friendships and creative partnerships; it has meant another platform in Chicago's brand of truth telling and joyful noise.

Aymar Jean Christian

Aymar Jean Christian is an associate professor of communication studies at Northwestern University. His first book, *Open TV: Innovation beyond Hollywood and the Rise of Web Television* (New York University

Press), argues that the Web brought innovation to television by opening development to independent producers. His work has been published in numerous academic journals, including the *International Journal of Communication*, *Television & New Media*, *Social Media & Society*, *Journal of Cinema and Media Studies*, *Continuum*, and *Transformative Works and Cultures*. He has juried television and video for the Peabody Awards, Gotham Awards, and Tribeca Film Festival, among others. He leads OTV | Open Television, a research project and platform for intersectional television. OTV programs have received recognition from HBO, the Television Academy (Emmy Awards), the New York Television Festival, the City of Chicago, the Streamy Awards, and Independent Filmmaker Project (Gotham Awards). Its programming partners have included the Museum of Contemporary Art Chicago, the Art Institute of Chicago, the Block Museum of Art, and the City of Chicago, along with numerous galleries, community organizations, and universities. Dr. Christian's blog, *Televisual*, is an archive of over five hundred posts chronicling the rise of the Web TV market, and he has written regular reports on TV and new media for *Indiewire*, the *Wall Street Journal*, *Slate*, and *Tubefilter*.

Tell me about your background. When did you get into arts and what brought you to Chicago?

AYMAR JEAN CHRISTIAN: Yeah, it's all about academia for me. While in Chicago I frankly had time to have a life. I just had worked so much in grad school, I didn't really have a social life until I went out into Chicago. I was really inspired by the performance art here, the nightlife, theater, the really robust but also community-based arts scene. That led to a project called Open TV, now OTV, which is a platform for intersectional television in Chicago. And it was while I was thinking about doing Open TV that I found the Home Theater Festival. Because I actually met Irina at like a Black Lives Matter event at the Logan Center in 2013.

How do you think about relationships between media and live theater?

I think it's a tension that I like to lean into: the relationship between liveness and mediated performance. One of the first performers in Home Theater for me was Erik Wallace. Wallace ended up being my first collaborator on OTV. Seeing Wallace not only as a dancer, but also as someone who did music. I was like, "Oh wow, you have a useful set of skills for making indie television."

Why did you decide to join the Chicago Home Theater Festival team?
I thought it would be an opportunity to meet people and meet artists. I liked that they were in so many houses, and they had so many different kinds of artists coming to the festival. I was in the space where I wanted to just absorb all that Chicago had to offer. It's a process—some of the hosts are really great people who are difficult to get to meet because they're very busy. And so I was like, "Oh, I can meet Faheem Majeed."[11] But initially I just wanted to host. I started off as a host. I wasn't producing anything. So, I think my initial goal was let me just get as many different types of people in my house as possible.

I just loved hosting. I really wanted to just make my home a space [where] people felt welcome. Invite some of my neighbors. And Ms. Mr. Junior, who was also performing that night, I had seen publicly, and didn't really have a chance to like speak to them. So it was like a way for me to say, "Hey, I love your work. Would you mind performing in my house?" And of course the festival brought all these other people in there that I didn't know about, but it's interesting how even some of those connections have continued. Like Nicholas Ward performed a poem in my house. And he was dating Fatimah Asghar, who was the writer for *Brown Girls*. So it was two years before *Brown Girls* was a thing. And Precious Davis was there. And she had been in my neighborhood and she was a famous Black trans woman in Lakeview who I had never really been able to engage with before. So it was a great way to meet and connect with people.

What was your approach to hosting? What were some interesting things that happened in your space?
I have a duplex in Lakeview, an old building. So I cleared out all the furniture, put all the seating on the side. I cooked a ton of food.

What did you cook?
I usually do a kale and avocado salad. I had a pasta. I had roasted tomatoes, roasted veggies. I definitely made some kind of chicken. Could have been homemade, could have been some Chicken Hut from around the corner. That was my standard menu at the time. A lot of roasted veggies and roasted things.

We started out with the main stage. We moved upstairs to my little lofted space, and there was a sci-fi theater show that happened there. Then they had a little stage, they had special effects and that was cool. And then Ms. Mr. Junior performed burlesque up there. Ms. Mr. Junior performs kind of like non-binary burlesque, but definitely femme-centric. And then we moved downstairs, that's when Nick Ward read his first poem. So, my apartment is really long and so Nick performed a poem about taking the Red Line from the North Side to the South Side with a woman of color that he was dating, and sort of like using my apartment to descend into the crowd. It was difficult because the acoustics aren't great in my apartment for that kind of thing.

Precious Davis made a sort of really powerful statement about what it means to be a Black trans woman in Lakeview. And like what it means to occupy space for her, and the danger she feels like she's in, but also the way in which some of these white-bodied people assume things about her, without actually asking her. In my experience it was one of the more intense discussions I've witnessed.

What is the most intense conversation you've had? You alluded to that.
It was in Humboldt Park. It was about gentrification and NIC Kay had said something about the ways in which white people take up space, and one white person was like, "I don't want to be this person. I want to help," or whatever. And NIC kind of just shut that down. And was like, "This is not about you, we're not here to sort of absolve you of your whiteness." I think there was a reference to their ancestors, and people who came before them. And so the white person was like, "But no, I know where my ancestors are from." And NIC was like, "Do you really though, do you really?" And she was shook and started crying. And then people just spoke over her tears, I think she just cried. For like twenty minutes.

We just sort of had to move on. The Black people were not going to stop for white tears. Which I sort of agreed with. So we've never had, from my knowledge, a conversation with someone who has literally cried for ten, twenty minutes. And had to keep going.

But actually a lot of people after that wanted to hug that person. She got support in the end. I feel like there's something about the home where it is about hosting and is about embracing openness.

When you joined Chicago Home Theater Festival, when you started hosting, what was the environment of Chicago like at the time?
I was pretty new to Chicago. By the time I was hosting I was two years into being here. So, I was still learning the city. I believe Rahm [Emanuel] was mayor. So that has always felt like an important political marker of Chicago, and the ways in which we were segregating the city,

the school closings happened. That was a really important introduction to Chicago, with schools closing. Because I had just come from Philly, where they were also closing schools, but not even as many. So I was hyperaware that that was a really aggressive segregationary tactic. I think segregation was particularly pronounced in Chicago at that time, and the need for people to understand what's happening in other Chicago neighborhoods, especially neighborhoods that were getting vilified by Rahm [Emanuel] as being crime-ridden and underpopulated, I think was super important, and maybe added a sense of intensity to the festival.

How have you conceptualized the concept and practice of home both within the home spaces and also in institutions?
The idea of home definitely got complicated when we were at the MCA and Garfield Park Conservatory. But for us, there was always the talk about home. It was definitely about site specificity. Because every space would not only look different, have different things you could do in it, but also have very specific art. It would be located in a specific neighborhood going through specific political, cultural, social, economic shifts.

Being in homes allowed us to be in spaces where institutions weren't. And we would have to grapple with the neighborhood, the site, what is around the home, before even talking about, okay this is somebody's home that has to be introduced in a very specific way. Every night the host of that home introduces the space, gives context to how long they've lived there. What is their relationship to the neighborhood? What are some of the things in the home that you should look out for? Both in terms of like don't touch, but also in terms of like this is something I'm really proud of. Or this is the way we normally use this space. So, there was an interpersonal, a geopolitical, and cultural sort of dimension to space always because we were in homes.

There was the idea of being welcoming. Homes are a space where we welcome people. That we are all presumed as sort of equal in a way, because we're all guests in a home. That was super key. There was always a discussion about how do we welcome people. Every year we sort of changed up a little bit. What do we say? How do we introduce the festival? But also, like how do we make it clear that we are both acknowledging that we are equal in the space, and yet also acknowledging the ways in which we're not all equal in the space? Which is what goes beyond the home. So how do we bring those neighborhoods, [those] cultural political dynamics into the space? To make space for

Ivan Resendiz, the musician who crossed the border four times, in Edgewater, 2017. Photograph by eedahahm. Courtesy of the photographer and the Chicago Home Theater Festival.

them. Make space for people to say, "I feel uncomfortable in the space," or "This space is not accessible to me, it was really hard to get to this space," and not feel shame for that. The home opens up so many different kinds of conversations that you can't really have in institutions.

What are your thoughts about the word "makeshift" and how, if at all, that word resonates with the festival?
When I think about makeshift I think about improvisation. I think about utilizing whatever resources are available. And I think those are definitely things that we had to do with this kind of festival. There were times when I hosted where right before the night started, we weren't entirely sure, once all the bodies were in the room, how things would go. So, once we got into the space, they're like, "Oh, you're doing this, let's actually shift this and make this performance over here." Or sometimes it would rain, or we were planning to be outside and we couldn't do that. Then there would be something in the house that would have to be like moved last minute or something some performer would realize they could utilize in the performance. A lamp for lighting.

I definitely think one could call it makeshift. You're making the work in that space almost as it is happening or like right before it's happening. You're shifting around things to make that space happen. To make the space available and open.

What does the Chicago Home Theater Festival, including its history and impact, mean for the city of Chicago?
Chicago has so many histories of community-based art, and art for artists. I think the Chicago Home Theater Festival deserves to be in that lineage and canon. Laley and Irina have said that the Home Theater Festival is a global thing, but it's sort of a little bit bigger in Chicago. That strikes me as very appropriate, because there are so many homes in Chicago, and compared to other big cities, people have more space. But also, Chicago has been a city where it's understood that being out in front of the people that know you—in your neighborhood, other artists who are working in your city—is super important for your development. As an artist but then also of course that the artist is supposed to be in the community.

There's the fact that we were focused on cross-pollinating artists and picking artists who maybe only showed on the South Side and bring them into the North Side. Or picking artists who have only shown on the West Side, bringing them to the South Side. Going to neighborhoods where there weren't any art institutions, or the city was underinvesting. All of those were super important to us. You know, acknowledge that that was part of this history of Chicago, because the history is going to get written that we were segregated, and people were leaving, and there was over-policing, and all the trauma. That was all very true. But I think the marginal ways . . . I want to remember that there were people here in Chicago that were trying to go against those dynamics. Bring people together and forge connections across the city, that we are tighter, and we are more aware of each other now as a whole.

Meida McNeal

Born and raised in Chicago, Meida McNeal works with the Chicago Park District as arts and culture manager supporting community arts partnerships, youth arts learning, cultural stewardship, and civic engagement initiatives across the city's parks and cultural centers. She is also artistic and managing director of Honey Pot Performance, an

Afro-feminist creative collaborative that integrates movement, theater, and first-voice to examine the nuanced ways people negotiate identity, belonging, and difference in their lives and cultural memberships. In 2014, she performed at the Chicago Home Theater Festival, and starting in 2015, she worked as a producer for the festival.

How did you get into the arts, theater, and performance?
MEIDA MCNEAL: I've been doing performance all my life. I started out with dance classes at the park district, one of the facilities right next to my house. Then went on and started taking dance classes at a place called Joseph Holmes here in Chicago, a multicultural dance company back in the eighties and nineties. And while I was in high school, we had a really vibrant arts and culture theater program. So I was really involved in that and musical theater and really started to try my hand at choreography there. I got into cultural anthropology and started thinking about cultural issues and dance and movement and performance. So, then that took me into grad school—I think I've always been kind of a bit curious. That took me into an MFA at Ohio State and the PhD in performance studies at Northwestern, really thinking about the history of movement languages and movement techniques, and how those are codes of belonging. So my work in Trinidad during my PhD was looking at and working with four different dance companies there to think about how each one of those companies was using a made movement language and training regimen to each think about their way of defining Trinidadian citizenship, and ways of belonging.

Then I transitioned into being an educator, being in academia for a while and chipping in to arts administration work. So now I'm with the parks [as] the arts and culture manager there and have a team now that works around supporting and bringing arts and culture resources to parks across the city. I do work with the performance collective I'm part of, Honey Pot Performance, and have been for about twenty years.

How did you become part of Chicago Home Theater Festival?
Irina or Laley reached out to me and asked if we [Honey Pot Performance] were interested in performing. We liked what they were doing. It aligned with things that we were doing across the city and so we said yes. That year they had a format where they had—I think most of their artists did multiple homes. So we were [at] three different locations: Hyde Park Art Center as part of the opening, a house in Pilsen with the closing, and one in the middle, the Solarium in Rogers Park.

We just loved it. It did align with the way that we made work and presented work, because our work was often presented in intimate spaces and our processes certainly have always been about involving the public or communities in gathering some of the information or having input in what we're making. Really appreciated the dialogic nature of what they were doing. That they were bringing together folks to experience performance, but that was also with food and other things happening as well.

How would you describe the festival in three words?
Intimate warm gatherings.

So how did you transition from being a presenting artist to being a producer of the festival?
Again, they invited me. It was Irina and Laley who reached out and said that they wanted to expand the number of producers to widen the circle, the network of artists and other folks that they were able to reach out to with CHTF, and I was down for it because I really had enjoyed it and felt like it was something that we needed in this city.

Tell me more about that. Why is CHTF something that Chicago needed?
I think it's something that lots of cities need. We talk about [it] all [the] time [how] Chicago is, you know, a highly segregated city. I think most cities are that way as well. I think it really behooves us to use performance as activator and a way to draw people together, to experience something together for a space and time. Then when you add food into that and dialogue into that, I think it creates an opportunity for something else to happen, to resonate outside of that occurrence. You don't know what it is. But you can't predict what will happen. I think we've seen that happen. Collaborations have come out if it. Friendships have come out of it. People will have experienced and gone back to neighborhoods that they hadn't really spent time in before. So I think it has a lot of impact.

Do you have any significant memories from either a show or event that you were performing in or that you produced, or even that you attended from the festival?
Oh. Several. So, one was definitely the first year we performed. The first performance was in the Hyde Park Art Center, and it was inside of this amazing immersive installation by John Preus. He had built this

thing called *The Beast* out of discarded furniture from CPS schools that had closed. And it was just amazing huge . . . it had this enclosed space inside that was smaller and intimate and we performed inside of that. It was just great. It created this interesting heat. So that was really good, and it was participatory.

That same festival year, when we ended—the last—we were part of the opening and closing. So the last one was in Pilsen. They did a really ambitious thing where they had three homes [and] people were moving from [house to house]. So it was kind of a marathon. We weren't at the house before, but I guess there were some really challenging things that happened in that one. And so people were hungry and kind of mad and irritable coming to the last house. I remember, Laley—or Irina—was like, "We got to have food and alcohol. We got to have some stuff for people to recharge." The performance we were doing was this first section of this work that we did about House culture. It was just really uplifting and warm and community. So it worked really well to get people in good spirits at the end. So those are two really strong memories I have.

You now work for the Chicago Park District. The Chicago Home Theater Festival started to work in parks. I'm curious how the use of parks compared with the use of homes, if at all, in the later iterations of the festival.

I really encouraged them [Laley and Irina] to bring the works out into the parks because I felt like it was just like an extended metaphor. The parks are our public homes. They are these public spaces that are in every seventy-seven of our neighborhoods in Chicago. Our parks system is massive. I just felt like there was a great link to be made between these very intimate gatherings that were happening at peoples' homes across the city and these public spaces, that don't always get navigated as such, depending on the neighborhood. But the spirit of Home Theater Festival I felt could open up that energy about these as our kind of public home spaces, intimate spaces where communities can gather for programing or they, you know, experience all kinds of different things.

So I think it was a great thing that it happened. We were at Garfield Park Conservatory. I thought it was a lovely evening. That kind of space is beautiful and amazing. Some people who came had never been in to the conservatory and were just blown away that that's a free space in the parks system.

Chicago Home Theater Festival performance at Garfield Park Conservatory, 2017. Photograph by eedahahm. Courtesy of the photographer and the Chicago Home Theater Festival.

It seemed like there was kind of an evolution you articulated very well with the festival. Kind of going from homes to homes and parks. Do you have anything more to say about that, how parks might have broadened or deepened what the festival was doing?

I guess on a larger scale it kind of opened up this idea of we need to encounter each other more. We need to find ways and reasons to be in each other's neighborhoods and spaces and to allow interactions to happen, through which we might not know what will happen. But just the impact of getting to know people who are not like you, or who are not from the same place that you are from. Even within the city that we all share.

Do you think that the spaces, the homes, and the parks were "makeshift"? If so, why? And if not, why not?

Makeshift. Hmm. Well, one side of me says, "No, they're not makeshift." These are all spaces that have prior histories and that's one of the great things [about] that festival, as it took lengths to try to really make sure it was part of the environment of the evening that was on people's minds.

Through those tours, through trying to connect the artist or the host to their neighborhood and sometimes telling stories or sharing contextual information about those spaces, you really could see some of the richness of some of these neighborhoods that don't always get talked about.

Makeshift, maybe yes, if I think about. . . . It's a bunch of people coming together mostly on a volunteer basis to figure out how we're going to share some food together, how we're going to figure out how to put performance in these home spaces that are not necessarily black box theaters, so how do we make something fit in a basement and then how do we make it fit in that living room? Or how do we move things to the kitchen? So there were a lot of quick decisions being made about how to figure out that whole flow of how to use these temporary spaces to hold the performances.

What did the Chicago Home Theater Festival mean for the city of Chicago?

It is one in a long line of—Chicago's a DIY city. I feel artists have visions of things and then make them happen. It fits into that tradition. I'm going to give it to Blake and Irina and Laley—as the first kind of brain trust behind it. They brought something really rigorous in the format that they conceived with this tour plus performances plus a meal and were very steadfast in making sure that that kind of format was retained in some way throughout.

Are there any other thoughts you'd like to share?

Just that we need to continue to make platforms like the Home Theater Fest. And we will, and we are, and we got to figure how to keep promoting those and putting them forward and uplifting them as much as we do any traditional theater or dance production venue.

Notes

1. These excerpts are from the website for the Chicago Home Theater Festival: http://www.chicagohtf.org/.

2. School of the Art Institute of Chicago.

3. Named for the SoMa—which stands for "South of Market"—neighborhood in which it exists in San Francisco.

4. Millennium Park is a twenty-four-and-a-half-acre public park located in Chicago's downtown that opened in 2004 under Mayor Richard M. Daley.

5. The Chicago Cultural Plan was published in October 2012 under then Chicago mayor Rahm Emanuel, whose term began a year earlier in 2011. Led by the City of Chicago's Department of Cultural Affairs and Special Events (DCASE), the drafting of the cultural plan took place in part through community meetings and town hall events throughout 2012. The document was the City of Chicago's second; the first cultural plan for the city was published in 1986 under then mayor Harold Washington.

6. See also Shannon Jackson's reference to "municipal housekeeping" in *Lines of Activity: Performance, Historiography, Hull-House Domesticity* (Ann Arbor: University of Michigan Press, 2000), 198.

7. Short for "Do-It-Yourself."

8. Youth Empowerment Performance Project, founded in Chicago in 2011 as a performance project for LGBTQ youth experiencing homelessness.

9. Darling Shear is a mixed-media artist whose work engages fashion, movement, and therapy.

10. Bill Ayers is a former leader of the Weather Underground and a retired education professor who taught at the University of Illinois at Chicago.

11. According to his website, "Faheem Majeed (American, b. 1976) is a builder—literally and metaphorically. A resident of the South Shore neighborhood in Chicago, Majeed often looks to the material makeup of his neighborhood and surrounding areas as an entry point into larger questions around civic-mindedness, community activism, and institutional critique."

EPILOGUE

Chicago Theater amid Pandemics

Megan E. Geigner and
Jasmine Jamillah Mahmoud

In February 2020, officials from Washington State reported the first known death in the US caused by COVID-19, a novel coronavirus. In the following months, cities and states began to "shut down" and enforce physical distancing policies to reduce the spread of the virus. J. B. Pritzker, the governor of Illinois, and Lori Lightfoot, Chicago's mayor, prohibited large gatherings and issued "shelter-in-place" orders that took effect on March 21. Countless theaters in Chicago suspended operations, disbanding rehearsals, leaving sets and costumes mid-build, canceling previews and openings, closing runs early, and moving fund-raising efforts to virtual spaces.

On May 25, 2020, a white Minneapolis, Minnesota, police officer kneeled on George Floyd, a Black man, for 8 minutes and 46 seconds, killing Floyd.[1] Protests erupted across the country decrying this act, as well as the lynching of Ahmaud Arbery in Glynn County, Georgia, on February 23 and the murder of Breonna Taylor in Louisville, Kentucky, on March 13, along with dozens of other Black Americans killed at the hands of police and white supremacists. Protests in Chicago began in late May and continued throughout the summer.

As we send this book to publication in early 2021, we are living through a new phase of makeshift space. City-issued curfews and state-issued stay-at-home orders mean many Americans are looking at one another through screens and encountering other people in person rarely. Both COVID-19 and the social uprising to demand racial justice have changed theater in the United States.

Theater in Chicago has responded in myriad ways to keep producing during these pandemics.[2] Some theaters worked with playwrights, agents, and Actors' Equity Association (AEA or "Equity," the actors' and stage managers' union) to stream past productions. In many cases, theaters advertised via email and social media to notify patrons that they could purchase a virtual ticket to receive a link to the show. Many companies set up Zoom play readings for audiences to attend. Others began making short films or doing radio plays. Still others worked to make original, short, live plays accessible online.[3]

Some theaters, such as Victory Gardens, became sites of protests. After the theater covered its storefront windows with plywood boards, artists from across the city painted and wrote on them to express their frustration with the theater and to demand greater representation, justice, and transparency for BIPOC artists. Other theaters became sites for respite and donations, opening their lobbies to protestors and organizing volunteers to collect items for those in need.

As the pandemic stretched on, many theaters found themselves facing difficult financial situations. Two of Chicago's largest theaters, Goodman and Steppenwolf, paid their complete staff to stay home between March and July 2020 because each theater received a Paycheck Protection Program (PPP) loan from the federal government. When the PPP expired, though, both theaters laid off or furloughed employees: Steppenwolf eliminated fifteen positions on July 10, and two-thirds of its staff was furloughed or laid off.[4] Steppenwolf has been able to keep some of its shop production staff in place and repurpose their labor to ready the opening of their new building, but Goodman has not had the same ability.[5] Both theaters held weekly all-staff Zoom meetings to discuss the financial situation and make plans for the 2020–2021 seasons.

Smaller theaters struggled more. The *Chicago Tribune* reported that House Theatre, with a full-time staff of eight, a part-time staff of three, and six hourly employees, had only two part-time employees as of July 2020.[6] Lookingglass Theatre gave up their offices in the building formerly known as the John Hancock Center and had only a few employees working from home.

But despite these hardships, the following examples show how Chicago theater and performance continues to engage in tactics of the marginalized and makeshift—as it has for the last century—while enduring a social justice reckoning and a global pandemic.

Court Theatre's "Liminal Space"

Court Theatre on the University of Chicago's campus closed the theater a few hours before the first preview of *The Lady from the Sea* in March 2020. Starting in June 2020, patrons were able to access to a livestream of the empty theater, a project called The Liminal Space.

Director of Production Jennifer Gadda described returning to the theater to check on the building weeks into the pandemic as "a sort of punch in the gut. Everything was right where we'd left it. The stage manager's prompt book lay open on her table. The director's music stand. My special tech coffee mug. Props on shelves backstage and costumes hung up haphazardly in the dressing rooms. The circle of chairs on stage where the acting company gathered as we wrestled with whether or not to close the show. It reminded me of my first visit to Pompeii, the way everything was just frozen in time."[7] Gadda sat alone in the dark theater that day, as she had often done when the theater was still open, which "gave [her] a chance to sit in a seat and absorb all those feelings. . . . It felt raw and beautiful and tragic—exactly the way live theater should be." She wondered if there was a way to capture and share that experience. This is how The Liminal Space was born.

Gadda borrowed a set of ghost lights from Chicago theater company Manual Cinema and asked Court's master electrician to get a set of programmable LED light bulbs. She asked Court's sound and video supervisor to set up a livestream of the theater and operate the video projectors and audio remotely. The sound effects, music, video, and visual elements were all from *The Lady from the Sea*. Access to the livestream launched at the end of June 2020.

Gadda said via email, "Some days I visit (virtually) and monkey with the lighting multiple times a day, other days it feels too raw for me to open the link at all. In my work as a production manager, I support/shepherd/facilitate the artistic process, but I rarely get to curate any work of my own. I was touched by the response from many of my fellow theater artists."

The first phase of The Liminal Space ended in the late summer of 2020, and audiences watched the crew strike the set of *Lady from the Sea* in fall 2020. The theater sat empty for the rest of the year, but audiences could still view it on the Liminal Space livestream. Starting in late winter of 2021, audiences could watch Court's production staff research and design scenery for a future production of *Othello* (although the theater did not have a sense of when the production may be able to happen). The university's COVID restrictions kept Gadda from expanding the project to host livestreamed concerts. Via email in February 2021, Gadda said, "there hasn't felt like a time to unplug the cameras and go dark. Maybe I'm still looking for some symbolic or poetic gesture that tells me it's time to end the project?"[8]

The Second A.C.T.

The moment of converging pandemics birthed a new organization in Chicago: The Second A.C.T., called that because it hopes to abolish the problematic traditional way of doing American theater, the first act wherein BIPOC[9] artists feel excluded, exploited, undermined, and abused. The acronym A.C.T. stands for Accountable Coalition of Theatres, and the organization seeks to "dismantle racism, systemic oppression, and power in the Chicago theatre community by conducting a safety and return-to-work audit of all theatre institutions resulting in a full evaluation of standards, ethics, and practices within an organization with the goal of determining the institutions and organizations who are doing the work to make their spaces not just equitable but clearly and loudly antiracist multicultural spaces that lift up and support the work of BIPOC artists."[10]

According to the actor, director, and activist Wardell Julius Clark, The Second A.C.T. is specific and unique to the Chicago theater community but parallel to the larger WeSeeYou movement, which was collaboratively authored by BIPOC artists in Chicago and across the country. WeSeeYou began with a letter to White American Theater about their heinous treatment of BIPOC artists, posted online in April 2020. In July 2020, the WeSeeYou movement posted a list of demands for Equity, non-Equity, and educational theaters. As Clark points out, "This is Chicago, we do things differently here than they do things in the rest of the world"; Chicago has a different hierarchy of theater systems than most American cities given that Chicago theaters exist on Equity, League of Regional Theatres (LORT), Chicago Area Theatre (CAT), and non-Equity contracts.[11]

Chicago theater artists Sydney Charles and Melissa DuPrey began conversations about how to make sure Chicago theater took up the changes advocated by WeSeeYou, and then reached out to Clark, Regina Victor, and Pat Whalen in the spring and early summer of 2020. On July

12, 2020, The Second A.C.T. livestreamed a rally on Facebook stating the needs and goals of the organization, with artists Sydney Charles, Ron OJ Parson, Wardell Julius Clark, Lili-Anne Brown, Regina Victor, Pat Whalen, Gloria Petrelli, Molly Brennan, Melissa DuPrey, Miranda González, Angelica Grace, Vic Musoni, and Bella BAHHS. The speakers addressed topics such as giving credit to the ancestors who have fought oppressive systems for decades, the need for antiracism training, the need to decolonize theater and education, how to be an ally, how to advocate for others and get artists in the younger generation into the room, self-care, the sacred space of theater, and how to speak Black liberation into existence, among others. Since the video, the group has shared a survey to assess the harm BIPOC and other artists have experienced working in Chicago theater and completed an audit of theaters.[12]

As Clark points out, the most successful shows in the last few decades have been those centering marginalized people. As theater companies anticipate going back to work after the pandemic, The Second A.C.T. requires Chicago companies to understand that the WeSeeYou demands are not just for Los Angeles and New York. (As of the writing of this book, Baltimore Center Stage is the only professional theater in the United States to take up the WeSeeYou demands.) Clark says the coalition will ask theaters to "show their receipts": Are they having their staff engage in equity, diversity, and inclusion (EDI) training regularly? Do all directors make the same amount of money per show? Does the theater make their hiring practices transparent? How do theaters choose seasons? Who is in the room and who is at the table, and can the theater account for who is not there?

As Clark says, "Ultimately, I don't know at what rate people will choose to do what they need to do to keep their house in order. The complicit nature and quiet suffering, that lid is gone. It will never exist again like it did in [and before] March [2020]."

The Neo-Futurists: The Infinite Wrench Goes Viral

The Neo-Futurists have done a production of thirty plays in sixty minutes for fifty weekends every year for over thirty years. Since late 2016, that production has been titled *The Infinite Wrench*. The show, and Neo-Futurism more broadly, is predicated on chance, audience participation, and truth-telling in shared space. According to Artistic Director

Kirsten Riiber, "The Neo-Futurists make decisions based on consensus; so the full ensemble voted on the decision to prioritize the safety of our audience and performers by canceling the show [on March 13, 2020]. The very next day, we met to begin strategizing around how we could continue to make work safely. The following day we voted to adapt our show to the digital format, and by the following Tuesday, we were in rehearsal for our new show."[13]

The new show, *The Infinite Wrench Goes Viral*, debuted in late March 2020 with the group reaching out through their "substantial social media following" to give instructions for audience members to subscribe for as little as three dollars a week: in less than six months, the theater had nearly seven hundred subscribers from all over the world. Subscribers received an email each week with a link to the show on YouTube that expired after seven days. Through the end of 2020, ticket sales for the digital show were roughly the same as ticket sales for the live show, which was, as Riiber said, "frankly, miraculous." Furthermore, the new form made the show more accessible: "Every play is closed-captioned, and for longtime fans who've left Chicago, they're able to return to their favorite weekly show."

In transitioning between live theater and film, Riiber said that "the greatest challenge has been the necessary distance between the performers and the audience." She went on to say that the ensemble discusses "balance" for the weekly show, and one criterion of balance is audience participation. "Audience involvement in our show is a signature quality of our work, and now we're tasked to discover new ways of achieving that. We've emailed our followers and requested story submissions, we've invited them to a Zoom room to sing a karaoke song, and we've asked them to send in videos of themselves doing a spit-take. We see the audience as an integral part of the show, and I know we'll continue to experiment with that aspect."

The theater's innovative shift from live theater to film not only enabled them to keep paying their ensemble and staff, but also allowed the theater and the audience a site to process everything happening during the converging pandemics. As Riiber points out, "Our audience comes to our show to see the world reflected with honesty, and this felt and continues to feel like a crucial moment for us to remain connected to our audience." As such, "the week that George Floyd was murdered, the cast of the show decided to only release work that was written that week rather than release the full show that included work from previous weeks. They met, they agreed our show should be a response to the moment, and they created an extremely impactful show." Riiber continued:

> Around the same time, one of our ensemble members connected with another non-profit to utilize our space as a drop-site for baby & parent supplies, to be distributed to Black families on the South and West sides of Chicago. Throughout quarantine, we have been discussing what possible opportunities for community engagement there might be with our now empty space. Neo-Futurist art brings people together to collectively digest the world around us. We see this as a communal experience that demands that we see each other; by hearing each other's stories told honestly. As an artistic institution, we are excited to nurture this desire to engage with communities and to live up to our stated mission: to create work that inspires our audience to thought, feeling, and action.

Riiber shared that the staff and ensemble are "incredibly grateful to have a place to make work right now. These are trying, exhausting, and terrifying times; and I think our continued following is a testament to the necessity of Neo-Futurism. We're responding to the world with honesty, and I believe this resonates with our audience."

Jocelyn Prince: Honk for Justice Chicago

On a street corner on Chicago's North Side, a Black woman sits in a beach chair on the sidewalk. She wears a white flowy dress and soaks her feet in a white tub. A straw hat adorning her head protects her from the sun; across her face, a medical mask protects her from COVID-19. Seated, she reads a magazine, seemingly immersed in its pages. Although there is quietness[14] to her position, this performance is a protest.

Around her is noise. Depending on the day, dozens or hundreds of people, mostly white people, accompany[15] her presence. They mostly stand, at a physical distance, some holding signs that read "Black Lives Matter" or "Solidarity Not Just Sympathy." Other protestors drive by in cars, honking to show support for Black lives.

This was Honk for Justice Chicago, a series of street performance protests devised by theater artist Jocelyn Prince. It began in June 2020 and ran every day, from 4:00 to 6:00 p.m., for the next two months, on street corners across North Side neighborhoods.

Prince grew up in South Shore, a mostly Black neighborhood on Chicago's South Side. She "grew up going to the theater"[16] since her mother, a high school teacher, directed school plays. Later, Prince worked in theater in New York City (cofounding the New Black Fest) and at the Yale School of Drama, before returning to Chicago a few years ago.

Prince was "extremely disturbed" by the video of George Floyd "pleading for his life while people in the community were forced to watch this happen." Soon after Floyd's murder, Prince participated regularly in Chicago protests—encountering police batons and rubber bullets—on the South Side. She chronicled:

> I live on the North Side; I would come back up here and [notice] people going about their normal lives. So a friend, Madison Kamp, contacted me and wanted to know if I knew if something [was] going on. I said, "I don't, but I have an idea. Let's create one of our own." Honk for Justice Chicago started out as just a regular street protest, where we asked people to come out on the sidewalk, hold a sign, create a visual spectacle, and get people to honk their horns.

Soon after, Prince developed a daily schedule across North Side neighborhoods, where antiracist protests were largely not happening: Mondays in Uptown at Foster and Sheridan, Tuesdays in West Town at Milwaukee and Chicago, Wednesdays in Logan Square at Milwaukee and Logan, Thursdays in Lincoln Square at Western and Montrose, Fridays in Lincoln Park at Halsted and Lincoln/Fullerton, Saturdays in Rogers Park at Greenleaf and Sheridan, and Sundays in West Ridge at Western and Pratt.

"Those two forces of COVID and George Floyd definitely influenced the creation and what the work evolved into," Prince said. Handmade antiracist protest signs, participants wearing masks, and physical distancing on street corners and in honking cars (which extended the sensorial reach) theatrically framed this work. Prince described "noise for justice . . . disturbing the peace," amplifying the frequent "No Justice No Peace" signs.

Prince's staging also enunciated the unacknowledged labor of Black women in social movements. She narrated:

> What if I showed up in a pretty, white summer dress and actually just sat down, while my white volunteers led other white people to protest? So it evolved from there. It's unfair for Black women to be continually asked to do this work and labor. White people are enacting racism, benefiting from racism. They need to take on the responsibility of dismantling it.

During each performance, Prince talked only to designated volunteers, nonverbally directing others to them. She added: "The 'yellow jacket' volunteers would, at times, have to intercept situations where someone wanted to complain about the protest."

Prince sought to include children and families. "Black helium balloons" were given to children, and through a partnership with Chicago Children's Theatre, micro-performances[17] featured puppets and music. Players included "sad clowns," yoga instructors dressed in black, and "stilt walkers from Walkabout Theater." Prince further depicted the scene: "Imagine a stilt walker holding Black Lives Matter signs in the air." The purpose: to imbue joy. "Joy is important in movements," Prince told us. "I wanted to create an environment that would be a marker in the lives of children that they might be inspired by when they get older."

When we asked if Honk for Justice Chicago was makeshift theater, Prince replied affirmatively:

> All of the costumes were things I found in my apartment. The signs were made, all of the materials were donated. Some people drop[ped] off bottles of water, sunscreen, snacks, and poster board and markers. It was a mashup of gathering resources. The street [wa]s our stage. Decisions were made based out of necessity, in the moment, in a highly flexible way.

She added: "I think all theater right now is makeshift theater. Whether it's how to make this work in this digital space, or performance without the support of a nonprofit theater industry. . . . When I think about makeshift, I think about doing what you can with what you have."

Final Thoughts

Our notion of the makeshift as a staple of Chicago theater, as articulated throughout this book, has taken on a new challenge with recent crises. We believe, judging from past experience, that how Chicago theater responded to the coronavirus pandemic and a new wave of racial strife is in keeping with this larger makeshift pattern and will most likely reemerge in kind. As Stuart notes so eloquently in the beginning of the book, Chicago theater emerged from the ashes of fires. Our hope is that Chicago theater will flourish again once we are in the wake of our present-day disasters. Perhaps our book will provide something of a blueprint to reassure, provide insight, and offer some sense of how Chicago and its theater might survive, grow, and change in reflection of these crises.

Notes

1. The filed criminal complaint reported that the officer kneeled for 7 minutes and 46 seconds, and prosecutors established it was 9 minutes and 29 seconds. But the rallying cry at protests was 8 minutes and 46 seconds.

2. Many have called the crises of COVID-19 and systemic racism the "twin pandemics." See "The Twin Pandemics of COVID-19 – 1619," *The Infused Classroom Podcast*, December 27, 2020.

3. Theaters that made previous productions available for remote viewing included TimeLine Theatre (*Kill Move Paradise* and *To Master the Art*), the Goodman (*School Girls, or, The African Mean Girls Play*), and Victory Gardens (*Fun Home*), among others. Lookingglass Theatre made a short film play titled *Sunset 1919* and collaborated with Chicago's local NPR affiliate, WBEZ, to translate *Her Honor Jane Byrne* to a radio play that aired on Thanksgiving weekend; Collaboraction ran an all-virtual 20–21 season; American Blues Theater started an online Zoom play-reading series called The Room; Black Lives, Black Words presented shows virtually and collaboratively with actors across time zones and continents; the Chicago Academy for the Arts started an online "Coffeehouse" variety show for their students; Muntu Dance Theatre staged a Juneteenth celebration in summer 2020 available online; Season of Concern worked with Theater Wit to do a benefit online performance of *Fefu and her Friends* in December 2020; and Manual Cinema produced a livestreamed version of *A Christmas Carol*. These are just a few of the examples from theaters in Chicago during 2020 and beyond.

4. Chris Jones, "Artistic Chicago Is Hemorrhaging Jobs: 'We Are Looking at the Decimation of an Industry,'" *Chicago Tribune*, July 16, 2020.

5. Chad Hain, associate technical director, Steppenwolf Theatre, interview with Megan E. Geigner, July 19, 2020.

6. Jones, "Artistic Chicago Is Hemorrhaging."

7. Jennifer Gadda, director of production, Court Theatre, email to Megan E. Geigner, August 5, 2020.

8. Jennifer Gadda, director of production, Court Theatre, email to Megan E. Geigner, February 26, 2021.

9. BIPOC stands for Black and Indigenous People of Color. It became the preferred nomenclature in the spring and summer of 2020. For more, see Sandra E. Garcia, "Where Did BIPOC Come From?," *New York Times*, June 17, 2020, https://www.nytimes.com/article/what-is-bipoc.html.

10. "Load Out and Strike: The Intermission Is Ova," Facebook video, July 12, 2020, https://www.facebook.com/112209697228130/videos/282216183101641.

11. This and subsequent quotes from Wardell Julius Clark, interview with Megan E. Geigner, July 16, 2020.

12. "Load Out and Strike."

13. This and subsequent quotes from Kirsten Riiber, artistic director, Neo-Futurists, email to Megan E. Geigner, August 5, 2020.

14. This use of "quiet" evokes Kevin Quashie's in *The Sovereignty of Quiet: Beyond Resistance in Black Culture* (New Brunswick, NJ: Rutgers University Press, 2012).

15. This term follows Laurel Mei-Singh's use in "Accompaniment through Carceral Geographies: Abolitionist Research Partnerships with Indigenous Communities," *Antipode: A Journal of Radical Geography* (2020): 1–21.

16. This and subsequent quotes from Jocelyn Prince, interview with Jasmine Jamillah Mahmoud, August 11, 2020.

17. Following John Muse, *Microdramas: Crucibles for Theater and Time* (Ann Arbor: University of Michigan Press, 2017).

CONTRIBUTORS

Rosemarie K. Bank is the author of *Theatre Culture in America, 1825–1860* and the editor (with Michal Kobialka) of *Theatre/Performance/Historiography: Times, Space, Matter*. She has published in many periodicals, including *Theatre Journal*, *Nineteenth-Century Theatre*, *Theatre History Studies, and Modern Drama*. A member of the College of Fellows of the American Theatre and a fellow of the Mid-America Theatre Conference (MATC), she was the editor of *Theatre Survey* and serves on several editorial boards of scholarly journals in theater. Several times a fellow of the National Endowment for the Humanities, Bank is professor emerita of theater at Kent State University.

Shannon Epplett has had articles appear in *New England Theatre Journal* and *Theatre History Studies*. His dissertation, "The Steppenwolf Scenario: The Habitus of Chicago's Off-Loop Theatre," traces the cultural and sociological origins of Chicago's Off-Loop theater community. He has been a fellow of the Newberry Library twice, first as part of the Newberry Consortium in American Indian Studies and then as the Susan Kelly Power and Helen Hornbeck Tanner Fellow. Epplett is an enrolled member of the Sault Ste. Marie Tribe of Chippewa Indians and is developing a performance piece based on the life of Anishinaabe poet Jane Johnston Schoolcraft. He is an instructional assistant professor of theater at Illinois State University.

Megan E. Geigner has published in several periodicals, including *New Theatre Quarterly*, *Theatre Journal*, and *Modern Drama*. Her research focuses on how performance creates ethnic, civic, and racial identity in and at such events as parades, world's fairs, commemorative monuments, and traditional theater. She serves in leadership for the Association for Theatre in Higher Education and an artistic associate with Chicago's TimeLine Theatre. Geigner has served on the board of directors of the Neo-Futurists (Chicago), and, since 2009, has worked as a dramaturg at several theaters in Chicago. She is an assistant professor of instruction in the Cook Family Writing Program at Northwestern University.

Cat Gleason has published in *Theatre/Practice* and the *American Journal of Semiotics.* Her dissertation, "Mapping the Lincoln Park Nexus: The Origin of the Chicago Off-Loop Theatre Movement," asserts that the beginnings of Chicago's Off-Loop theater are intimately intertwined with political and social performances of the era. Her research focuses on Chicago theater, theatrical design, theater pedagogy, and the nature of collaborative practice. Her theatrical practice includes directing, dramaturgy, choreography, and an occasional scenic design. Gleason has specialized in physical theater and devised works, and was trained by Chicago institutions such as Plasticene and Goat Island. She is a lecturer at Truman State University and serves as the Region 5 dramaturgy coordinator for the Kennedy Center American College Theatre Festival.

Stuart J. Hecht has published more than thirty articles in journals including *Theatre Journal, The Journal of American Theatre and Drama, and Chicago History.* He has written chapters in five major books as well. His book *Transposing Broadway: Jews, Assimilation, and the American Musical* was recommended by the journal *Choice*. He is the long-standing editor in chief of *New England Theatre Journal* and is an editorial board member for *Theatre Annual, Journal of American Drama and Theatre* and *Studies in Musical Theatre*. Hecht also sits on the boards of the New England Theatre Conference and the Chicago Theatre History Project, is an officer of the American Theatre and Drama Society, and was named a Fellow of the Mid-America Theatre Conference. He is an associate professor of theater at Boston College.

Aaron Krall published "Building the Entertainment Machine: Charles L. Mee's *Time to Burn* and the Performance of Postindustrial Decay in Chicago" in *Theatre Survey*. He was also contributor to the Shakespeare 400 Chicago City Desk blog. He is the coordinator of the UIC Summer Enrichment Writing Workshop, a pre-matriculation program designed to advance students into credit-bearing writing courses, and the executive vice president of UIC United Faculty, Local #6456. He is a senior lecturer in the English department at the University of Illinois at Chicago.

Laura A. Lodewyck has been published in *The Oxford Handbook of Greek Drama in the Americas*, *Shakespeare Bulletin*, and *Theatre Survey*. Her research focuses on the transformative power of theater, particularly during times of crisis, and she is a scholar with the Latinx Theatre Commons' *El Fuego* initiative, whose mission is to produce and document new Latinx plays. She is also a contributor to the Humanities and Human Flourishing Project, which aims to evidence the role of the arts in enriching societal and individual well-being. As a practitioner in Chicago, Lodewyck has worked with the former Chicago Fusion Theatre/Wayward Productions, Remy Bumppo Theatre, Chicago Shakespeare Theater, Court Theatre, Illinois Theatre Center, Teatro Vista, and Victory Gardens Theater, and she has appeared on *Chicago Med*. She is an associate professor of theater at North Central College in Naperville, Illinois.

Jasmine Jamillah Mahmoud has published in several journals, including *Modern Drama*, *Performance Research*, and *TDR: The Drama Review*, and in several edited collections. An urban ethnographer and performance historian, her research examines experimental theater practices staged in urban margins; relationships among aesthetics, race, policy, and space; and the role of artistic practices in decolonial, antiracist neighborhood processes. She has served in leadership positions with the Association for Theatre in Higher Education. Mahmoud is an assistant professor in the department of performing arts and arts leadership at Seattle University.

Travis Stern focuses his research on two primary areas: the history and theory of improv and comedy, and the intersections between American theater and professional baseball at the turn of the nineteenth to the twentieth century, including the interplay of a ballplayer's persona between the two entertainment forms. He has presented this work at the Baseball Hall of Fame in Cooperstown, New York, among other places. Stern serves as webmaster and as a member of the executive committee for Mid-America Theatre Conference. He is an associate professor of theater arts at Bradley University.

LaRonika Marie Thomas has a chapter titled "Digital Dramaturgy and Digital Dramaturgs" in *The Routledge Companion to Dramaturgy*. She was the 2016 recipient of the American Theatre and Drama Society Graduate Student Travel Award for her paper "Toward a Civic

Dramaturgy: Performances of Urban Planning in Chicago from Daniel Burnham to Theaster Gates." Thomas is developing a theory of civic dramaturgy in urban planning, cultural space, cultural policy, and the role of art and art-makers in twenty-first-century Chicago. She is the vice president of membership for Literary Managers and Dramaturgs of the Americas (LMDA), and her creative and scholarly work has been funded by LMDA, the University of Maryland, and the City of Chicago. She has taught at Loyola University Maryland, the Community College of Baltimore County, and Washington College.

INDEX

Page numbers for figures appear in *italics*; page numbers for maps appear in **bold**.